POETICS OF CONDUCT

Poetics of Conduct

Oral Narrative and Moral Being in a South Indian Town

Leela Prasad

COLUMBIA UNIVERSITY PRESS NEW YORK

COLUMBIA UNIVERSITY PRESS
Publishers Since 1893
NEW YORK CHICHESTER, WEST SUSSEX

Library of Congress Cataloging-in-Publication Data
Prasad Leela
Poetics of conduct : oral narrative and moral being in a South Indian town / Leela Prasad.
p. cm.
Includes bibliographical references and index.
ISBN 0-231-13920-9 (cloth : alk. paper) — ISBN 0-231-13921-7 (pbk. : alk. paper) — ISBN 0-231-51127-2 (ebook)
1. Sringeri (India)—Religious life and customs. 2. Sringeri (India)—Social life and customs. 3. Narrative poetry, Kannada—Moral and ethical aspects—India—Sringeri. 4. Folk literature, Kannada—Moral and ethical aspects—India—Sringeri. 5. Hindu ethics—India—Sringeri. I. Title
BL1226.15.S75P73 2006
294.50954'87—dc22 2006017788

Casebound editions of Columbia University Press books are printed on permanent and durable acid-free paper.

Printed in the United States of America

c 10 9 8 7 6 5 4 3 2 1
p 10 9 8 7 6 5 4 3 2 1

For Sringeri

Contents

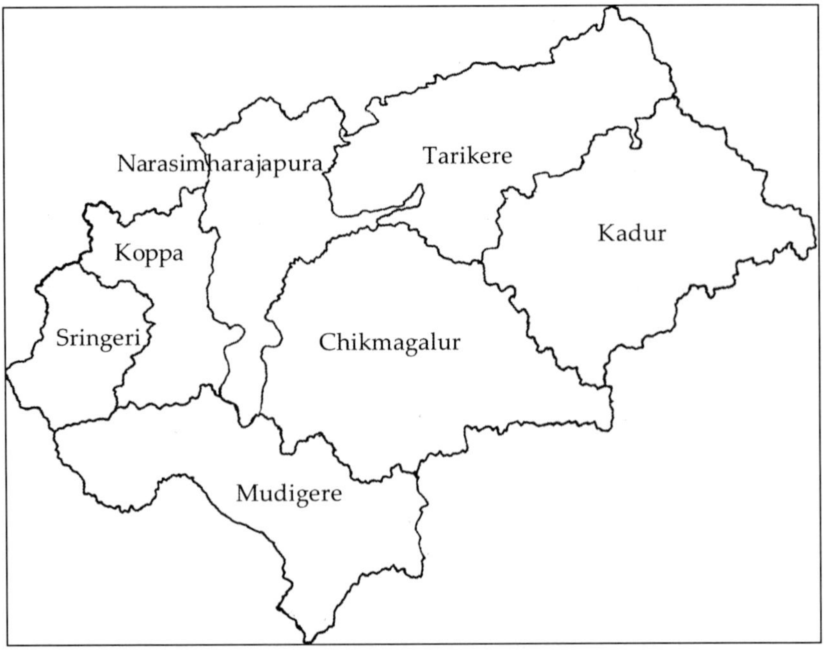

MAP 1. Taluks of Chikmagalur district. *http://www.kar.nic.in/district_glance.asp?distname=Chikmagalur*

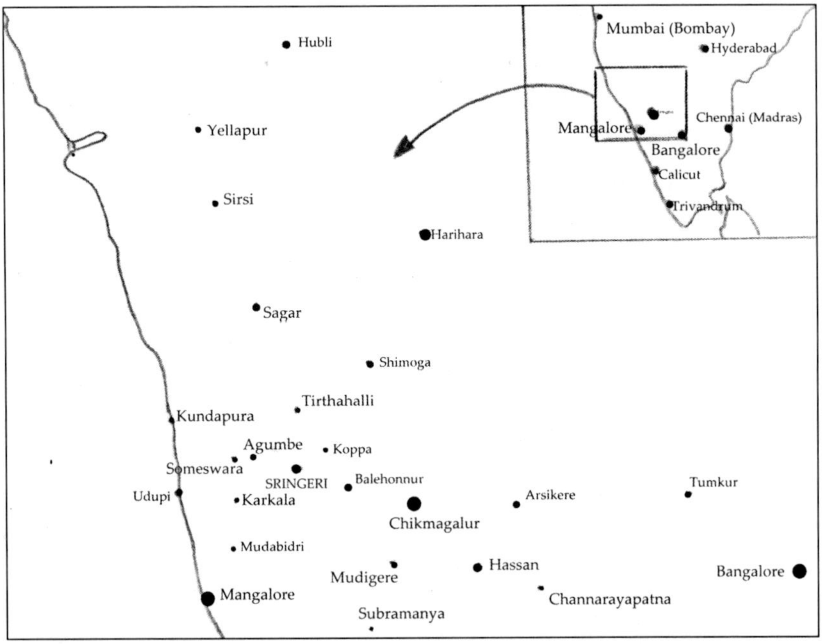

MAP 2. Towns around Sringeri. *http://www.tattvaloka.com/mapofsringeri.htm*

Acknowledgments

Somewhere along the writing of this book grew a sense, now distinct, of how this book had never really been mine. My authorship is made but a formal gesture by the many individuals and institutions that have enabled this work and by the divine play and grace that has eventually led to its completion. During a darshan I described this book to Shri Bharati Tirtha, the present guru of the Shankara matha in Sringeri, and sought his blessings. He smiled and said, "How can a book about Sringeri not have my blessings?" Sringeri understandings of propriety, which inspired this book, also made it happen: my deep gratitude to all the people in Sringeri who appear in this book. I am indebted also to the many Sringeri friends who are implicit, but nevertheless important presences in the book: in Koulkudige, the Srinivas Rayaru family; in Sringeri town, Nagabhushan Rao and Vasanthi, Uma and Rajanna, "Ayurveda" Ramaswamy and his family, Mr. and Mrs. M. M. Subramaniam, "Photo" Shastry and his family, and Parvati and Bhavani; and in Vidyaranyapura, the Bapats, and Vatsala and Michael. I also thank the many friends within the matha for making the often crowded temples become familiar places for me.

Outside Sringeri, I am grateful to Margaret A. Mills, my academic adviser at the University of Pennsylvania, who unobtrusively taught me the great value of listening (not just in "fieldwork"), even if it takes years to learn how to hear. My intellectual debts to Roger Abrahams, Dan Ben-Amos, David Hufford, and Janet Theophano will be evident throughout the book. I owe special thanks to Joyce Burkhalter Flueckiger for her magnanimous friendship and support over the years. Among the many other scholars who have shared their intellectual riches with me over the years are Anne Feldhaus, Pika Ghosh, Velcheru Narayana Rao, the late A. K. Ramanujan, and Sumathi Ramaswamy; to each my gratitude. My thanks to my colleagues in the Department of Religion at Duke University: Ebrahim Moosa and Melvin Peters cheerfully read various chapters, providing me perspectives from their own fields that helped me broaden my view; Bruce Lawrence's close and perceptive reading of the entire manuscript was tremendously helpful especially when I was too close to the trees to see the forest. For their generous help with Greek etymologies and references, I take pleasure in thanking Melvin Peters, my father S. Nagarajan, and my colleague Micaela Janan from the Department of Classical Studies at Duke. Patrick Olivelle, Deepak Sarma, and Sudha Shreeniwas read and provided incisive comments on the chapters on shastra and sampradaya. I must very specially thank Ludo Rocher, Kirin Narayan, and an anonymous reviewer of the manuscript. Ludo Rocher's supportive comments greatly encouraged my explorations into the problem of shastra in everyday life. Kirin Narayan's insightful reading of the manuscript helped me reorganize the book for the better. For her unwavering encouragement on this and other projects, I thank her. The detailed and imaginative feedback of the anonymous reviewer has been of singular value.

I will not have the joy of sharing this work with my paternal grandfather, the late S. Srinivasan who retired as a magistrate in the judicial service of the old princely state of Mysore and lived in Sringeri during the mid-1950s for three years. I am deeply grateful to him for the reputation he left behind him in Sringeri; forty years later, his name opened many conversations and doors for me. In the course of my fieldwork I discovered another connection to Sringeri that similarly helped me. My maternal great-granduncle, Shri Satyananda Sarasvathi Swami, I learned, had formally initiated Shri Chandrashekara Bharati, the thirty-fourth guru, into sanyasa in 1912 since the previous guru (who traditionally conducts the initiation) had passed away before Shri Chandrashekara Bharati could reach Sringeri. After the initiation, Shri Satyananda Sarasvathi left Sringeri to reside in Kovvur, in eastern Andhra Pradesh.

My parents, Professor S. Nagarajan and Srimathi Nagarajan, read, queried, made suggestions, and reread. My father's questions kept the entire process in an exciting and continuous mode of "rethinking," whether it was about concepts, assumptions, or language. My mother, also a teacher, was my cheerful companion for a few months when she lived with me in Sringeri; her searching questions and reflections often helped me clarify my thinking and writing. As always, I have drawn on my parents' optimism and faith in me. They, and other members of my family, have many times undertaken—with affection and wry humor—global reorganizations to accommodate my needs. My brother, Wg Cdr S Shankar, and my father drove more than seven hundred miles in two days to take photographs of Sringeri for this book because some that I had taken turned out hazy. Shankar and Vijaya—a classmate during our M.A days and later my sister-in-law—have been valuable intellectual partners all through the project. My younger brother, S. Chandramouli ("Shekar") kept the project in play-frame with irresistible humor, but he also often sacrificed his professional badminton to make my logistics happen. I also thank Indira Chandramouli, my sister-in-law, for her support during a critical stint of research. Discussions with my grand aunt Sarojamma illuminated this book in ways I could not see then. My father-in-law, C. S. Rao, shared his grounded understanding of the region with me. I cannot adequately thank my extended family, especially my grandparents in Hyderabad, and my close friends for their interest and inexhaustible support.

The generosity that has shaped this project is evident also in no small way in the unhesitating sharing of artwork and photographs. I am thankful to my longtime friend Kusum Viswanath for sharing her exquisite pencil sketches of Sringeri streets. I thank Mr. T. R. R. Ramachandran, Mrs. Sarala, and Mrs. Shardha Chityala of *Tattvāloka* for permission to reproduce maps relating to Sringeri. K. R. Sanjay faxed me his permission from India for his photograph of the temple at Kigga that I found on the Internet. Krishna ("Calvinkrishy") changed his copyright licenses on Wikipedia to make his photographs of Sringeri accessible to me for reproduction in this book. I hope to meet Sanjay and Krishna someday in non-Internet worlds to thank them in person.

Working with Columbia University Press has been a great pleasure, professionally and personally. Wendy Lochner and Christine Mortlock have brought an enthusiastic commitment to this work from the very beginning that, along with their remarkable efficiency, has sustained me. Susan Pensak has been a gracious and fine manuscript editor, a poet rather, making suggestions that showed she understood the book "from the inside." This team along with the production staff at Columbia University Press has been a writer's dream-come-true. I am grateful to Rukun Advani at Permanent Black for making the South Asian edition of this book possible.

I owe deep thanks to the American Academy of Religion, the American Institute of Indian Studies, the American Philosophical Society, and the National Endowment for the Humanities, all of which generously supported various phases of this research. I am also indebted to Duke University for its support of this project through several grants and periods of leave.

Material from some chapters of this book has appeared elsewhere. Portions of chapter 6 were first published in my article in the *Journal of Religious Ethics* 32.1 (2003), parts of chapters 3 and 4 appear in my essay in *Numen* 53.1 (2006), and material from chapter 2 appears in *Region, Culture, and Politics in India*, an anthology edited by Rajendra Vora and Anne Feldhaus (New Delhi: Manohar, 2006). I appreciate the permission from these editors to reuse material from these articles.

Finally, my gratitude beyond expression to Prasad, my husband, who engaged with every word and idea in this book. His intellectual and ethnographic presence in the book through all its stages has made it better. Prasad knows how much I share this work with him. Anandini and Akshayini, our daughters, have tolerated steep cuts in family play time and actually believe they want to be "awthurs" when they grow up. They have presented me several of their own "drafts" with "close your eyes . . . open . . . tha-daan!" I can only attribute this to the magic spell of Prasad and of Sringeri.

Note on Translation and Transliteration

Translating conversations and stories into English from Kannada has been a deeply engaging process within which to negotiate the complexities of oral and written textualities. For readers who may be interested, the process was roughly the following: I usually began by translating fairly literally, making sure that the English meanings of Kannada words were contextually appropriate. I then relistened to tapes many times for linguistic and extralinguistic traces such as emphases, pauses, or elisions so that the printed text could reflect something of the ways of speaking. My translations draw on my familiarity over the years with individual styles and rhythms of speakers. However, to avoid burdening readers with overly notated texts, I use a simple transcription system in which indentation indexes orality, line breaks indicate breaks in speech or shifts in thought, and text enclosed in * * indicates words or phrases originally spoken in English by speakers (the asterisks notation I modify from Kirin Narayan's *Storytellers, Saints, and Scoundrels*). Within oral narrative my "stage directions" appear in italics in parentheses, such as (*Leela laughs*), while all glosses and brief explanations remain in roman, also in parentheses, for example, "aviveka (indiscrimination)." Emphasis in oral speech is indicated through italics.

Diacritical marks for Indian language terms and phrases that appear frequently in this volume are indicated in the list below, but, in the book, these words appear without diacritics. However, diacritical marks are retained for titles of works (*Śaṅkara Digvijaya*) and words or phrases that appear infrequently.

I spell names of people, caste groups, and places in accordance with undiacritized standard usage in English. Thus Sringeri, not Śṛṅgeri, Krishna, not Kṛṣṇa, and Virashaiva, not Vīraśaiva. The only caste name I do not capitalize is "brahman" in order to keep it distinct from the metaphysical concept "Brahman."

Diacritics

abhisheka	abhiṣeka	darshan	darśan
abhyanjana	abhyañjana	dashanami	daśanāmi
acara	ācāra	deshi	deśī
adrishtha	adṛṣṭa	devi	devī
adda pallaki	aḍḍa pallakki	dharmadhikari	dharmādhikāri
adige	aḍige	dipa	dīpā
agama	āgama	drishtha	dṛṣṭa
agrahara	agrahārā	durve	dūrve
ahvana	āhvāna	Gayatri	Gāyatrī
Alvar	Ālvār	grihasta	gṛhasta
apacara	apacāra	inam	inām
apaurusheya	apauruṣeya	jagirdari	jāgirdāri
arati	āratī	janivara	janivāra
ashirvada	āśīrvāda	kadita	kaḍitā
ashis	āśis	kama	kāma
atithya	ātithya	Kartaviryarjuna	Kārtavīryārjuna
auchitya	aucitya	madi	maḍi
bhiksha	bhikṣā	Mahabharata	Mahābhārata
brahmachari	brahmacāri	mahajana	mahājana
Chandi	Caṇḍī	Malnad	Malnāḍ
Chitpavan	Citpāvan	mangala gouri	maṅgaḷa gourī
dakshine	dakṣine	mantrakshate	mañtrākṣate
dana	dāna	marga	mārga

matha	maṭha
Mimamsa	Mīmāṁsā
moksha	mokṣa
muhurta	muhūrta
murne	mūrne
murti	mūrti
naivedya	naivēdya
namaskara	namaskāra
navaratri	navarātri
panche-shalya	pañce-śalya
Pancharatra	Pañcarātra
pangada	paṅgaḍa
pankti	paṅkti
parayana	pārāyaṇa
paurusheya	pauruṣeya
phala	phalā
pitha	pīṭha
prasada	prasād(a)
prayaschitta	prāyascitta
puja	pūjā
Purana	Purāṇa
raja dharma	rāja dharma
rakshasa	rākṣasa
Ramayana	Rāmāyaṇa
rina	riṇa/ṛṇa
sadachara	sadācāra
sadhana	sādhanā
sahridaya	sahṛdaya
shakti	śakti
samadhi	samādhi
sampradaya	sampradāya
samsthana	saṃsthāna
sanyasi	sannyāsi
Sharada	Śāradā
shastra	śāstra
seve	sēve
shistha	śiṣṭa
shisthu	śiṣṭu
shloka	śloka
smarta	smārta
smriti	smṛti
shraaddha	śrāddha (annual rite of feeding ancestors)
shraddha	śraddhā or śraddhe (faith)
shruti	śruti
Shringapura	Śṛingapura
sthala purana	sthaḷa purāṇa
sukshma	sūkṣma
tambula	tāmbūla
tirtha	tīrtha
turiya	turīya
upacara	upacāra
upakarma	upākarma
Upanishad	Upaniṣad
Vaishnava	Vaiṣṇava
vakya	vākya
vichara	vicāra
Virashaiva	Vīraśaiva
vyavahara	vyavahāra

Introduction

Puranas like to stretch their own genealogies. If I were to tell the story of Sringeri, a pilgrimage town in south India, as a Puranic narrative, it would begin many, many centuries ago. That beginning is beyond my power to recall, but the part familiar to me began in the summers that my parents would take us children to Sringeri on a pilgrimage. I remember those visits not as a pious pilgrim, but as providing an escape from summer school homework, a series of exhilarating rides on trains, buses, and, best of all, on a boat across the river Tunga. We would board the night bus from Bangalore, get tossed around as we dozed while the bus steadily climbed the winding, often rain-soaked roads of the Western Ghats (mountain ranges). We would finally wake up at dawn to look out at the misty, cloud-packed green valleys of areca palms and paddy fields and deep forests before we reached Sringeri in a few hours.

Sringeri, with a population of about four thousand people, is a small town in northwestern Karnataka. At Chikmagalur, the district headquarters,[1] about four hours before Sringeri, the bus would nearly empty, leaving just disheveled pilgrims and tourists and, occasionally, some residents returning

FIGURE 1. The river Tunga flowing next to the matha. *Photo by Baba Prasad*

home, to journey bumpily upward into the ghats. The bus would stop many times, often at one-house "villages," dropping off or picking up milkmen, school-bound children, or those shuttling to workplaces. Once, it is said, Krishnaraja Wodeyar, the maharaja of Mysore, was so overcome by the tranquil beauty of Sringeri, and by the friendly fish that rush to meet you on the steps of the temple leading to the Tunga river, that he took off his gold ring and slipped it onto the pouting nose of a fish. And you hear that even today, if you are lucky, you can see the fish with its royal nose ring, a fleck of gold in the holy Tunga. I loved the story, and always wondered if I would ever see the gold-ringed fish when I sat on the riverbank and watched the fish rush to catch the puffed rice we threw into the water. On the steps, carved into the stone, is an imprint of the sight that the philosopher Shankara is popularly believed to have seen twelve centuries ago: a cobra shielding a frog from the sun's rays. Stories, journeys, have a way of enticing you, and it must have been on one of those awe-inspiring, journeys that our family made every year that I fell in love with Sringeri.

Gradually, I came to know Sringeri as almost everyone who visits it occasionally knows it: temples and the matha (monastery). Buses taking one into Sringeri stop in front of the arched gateway of the temple complex, over which a large sign declares that this is the Sharada pīṭham[2] established by Shankara in approximately CE 800 for the dissemination of Advaita, the philosophy of nondualism. Shankara established mathas at three other places: Dwaraka on the west coast, Puri on the eastern seashore, and Badrinath in the Himalayas in the north. My father would book a room for us in one of the matha's guesthouses for three days, and, rising early, we would get all the pujas performed, one by one. To have pujas performed for some of the past gurus of the matha, we had to cross the Tunga in a wooden boat, *dōṇi*, to the Narasimhavana (Narasimha Gardens), which were separated from the Sharada temple complex by the river. One could not do that in the monsoon season, from June to late August when the river rose and raged. (There is now a concrete bridge linking the temples to the Narasimhavana where the guru resides.)

The only people we really knew in the town were the Murthys: Dodda Murthy and his wife, Chayamma. Dodda Murthy (the "elder" Murthy), or, officially, N.S. Lakṣhminarasimha Murthy, is a retired schoolteacher, who, in 2004, is in his mid-eighties. We used to eat the prasada (sanctified food) in the temple until the last day of our visit when the Murthys, who live in one of the oldest homes in Sringeri, over two hundred years old, would invite us for dinner before we caught the bus back to Bangalore. We would eat the wonderful meal on banana leaves and enjoy the sweet water of the Tunga. "Gangā snāna, Tungā pāna," goes the saying: Bathe in the Ganga, drink from the Tunga.

Dodda Murthy is a good friend of my father, just as his father had been a good friend of my grandfather, who had been a district judge in the Sringeri area for a few years. After my grandfather retired, he had lived in Sringeri from 1950 to 1955 in a small house opposite the Murthys. The house was called Lakshmi Nivas after the mother of the then guru of the matha, Sri Chandrashekara Bharati, who had asked my grandfather to live there following a personal tragedy in my grandfather's life. While living in Sringeri, my grandfather became an occasional honorary correspondent for the Madras-based national English newspaper, the *Hindu*. Many Sringeri residents and officers of the matha also consulted him informally for legal advice. He and Dodda Murthy's father, who was a local landlord, would meet in the evenings after their evening pujas and (sitting on the stone bench outside the Murthy house) read with the help of a Sanskrit pandit the *Chāndōgya* and the *Taittirīya Upaniṣads.* My father, who taught English in Government colleges in Jabalpur and Amaravati in central India, spent his summers in Sringeri, a practice he continued after his return to India in 1960 from Harvard where he got his doctorate in English. He used to visit Sringeri even after my grandparents had moved to Bangalore. When I told Dodda Murthy years later that I was going to live in Sringeri for doctoral research, he said, as he was to say many times during my stay, "Nimma grandfather kālada ninda hāge iṭṭukonḍu bandiddīra" (you're maintaining the tradition from your grandfather's times).

In the days when I visited Sringeri with my family, I spoke no Kannada, having grown up in Pune speaking Marathi and my mother tongue, Telugu. So while my father, who was raised in Karnataka, chatted in fluent Kannada with the Murthys, my mother and my two brothers and I participated in the conversations through smiles and nods. After I got married, when my husband, Prasad, and I went to Sringeri, we had the customary meal with the Murthys, of course, and I still spoke no Kannada. When Prasad and I met in graduate school at the University of Hyderabad, I did not know that his Kannada-speaking family also followed the teachings of the Sringeri gurus, nor did I know that when I would next visit Sringeri from the U.S., where we had gone for graduate study, I would return speaking Kannada comfortably. Rather oddly, I had learned to speak it in the small university town of Hanover, New Hampshire, talking to Prasad, who was the only other Kannada speaker in town. In Sringeri, Dodda Murthy was amused and Chayamma was incredulous.

Dodda Murthy and Chayamma

"Nobody else has seen these in forty years," said Dodda Murthy, as he carefully handed me some books and newspaper clippings. "Take them home and read them. It's too noisy around here with the kids." Stunned, I held the barely yellowed and dry-and-crisp papers. How could he preserve them so well in Sringeri, I wondered, my mind jumping to the damp books on my bookshelf in my Sringeri apartment. This was the facet that I have come to associate with Dodda Murthy—with his small-built frame and thick black-framed glasses, muslin undershirt and white dhoti, and a passion for history and the documented past.

I stopped by Dodda Murthy and Chayamma's house virtually every other day, for at least ten minutes, drawn both by the fact they were my longest, most familiar, connection to Sringeri and because I fell into the habit of sharing the day's "events" with them. I used to gravitate to Chayamma for everything during my first full year in Sringeri. Once I frantically rushed across to her house (my apartment was about a hundred feet away from their house) after misplacing my gold ring. She asked me to have a puja done to Kartaviryarjuna, a deity who helps to recover lost objects. "Hurry, the temple will still be accepting puja tickets," she urged. I had the puja done, the priest and I standing on a stone ledge along the outer wall of the Vidyashankara temple near a relief of Kartaviryarjuna that is always freshly adorned with kumkum and flowers. I found my ring that evening. Thanks to this and my absentmindedness, I have since had to have countless pujas performed to Kartaviryarjuna. Ten-minute visits frequently turned into absorbing two- to three-hour conversations with Dodda Murthy and Chayamma. Chayamma, sprightly and petite, usually walked in and out of the room, adding details, explaining things that she felt I perhaps did not know. Dodda Murthy retired as a schoolteacher, a profession that he said he had simply wandered into—nobody in his extended family had ever been a teacher. I could not, however, imagine Dodda Murthy in any other profession. I heard from others that he had been a strict, but fine teacher. He lost most of his agricultural lands to tenants following land reforms, and the remaining continue to be managed by his nephews, Panduranga and Nagaraja, since Dodda Murthy and Chayamma do not have children. Dodda Murthy was twenty-seven when he married fourteen-year-old Chayamma, who came from Hassan (in the plains) in 1947. A photograph taken right after the four-day wedding hangs in the inner room where Dodda Murthy stores his precious papers and mementos. Dodda Murthy has a way of preserving things; in 2004 he showed me the still-new-looking umbrella I had given him in 1995. "I use this all the time," he told me, and Chayamma added, somewhat irritated, "And he doesn't let anybody touch it."

Dodda Murthy's narratives were typically about the past, and as I now synthesize my experiences of Sringeri into this book, I realize that much of the detail I know about Sringeri in relation to the world outside it comes from both the fine and broad strokes that Dodda Murthy's reminiscences have painted on the canvas of my mind. His history of the house itself was braided with a history of Sringeri's development and personages. The first bank to open in Sringeri, Sharada Bank, and its associated Sharada Co-operative Society, were owned by his father (C. N. Subba Rao) and operated from one of the rooms. Dodda Murthy's stories about pilgrims who came annually to Sringeri from South Kanara and camped in the Murthy courtyard and his descriptions of the royal Mysore durbar evoked for me a sense of the concrete ways in which relationships were forged across regions. Along with these stories, narratives about the initiation of different gurus into sanyasa, the presanyasa days of Sri Abhinava Vidyatirtha (the thirty-fourth guru), who had been Dodda Murthy's childhood playmate, British Residents, the power play between the matha's "Agents" and local communities, and everyday life in Sringeri during the 1930s, 1940s, and early 1950s, before the jagirdari (land-grant state) was abolished, filled countless hours and my audiotapes. An avid follower of world events and Indian politics, he made the Indian freedom struggle familiar to me with accounts of visits to the Mysore region by well-known leaders of the Independence movement. He had a photographic memory of how some of them spoke in public. He occasionally illustrated his recollections with extremely well-preserved photographs, old invitations, journal issues, newspapers, and—most precious of all to me—his own diaries, which he wrote weekly from 1940 to 1950. Once when he was narrating his travels through India, Chayamma interjected that Dodda Murthy "never drank water on his travels"—for health reasons, but I burst out laughing when she said, "Can you believe it? He asks instead for sāru [steaming hot spicy, watery soup]." Over the years Dodda Murthy and I settled into a comfortable raconteur-listener relationship, one that became doubly enthused when Prasad, my husband, joined the conversations. We traded stories and experiences.

Many of Dodda Murthy's narrations compared times past and times present or compared practices across cultures. Deferring judgments, he ended such stories with variations of "āgina kāla hāge ittu" (Those times were like that) or "avattina prapañca bere; ivattina prapañca bere" (The world of those times was different; the world today is different). For Dodda Murthy, more than anyone else I knew in Sringeri, it was a matter of "sticking to fact," not to give in to embellishment, when narrating or describing. It was perhaps this fidelity to "things as they are" as he knew them that explains the fact that his narratives, ten years apart, on my tapes are almost exactly the same in detail and emphasis. From Dodda Murthy I learned that narration itself is an ethical act: One evening in late May in 1995, as my stay in Sringeri came to a close, when he was visiting Prasad and me in our apartment, talk turned to Sringeri matters, and I mentioned someone with whom I'd chatted that afternoon. He asked me if I knew the tragic manner in which the resident's father had passed away many years ago. When I said no, he started to recount the incident, but then stopped in mid-sentence, noticing that I had brought a cup of boiled milk for him. "Let me finish this first," he said. "It isn't right to drink milk after narrating such a story," he explained briefly. Finishing the milk quickly, dwelling for a few minutes on mundane issues like how hot or how cold he liked his food to be, he returned to a description of the tragic episode. To have drunk the milk after narrating such an episode would have been an inappropriate and callous mixing of "tragedy" with "satisfaction."

For centuries the Shankara matha has been a prominent exponent of, and an authority on, Advaitic texts and Hindu codes of conduct known as the Dharmasutras and the Dharmashastras for a vast following of Hindus all over India and, of late, in the Hindu diaspora.[3] The Dharmasutras and the Dharmashastras themselves, in astonishing diversity and detail, discuss a wide variety of topics relating to social and religious conduct, law, and righteousness. By no means uniform, these vast normative compendia, commonly referred to as the "shastras" in everyday parlance, have been compiled by different authors approximately between 500 BCE and 400 CE. In an unbroken lineage of over twelve hundred years, the gurus who head the matha, and matha-appointed scholars, have interpreted the Dharmashastras

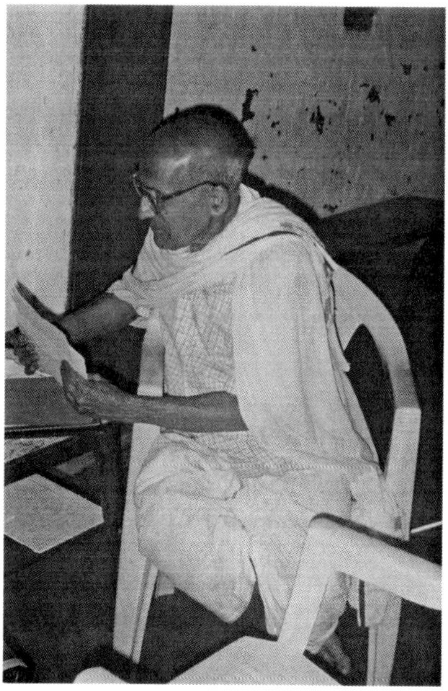

FIGURE 2. Dodda Murthy with his archive. *Photo by Leela Prasad*

FIGURE 3. Chayamma. *Photo by Leela Prasad*

and counseled royalty and the lay public on matters ranging from military campaigns and land disputes to the suitability of marriage alliances and the ethics of business practice. Historical records, including the kaditas (ledgers) of the matha, from the fourteenth century, show that powerful rulers like the Vijayanagara emperors, the Muslim kings Hyder Ali and Tipu Sultan of Mysore, the local Keladi Nayakas and the Mysore Wodeyars, and the colonizing British engaged in complex politicoreligious exchanges with the matha, perceiving its strategic importance in regional politics. Until the 1960s and 1970s, when land reform legislation altered its powerful economic status, the matha owned and governed Sringeri as an independent land-grant state through an intimate web of tenancy relationships with local populations.[4] Pontifical authority gradually grew to be politically empowered, transforming a hermitage and temple into a powerful monastic institution with political leverage. To a visitor the monastic institution that sprawls in the middle of the town seems to symbolize its indisputable centrality in the normative and cultural life of the region.

FIGURE 4. Shankara matha and Sharada temple. *Photo by S. Shankar*

Yet *what* exactly constitutes the "normative" in practice, I was to discover, would manifest itself as a problem to investigate. In 1992, many years after my summer visits to Sringeri had come to an end, I returned to it as a Ph.D. student at the University of Pennsylvania, troubled by prevailing academic classifications of the cultural knowledge systems of India. My training in the social sciences and humanities in the U.S. had been invigorating, but I felt burdened with analytic dichotomies that are a familiar part of Western discourse about "Indian culture." The grand dichotomy was the division of cultural traditions into "classical" and "folk." In the Hindu context "classical" had for long been characterized as pan-Indian, high caste, and Sanskritic, and the "folk" as localized, low caste, and vernacular. In early conceptualizations of this categorization, folk or little traditions were appreciated as derivative ones that drew inspiration from the classical or Great Tradition.[5]

However, as wide-ranging empirical research on oral and written epic traditions, art forms, and cultural practices began to register the crisscrossing ways in which expressive forms relate to one another and respond to changing political climates, scholars found it difficult to work with this partitioned analytic hypostatization of Indian culture. Instead, they began to consider the complex exchanges between expressive traditions, arguing along the lines of Stuart Blackburn and A. K. Ramanujan that both folk and classical traditions are "coexistent and available (in varying degrees) to everyone, as codes switched by rules of context like speech varieties in a speaker's repertoire."[6]

Although I was excited by the reenvisaging of Indian cultural traditions as plural and elastic, a view that came down heavily on an "upstairs/downstairs view of India,"[7] I was still uneasy with the categories themselves since they were based on studies of specific performance genres and ignored the "everyday" contexts of cultural experience.[8] How would one classify an everyday conversation, for instance, in which a personal experience narrative triggers a reference to a popular film, which could in turn lead to a scriptural citation or an allusion to the epic *Mahabharata*, and end in a joke or an anecdote? The need for locating theory building about culture in ethnographic understandings of everyday contexts had been voiced by Roger Abrahams in his call for the study of conversational genres and had even earlier found particular admission in the ethnography of speaking school.[9] Although we now talked of a continuum and not a hierarchy of traditions, how individuals actually selected and ordered their knowledge of various cultural traditions in daily discourse remained a puzzle.

In one sense Sringeri seemed to embody "classical" culture. Its temples and the twelve-hundred-year-old matha were virtually icons of Vedic traditions: the daily pujas in the temples, the philosophical debates (*vidvat sabhas*) organized by the matha in which Sanskrit scholars from all over India participated, and the Sanskrit Vidyapitha (university) spoke for the Sanskritic persuasion of Sringeri. However, when I began to live in Sringeri for extended periods of time on my visits in 1992 and 1993, I became aware of the diversity of the region's expressive culture. I learned about the popular dance drama, the *yakshagana*, the *anṭige-panṭige* festival of the Vokkaliga community during Deepavali, the seasonal *jātre* (fairs), and the harvest celebrations.

During 1992–1993 I also began to gain a more grounded perspective of Sringeri's demographics and geography. I met N. S. Chandrashekar (Putta Murthy, or "the younger Murthy"), Dodda Murthy's younger brother, and his son, Panduranga, who is editor and owner of *Srunkona*, a widely circulated local weekly. Then in his mid-sixties, Putta Murthy had been president of the Sringeri municipality, and, although he had retired, he remained influential in the public affairs of the town. A visionary community presence, Putta Murthy campaigned for the inclusion of women in the political administration of Sringeri (Lakshmidevamma, his wife, had served as municipal councillor for many years). He had convinced the municipality to construct roads and bridges in the interior rural areas and had organized numerous forums for debating and resolving communitywide issues that cut across caste and religious lines. When I described to Putta Murthy and Panduranga the academic debate about folk and classical categories, elaborating that I had felt this categorization did not account for everyday life, they suggested that the conversations that occurred during the seasonal processing of harvested areca nut in Sringeri might give me a structured setting in which to examine the mingling of cultural forms.

Areca nut, occupying more than 25 percent of Sringeri's arable land, is cultivated by most of the local land-owning community, and, because it is not labor intensive, it offers viable supplementary occupation for those employed in other means of livelihood. Between September, when the lashing monsoon dwindles into a thin drizzle, and mid-January, when Sankranti, the harvest festival, arrives, the nuts are plucked from the soaring palms by skilled workers and brought to the homes of the owners. Families of owners as well as hired workers—a heterogeneous group in terms of caste, age, and gender—husk the nuts late into the night for several days, and keep awake and engaged through conversation and occasional cups of tea and coffee. So, in 1994, I returned to Sringeri to study the talk that takes place during the processing of the areca nut. As I listened to the conversations unpredictably unfold (as conversations often do), with anecdotes, jokes, and gossip tumbling into each other, it became vividly clear to me that the matha was only one among many other markers of Sringeri culture. Most important, I also came to realize that the matha is not the sole influence on normative thinking in the region. In everyday life the matha (rather, the Dharmashastric practices and models it endorses) is but one among many sources of the normative that compete, collaborate, or even ignore one another in the moral imagination of individuals.

Thus independent of the matha's sponsorship is a culture that celebrates regional festivals, dance dramas, and especially the wider region's famous traditions of hospitality. *Upachara,* the term for hospitality in Kannada also means "right conduct." With considerable normative implications that permeate everyday practice and parlance in Sringeri, the notion of upachara enjoys a long cultural history in the region, and, as I show in this book, the practice of upachara has come to claim its own poetic. I tried to clumsily follow up on commentary and anecdotes that I had recorded and noticed during areca-nut-shelling sessions, often stubbing against complicated responses to my identity as guest, young married woman, brahman, Ph.D. student (and so on).[10] I soon learned that seemingly ordinary day-to-day proprieties—who visits whom and for how long, what modes of speaking are employed, what food is cooked and how it is served, for instance—belonged to fine-grained but pervasive understandings of upachara.

A prominent expression of upachara that is unique to Sringeri is an oral performance tradition known as *ashirvada* (ceremonial blessing). In ashirvada priests or male elders are invited to make exegetical "speeches" to audiences at the end of festive ceremonies conducted in homes or temples. These extemporaneous speeches, which seek to provide the "essence" of the ritual event in terms of purpose, enactment, and effect, present idealized ethical models, and thereby make a rhetorical statement about what constitutes appropriate conduct. While the ashirvada tradition is a performative expression of upachara, and explicitly emphasizes ideas that are underwritten by treatises on conduct such as the Dharmashastras, the cultural consciousness about appropriate conduct that is central to upachara is seen not only in grand gestures of hospitality or ritual performance but also in acts of everyday life.

Although I had arrived in Sringeri assuming that the matha would be unquestionably central in the normative worldview of Sringeri residents, Sringeri conversations brought to the surface plural sources and vocabularies of the normative that often, in fact, did not always reflect views endorsed by the matha in its official capacity. The countless lifestories, narratives of local history, and stories about deities, miracles, and itinerant ascetics compellingly unsettled my initial perception, and I began to ask how quotidian contexts (characterized by gender, age, economic status, caste identity, and social situation) and everyday conversations reflected the cultural attention given to the notion of appropriate conduct. Put another way, if the ashirvada tradition, with its emphasis on shastric idealizations of conduct, constitutes the performative expression of Sringeri upachara, how do narratives shared in spontaneous conversation reflect and shape moral being and becoming and display the more likely labyrinthine relationships between canons that prescribe conduct (even as they express canonical ambiguities) and complex exigencies of everyday life? How do smarta brahmans situate the normative authority of the matha and the Sanskrit codes of conduct in their daily lives? Or do they?[11] Definitionally, smarta brahmans take their name from their adherence to the smriti ("remembered") tradition that mainly comprises the Dharmashastras and the Dharmasutras.

Thus the central questions of this book are: How do people living in the vicinity of a powerful institution, with a local and panregional reach, that for centuries has been an influential interpreter of the Dharmashastras, imagine and express their moral worlds? What indeed is normative for whom and when, and what vocabulary defines it? How do individuals make connections between "knowing" and "doing" the right thing when sources of the normative are many? In attempting to answer these questions, this book presents and discusses stories that Sringeri residents shared with me in everyday conversations, stories about renunciates, ritual worship, commensal eating, domestic activities, and human relationships with the divine, for example. Translating these stories from Kannada, I argue that although such topics may be treated extensively in Dharmashastra texts and authenticated by the monastic authority in the vicinity, these stories from everyday life reveal intricate and dynamic relationships between "prescribed" and "practiced" conduct. Drawing also on conversations and observations outside narrated contexts, the book shows, first, that "shastra" in lived Hinduism is truly elastic in its creative engagement of tradition, text, practice, and moral authority and, second, that as a moral concept, shastra coexists with other concepts of the normative. At the same time, the book also analyzes the explicitly prescriptive ashirvada tradition, presenting one illustrative ashirvada performance. In the face of "Hindu" fundamentalist rhetoric or generalized Marxist readings that privilege monolithic, exclusionary narratives about morality, this study hopes to crucially illustrate the plurality of moral discourse even in a scripturally conscious setting, and raise an important larger question. How do, or do, multiple discourses about conduct relate to each other in the daily lives of people? As I try to understand the many kinds of diglossia that are at work in the articulation of moral experience, I find the work of language philosophers like Paul Ricoeur and Mikhael Bakhtin helpful.[12]

I also had to dismantle another assumption: that institutions such as the matha that are centers of brahmanical ideology are unidimensionally dominant. Oral and written histories about the matha and ongoing engagements with it reminded me of what the public eye is prone to miss: the matha is a *peopled* place with historically located *relationships* to local communities, individuals, and families. Once I recognized this, I began to perceive that there are several structures of authority within the matha, multiple reciprocal agreements and possibilities for negotiation between the matha and families, and differences of opinion among individuals in administrative positions in the matha. Ultimately, one is compelled to rethink the constructs of "the matha" and "the community." Even though many in Sringeri's community work in the matha, they lead lives quite distinct from it, and the phrase "the matha " does not always mean the *same* structure of pontifical authority to everybody, or always. By the term *the matha,* individuals could refer to a geopolitical authority, to a cultural institution, to an institution that is embodied by particular persons, or to a symbol of certain historical periods. Principally, however, many individuals and families regard particular spiritual heads of the matha as their guru(s), and such relationships inform their daily lives and their assessments of current practices of the matha. Evaluations of the matha are critical of specific policies—and personages—of the matha. At the same time, people are generally aware of the complex position of the matha, especially since it has seen significant sociopolitical transformations in its own structure especially in the 1960s and 1970s. Individuals in Sringeri also pointed out that the matha has obligations as a social institution, obligations that are likely to clash sometimes with local priorities.

I carry a backpack of theoretical perspectives, oddly mirroring what Putta Murthy once said about me (and my husband, who was visiting) when we came rushing into their house, late for lunch, "Bandru ibbaru, benna mēle cīla hākkoṇḍu!" (Here come the two, with bags on their backs!). The book's theoretical bases derive from "oral literary criticism" from Sringeri,[13] from early Indian sociophilosophical theories, from Sanskrit poetics and performance theory, from folkloristic performance studies, and from Anglo-American perspectives on narrative. Thus not only does theory appear in many shapes and forms, but it also asks that we reexamine the concept of theory itself. I take more seriously than perhaps intended by "new ethnography" that reflexive ethnography is an attempt to engage with theorizations occurring in varied and particularized contexts of human life, theorizations that, at the minimum, go beyond the academe and beyond Euro-American notions of what might count as theory.[14] What is theory, who makes it, and who validates it as *theory?* What, and by whom, is a way of thinking designated as *not theory*? Margaret Mills, pointing out gender blindness inherent to visions of what theory is in the study of folklore (and one might consider such myopia to be even more glaring in other disciplines) says, "If you buy (as I do) Marta Weigle's idea that gossip-anecdote can speak (constitute *and* articulate) cosmic order(s) just as much as cosmotactic *myths* do, then our data—are *always already* speaking 'theory'—somebody's theory, theory in the everyday—and it's our job to sort out *whose* theory . . . we might best make our high claim be low theory, to see how 'experience near' (from our subjects' point of view) our theoretical constructions can be."[15]

As we interrogate the construct of theory, we might also ask, what relationships are possible or imagined between theory and practice? James Laidlaw insightfully explores this question in his rich ethnography of religious practices prevalent in a Jain community in Jaipur, Rajasthan, a study with which my own work finds affinities. Taking up the problem of how in everyday life Jains (a largely prosperous business community) interpret and live out what seem to be "impossible ideals and values" of austere renunciation, Laidlaw points out how necessary it is to recognize Jainism not simply as an unfolding of doctrines but as an "enduring form of life . . . [that] seems to provide its followers with ideas, institutions, relationships, and practices—a set of ways of going on—which together make conflicting values compossible, and impossible ideals compelling."[16] If "doctrines" are understood as "theory," Sheldon Pollock concludes after an extensive study of the notion of shastra that, in contrast to the West, in Sanskritic culture "'theory' is held always and necessarily to precede and govern practice; there is no dialectical interaction between them. Two important implications of this fundamental postulate are that all knowledge is pre-existent, and that progress can only be achieved by a regressive re-appropriation of the past."[17] This is an important unsettling of the idea in Western cultures that theory follows *from* practice or data. Still, relationships between theory and practice need not necessarily exist, as Laidlaw finds: "Much religious practice takes place in the absence of a theory to explain it; and even where such theories are formulated, it would be a mistake to assume they underlie experience or practice, or that people's religious lives are in any sense based upon them."[18] However, the chapters that follow in this book modify both Pollock's and Laidlaw's observations somewhat to suggest that once you admit moral theorization as taking place in everyday life where "practitioners" identify, historicize, and improvise upon plural sources of the normative, "dialectical" relations between "theory" and "practice" necessarily follow. Theorization that occurs in everyday life dissolves lines between "theory" and "practice," and the challenge comes from such theorization being both explicit and embedded in everyday practice, and maddeningly plural. Can we, as Yeats asked, know the dancer from the dance? As Roger Abrahams, one of the most prolific scholars of modern everyday experience and expressivity, has remarked recently, "We look for meanings, not behind our vernacular artifacts and interactions, but *in* them" (emphasis mine).[19]

My location helps me find perhaps surprising dialogue between theories that emerge in Sringeri self-representations and Hindu written texts, on the one hand, and theories that are external to both (Wittgenstein, Ricoeur, for example), on the other. For example, one of the most exciting explorations for me in this study has been an engagement with Sanskrit poetics, specifically with the concept of dramaturgical propriety (*auchitya*). Understood as the appropriate adaptation of poetic means to the poetic end, the concept of auchitya was systematized by the eleventh-century critic, Kshemendra, in his *Aucityavicāracarca* (Inquiry into deliberations on propriety). Although Sanskrit critics debated for centuries what the most important constituent of poetry was (was it figurative speech, style, or suggestion, for example?), they all agreed that auchitya was an indispensable regulatory principle in judging the poetic merit of a work of art. But Kshemendra took this argument further to say that only when every aspect of artistic representation—character, diction, style, and intent, for instance—is deployed in the manner most befitting the whole could a work of art effectively evoke aesthetic emotion (*rasa*) which was the goal of all poetic effort. I find parallels between dramatic propriety conceptualized more than ten centuries ago and the contemporary oral poetics of the ashirvada tradition as well as the moral propriety in everyday life in Sringeri. Such a dialogue has uncovered connections between aesthetics and persuasiveness, areas that imply one another but have remained hermetic in scholarship. By bringing performance studies—understood not only as a recent development but also as formulated in India two millennia ago—to ethical inquiry, this book posits that moral narration is intimately tied to the aesthetics of narrativization so that the socially situated moral self and the artistic self are continuous with, and shape, each other or, sometimes, provide ironic commentary on each other.

Diverging from studies of ethics that center on written compendia of moral codes designated by cultural historians as normative, this book builds on the recognition that the moral lives of people are not ossified products of "authoritative" texts. Instead, narratives, spontaneously shared and ceremonially delivered, hold up the moral self as dynamic and gendered, with a historical presence, a political agency, and endowed with a capacity for artistic expression that mediates many sources of knowledge to articulate appropriateness in conduct. In writing this book, I am persuaded by oral narratives and narrators that relationships between ethical precept and practice are intertwined and that conceptualizing an ethics-in-practice necessitates understanding the tremendous role of imagination in configuring the moral self in relation to "text," authority, and community.[20]

For centuries the Hindu context with its Puranic stories, epics, folktales, and hagiographies, in all their limitless variations, has recognized that narrative—encompassing the oral, the written, and the visual—is a brilliant and enduring medium for the expression of moral discourse.[21] Two wonderful folkloric collections immediately come to mind. Kirin Narayan shows how Swamiji, a holy man in Nasik (western India), with great compassion, humor, and wisdom employs storytelling to enliven moral teaching. While sometimes Swamiji's stories resemble known literary story traditions, his stories are ultimately narrations that are deeply sensitive to the situational contexts of the listening audience. In this he exemplifies and particularizes one of the oldest thriving ways in which the moral life is imparted and learned in India.[22] More recently, in a hundred oral tales shared with him in various villages in Tamilnadu, Stuart Blackburn finds that the tales are explicitly moral in orientation and reflect not only moral content but tellers' perspectives on that content. In their focus on crime and justice, Blackburn suggests that these "Tamil tales of morality" outline a moral system that is "parallel" to a karma-centered ethics.[23] The moral content of the tales is hardly static or contained only in symbols; rather, it is shaped by tellers' perspectives that operate within "the boundaries of historically transmitted understandings attached to specific characters, motifs and episodes."[24] While the Sanskrit epics of the *Ramayana* and the *Mahabharata* themselves accommodate multiple, competing moral visions within their narrative frames, innumerable retellings of these epic stories accentuate this interrogative tendency.[25] Hagiographic narrative is frequently seen as exemplifying moral teaching through the devotionalism and life story of the saint.[26] Indian narrative traditions, wide-ranging in genre and content that have back-and-forth reverberations, indeed provoke us to think about how we frame the moral debates they encode.

Our reading of "moral content," already complicated by contexts and genres of communication, is further challenged by narrative that takes non-verbal forms. C. S. Patil, for example, describes how various architectural structures—pillars, temples, wells, rocks—from the seventh to the twelfth centuries spanning India, Bangladesh, and Indonesia fascinatingly display episodes from the morally didactic tales of the *Panchatantra* with their lively animal and human protagonists. These architectural depictions, Patil argues, indicate ways in which *different* literary traditions of the *Panchatantra* are deployed. Although the question is not relevant to Patil's inquiry, we could ask whether the sculptures themselves reflect any shifts in moral emphases depending on the literary traditions they express.[27]

In the Euro-American context, dissatisfaction with rule-oriented moral theory (Descartes, Kant) has led to the formulation of "narrative ethics" in the last few decades. The objection has been that rule-driven moral theory, in its attempt to universalize ethics, forgets to adequately factor in the enormous significance of individual experience, of contexts of time and space, or of contexts of communities and cultures in the formation (and expression) of moral understanding. The recognition that narrative accounts for these various contexts, and is also attentive to individual experience of language and social process, has informed the work of various scholars who, although differing in their emphases, share the view that it is primarily through narrative—more than by propositions or rules—that moral knowledge is formed and moral knowing occurs.[28] Narrative ethics argues that ethical deliberation is a narrative endeavor, one that allows the individual agent to explore through reflection, recollection, and retelling, the all too common human predicaments of ambiguity, uncertainty, failure, or possibility. The anxiety that narrative ethics could breed moral relativism is answered by the recognition that narratives are social products, linguistically mediated and culturally conditioned—and that therefore narrative always expresses a *relation* to something larger than itself.

As I discuss in chapters 5 and 6, in fact in Sanskrit poetics of the seventh to eleventh centuries a serious concern was how to make narrative align itself to its larger goals—of creating a particular emotion or evoking a moral perspective.

These important insights highlight the ethical underpinnings of the narrative experience, but leave open, or altogether ignore, the implications of *oral* narrative for ethical inquiry. In fact, narrative ethics has largely concerned itself with written narrative, particularly Western literary and parabolic narrative, leaving out human voices and visages and the lived cultural contexts that form the rationale for this field.[29] I argue that the dynamic nature of oral narrative and the seeing-and-doing orientations—a literacy of practice—that are part of everyday life brings fresh questions to studies of ethics, compelling that we ask how individuals imagine or create the normative and negotiate and express it amidst their gendered identities, their belongings to family and community, and their varied circumstances of time and place. Oral narration, by virtue of being embedded in everyday life, captures "texts" that often defy fixity, that are emergent and contextual, and whose authorship is frequently coconstructed.[30] If the oral performance of ethical discourse (as in the ashirvada tradition) underscores social consensus on appropriate conduct, how do conversational narratives and the life situations they embody disturb that consensus or identify more complex processes of moral reflection? A consideration of oral narrative takes the study of ethics beyond the literary experience and fosters critical recognition of its own distinct dramatic, compositional aesthetic. Even as this book focuses on narrative, implicit in its various chapters is a central understanding that has shaped this exploration: moral learning and "appropriateness" in conduct are to a great extent imbibed through what I have just called seeing-and-doing orientations. Thus, my study of narrativized experience often encounters the verbalized construct, in Wittgensteinian fashion, "that's just the way it is done" or "I just know this." Such knowing is embedded in nonverbal transmission gained by being immersed in an environment. As somebody remarked to me in Halanduru, a village five miles into the forest from Sringeri town (where I used to live in a rented apartment), how will you know what to do and how if you stay with us for two days and go away?

The interpretations I propose of stories and performances are shaped either explicitly through "oral literary criticism" or through the interpretive agency that necessarily suffuses (and surrounds) the narrations I present. Since the ashirvada tradition is considered formal "performance" in Sringeri,[31] I draw on performance theories developed both in folkloristics (since the 1960s, with the coming together of sociolinguistics and ethnography) and in Sanskrit poetics of the tenth to eleventh centuries, particularly the concept of dramaturgical propriety. On the other hand, since conversationally shared stories (which are many times personal experience narratives) are for the most part not seen as "performances" by narrators, I rely more on conversational rhythms and contextual knowledge for interpretation.

Linguistic anthropologists (whose work interfaces folklore, phenomenology, and developmental psychology) have usefully identified aspects that "quotidian narratives" perhaps share across cultures despite being always locally situated. Elinor Ochs and Lisa Capps identify such "dimensions" as "tellership" (who narrates), "tellability" (what is and is not selected for narration), "embeddedness" (discourse context), "linearity" (ordering of narrative time), and "moral stance" (perspective on experience).[32] Indeed, for folklorists studying verbal artistic communication, these dimensions have for decades been integral to providing one kind of "context."[33] However, I am deliberately reticent about drawing on sociolinguistic approaches to conversational narrative. While thinking of stories and conversations in terms of interactional "frames," emphases and elisions, topical detours and repetitions, and so on does help me attend to the individuated poetics of speaking,[34] I must ask that the conversational stories I present be understood ultimately within the context of the *relationships* that I have come to share with the individuals whose stories appear here. Particular interactive moments perhaps produce narrations, but these moments belong in relationships and speak in complex ways to the memory and self-understandings of narrators—indeed, scholarship on life story illuminates this complexity, weaving as it does the "macros" and the "micros" of living and speaking that build on a process of sustained engagement.[35]

Also shaping my study is the recognition that the work of interpretation is perpetual, neither beginning with the ethnographer nor ending with her. Therefore, the challenge becomes not how to provide a conclusive interpretation, but how to keep interpretations provisional, so that the oral text remains "open" despite its fixity in print. Margaret Mills explores several mechanisms by which texts could be rendered open on the printed page—for example, by providing continuous transcripts of narrative, rather than frequently interspersing the narrative with the ethnographer's directorial interpretations, or by presenting material that seems muddlesome or contradictory to the ethnographer's perspective. But, as Mills reminds us, despite these attempts, complete textual openness may well remain a chimera.

I have shared the book in drafts at first and then in entirety with many people in Sringeri, but particularly with those whose voices are recorded in these pages. Apart from the lengthy discussions we have had about perspectives when I visited Sringeri, most recently in summer 2005, Sringeri residents have provided continuous and active feedback through phone calls and e-mail. When levels of English fluency did not match, and I could not physically be present to provide the Kannada translation, Sringeri residents shared the chapters (or at least sections of it they wished to have read) with those who could translate for them to be able to engage. Thus this process has been one of serious, mutual engagement through varying means. For example, Ramachandra Bhatta reviewed recordings of the stories he narrated to me, read my translations, and also commented specifically on chapter 3, saying he agreed that what was lost during colonial intervention was the sense of flexibility that goes with shastra. When I asked Giridhara Shastry—somebody who read every word of this book as well as its many drafts—whether I could present the story of the meal event hosted by the matha (in chapter 6), he said I could present it provided I did not use it to "prove" an agenda that was external or hostile to the context of that episode. I discussed the story, as I did with other narrators, and shared my translation and interpretation of it. Without exception, the interpretations I propose have been allowed to remain. Perhaps this is less a reflection of the correctness of my views than of the pluralism I encountered in Sringeri society.

The plan of the book is as follows: chapter 1 ("Place and Placeness") explores multiple Sringeri locations in order to evoke some of the many ways in which "a Sringeri ethos" is expressed. Moral articulations, the chapter suggests, occur in situated contexts that encode layered affinities and distances to place, history, and community. I thus present demographics, town histories, geophysical mappings of the region, festival celebrations, and the place of ashirvada in Sringeri consciousness to demonstrate how they contribute to differing and temporal senses of belonging. The chapter ends with the question that is at the core of Sringeri traditions of upachara: What is appropriate conduct?

Chapter 2 considers this question in the light of Sringeri's history, particularly in the context of historical relationships between the matha, various kings and governments, and diverse local communities. Drawing on different sources of history—place lore, oral accounts, monuments, inscriptions, and ledgers—this chapter traces the wide web of obligatory linkages between king and ascetic, landlord and tenant, guru and communities, and deity and devotee. The modes in which these linkages were forged, maintained, or repudiated, I suggest, reveal conceptions of what constitutes appropriate conduct. I draw on traditional Hindu sociophilosophical theories of *rina* (debt), *dana* (gifting), and upachara to demonstrate the complexity of these linkages and especially their invisible and indirect impetuses.

The perpetual question of what constitutes dharmic conduct (dharma being duty, righteousness, law) and how to enact it is often linked to the notion of shastra, a concept that fuses precept and practice and that even defines itself as a "theory of practice."[36] So powerful is shastra as a normative concept that it has sustained debate and deliberation on its nature across the millennia. Contemporary Hindu society, including the society of Sringeri, continues to grapple with shastric questions about the nature and source of moral authority, jurisdictions of moral knowledge, and the efficacy, permissibility, and the rigidity of prescriptions. In chapter 3 I turn to the identity of the matha, as it crystallized around the fourteenth century into a Dharmashastra-interpreting authority, to explore conceptualizations of shastra in early India across various schools of philosophy and in medieval bhakti and court literature. European protoethnographic observations about a fluid, largely oral system of jurisprudence in precolonial south India seem to contradict British colonial policy, which relied on a parochial book-based understanding of shastra to effect profound changes in indigenous judicial systems. Understanding these broader developments, I argue, helps us perceive the changes that occurred consequently in the judicial reach and authority of the Sringeri matha.

The stories and conversations in chapter 4 challenge us to widen our understanding of text and textuality so that we can recognize that the world of material and oral practices also provides "texts" that function as vibrant forms of moral guidance for Hindus. From such a widening emerges a lived grammar of the normative, a sociosemantic field of normative discourse and praxis marked by lively, though not always friendly, interplay between shastra and other concepts like sampradaya (tradition), niyama (rule), achara (practice), and paddhati (custom), all of which make competing claims to authority. The profusion of a vocabulary of the normative prompts me to ask, drawing on Wittgenstein, whether it is possible to discern patterns that constitute a "grammar of our concepts" about the normative. While Indian contexts robustly admit oral texts that guide conduct, along with written texts, sung texts, and heard texts, I find that Sringeri theorizations necessitate that we also think of conduct being guided by, and expressed through, *imagined texts*, texts that are dynamically put together, are situational, and historically accountable.

Chapter 5 translates and interprets one ashirvada event that marked the conclusion of a Durga puja in 2004. Ashirvada texts and their performative contexts constitute one significant kind of normative discourse in Sringeri that emphasizes (and exhorts) a fidelity to shastric norms prescribed in specific Dharmashastras, Puranas, or the epics. Cited ubiquitously as illustrating Sringeri's continued participation in the famous regionwide tradition of upachara, ashirvada performances celebrate guest-host relations in a stylized manner and are seen as bearing a dual obligation: to enunciate dharmic "precepts" and to adhere to poetic propriety. Drawing on observations, and on conversations with performers and audiences over many years, I present an oral poetics of ashirvada. I then explore how such an oral poetics is continuous with, or diverges from, Sanskrit poetics. The shared conceptual basis, I argue, is the theory of auchitya or dramatic propriety. Juxtaposed against the deliberately stylized ashirvada tradition, which is conscious of its ethical and aesthetic accountabilities, are personal-experience narratives shared in "everyday" conversations expressing another sort of vivacity that characterizes moral imagination.

Chapter 6 presents six such conversational narratives, locating them in the lives of narrators, in relationships with me, and in the fluid contexts of our interactions so as to not impart to the narratives a fixity they may not have possessed. In a sense this chapter presents a form readers will already have encountered throughout the book: oral narrative shared spontaneously in conversation. But this chapter seeks to foreground the use of narrative in self-presentation. The stories in this chapter thus reflect how moral being and becoming come not from an unmediated allegiance to a fossilized normative, but rather from a crisscrossing engagement with diverse sources of the normative. Instead of "scriptural stipulations," they foreground values such as sukshma (subtlety), viveka (discernment), nigarva (humility), and seve (service) that take diverse locations—a Sringeri kitchen, Gandhi's ashram, a temple, a public meal event, and so on. These values emerge as powerful forces—but not exclusive or exhaustive—in individual constructions of a moral universe.

It is almost impossible to untangle the many voices and presences that have filled the ten years in the making of this ethnography. As I suppose happens with those who do ethnography, cultural "data," even when it is not marked as such, imperceptibly presents itself in bus stops and shops, on streets and in markets, in one-time interactions and in long-term relationships. Appearing in different places in the book are vignettes of several people whose voices permeate its pages. The vignettes are just that—they are not life sketches, nor are they representative of Sringeri people, nor do they constitute essential characteristics of Sringeri life. Nevertheless, I hope they will say something about the relationships I share with these individuals and trace the spaces of my interactions with them. Most important, I hope they will evoke the presence of the persons who narrated the stories that appear throughout the book, but especially in chapter 6.

This book is situated in the lives of Sringeri brahmans, who, in the majority, follow the smarta tradition. My own identity—a changing compilation of many identities (U.S.A.-living researcher interested rather imprecisely in "Sringeri culture," friend of the Murthy family, a Telugu-Kannada-Marathi mixed breed city-bred Hyderabadi, for example)—took me to the homes of many families where I found that my smarta brahmanical identity gained a new prominence. Until my stay in Sringeri, I had paid little conscious attention to (and hence was not conversant with) the specifics of the texts, traditions, and practices that were believed to characterize my smarta background. My personal locations and my little-little identities were transparent to those I interacted with—a transparency aided by my own narrations of experiences—and doubtless influenced conversations that took place and the stories that people in Sringeri shared with me.

1 *Sringeri*

Place and Placeness

Sringeri is part of the region in northwestern Karnataka known as the Malnad that takes its name from *male* (hill) and *nāḍu* (land).[1] It receives on an average 130 to 150 inches of rain every year, and one rarely visits Sringeri—or leaves it—between June and September when the rains can be torrential. Lying east of the Sahyadri mountain range in southwestern India, the Malnad includes the taluks of Sringeri, Koppa, Narasimharajapura, and sometimes Mudigere. The roughly 400-mile long and 40-mile wide stretch of the Malnad is at a height that ranges from 500 to 3,000 feet above sea level.[2] The Malnad is one of those regions that is not marked on a map, but charted very tangibly in public imagination. One of the most popular constructs of collective identity in Sringeri is its identification with "Malnad culture."

Being part of the Malnad, however, is only one way in which Sringeri communities imagine themselves. This chapter explores some of the many ways in which it is possible to characterize collective ambiences of Sringeri—through demographics, architecture, oral histories of the town, festival celebrations, regional consciousness (particularly about upachara, the practice of hospitality), and the ashirvada tradition considered unique to Sringeri. These intersecting, shifting, mediated, and material expressions constitute in different ways the ethos of Sringeri. The word *ethos*—indeed the very word from which the term *ethics* has arisen—fittingly captures the many terms and phrases used colloquially in Kannada to preface or contextualize "Sringeri culture"—*illi vātavaraṇa* (the atmosphere here), *rītī vidhānā* (ways and means of being), *Sringerīya viṣeśa* (the special thing about Sringeri), *namma Sringeriyalli* (in our Sringeri), and *ī kaḍe ella* (in these parts), for example. While the Oxford English Dictionary glosses *ethos* as "the characteristic spirit, prevalent tone of sentiment, of a people or community; the 'genius' of an institution or system," early Greek usage includes "place" as one of its meanings.[3] Although Aristotle's use of ethos focused more on moral "character" honed through "habits" of virtuous living that provided authority to public speakers, "the most concrete meaning given for the term in the Greek lexicon is a 'habitual gathering place.'"[4] Another important denotation of ethos is "manners, customs."[5] Ethos, then, is a word that brings together senses of place, placeness, public, community, and moral ambience—that are all implicated in the ways Sringeri is experienced and imagined.

This chapter builds on a threefold understanding: first, there are almost always multiple configurations to the ethos of a place, second, these configurations are temporally, spatially, and communally differentiated, and, third, these diverse characterizations of ethos embody diverse approaches to the practice of ethics. As Nedra Reynolds has put it, "careful attention to the etymology of ethos—its connections to space, place, or location—helps to reestablish ethos as a social act and as a product of a community's character."[6] The ethos of Sringeri—as of any place—is a social construct that not only is produced by shared experiences and memories but also simultaneously itself can produce insider-outsider demarcations in such a way that landscapes of culture and place become integral to moral articulations.

Sringeri's Place Stories

Sthala puranas, or place stories, are a robust oral and written genre in Hindu culture, remembering and vivifying the past of a place in terms of deeds of deities and holy people. Sthala puranas sometimes localize wider narratives, for example, making Sita of the *Ramayana* epic tradition rest under the shade of a local tree or a rock, but their primary loyalty is toward delineating and developing a vernacular, ethos. Origin stories, place names, architectural and geological features, local events, and political episodes—all contribute to the making of sthala puranas, although the *māhātmyās*, their more visible subgenre, concentrate on the glorification of a particular place.[7] As new events and newer histories continually write themselves into a place, they are many times absorbed into its sthala puranas (which usually exist in the plural) and so sthala puranas in the oral tradition grow and change and admit considerable variation. Topography constantly multiplies and is transformed into symbolic geography.

One well-known place story in Sringeri recounts how Sringeri got its name. I had heard the story many times during my stay in Sringeri, and variants did not differ substantially. But the most elaborate version was one that I heard from Ganapati Avadhani. Until 1997 Ganapati Avadhani had been the matha's *dharmadhikari*, the appointee of the matha for adjudicating matters of conduct. His family went back many centuries in Sringeri. On my extended stay in 2004 I used to see him sitting on the front porch of his house, elegantly draped in his shawl and traditionally worn dhoti, almost every time I walked to one of the main streets of Sringeri. One day I stopped to talk to him, and one long conversation led to many during that summer. At some point I remarked in Kannada, "I don't know if you'll remember my grandfather who lived in Sringeri in the 1950s. Srinivasan . . . " Recognition was instant. "Oh, Judge Srinivasan's granddaughter? Of course I knew him. You didn't mention this to me until now? And you talk to me in Kannada? Come, you're *manavāñḍlu*! (our people)." I immediately remembered with amusement Chayamma's remark from a decade ago when I had mentioned to her that a particular Telugu woman had visited me in my apartment. Although this woman had been a resident of Sringeri for many years, it was probably among the very few times she had visited anybody. Chayamma had quipped, "Eṣṭādru manavāñḍlu!" (what it comes down to is "our people"!). Chayamma, who does not speak Telugu, had combined the Kannada *eṣṭādru* with the Telugu *manavāñḍlu* by which Telugu people popularly indicate "one's own community." Through this brief and witty linguistic invention, she had critiqued insiderness and ethnic identification.

So, with Ganapati Avadhani, conversations from then on were in Telugu. "I'll tell you a story about Sringeri's *mūla* [root; origin]," Ganapati Avadhani said, as I settled on the bench in the veranda of his house. "Once you know this story, you won't need to know anything else," he added. He then began the story of the rain-bringing sage Rishyashringa from whom Sringeri gets its name. Rishyashringagiri (giri = hill) is the hill where Rishyashringa is said to have lived and performed penance.

GA: Brahma's son, Kashyapa, had a son called Vibhandaka, the great sage who lived in these parts. Vibhandaka desired to remain a brahmachari (celibate student), and to seek Shiva through penance. The gods noticed the rigorous penance but felt that so illustrious a lineage needed to be continued for the good of humanity.

"Let us awaken desire in him for a woman, he'll then want to marry and will have children,"

they reasoned.

So they send Urvashi (a celestial dancer), who tries to seduce Vibhandaka.[8]

He was unmoved. And she was resolute.

L: She had come with that very intention!

GA: Both of them were obstinate!

But one day Vibhandaka was bathing and he was aroused. In all this hustle and bustle, he ejaculated into the water.

And went back to penance.

But the gods thought their purpose achieved. They asked Urvashi to become a deer and accept the seed. The "deer" became pregnant.

Meanwhile the unknowing Vibhandaka had been continuing his austerities.

One day he went for his bath to the river, and found a crying infant boy and a deer beside it.

The deer ran away as soon as it saw him.

Now he (Vibhandaka) could not abandon the tender infant.

L: After all, he was the father.

GA: But neither could he take in the child and shelter it, bachelor and ascetic that he was. The gods then intervene.

They say,

"This child is yours. It is your duty to protect him."

Now he was in a deep dilemma. No cradle, no milk.

So he prayed to Shiva saying,

"Only you can look after this child that you have given me."

And he placed the child among the Tulasi and Bilva leaves that he used in Shiva's worship.

With those very leaves as bed, Shiva protected the child.

Honeybees used to drop honey into the child's mouth.

This went on for eleven days.

Then it was time for the naming ceremony.

All the sages (rishi[s]) arrived at Vibhandaka's invitation.

They decided that he had to have "Rishi" in his name for he was a rishi's son.

Then they saw that the child had a deer-like horn (shringa) in his forehead.

So they named him Rishyashringa (one-horned, born of a sage).

Vibhandaka at last said,

"Since I allowed myself be charmed by a woman, let no woman ever be allowed to set foot in the forests of Sringeri."

And he withdrew into penance.

So Rishyashringa grew up with no mother, and with no knowledge about the existence of the female species, and in the company of his father. He too learned to live the ascetic life.

In the northern parts, Romapada's kingdom was struck by drought. The king sought sage Narada's advice.

Narada tells him,

"If a true ascetic visits your kingdom, he will bring the rains."

"Now where would we find such an ascetic?"

"There is one in Sringeri. However, it will be difficult to bring him here. He is protected by his father, a great ascetic but short-tempered. It is impossible to wean the son away from the father. But you could try."

Romapada sends a call across his entire kingdom but everybody is daunted, afraid of the elder sage's fury.

"What if he curses us?"

Then some courtesans come forward.

L: Hanh!

GA: They say,

"We'll bring him. If we perish, what could be a better fate than perishing because of a sage's curse? If we succeed, then it is a success—

L: a gain—

GA: If we succeed, it will be a victory for all of womankind.[9]

So please permit us (to bring Rishyashringa)."

Romapada gratefully accepted the offer. So the courtesans set out. And they arrived at Narve, right here, about nine miles from Sringeri, and they waited there. One day, as usual, when Rishyashringa was picking herbs and roots for his father, they beckoned to him from across the river.

"Come here, come here!"

Rishyashringa had never seen a woman before, and—

L: He must have wondered what creature that was!

GA: Right. He had no idea what that was. They gave him all kinds of exotic foods and enticed him, telling him,

"Come with us, our kingdom has even greater pleasures."

So Rishyashringa goes with them.

The minute he set foot in Romapada's kingdom, the rains poured. Romapada was happy. Rishyashringa conducted the putrakāmeṣṭi sacrifice[10] for Dasaratha, Romapada's close friend—and of course, you must know that Rama, Lakshmana, and all were born as a result of this sacrifice.

L: Uh huh.

GA: Rishyashringa married Shanta, Dasaratha's daughter, the elder sister of Rama.[11]

Back in the forest, Vibhandaka waited and waited. His son did not return. At first he was furious with Rishyashringa. Then he grieved for him. He increased his austerities.

Rishyashringa soon had a child. As he watched the womenfolk place his child in a golden cradle during the naming ceremony and sing songs, he was filled with grief.

He remembered his father:

"I never had a mother.

When I was alone, my father looked after me.

There he is, old, and I have abandoned him and am enjoying the world."

Tears streamed down.

Crying,

"Appa, appa" (father, father),

he left his wife, his child, his kingdom—he was an ascetic, after all—he returned to his father.

Vibhandaka had vowed never to see his son's face again. But you know the beauty in this? He was a father, and the instant he heard his child cry out,

"Appa!"

the fury melted.

They recount their experiences to each other, and decide they would seek moksha (liberation). Vibhandaka's prayers are answered first.

When Shiva appears to him, he says:

"I desire to be united with you."

And in the temple up there (*pointing to the steps to the Mallikarjuna temple visible from Ganapati Avadhani's house*) you have the linga into which Vibhandaka merged.

Rishyashringa intensified his penance.

The gods were alarmed by the intensity, and appealed to Ishwara (Shiva) to grant Rishyashringa his wish. Ishwara appeared before Rishyashringa, saying,

"What is all this furor you're creating?"

Rishyashringa answered,

"Well, you granted moksha to my father. I too desire moksha."

"But your father had performed penance for many, many years."

"But what did he ask of you, and what did you grant him?"

insisted Rishyashringa.

See (*addressing me*), how powerful his asceticism must have been that he could talk to Ishwara in this manner!

"Your father asked that he be united with me."

In his eagerness to emulate his father, Rishyashringa, said,

"I too desire that you be united with me."

He was a youth, after all.

But since that was how he had asked, that was what he got!

Up there in the temple in Kigga, the *shivalinga* has a horn: Ishwara had merged into the being of Rishyashringa.

Here (in the temple up the street), Vibhandaka is indistinct from Ishwara (i.e., the linga) because he merged into Ishwara.

For a long time, Kigga was not a happy town.

If there was a wife, there was no husband, if there was a husband, there was no wife, if there were both, there was no child, and if there were children, the businesses did not prosper—there was always some trouble in Kigga.

However godly Rishyashringa had been, he had his human drawbacks.

In recent times, the townspeople of Kigga finally approached Sringeri. Then, Sachidananda Sivabhinava Narasimha Bharatigalu (the guru of the matha from 1879–1912) established the vigraha (image) of Shanta devi (Rishyashringa's wife) in the temple in Kigga.

It was only after that goddess was installed in the temple that Kigga saw good times.

FIGURE 1.1. Entrance to the Ishwara temple at Kigga. *Photo by K. R. Sanjay*

When I played the tape back to Ganapati Avadhani a few days later, both of us occasionally straining to catch a phrase or a detail above the maddening din of Sringeri traffic also captured on tape, he was satisfied with the narration. "I never thought I would tell this story on tape," he said, "but it is Sringeri's story, and your book is about Sringeri." On thinking about this, I realized that although such stories are not exchanged every day nor are they foremost in people's minds in the humdrum of life, they do get narrated, in scattered ways perhaps, when the question of Sringeri's place identity comes up. Also, it is believed in Sringeri that you do not visit the Kigga temple and not come back to visit the Mallikarjuna temple on the hill.[12] While the Rishyashringa story lends itself to many levels of analysis, for our purpose, it brings together a few key aspects that I found reiterated in Sringeri's moral discourse(s): a high regard for the monastic life and the complexity of its interactions with the life of a householder and an unrivaled high place accorded to the goddess (whether it is Shanta or Sharada). Virtually everybody who has lived in Sringeri for some time can tell anecdotes about sanyasis (renouncers)—either about the gurus of the matha or about itinerant sanyasis who visit Sringeri. These narratives reverentially, affectionately, and sometimes even humorously highlight the spiritual achievements of sanyasis, their idiosyncratic ways of living, but also particular principles they embody. Similarly, reflections about personal struggle, stability, and creative endeavor often refer to ammanavaru (the goddess) in intimate ways.

A second popular sthala purana is associated with Shankara's founding of the Sringeri matha. One evening in 1994 at Kadavadi, Nagaraja, Indira,[13] and I settled in the inner room of their house after dinner to listen to the weekly "National Program" of music on the radio. I asked Nagaraja about the stone carving on the river steps depicting a frog and a snake. Nagaraja began:

The story goes that when Shankara first came to Sringeri,he saw, on the sandy banks of the river, a cobra and a frog, and, as you know, cobras prey on frogs. The frog was struggling in labor, and the cobra had spread out its hood to protect the frog from the sun's glare. Shankara, beholding this sight, thought, here is a place where even sworn enemies live as friends. And with this vision, he established the Sringeri matha.[14]

The story then goes to describe how Shankara, after defeating in debate Mandana Mishra, a reputed advocate of the Karma Mimamsa school,[15] renamed him Sureshvaracharya and appointed him the first head of the Sringeri matha—thus initiating a continuous lineage of gurus of the Sringeri matha. The four directions of Sringeri are also graced by smaller temples that Shankara is believed to have installed. In the east is the Kāla Bhairava (Shiva) temple, to the north is the Kāḷikāmba (Kali), to the south the Durgāmba (Durga), and to the west the Kere Āñjaneya (Hanuman) temple by the lake.[16] For Nagaraja, as for many Sringeri residents, such stories about the founding of Sringeri, kept alive through contestation and retelling, locate Sringeri 's historical beginnings in the establishment and growth of the Shankara matha. The popularity of this narrative is apparent from its reproduction in varying detail and emphasis in verbal accounts, stone carvings, commercial paintings, tourist brochures, museum depictions, state and district gazetteers, and popular songs.

Popular songs, incessantly booming from cassette shops, showcase images of Sringeri abstracted from such place legends for visiting tourists and pilgrims and situate Sringeri in a spiritual, ancient past and a peaceful present. Pervasive in most depictions of Sringeri is a complete romanticization of its character. For one, its location in thickly forested mountainous country makes Sringeri available for claims that it is "protected from civilization." The publication of the matha, *The Greatness of Sringeri,* declares, "When peace eludes you, when the world is too much for you, when the fever of life torments you, come to Sringeri," where "peace is palpable, tangible!"[17] Most of this literature—written from the perspective of devout adherents of the matha and followers of particular gurus—focuses on the religious activities of the matha and glorifies it.[18]

Sringeri Jains and Muslims: Shared Space

Prominent sthala puranas such as the ones narrated above obscure the pre-Shankara times when there were Jain settlements in Sringeri. Largely written as the story of defeated heterodoxy, these times, of which little is really known or documented authoritatively, are not generally perceived as belonging to Sringeri's showcase items. Historical writing on the pre-Shankara period speculates that, prior to Shankara's arrival in Sringeri around the eighth century A.D, Jains lived in these parts, enjoyed the support of regional rulers,[19] and were "well-esconced [*sic*] in the patronage of traders, merchants and officers of the state."[20] Lewis Rice, a British official known for his work with stone and copper-plate inscriptions in the old Mysore area, presents evidence suggesting that, around 350 BC, Jains moved into the Mysore region to escape from a famine in northern India.[21]

The added presence of Tantric sects like the Kāpālikas and the Pāśupatas[22] against whom the Jains competed for religious dominance further argues against an idyllic, unpopulated vision of Sringeri.[23] Scholars have noted that Shankara himself met opposition from both the well-established Jains and from these other sects. His encounters with the Kāpālikas is poeticized in collections such as the Sanskrit *Śaṇkara Digvijaya*.[24] Critical assessments of this competition for religious high ground make it clear that the Sringeri in which Shankara chose to establish the matha was occupied by diverse sects who competed with each other on many levels; the Jains being the most powerful community in the region at that time.

Interestingly, it is not disputed in Sringeri today that Jains once lived in the area and were compelled to leave, but the knowledge does not shape most formulations of "Sringeri's past." Histories of Sringeri are simply seen as beginning with the founding of the matha. When I mentioned this to Lakshmidevamma, she said, "True, they say that there were basadis (Jain temples) here. It is said that the Jains were defeated in debate by Shankara, who laid the condition that they either follow his philosophy or leave the region. They didn't leave these parts, of course, but built basadis in the outskirts, and settled there. That stone pillar in the temple and the Janardhana temple in front of it belonged to Jains. So, before Shankara arrived, the Jains were already settled here, with their temples and their streets."

When I visited the Jain basadi down Bharati Street, I was struck by the quiet way in which it spoke of its history. An inscription in the basadi states that it was built in AD 1150 in the memory of Marishetty, a descendant of a Jain family in Belur (about 165 kilometers southeast of Sringeri). The main deity, Parshwanatha swamy, is a one-foot-high black stone image that depicts two coiled serpents with their hoods spread out over the deity. There are also vigrahas (images) of the goddess Padmavati and the twenty-four tirthankaras, the Jain teachers, in the enclosure in front of the main deity. As I walked around the temple more recently in June 2004, looking at sculptures that had been freshly washed in the light drizzle that had set in, Shamanna, the caretaker of the basadi, told me that some of the statues in the pillared courtyard (the navaranga) had been brought from ruins of basadis around Sringeri. Plans were underway for renovation, but the funds were slow in coming. All the same, the sanctum had been completed, renovated with new flooring, puja was being conducted daily. The annual Jain celebration at Mahavir Jayanti clearly indicates that Sringeri's Jainism is an ongoing tradition.

Almost across the street from the basadi is the house of one of the oldest Jain families in Sringeri, whose ancestral roots are in South Kanara. There, I met the young doctor couple, Drs. Niranjan and Bhuvaneshwari, who are active in Jain revival in the Sringeri area. Dr. Niranjan had just returned from work, and Dr. Bhuvaneshwari came in and out of the private clinic she ran in front of their house to chat with us in the living room. "There are only five Jain families now, but there was a time when the matha used to invite our family along with Sringeri's well-known people as the *paṭṭanada sheṭṭaru* (the town's business people). My grandfather was member of the Mysore *praja pratinidhi sabha* (Representative Assembly) of Krishnaraja Wodeyar (the Maharaja of Mysore, from 1902 to 1940)," said Dr. Niranjan. I looked at the framed photograph of his grandfather with the maharaja in their living room. "When my father returned to Sringeri in 1969 after a long stay in Udupi, the matha's guru, Sri Abhinava Vidyatirtha, sent for him. He met the guru, and said, 'You're all brahmans, and I don't know if you know we're Jains.' The guru replied, 'I *know* you are Jains. Jains go a very long time back in Sringeri—there was a time when all this belonged to you (i.e., to the Jains).'" Indeed, Mudibidre, Karkala, Venuru, and Narasimharajapura are among the many towns around Sringeri that form a strong network of places mapping Jainism in this part of Karnataka.[25]

FIGURE 1.2. Parshwanatha swami shrine in Sringeri's Jain basadi. *Photo by Baba Prasad*

Today, the town's population is 4,253.[26] While brahmans, and the few Jains in Sringeri, live in the immediate area around the matha, Hindus of other castes (Vokkaligas, Vishwakarmas, and Bunts, for example) and Muslims, many of whom have generational ties with Sringeri, live in different parts of the town. These generational ties, I learned, are quite significant and deep, shaping interreligious dialogue and coexistence. I showed up unannounced one mid-morning at the house of Ziya Ahmed, who was well known in Sringeri as a respected member of the Muslim community and also as former vice president of Sringeri's municipal council from 1979–1981. Ziya Ahmed and Putta Murthy had worked together in town planning and development, and I had heard often that they had made a dynamic team. We started talking initially in Kannada, but as we leafed through his family's photo albums

I could not repress my Hyderabadi self from switching to a Hindi-Urdu dialect known as Hyderabadi Hindi. Ziya Ahmed and his daughter switched to Mysore Urdu, and thus we had our long conversation.

Most Sringeri Muslims—a little less than 10 percent of Sringeri's total population—have ancestral origins in the Mysore and South Kanara areas, but retain strong ties to Sringeri that go back several hundred years when they came as mahouts for the matha's elephants, tin workers, chariot artisans, palanquin bearers, and umbrella makers. Other nearby Muslim communities are in Kigga, Nemmar, Addagadde, Kunchebayalu, all within a ten-mile radius of Sringeri. I had seen an urs (procession) come up to the Mallikarjuna temple, looping through the main streets of Sringeri, and asked about its connections to Muharram—since this, for me, was one of the most vivid aspects of Muslim celebration in Hyderabad. He told me an interesting story in connection with this tradition about the discovery of a panja, a sacred replica symbolic of the hand of Imam Hussain (the martyred grandson of Prophet Mohammed) raised in battle:

> The guru Sivabhinava Narasimhabharati (the guru from 1879–1912) found a panja in the river and gave it to the elders in the Muslim community, saying,
>
> "You do the worship for this, and the matha will meet the full expenses of the ten-day celebration of Muharram."
>
> The matha also used to help during the ten-day Muharram celebrations by sending four men to hold the pallakki (palanquin) and also used to give kerosene lights in the days when there was no electricity.
>
> This continued for many years, but once the government land where the ta'ziya (temporary miniature mausoleum) used to be was acquired by a private party, the ta'ziya had to find a new place for each Muharram.
>
> It was considered inappropriate by the community to house the ta'ziya in the masjid given some of the physical demonstration that accompanied it.
>
> The panja used to be in the custody of a Muslim family, but, once they moved, although the panja is still in the masjid, the tradition of the Muharram ta'ziya and panja is no longer prevalent. We observe Muharram at home and visit one another these days.

We walked over to the new masjid that was being built—the older structure had been around since 1926—and as Ziya Ahmed showed me around, I

FIGURE 1.3. New masjid. *Photo by Leela Prasad*

began to see something of the various ways in which diverse communities in Sringeri had learned to live with one another, negotiating their copresence and a mutual cultural awareness.[27] Perhaps this was nowhere more evident than in two narrations about an unusual visitor to Sringeri—a wild leopard.

Samaka Ramachandra Bhattru and Amrutamba

Dodda Murthy took me splashing through Sringeri's monsoon-washed streets to Ramachandra Bhattru's house as I looked for an apartment to rent in 1994. Ramachandra Bhattru, a schoolteacher who was then in his mid-forties, had been cautious about the tenant to whom he would rent his house, and I would have clearly remained "an outsider" but for Dodda Murthy's introduction. "She comes from a family that is known to us from her grandfather's time," he echoed his favorite line. The endorsement was enough for Ramachandra Bhattru to rent the apartment to me, but he later remarked that the fact that I had come to Sringeri for "an educational purpose" had also persuaded him. "It is after all the Sharada peetha (the seat of learning)," he said. Ramachandra Bhattru became a tremendous resource in the research for this book, introducing me to people and places, arranging cultural events if it was not possible for me to be in Sringeri when they "naturally" occurred, or informing me of happenings of interest.

The family name of Samaka comes from the family's generational scholarship of the Samaveda, the Veda that renders in song (sāman) the hymns of the Rig Veda and provides instructions on their musical recitation (gaṇa). His father and uncle were noted scholars who taught in the matha's Sanskrit school. It is a rich family history that Ramchandra Bhattru does not take casually, and one that Nagaraja, his son (in his early twenties in 2004) has sought to continue through an M.A. and Ph.D. in Sanskrit and by becoming a professional purohita (priest).

Amrutamba, Ramachandra Bhattru's wife, is also a schoolteacher. She is originally from Konanduru, about fifty miles from Sringeri, where she had her education. As I got accustomed to their school routines, I began to time my visits to their house so that I could catch them at a more leisurely hour during the evening. Occasionally, I would find her and Ramachandra Bhattru cutting vegetables together for the evening meal, and we would sit chatting. These evening conversations literally fill many pages of this ethnography.

It was six months after I had begun to live in Sringeri that I was to see Ramachandra Bhattru's forte as a raconteur. My father was visiting and I had taken him to Ramachandra Bhattru's house. Amrutamba, Nagaraja, and Tejaswini (then five years old) were away in Bangalore. As we chatted, Ramachandra Bhattru seemed a little startled by my father's fluency in Kannada and by his familiarity with landmarks of the past and people of earlier generations, but joined him in reminiscing. The long anecdote-filled evening impressed upon me Sringeri's people and times so vividly that it stands out in my memory as I write almost ten years later. The entry in my journal for that evening says, "When I left RB's house, I felt that somehow the equation between RB and myself had changed."

What I had noted as striking during that conversation was that as Ramachandra Bhattru narrated episodes from the past he had addressed them to me, even though the conversation had been quite pointedly between him and my father. Over the next several days, as I reflected on the impact of that evening, I realized it would have been inappropriate for Ramachandra Bhattru, in the context of elder-younger dynamics, to have narrated stories intended to illustrate "greatness of human character" to my father, but it was acceptable for him to narrate those stories to me. So my father told him anecdotes about the gurus and "the old times," and Ramachandra Bhattru in turn recounted similar stories to me. Such sensitivity to the interpersonal dynamics of narration and to expressive effect, backed by an immense repertoire of "cultural knowledge" and stories (not from the Puranas or the like but from quotidian Sringeri settings and personal experiences) mark Ramachandra Bhattru as a master storyteller. Ramachandra Bhattru's style of delivery not only made me conscious of how stories that people narrated etched themselves on the landscape of Sringeri, time and again, but also made me realize that moral imagination goes hand in hand with the narrative experience.

I first heard about the leopard from Ramachandra Bhatta, who recounted this incident of the mid-1980s:

RB: Channa Reddy, the chief minister of Andhra Pradesh, was visiting Sringeri.

While he and his wife were in the Mallikarjuna temple on the hill, some rainwater leaked through the roof and fell on her, his wife.

FIGURE 1.4. Ramachandra Bhattru and Amrutamba in their home. *Photo by Leela Prasad*

When they took the guru's darshan, she said to the guru,

(*sound of autorickshaw with its musical horn*)

"I have a desire, and I pray that you bless it."

"What is it, amma?" he asked.

She replied,

"I would like to have this temple repaired using money from our trust."

L: Oh!

RB: The guru gave his permission, the money was sanctioned, and construction began. The facade was redone, and then a thought came to the guru:

"When so much construction is being done, why don't we have the pāṇipīṭha also redone?"

L: Uh huh . . .

(the pāṇipīṭha is the pedestal with a spout that surrounds the shivalinga and serves as the conduit for substances like water, milk, honey that are used in worship)

RB: So that work was also begun.

But it soon became obvious that they needed to know the base of the shivalinga. Because the linga had been installed into the pāṇipīṭha and needed to be *removed* first.

L: Yes.

RB: While these discussions were going on, a weird thing happened.

Suddenly there was a leopard in the town.

L: *What?!* (*incredulously*)

RB: We've seen this with our own eyes!

Right in the town!

For five days!

There was newspaper coverage too.

Who knows where it came from.

But, strange thing was, that leopard would go and sleep in cattle sheds.

If you raised an alarm, it slipped away.

L: Arre!

RB: Pilgrims coming at night got wind of it and were terrified:

"There's a leopard in this town."

(*bus honks loudly*)

We also saw all this happening.

But we could not catch it.

I mean, even with all the advanced facilities in this world, it could not be trapped.

It would sleep in some cattle shed at night, or just walk around.

(*Leela is amazed*)

At that point there was a young school headmaster who had just arrived in town.

I had helped him move into a house.

Right down the lane—in that house; huli-mane, "Tigerhouse" we now call it.

So one day,

in broad daylight around 11 o'clock, the leopard was found sitting on a tall tree,

a really tall tree.

A huge crowd had gathered.

(*speaking rapidly*)

The Forest Department came with cages, traps, and whatnot.

In the hue and cry the thing did not know where to go, but somehow it managed to get into the rafters of this poor headmaster's house—which had an opening.

L: Ah!

RB: Now, he was bathing.

L: Oh, no!

RB: When he heard this yelling, and heard the leopard on the roof, he came charging out in just his towel.

He came running all the way to my house, shouting,

"I am finished, Bhattre!"

I said,

"Let's go see where it is."

But he was shaking,

"There's no way I'll come; you go if you want."

(*Leela laughs*)

When I went to see—

He (*the headmaster*) had managed to bolt the door behind him—

but a window was *open.*

I peeped in.

There was this full-length mirror hanging on the wall.

L: Hunh!

RB: The leopard was throwing itself against the reflection.

Again and again. Scratching it.

L: Poor thing!

RB: The scratching had left its claws all bloody.

Finally, when they opened the door and tried to catch it, it escaped (*switches to a somber tone*).

L: Ayyah!

RB: The guru became worried (*speaking in a serious tone*):

"Why did I undertake reconstruction of the shivalinga?"

Then he prayed, saying,

"Please don't harm anybody. I will finish this task quickly.

I did not know that I had disturbed something that has been there for generations."

Then, soon after that, everybody saw the leopard run up the hill,

L: The leopard?

RB: up the steps of the Mallikarjuna temple.

Nobody saw it ever after that.

L: Isn't that strange!

RB: You know, the man who eventually bought that house was a student of mine.

And his family name happened to be "Hulimane" (lit. "Tiger-house").

When he came to me to ask what he should name the house, I said,

"You are from Hulimane.

Such is the story of that house.

Call it "Vyāghri Nivas!" (Residence of the Tiger).

And he did!

I was to hear about this incident once again from Ziya Ahmed:

ZA: Sometime, in 1980s, maybe 1984, a tiger—actually a leopard—came into town.

L: Yeah, I heard about that.

ZA: It came right into town. It created a real scare, and went straight into one school headmaster's house.

It stayed there all day.

The Forest Department showed up and tried different things to catch it.

They couldn't.

Now what had happened meanwhile was that—now this is what I have heard; I haven't seen this—

L: Yes, oh sure—

ZA: There on the hill is a mazar (tomb of a Muslim saint), and the *plan* was made to dig it out.

At the time this decision was made, the leopard appeared.

The swamiji (the guru of the matha) came to know about the leopard.

He immediately sent word.

"The mazar—don't touch that spot, leave it alone."

And you know, after this, strange thing,

nobody knows where that leopard disappeared.

It came out of the house, they tried to catch it,

but it vanished.

L: So there must have been some connection?

ZA: So this is what took place, so we've heard.

(*then, in lowered tone*)

You know, the swamiji has some mohabbat (love) for us.

L: The current guru?

ZA: Yes, even today.

We organized a feast recently and he sent us a message, "You're doing a good thing; it will go well."

L: I heard the temple was being renovated and the shivalinga was disturbed—some people in Sringeri say that the leopard came because of this!

ZA: Yes, they say that too.

The two narrations are clearly more than about the space shared on Mallikarjuna Hill on which both the mazar and the shivalinga are located. When I mentioned to Ramachandra Bhattru that there was a Muslim story about the leopard, he acknowledged that he'd heard about it and said, "Who knows for sure with regard to such things?" It was intriguing to me that neither Ziya Ahmed nor Ramachandra Bhattru had mentioned the "other" story until I asked, and it was all the more intriguing that they did not dispute the other story. However, both stories seem to reveal a space of shared understanding: human vision is limited and the divine manifests itself through "signs," especially when a cosmic order is liable to be disturbed by human action. Just as the mazar and the shivalinga had existed beside each other for generations and there was little reason to alter that arrangement, there seemed to be little reason for narratives to encroach on each other.

Perhaps it was because of the resilience of these older, more complex ties to each other and to Sringeri that, despite the political success of the Bharatiya Janata Party in the region, right-wing formations in and around Sringeri (like the Bajrang Dal and the Rashtriya Swayamsevak Sangh) have failed to make negative interventions in the relationships between Sringeri's Muslims and non-Muslim communities. As we talked about contemporary nationalist politics, particularly played out over the Ayodhya issue, Ziya Ahmed said, "It is only in India's recent history that politicians have begun to see people only as Hindus or as Muslims. If they (politicians) sit down and talk, can't differences be sorted out? But they only give loud speeches."

Sringeri's Agraharas: Layout, Architecture, and Affiliations

Older Sringeri homes were constructed in brahman localities called agraharas (land donated to brahmans by royal patrons). The Shringapura grant in 1346 by the first Vijayanagara emperor, Harihara I, founded the first Sringeri agrahara in the immediate vicinity of the matha.[28] Along the banks of the Tunga, each with its own temple, are Sringeri's other agraharas (which, following tradition, had to be situated close to a river and a temple to facilitate the religious life of brahmans). Along the eastern bank of the Tunga, with its many temples, is Vidyaranyapura, established in 1386 by Harihara II to honor Vidyaranya, the twelfth guru of the matha and the principal adviser to the Vijayanagara emperors. Later, in the seventeenth century, were built the agraharas of Sacchidanandapura and Narasimhapura. Around the same time was built the winding agrahara of Vaikunthapura along with its temple dedicated to Vitthala.[29]

Oral history in Sringeri recounts that three hundred brahman families were invited from various parts of south India to reside in Sringeri's agraharas. In return for land and livelihood, the brahmans taught at the matha and performed ritual worship at the temples.[30] The brahman community in contemporary Sringeri consists of subsects like the Babburkamme, Mulakanad, Chitpavan, Havyak, Hoysala Karnataka, Ippatnakaru, Kandavara, Kavarga, Kota, Panchagrama, and Shivalli. This diversity is downplayed in contemporary self-representation (with marriages taking place between subsects), but historically subsects have affiliated with mathas *other* than the Sringeri matha. For instance, Shivalli brahmans associate with the matha in Hariharapura (about six miles from Sringeri), while Kota brahmans associate with the Bhandigadi matha (in the neighboring taluk of Tirthahalli), and

Havyak brahmans with the Ramachandrapura matha (also in Tirthahalli), all in affiliations that are not exclusive. During the important annual rite of changing the sacred thread (upakarma), Shivalli brahmans used to go to the Sri Raja Gopala Krishna temple "right there in the town" or to the Vitthala temple in nearby Vaikunthapura, while Kota brahmans to the Mallikarjuna temple on the hill, and not to the Sringeri matha where the Babburkamme, Andhra, and the Hoysala Karnataka brahmans would go.[31]

The main roads of the town, Bharati Street and Harihara Street, which start at the entrance of the matha, and form the arms of an L-shape as they run through the town, are characterized by innumerable small hotels and lodges, and stores that stock prerecorded audio cassettes, photo film, *japa mālās*,[32] toys, and other religious paraphernalia. Bharati Street is packed with busy provisions stores, silversmiths, banks, a post office, vegetable sellers, telephone booths and photocopy shops, an ice cream parlor and Internet cafés. Roadside vendors line the streets, selling fresh flowers, tender coconut, and puffed rice to feed the fish in the river.

The long Bharati Street takes you out of town through the Muslim neighborhood till it bifurcates near the new masjid. The left branch takes you out of Sringeri, and the right takes you to the J.C.B.M. College and the Rajeev Gandhi Sanskrit College. It always struck me as appropriate

FIGURE 1.5. Bharati Street leading to the matha's entrance. *Photo by K. Gopikiran*

that in this town that is home to Sharada, the goddess of learning, education should enjoy a conspicuously high place. Sringeri today has a literacy rate of about 90 percent, unusually high for a rural community in India, with an 86 percent female literacy rate (48 percent of the literate population are women).[33] The Girls High School that is run by the matha established in 1972 has set a state record for 100 percent matriculation rates.[34] (The present government-run Higher Primary Boys School was formerly the "Anglo-Vernacular" School, which, in colonial tradition, taught English and Kannada. The present Government Junior College was the first high school to be established in Sringeri by the matha.) These statistics have come a long way from the 1930s, however, when students had to go to Shimoga (about one hundred kilometers away) for high school and come home only during vacations. Consequently, girls in Sringeri typically studied only till middle school, with only four or five girls in the entire high school in Shimoga.

Most of the small stores along the main streets of Sringeri are the newly constructed fronts of centuries-old houses, which often have courtyards, cattle sheds, private temples, and many living quarters behind the crowded storefronts. For instance, Srungagiri Xerox, a tiny fifty-square-foot photocopy and stationery store, is the main, if undetectable, entrance to Nagabhusana Rao and Vasanthi's house, a house that actually sprawls for a quarter mile behind the store and is complete with an areca nut garden that stretches to the northern bank of the Tunga, a twenty-room lodge, and four apartments. It was inexhaustibly thrilling to discover the intricate interior behind a storefront: the low-roofed, wood-beamed rooms with shelves built into beams close to the ceiling, the narrow corridors leading to storage areas and dining halls, the engraved solid wooden doorways, an open well usually fitted with an electric pump, the elaborate devara mane or place of worship, the kitchen with separate areas for festive and everyday cooking, and the bathing area with its deep hanḍe (wood-burning stove with a brass or copper pot) for heating water.

The architecture of Sringeri houses speaks of an ethos in which deities are the first owners of property.[35] Most homes have small family temples in their central courtyard, standing independent from the living quarters, following the tradition that the construction of a residence must first be dedicated to a deity. "It's a very Malnad thing," Putta Murthy said, talking about the small Rameshwara temple in the inner courtyard of their 250-year old house.[36] According to their family history, after his great grandfather left

FIGURE 1.6. Rameshwara temple in the courtyard of Dodda Murthy's house. *Photo by Baba Prasad*

Nagara, about sixty miles south of Sringeri, in the late eighteenth century, he initially settled down near Vidyaranyapura, about two miles from the present-day town of Sringeri. As the story is told, he found considerable wealth buried in one of his fields and built the house they live in today. He first endowed a small portion of his agricultural land toward the construction of a private home temple that stands in their courtyard, distinct from the shrine inside the home. The revenue from the agricultural land helps to meet the expenses of the temple and supports a priest in residence who conducts daily worship at the temple. The priest's family often lives in the same courtyard and is associated for generations with the family and the temple—or at least as long as somebody in the lineage takes on priestly duties. There is much "family folklore" surrounding such temples. In the Murthy family I came to hear stories about the specially sculpted pillars of the temple, the story of the sudden crack in the shivalinga that was predicted by an astrologer in Varanasi, and the annual celebration of its subsequent reinstallation.

Agriculture: An Ethos

Although some of Sringeri's brahmans are employed by the matha in administrative positions, as teachers in the Vedic school, as priests, or in the matha's kitchens, many are independent of the matha, and farm, teach, or own stores and lodges. In recent decades burgeoning tourism and pilgrimage has further diversified the occupations available to Sringeri residents. Professions outside the matha also allow for the greater, in many cases primary, participation of women. The economy of the region is supported principally by areca nut, coconut, and rice farming, as well as by coffee, black pepper, and cardamom orchards, and thus many brahmans, like Vokkaligas (who form the other major community in the area), are agriculturalists.

Agricultural seasons, especially those associated with areca nut, bring with them a culture of community. For example, often, after the areca harvesting season, the thatched roofs of sheds attached to houses would need to be rethatched. Word would be sent around, "Namma maneli hacche!" (thatching in our house). Dodda Murthy described how all the boys from the surrounding area would come in the morning. "'Sogasāda coffee-tinḍi māḍukoḍa avaru, *first-class* coffee-tinḍi!' (They would give us first-class coffee and snacks). Once we had eaten a good breakfast, we would all climb the roof, and remove the old areca leaves and put in the new ones. And this job would take up to 4 in the evening. Then water was made ready for the boys for a hot bath. We would rest, and then eat a festive meal. And this would go on in every house."[37] When labor is shared by small growers, people are conscientious about reciprocal commitment. A couple who did not pitch in one season for grain threshing when I was in Sringeri said ruefully, "You break the rule and you're stuck alone. Had we gone to help them, they would have come today."

Dodda Murthy reminisced about the 1930s when sacks of processed areca nut from various homes and villages in and around Sringeri used to be lined up in their courtyard and then piled on to passing carts to be taken to the markets in Birur (the Shimoga markets came much later).

> Grains used to come into Sringeri in bullock carts and would be sold at the sante (fair) held at the open ground by the river—where today buses are parked and washed.
>
> People bought up their yearly stock of supplies, because getting even to the nearest market in Tarikere was almost impossible with the rains and the fevers that came with them.

The carts brought whole unprocessed grain, and these had to be cleaned, dried, pounded, roasted and readied to last through the monsoon.

The returning carts took the sacks of areca nut to the markets. Whoever accompanied the carts to the markets sold the areca nut, and the money from the sales was distributed to the respective owners in the taluk.

Nobody worried that areca nut would get lost or stolen along the way.[38]

Later, in the library at the University of Pennsylvania, I read L. B. Bowring's 1871 note which reports that areca nut growers in the Malnad region had conflicts with growers in Bombay who were excused from the high excise duty levied on Malnad farmers.[39] In contrast to Dodda Murthy's recollection, Bowring's note further says:

By far the best betel-nut [areca nut] is grown in the Malnad of the Kadoor district. As there are few cart-roads in the hill country, the betel-nut is generally carried on pack-bullocks and donkeys, of which large droves are brought in the cold weather months by gangs of Lambadis and Korchars, two of the wandering tribes, who have the reputation of combining with

FIGURE 1.7. Koulkudige Sridhar with apiary. *Photo by Leela Prasad*

> their more honest calling a predilection for thieving and gang robbery. The principal depots are Birur in the Kadoor district, and Tipatur [Tiptur] and Gubbi in the Toomkoor district.[40]

Festivals: Ambiguated Senses of Belonging

Festivals, for instance, visibly teased out the shifting affinities of Sringeri residents toward the matha and toward the community.[41] The ten days of Navaratri festivities (honoring the presiding goddess), organized by the matha and attended by pilgrims from all over south India, are popularly seen to index a "Sringeri identity." Sringeri remembers, in a singular way during Navaratri, its historical transition from a pilgrimage center to an area with a powerful political presence and identity. In addition to the special worship in the temple that includes recitations from various sacred texts, pujas, and festive meals, the matha organizes chariot processions during which the goddess rides grandly out into the streets of Sringeri every evening, nightly music concerts, and the durbar (royal court) held only during the Navaratri nights by the guru, attired in his special regalia.

Residents, who dress festively to come to the matha, take this opportunity to catch up with friends from neighboring towns, to participate collectively in special worship at the various other temples of the matha in the town, and, often, to sponsor a puja at the main temple. During my visits to nearby villages and towns, people told me that they would visit the matha at least once during Navaratri, even if it was their only visit to the matha for the year. Sringeri residents, irrespective of caste, gender, age, or social standing, express cultural ownership of the matha's festivity, unequivocally calling it "our Sringeri thing." This community identification during the festival can perhaps be likened to the cohering force behind what Joyce Flueckiger calls a "folklore group," a transient collectivity that assembles in the context of a performance and "dissipates" soon after the performance is over.[42] At the same time as the Navaratri festivity centripetally draws Sringeri residents to the matha, they also worship the goddess in other forms and in other places in Sringeri. Atop a small hill in the Muslim neighborhood is the small temple of the goddess Choudeshwari that is especially well-attended during Navaratri, mostly by Bunt and Lingayat families but also by a few brahmans and Muslims from the neighborhood.[43]

If, during Navaratri celebrations, the community suspends the ambivalence felt at other times toward the matha and submerges local demarcations between insiders and outsiders that *continue* to be observed during the festivities—during the festival, for instance, of Ramanavami—it is a remarkably different story. Public celebrations for Ramanavami in Sringeri are localized in neighborhoods. Brahmans from surrounding agraharas of Vaikunthapura, Vidyaranyapura, and Sachidanandapura form committees that organize independent local celebrations that span ten days. An intensely "local" flavor permeates Ramanavami festivity (which include processions, pujas, community meals), and the sense of locality is underscored by the fact that residents of Vidyaranyapura, for example, barely three miles away from the town of Sringeri, have "their own" Ramanavami celebrations and are invited as "guests" to the Sringeri celebrations. There are Vidyaranyapura Rama bhajans and there are Sringeri Rama bhajans, and when the Vidyaranyapura group sing "their" songs at the Sringeri celebrations, they are formally felicitated for their participation. At other times Vidyaranyapura residents are not in any way considered separate from the Sringeri community.

As far as Ramanavami celebrations go, these local bodies claim an autonomy that is expressed through statements like, "We don't have any sambandha, any connection, with the matha. This is our own thing." And yet it is also important to remember that the "Sringeri identity" generated during Ramanavami is primarily a "brahman" collectivity. These "differential

FIGURE 1.8. Ramanavami celebrations in Vaikunthapura. *Photo by Leela Prasad*

identities," to use Bauman's term, are similar to the ways in which Joyce Flueckiger finds Chhatisgarhi communities in central India draw and redraw elastic regional boundaries around folklore genres and make contextual claims to the ownership of traditions.[44] "Localness" then, is clearly an identity that moves between and across the larger-than-local,[45] the local, and the smaller-than-local.

Malnad Upachara

"Malnad upachara kēḷa bēka?" (As for the Malnad's hospitality, does one need to ask?) People who lived outside this region rhetorically asked me this question many times on my journeys between Bangalore and Sringeri. In common parlance the Malnad is contrasted to the Maidan (the plateau), which is to the southeast of Sringeri and includes the districts of Hassan, Tumkur, Mysore, and Bangalore. When I used to describe my travel through Maidan areas to friends in Sringeri, I would often hear, "avaru bēre!" (they are different!) along with a tongue-in-cheek reference to "Maidan oraṭu" (the Maidan's coarse manners).[46] Malnad residents articulate this difference more elaborately in a discourse around the phrase "namma Malnadinalli" (in our Malnad) that characterizes the Malnad's foodways, social customs, and language use, but the highlight of this discourse is Malnad hospitality, or upachara, which centers on an aesthetic of social propriety.

By "Malnad upachara" people outside Sringeri refer to what they perceive to be the long-continuing, bounteous traditions of hospitality of the Malnad. Malnad hospitality was exemplified, for instance, by such luxuries as the famous abhyanjana, or oil baths, provided to visitors to the Kuthgodu home, six miles from Sringeri, or by the generous meals that the goddess Annapurna is (still) believed to provide her pilgrims in the neighboring town of Hornād irrespective of the time of day or night they arrive, or by the feasting and entertaining of guests in Malnad homes for weeks during the long monsoons.[47] Travel to Sringeri was difficult in older days through thick mountainous forests, long spells of heavy rain, and rather rough transportation. Malnad homes, which on account of land-owning patterns in the region were virtually single-home villages, became the loci for elaborate traditions of hospitality toward visitors.[48]

In fact, the first bus service in Sringeri was started in the 1930s by S. J. Krishnamurthy's father, Shringa Rao, and Krishnamurthy's uncle, Rama

Rao. The company soon ran into heavy losses because of lack of traffic and rough road and weather conditions. The bus used to leave Sringeri at 7 AM, taking passengers and outgoing mail to Chikmagalur, which it reached around 5 PM (the journey today takes four hours or less), and returned to Sringeri only next morning. It was called the "mail bus," and it brought the newspaper—just eight copies of the national newspaper, *The Hindu*—to Sringeri. The news inevitably would be three days old because it was mailed to Sringeri and came in as regular post. The bus had a roof so low that one could not stand in the bus, and it had no side walls. It flooded when it rained, forcing passengers to toss a tarpaulin over the bus. In the 1940s there used to be a "light railway," a tram so called because of its small size, from Narsimharajapura to Tarikere. To travel the distance of twenty-five miles, the tram took four and a half hours. The route lay through the ghats, and those who can remember traveling on the "light railway" recall the journey as the most scenic one they have ever made.

In those days of trickling transportation, dance dramas, like yakshagana, provided occasions for the area's families to socialize, and visiting performance troupes would stay with a family for weeks. Families took turns at sponsoring performances, and whoever attended these shows stayed for a few days with the hosting family. As if echoing the observation in the 1981 *Census of India* about the "distinctive settlement patterns" of the Maidan and the Malnad,[49] Putta Murthy said:

> In the Maidan homes are clustered together, but here a village means a single home.
>
> You've gone to Halanduru often,
>
> *tell me, is it easy to get there?*
>
> You've seen how difficult it is even today to get to one of these homes.
>
> Imagine the days when you had to go by foot; you'd cross a river, which was in flood half the time.
>
> No *buses,*
>
> no communications.
>
> How were we to *manage*?
>
> A temple, the matha, about four or five houses.
>
> If one person performed the puja, another did something else, and, if others were available, they took on some other work.
>
> In this way the few *families* in a village would be close-knit.[50]

And, indeed, even in contemporary times, for many months, gratefully enjoying the rich welcome I received at every home I visited and lived in, I was swayed by this popular perception of Malnad culture. Then one afternoon, the following conversation in Putta Murthy's house overturned my idyllic and limited understanding of Sringeri upachara.[51]

L: One hears the *matha's culture dominates* in this area. In *academic circles*—[52]

P: Also, they say that brahmans in this *area*—

PM: Let me tell you. To be a brahman is a **burden.**

You see, it's difficult for you to understand, but we know from experience.

People we know think,

"Let's go to Sringeri. We know this family there.

Let's go to their house, there's a place to stay."

And they come.

Why do they come? They come out of *affection* for us, just the way you have come.

Your grandfather was here, your father used to visit us.

"There's a family we know, let's go there. It doesn't matter if the matha does not have room for us, we still have a place to stay."

So you come here out of *affection* for us.

But, what happens is that somebody says,

"Oh you're visiting the Sringeri matha? Our friends live there, you could go and stay with them."

And so people come with a letter. This creates a constant stream of visitors who want to go to the matha.

So let's say you come to Sringeri. We invite you saying,

"You are a rare visitor, please have a meal with us."

But you say,

"No, no. We have to eat prasada, so we'll have our meal in the matha."

Should we say OK or should we insist that you eat with us?

Just as when we go on a pilgrimage, we too like to eat prasada in the temple. You come from far, you want to partake of the matha's prasada, and so you go to the matha.

To tell you how Sringeri upachara was in the past, if you came to Sringeri, upachara here meant to *serve*. And serve—call it *hospitality,* in a way.[53] And serve *generously.* Even if you stayed for two or three or four days, you were welcome. If it was the monsoon season, you would be served fried happalụa and sondụige (types of fried crisps). In *this* way, cooking and eating—having a good time—that was *hospitality.*

(*L and P respond appreciatively.*)

Now, in Bangalore and Mysore, "Sringeri upachara" has come to mean—(*breaks off to explain carefully*)

Suppose someone comes to Sringeri, and says,

"We'll go to the river to bathe."

Can we say, "No"?

Sometimes we say,

"Don't go to the river to bathe. The water may be too cold for you."

And yet, they go.

Now, somebody who has seen guests go to the river to bathe, comes along and alleges,

"If you go to Sringeri, they (people in Sringeri) will say to you, 'You prefer to bathe in the river, I suppose,' or,

'You want to eat in the matha, I suppose.'"

That's what we are alleged to say. This is how Sringeri upachara has been misinterpreted and made *notorious.*

PM: You asked about "*Sringeri's culture.*" Our upachara is ignored.

L: Oh . . . (*not quite sure where this is going*).

PM: This *heritage,* what people here have been doing *traditionally*—welcoming you as soon as you arrived, asking you to stay for long. In the past the famous thing in every home was abhyanjana (oil massage followed by hot bath). There's the Kuthgodu home (about six miles from Sringeri), which was *famous* for abhyanjana. There, when natural water supply was insufficient, they would arrange for *artificial* means of supply through pipes or conduits made of areca and make sure that there was water supply *twenty-four hours* a day. They actually used to invite people, saying,

"Come, get abhyanjana done!"

Visitors would have oil massages and hot baths, stay for a few days, enjoy themselves, and then return to their homes.

That is what you could call *heritage.* Or take Hornad (a nearby pilgrimage town) where you have Annapurneshvari (goddess of food). Even there they used to give you coffee and breakfast as soon as you arrived in the morning, both sweet stuff and spicy stuff for breakfast and then coffee. Then you'd have a hot bath, and after that if you wanted to drink milk or something, they'd give you that. There would be a sumptuous lunch. Coffee in the afternoon. Something to eat in the evening, and at night too—they would give all this in the temple. Water was plentiful: you could have as long a bath as you wished, they would give you oil and shikakayi (soapnut powder).

All this in the temple.

This is what we'd call *Malnad culture.*

But, as I said, today outsiders have made *Sringeri upachara* to be—

P: The "Will you go to the matha?"

PR: Those times and places!

PM: In those days, upachara was this.

People ignore this history, and instead challenge Sringeri's upachara.

If you like, *you* could write about *Sringeri upachara.*

What is meant by Sringeri upachara is that, in homes here, when there are small feasts and festivals, or marriages, after the meal is eaten, everybody gathers.

Then an *aged* purohit (priest) tells us a few things about the festival or ceremony: why one performed it, what benefits were obtained by it and what it all meant, and how we ought to conduct ourselves. Then, blessing the hosts, the priest distributes akshate (sacred turmeric-colored rice grains) to everybody.

And to the family that hosted the performance, he offers elaborate *thanks*: "You did this good deed in this place, and God will look after you well. You fed us well, and we are all satisfied. May God give you everything you want."

This is the ashirvada ceremony.

And *this* is what is special about Sringeri upachara.

People forget this—they don't even talk about it.

Instead, they have made out upachara to be—(*Panduranga laughs*).

Ashirvada does not take place everywhere.

L: True, I haven't heard about it.

PM: It lasts for about a half hour.

And depending on the person performing it, if he is good, it's a *beautiful event.*

But when somebody says,

"Sringeri upachara is no big deal. What's so special in your Sringeri upachara?"

it sets my body on fire!

In his gravelly voice, a voice that, despite its characteristic eloquence, sadly portended his final days, and one that I can hear now only on my audiotapes and in my memory,[54] Putta Murthy had described for me an ashirvada (ceremonial blessing) performance, an oral genre that, as I was to discover later, is unanimously cited by Sringeri residents as distinctive to Sringeri. Ashirvada performances, which are between twenty and thirty minutes long, are celebratory speech events that occur at the end of occasions like weddings, housewarming or naming ceremonies, and religious recitations (parayana). Conducted in homes and occasionally in temple courtyards, these performances center around an extempore recitation in Kannada by a priest or a brahman male scholar in the community who offers thanks to guests, hosts, and deities, provides an exegesis of the framing event, and dwells on the significance of the event for everyday conduct. While an ashirvada event includes the distribution of *tāmbūla* (the customary betel nut leaf with areca nut) and occasionally a devotional song or two by gathered women, the improvised speech stands out as an emergent text: it cites various shastras, abstracts stories from Sanskrit epics, weaves regional literature with devotional narrative. The "speech" displays a spectacular interplay of voice, scriptural allusion, audience awareness, and poetic mood.

But Putta Murthy's description of ashirvada had also posed a conundrum for me: *Upachara* in colloquial Kannada is the word for "hospitality" (equivalent to atithya, the attentive reception of guests), and its etymological root "come near, approach" leads to its association with attentive service, as in "waited on, served, honoured, adored."[55] What makes it possible to perceive the narrative-oriented performance tradition of ashirvada that outlines moral conduct as being a rejoinder to an accusation of inhospitality? How was verbal art, with its own performative aesthetics, connected to "everyday" guest-host relations?

Exploring these questions for many months after that conversation, I gradually came to understand that upachara is a connotatively rich construct whose central meaning in Sringeri is "right conduct" in speech, intention, and action. Anticipating a narration I was to encounter frequently from many other individuals in Sringeri, Putta Murthy holds up an encounter that can well be imagined as part of "everyday" life in Sringeri or in any pilgrimage town in India: a family of pilgrims shows up at the door citing a mutual friendship or carrying a letter of introduction. Sringeri householders find themselves caught between norms of hospitality and norms of pilgrimage, a predicament caused by several significant agrarian and political changes that had taken place in Sringeri since the times of "Kuthgodu hospitality."

The abolition of the land-grant status of the matha in 1960 depleted the matha's economic base and necessitated a dependence on pilgrims while land reform legislation of the 1970s limited resources available to Sringeri families. The boom in tourism and pilgrimage in recent decades has made Sringeri a "must-see" town in south India, and improved transportation today brings busloads of pilgrims and tourists throughout the year, even if for short stays, sometimes for a few hours. A state highway, widely networked by state-owned and private bus systems, efficiently transports one to Mangalore, Agumbe, Hornad, Kudremukh, Dharmasthala, and Kollur among many other places in packaged tours that combine the mountain and seashore experience with pilgrimage.[56] The thousands of pilgrims stretch the matha's subsidized food and lodging facilities, and, knowing in advance the "accommodation crisis" in Sringeri, many pilgrims and tourists arrive in Sringeri homes with the proverbial letters of introduction. Sringeri hosts are left to decipher intentions: does the stranger-pilgrim wish to bathe in the holy Tunga and eat prasada at the renowned matha along with hundreds of fellow pilgrims (both are ideals of pilgrimage), to bathe with water heated on woodstoves and eat hot meals with the family, or some combination thereof? When hosts attempt to understand pilgrims' preferences by inquiring about them or by making suggestions, their hospitality is itself called into question and cast into ambiguous repute. Putta Murthy's dramatization of a "typical" dialogue between a guest and a Sringeri family holds up the question at the core of Sringeri upachara, and one that is the broader inquiry of this book: *What constitutes appropriate conduct?*

Although there is no one way to describe the tangible sense in which one experiences "Sringeri's culture," this chapter has explored how Sringeri's ethos, a material-cultural-moral configuration, is shaped by location, by particular kinds of collectivity, and by particular senses of belonging. As I move into the next chapter to consider the matha's growth from a monastic establishment to a landed politicoreligious entity, another historical perspective on Sringeri's ethos will come into view.

Putta Murthy and Lakshmidevamma's Family

An immensely public figure, Putta Murthy was a member of the municipal council for thirty years, and president from 1979 to 1983. He was instrumental in forming and serving on many town committees and in convincing the municipality to construct roads and bridges in interior rural areas. He was famous for his success in getting the government to divert unused funds from other projects to pending Sringeri projects such as building houses, a water tank, a road, and a cinema hall. He told me, "People these days don't know how to fight for money, how to use funds unspent on one project on some other project!"

In oral histories of modern Sringeri Putta Murthy is reputed for his principled politics that was not afraid to challenge established authority. The story is told of the 1948 municipal elections in which, as a first-time candidate, he competed against the powerful K. C. Chandramowli Rao of Hulgar, a nearby village. Chandramowli Rao was one of the largest landowners in the region and a strong political voice in the municipal council, having been many times its president. Putta Murthy's parents tried to dissuade him from running against an "elderly respected person." But Putta Murthy himself recalled saying, "'It is my right (to run)! I am not saying I want to win, I simply want to run!'" After all, having lost a year in the Quit India unrest, he had finished his secondary schooling in Mysore barely two years earlier, in 1946. There had been fifteen electoral blocks in Sringeri, with representatives for each, and in the Matha block from where Putta Murthy contested, the total number of votes was eighty-seven. The matha's entire community supported Chandramowli Rao, and young Putta Murthy lost by thirteen votes. "But, in the spirit of the nationalism sweeping the country," he concluded, "I had proved that thirty-seven people did not support Chandramowli Rao, and that was important for a democratic election!" Putta Murthy ran against Chandramowli Rao a few more times, but lost each time by one or two votes. In 1964 both Lakshmidevamma and Putta Murthy ran, and they were both elected.

As Putta Murthy and his three brothers (he had three sisters also) completed their education, each of them resolved to work for some time "for the guru and for Sharada." An older brother who lives in Calcutta worked as peshkar (revenue officer) and in the taluk office for some time. Putta Murthy also worked in the taluk office for a brief period, then in the education and revenue departments, before turning full-time to the care of the family's lands. From Dodda Murthy I learned that Putta Murthy had a twin sister and heard about their other siblings who lived in Kolkata and elsewhere in India.

One afternoon I accompanied Putta Murthy to Kadavadi, eight miles from the town of Sringeri, where the family has a small areca grove and rice fields. Kadavadi's story begins in the late 1950s when Putta Murthy, who was employed in the matha's revenue department, resigned to work on the lands in Kadavadi. He used to cycle the eight-mile mud track from Sringeri every day and work from early in the morning to late at night. In one year he had the forest cleared and prepared the land for the cultivation of paddy and areca. It took the usual twelve years for the palms he planted to start yielding areca. The small mossy bridge over a rivulet of the Tunga that I used to cross almost every day during the areca harvest season had been constructed in the early 1980s by Putta Murthy. It had made, local residents told me, Kadavadi accessible from the main road even during the rains. "Getting a crop was like winning the lottery," Putta Murthy said to me, describing how the harvest was often lost to wild bison or mountain goats. The forest was thick then, and occasionally even a tiger called from the surrounding jungle. Those were times when Putta Murthy and some of the tenants kept vigil, cooking in the open, watchful of the crop. These graphic reminiscences, while making my Kadavadi stay feel adventurous during daytime, nonetheless made me nervous after dark especially as I would lie awake considering the lightly bolted door of the house where I used to stay with Putta Murthy's son and daughter-in-law, Nagaraja and Indira. There are no tigers now.

With Nagaraja and Indira, and Panduranga and his wife, Radha, I developed close friendships, trading with them stories of college life and of our travels. Nagaraja and Indira looked after Kadavadi affairs and would let me know when they were planning to spend a few weeks there—mostly during the harvesting season; I would quickly follow. These stays at Kadavadi were a deep education for me. For, more than anything else, I learned routines that were distant from my own daily life while sharing with Nagaraja and Indira a common outlook. Panduranga ran the family printing press (in the Sringeri house) and was editor of the local weekly, *Srunkona,* which covered happenings in Sringeri, Koppa, and Narasimharajapura. Our standard joke was that I would make "lakhs of rupees" from my "Sringeri book," as they called it, and buy a plot of land in Sringeri (on which I would cultivate areca and paddy).

Putta Murthy and Lakshmidevamma's youngest daughter was a few years older than me, and it pleased me that they addressed me in the more personal ekavachana (the singular) rather than the honorific plural form of address. Lakshmidevamma, born in 1936, grew up in Sringeri on Bharati Street and was brought up by her maternal uncle, Kavi Mahabala Bhattru, and her grandparents. She married Putta Murthy in 1953, and, like him, she became a committed social activist. In 1964, when it was officially mandated that a woman representative should run for a seat on the Municipal Council, she stood for election against a woman from a tinmaker's family and won the seat. Since Putta Murthy had passionately campaigned for the participation of women in Sringeri's political administration, Lakshmidevamma recalled, "When he (Putta Murthy) went around asking women to run, some said to him, 'Why don't you ask your wife to run instead?' I didn't want to at all—women did not do things like that in those times, and then, this family was so well-known—but he (Putta Murthy) really wanted me to try." Chayamma, joining this conversation, added, "In those days women would not venture across the river, even to seek the darshana of the guru. It is of course different today, with women standing in lines or discussing matters with him, but except when we would go to give him an invitation for a family event, we hardly went across to the other side of the temple complex (to the Narasimhavana, where the gurus reside). Even the temple, we would maybe visit on a Friday, but that was it." I asked, "Was there a rule that women couldn't go?" "No, there was no rule, but we just didn't have the *paddhati* (custom) for doing so."

It was clear that Lakshmidevamma not only enjoyed the five-year term as councillor, but was immensely successful. As the sole woman councillor, she was on a committee that persuaded the government to build the Girls Primary School and raised funds for it. Along with other women, she started a women's support group, a day nursery, and a library, and brought to Sringeri renowned musicians and dramatic companies. She was on the betterment committees for the Girls' Middle and Primary Schools, ensuring that the schools did not lack teachers or resources. "A lot of development happened during the term of that council because we had the support of the guru, Sri Abhinava Vidyatirtha," she reflected. Once the printing press was set up in the 1970s, she began to accompany Putta Murthy to printers' association conferences held in locations all over India. "I really enjoyed seeing new places and learning about different cultures (*jana jīvana*) and cuisines (adige)," she said, as she vividly described her visit to Jaipur in Rajasthan.

Marrying into the family only a few years apart, Chayamma and Lakshmidevamma had become inseparable companions. I began to get used to asking a question of one and getting joint, coconstructed answers. When I met everybody in 2004, there was the hustle and bustle of construction (Putta Murthy's side of the house was being made into a modern two-floored apartment) and Panduranga's young school-and-college-age daughters still kept the house busy with their chatter, but a cloud hovered over the usually lively home. Putta Murthy had passed away in 2002, and in 2003 Lakshmidevamma and Putta Murthy's youngest daughter, Vijaya, had also passed away after painful illness, leaving behind small children. The last time I saw her was during a picnic we had all gone to at nearby Sirimane Waterfalls, cramming into a tiller. We had cooked food, using boulders as supports for woodstoves. I was not surprised when Ziya Ahmed, former member of the Municipal Council and colleague to both Putta Murthy and Lakshmidevamma, told me that the entire town had come to pay their last respects to Putta Murthy when his body was taken away for cremation.

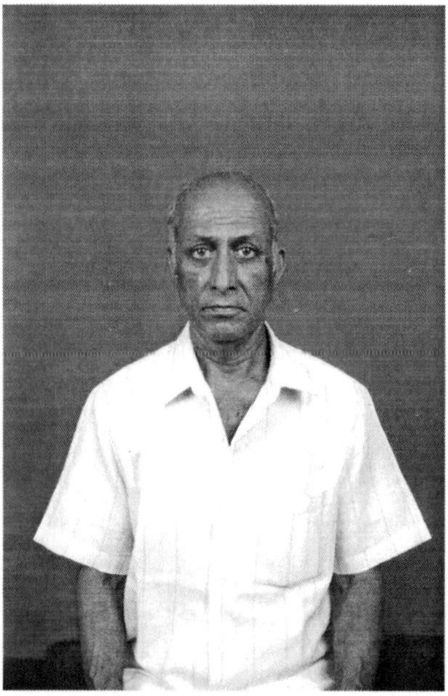

FIGURE 1.9. N.S. Chandrashekar (Putta Murthy). *Photo courtesy N.S. Panduranga*

FIGURE 1.10. Lakshmidevamma. *Photo by Leela Prasad*

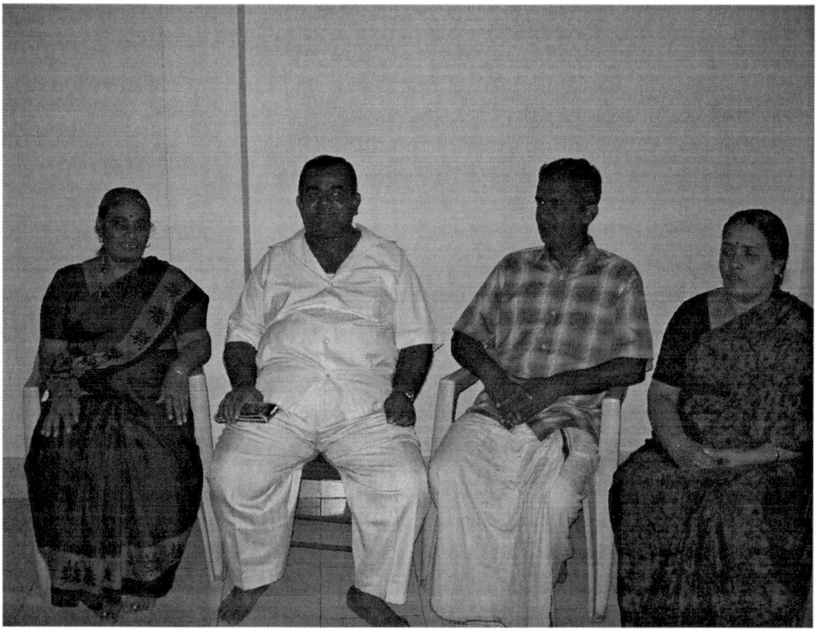

FIGURE 1.11. Indira, Nagaraja, Panduranga, and Radha. *Photo by S. Shankar*

2 *Connectedness and Reciprocity*

Historicizing Sringeri Upachara

The areca season drew to a close, bringing to an end my visits to Kadavadi, eight miles from the town of Sringeri, where Putta Murthy's family has a small areca grove and rice fields. Putta Murthy's eldest son, Nagaraja, and his wife, Indira, live in Kadavadi for most of the year, supervising the harvesting and processing of areca and paddy, returning to Sringeri to be with the rest of their family when festivals come round or when there is a lull in agricultural activity. Kadavadi is a twenty-minute bus ride from Sringeri. From the bus stop it takes about fifteen minutes to zigzag along the footpaths through the fields to the house. Often I used to reach Kadavadi on the late afternoon bus, at a time when Indira would be wrapping up housework and Nagaraja would be getting kerosene lanterns ready for the evening (Kadavadi got electricity in 1999 and phone service shortly thereafter). During my stay in 1994–1995 we used to fill buckets with water that we drew from the well, and Nagaraja would take these in to the house to fill the drums and other containers. Indira and Nagaraja's lifestyle and routine at Kadavadi were very different from their life in their Sringeri home, where cable TV provided evening entertainment and electrical appliances made cooking easy.

Indira often said how it was only during this long stay in Sringeri that I had become close to them. "You would visit the Dodda Murthy family and leave. But, you know, if there is some *rina* [debt from a previous life], you are bound to come back to us ["alla kaṇḍri, adu riṇa iddare bandēbartira"]". Chayamma too used to say that to me. Our attachment, she was convinced, must have carried over from some other life, *yāva jañmada riṇa no.* My mother, who stayed with me in my Sringeri apartment for some time, said that about Uma, my downstairs neighbor, who used to call her *amma* (mother). A young Bunt family,[1] Uma and Rajanna and their two school-age sons had rented the downstairs portion of Ramachandra Bhattru's house for many years before I came to Sringeri. Rajanna owned a lorry transportation business, and Uma and I became close friends. I used to accompany her to the Choudeshwari temple that she frequented on the hill just outside Sringeri town and attend her family's events. We exchanged confidences, and, when my mother came to live with me for a few months, some good food was also traded up and down. Uma had helped me adjust to day-to-day living in Sringeri, from making arrangements for firewood for our woodstove (for heating water) to taking care of my apartment during my absence. Once when Uma brought over a special sweet dish that she had cooked, my mother remarked, "I don't know what rina Uma has with me that she does so much for us." *I* certainly was indebted to Uma. Parvati, the woman we had hired to help with housework, said that rina makes women relate almost like *tāyi-magaḷu*, mother and daughter, or like *akka-tangi*, sisters.

Rina.[2] Debt, obligation, responsibility, bond, connectedness. Kittel's Kannada-English dictionary defines *riṇānubandha*[3] as "the connection of indebtedness, as contracted in some preceding birth and forming the ground of certain sufferings or enjoyments in the present." This definition does not distinguish clearly between debt incurred, for example, when one takes a loan from somebody, and debt in the sense of a duty that must be performed. Sanskrit texts discuss rina as three duties that an upper-caste Hindu male must perform. The *Āpastamba Dharmasūtra*;[4] states that every brahman is born with three debts that have accumulated through many lives: the first debt is owed to the gods, the second to the sages, and the third to the ancestors. A brahman fulfills his debt to the gods by worshipping them and by performing prescribed sacrifices; to the sages by keeping the Vedic tradition alive and active; and to the ancestors by continuing the lineage through male progeny. The *Śatapatha Brāhmaṇa* argues that every individual, not just a brahman, is born with rinas, and it adds a fourth rina, the obligation to humankind, repaid through appropriate hospitality toward guests.[5] Exploring various overlapping "ethical templates" that influence Hindu experiences, R. S. Khare posits that rina is one of four "moral co-ordinates" that regulate Hindu kinship.[6] The most abiding sense of the term *rina* in everyday use is connectedness, the belief that rina draws individuals to each other and binds events and people even when they do not seem explicably connected. Thus when Chayamma, Indira, my mother, or Parvati referred to rina, it was to describe and *account for* the affection between apparently unrelated individuals. This explanatory framework helps seemingly inexplicable obligations, relationships, and attachments become philosophically comprehensible.[7]

But the concept of rina also has a strong material basis. It binds givers and receivers in obligatory relationships that have material implications. It was this sense that began to impress upon me as I explored relationships between individuals, institutions, and communities in Sringeri across different historical periods. Histories of medieval south India note the profound nexus between religious establishments, political rulers, and diverse local communities, a nexus that is vividly expressed through intricate and checkered give-and-take amidst the triad. As this literature demonstrates, exchanges engendered not only political and economic reciprocity but also created a moral ethos in which sociality was expressed. Given that the present community in Sringeri traces itself mostly to post-Shankara times (after the matha was established and communities developed around it), I ask, what idioms of conduct and practice are evidenced in the engagement between the matha, kings, and local communities or individuals? How were cordialities enacted, how did breaches occur, and what negotiation was permissible through what modes? In what tangible and intangible ways was moral appropriateness expressed?

Drawing on different sources of history—place lore, anecdote, written record, and artifact—this chapter traces obligatory networks between king and ascetic, agricultural landlord and tenant, guru and townspeople, or even deity and devotee in Sringeri. The modalities through which these networks and linkages were instituted, sustained, or disclaimed, I suggest, hold important insights for what constitutes appropriate conduct or upachara in different contexts. The historicization I seek to make in this chapter draws on the Hindu sociophilosophical concepts of rina (debt) and dana (gifting). Rina and dana, I argue, underlie the formation and expression of networks and linkages, visibly and invisibly affecting social and political interactions and expectations. It is intriguing to see how despite profound transformations in political and economic landscapes, and consequent changes in networks and linkages, Sringeri's community displays a marked attentiveness to the observance of upachara, appropriate conduct.

As the matha grew into a self-governing establishment (*samsthana*), it gradually became a critical site in the region's political history. In particular, the volatile political conditions in the region between the fourteenth and the eighteenth centuries saw intense and continuous negotiation between the matha, local communities, and external rulers who sought to enhance their control over the region. It is interesting to note how, during these centuries, social relations concerning the matha came to be mediated through reciprocal arrangements, gift giving (dana), and patronage. For rulers, patronage of the matha, whether through lavish endowments or administrative support, was a significant means of maintaining cordial relations and augmenting positions of power. The Sringeri matha, in its turn, reciprocated the patronage it received not only by offering religious services, but by deploying its religious authority to validate the political authority of the patron-king. Historicopolitical events of the late twentieth century like the abolition of the Sringeri matha's land-grant status and land reform legislation introduced changes in the social landscape of Sringeri, affecting the nature of obligatory relationships between people and institutions.

It was not until the fourteenth century that Sringeri became visible as a political entity. Vidyaranya, a sanyasi associated with the Sringeri matha (he later became the twelfth guru of the matha in CE 1375) helped Harihara I and his brother Bukka[8] to establish what emerged as one of the most powerful and expansive Hindu kingdoms in Indian history, the Vijayanagara Empire.[9] Although scholars are uncertain whether Hakka and Bukka were independent rulers or ministers in the court of last of the Hoysala kings who ruled in the Karnataka region before the Vijayanagara kings, it is generally held that the brothers sought Vidyaranya's counsel to overthrow the Muslim conquerors of south India.[10] Soon after their victories, acting on Vidyaranya's advice, they founded the nine-gated city of Vijayanagara ("city of victory") in the shape of a Shri chakra[11] with a temple at its center. Vidyaranya is believed to have personally conducted Hakka's coronation. The *Vidyāraṇya Vrittānta* notes:

> Vidyaranya seated himself upon the throne before the coronation of Harihara and received from him with libations of water a gift of a lakh and a quarter, territory both above and below the ghats in the kingdom of

> Karnataka, which he [Hakka] had obtained [from the earlier ruler or rulers] for the maintenance of the matha and the *choultry* [resthouse] at Sringeri as well as the *agrahara* [brahman locality] and Paramahamsa choultry. Then seating Harihara on the throne Vidyaranya performed his coronation.[12]

Sringeri's ties to royalty are vividly displayed in the grand tradition of the durbar (royal court) that is held in the Sharada temple during Navaratri, when the pontiff in regal attire ceremonially conducts court at the end of each of the nine nights of the festival. The durbar is without question one of Sringeri's showcase items. But how is it that an avowed ascetic can become king, even if temporarily? According to historical records as well as popular belief, the Sringeri durbar has its origin in the guru dakshina[13] that Harihara and Bukka offered to Vidyaranya in return for his counsel in establishing the Vijayanagara empire.[14] The Vijayanagara kings are reported to have themselves lavishly celebrated Navaratri in Sringeri.[15] Sitting outside on the stone ledge running along the house in Kadavadi, Nagaraja and I talked about the upcoming Navaratri celebrations. He narrated the following story:

> After Vidyaranya established the Karnataka samsthana for Hakka and Bukka, he returned to Sringeri.
>
> One day the thought came to him,
> "Are my disciples still devoted to me?"
> He decided to test Hakka and Bukka and said,
> "I've built this kingdom for you, and you've been ruling it.
> But you have not given me my guru dakshina."
> They responded,
> "You have not asked for anything. We will gladly give you whatever you desire."
>
> And taking some tulasi (basil) leaves, and some mantrakshate (sacred turmeric-dipped rice grains), they offered oblations, saying,
> "We offer you our entire empire in guru dakshina."
> Immensely pleased, Vidyaranya replied,
> "I am happy with your guru-bhakti (devotion to guru).
> But of what use is an empire to me, a sanyasi? I asked only to test you."
>
> At this, the brothers said, "We have given away the empire to you, and we cannot now take it back.
>
> But, there is one thing—whatever regalia we use, we will hand those over to you.

And for at least ten days in every year, we would like you to conduct the durbar just as we do."

So they gave Vidyaranya their throne, the crown, the palanquin, and the scepter.

From that year, the matha has been organizing a durbar during Navaratri and the guru becomes an "emperor" for nine nights.[16]

Thus the story mediates two inappropriate actions: while it is unacceptable for a sanyasi to accept a kingdom and rule it, guru dakshina cannot be returned without repudiating the guru-disciple relationship itself. The durbar represents Vidyaranya's symbolic acceptance of the guru dakshina of royalty. Thus, every year, Sringeri residents remind themselves of the obligatory bond, the rina, between Sringeri gurus and the Vijayanagara kings. The historical relations that developed between the matha and the Vijayanagara empire over the succeeding centuries validate Jan Gonda's observation that dakshina also serves to maintain a mutually beneficial alliance between the giver and the receiver.[17]

However, inscriptions available today present a different manifestation of this reciprocation: Harihara and his brother reciprocated Vidyaranya's help by visiting Sringeri in 1346, and donating to the then guru of the matha, Bharati Tirtha, and his forty brahman disciples, nine villages that were deemed, like all the land grants that followed, *sarvamānyā*, or exempt from duties and taxes. Called the "Shringapura grant" by historians, and recorded in a stone inscription preserved in Sringeri even today, this is the first known land grant received by the matha.[18] Hermann Kulke notes that in the Shringapura grant inscription Sringeri is referred to only as "a 'place of pilgrimage' or 'holy ford' (tīrtha) where Bhārati Tīrtha and his followers were performing their services."[19] The Shringapura grant—acknowledged as a historic landmark—can be presumed to have fundamentally changed Sringeri from a strictly religious establishment described in the inscription into an independent, landed, politically empowered state.[20] Further, this endowment created the conditions for the emergence of Sringeri as a distinct geopolitical entity through the formation of the Shringapura agrahara, the first of many brahman settlements in the area.

For us, the most important aspect of the Shringapura grant and the circumstances of its genesis is that it had the indirect effect of initiating a six-century tradition of land and other endowments from various rulers and wealthy individuals to the matha, a tradition that I believe carefully charts reciprocities implicit in the grand gestures of patronage. In these gestures one can also see the gradual formation of a moral ambience that reinforces giving and taking through carefully structured idioms of exchange in a continuous process that weaves the "historical" with the "social." Several grants followed the Shringapura grant, and the numerous grants that the Vijayanagara kings made when Vidyaranya became guru in 1375 give us an idea of the kings' sense of personal indebtedness to him. In K.R. Venkataraman's words, "The creation of the *samsthānam* (independent government) marks the expression of reverence and gratitude on the part of the early emperors of Vijayanagar who were deeply conscious of the debt they owed to the [Sringeri] Jagadgurus."[21] In fact, Kulke records that land grants made during Vidyaranya's years as the *maṭhādipati* (the head of the matha) amounted to three times as much as the grants made during the first decade after the inception of the Vijayanagara kingdom.[22] In all, these endowments totaled to an annual revenue of 3,003 pagodas,[23] and hence Sringeri came to be known as *mūru sāvira mūru varahada sīme*, or "region [providing tax] of three thousand and three varahas."

The Sringeri Sharada temple and Shankara matha fit into a well-known ideological scheme in which gods and kings are believed to share a sovereign status: the deity is supreme sovereign and the king is the political potentate.[24] By pledging service to the deity through a system of endowments, the king fulfills the obligation of ensuring the continuity of worship at the temple. The temple reciprocates through an elaborate system of honors (*maryāde*) that in turn serves to continually vivify the king's territorial sovereignty. In all ritual processes and material redistribution emanating from the deity, the king, by virtue of being supreme patron of the deity, is the first to receive honors and the prasada.[25]

Murne Mane Rambhattru

Ramachandra Bhattru formally introduced Murne mane Rambhattru to my husband and me as we stood watching a procession on Bharati Street in May 1995, although we had acknowledged each other in the temple before this introduction. He remarked that he had seen me in the temple "in a sari," and I felt the reference also noted that I typically dressed in a salwar-kameez (Indian long tunic and baggy pants). Since he lived on an adjoining street that I took on my way to the autorickshaw stand and the market, I often saw him on his porch, and we chatted. A scholar of Rig

Veda like his father before him, Rambhattru had taught in the matha's Sanskrit school for forty-nine years, while also conducting private tuition. He had lost his wife at the time I met him and was living with one of his sons who worked in a bank in Sringeri.

Rambhattru came of a priestly family believed to be one of the earliest to settle in Sringeri. According to the historical records of the matha and oral accounts, in the mid-fourteenth century the kings of the new Vijayanagara empire invited about three hundred brahman families to Sringeri from other regions of South India. Vidyaranya, who was the guru of the matha and spiritual counselor to the Vijayanagara kings, sought the help of three scholars from among these families to write commentaries on the Vedas. The families of these scholars came to be known as the *Modalne mane* (First family), *Eraḍane mane* (Second family), and *Mūrne mane* (Third family). In addition, Rambhattru was also one of Sringeri's mahajana (eminent persons), a prestigious position that, in the past, was accorded by the matha and the townspeople to individuals of great learning and discernment. Rambhattru's accounts of these honors and positions were modest and detached. I became aware of more than just the eminence attached to such statuses; Rambhattru's descriptions brought alive for me interactions that took place between the mahajana, the matha's administration, British officials, and the representatives of the Mysore court and highlighted the dynamics of power that existed between various figures of authority in Sringeri.

The last person I saw in Sringeri, as our rented car bursting with the possessions of a nearly two-year stay pulled out, was Murne mane Rambhattru, standing on his porch—we waved to each other. It was also the last time I was to see him, since, on my visits in between to Sringeri, he had not been in town. In 2004, when I went to Sringeri, all set to give him a copy of an article that included a story he had narrated, I instead ended up attending the first anniversary of his passing away. I left the article with his sons and daughters-in-law from Bangalore who, since we did not know each other, in all probability also did not know until then that I felt the loss personally. Since none of Rambhattru's sons or daughters is employed in the matha, a tradition centuries old, has ended.

However in Sringeri, an interesting case that diverges from this well-recognized pattern displays the complexities of this redistributive process. The descendants of the Modalne mane, Eradane mane, and Murne mane families receive special temple honors that were instituted in 1386 that continue to this day for descendants of the three families.[26] Thus, when *arati*[27] is performed to the deities at the temples, it is first offered to the guru, then to representatives of these families in that order before it is taken around among other devotees who are gathered.[28] The redistributive process in this case accommodates more ambiguity than would seem possible in the transactional paradigm in which the temple/deity receives the royal gift and the king receives honors and sanctified returns.

Several readings are possible of the dynamics underlying the transactions between the king, the matha, and the scholars. While the king Harihara's gesture can be interpreted in general as his patronage of brahmanical learning (such patronage being incumbent upon Harihara's royal rank), it can also be understood as a public expression of his reverence to Vidyaranya, who was the guru of the matha and his spiritual preceptor. The temple honors accorded to the brahmans could also be considered part of the matha's remuneration to the brahmans for their scholarly assistance in an important project. At the same time, conferring temple honors could be the matha's way of underwriting the prestige involved in receiving land grants from Harihara II and communicating to the king that his gesture merited the matha's instituting a new temple *tradition* of honoring those brahman families. The management of such reciprocities, it appears, was critical for the maintenance of proper relations between the brahman community, the matha, and the ruler, all of whom occupied mutually advantageous, if different, positions of power.

The use of a language of honors to communicate positions in social hierarchy is seen in a decree passed by the Mysore Wodeyar administration in 1806–1807. The decree stated that in any meeting of religious personages the agratāmbūla (the first presentation of betel leaf and areca nut made to the most honored person in the gathering) should be first offered to the Sringeri guru, second to the guru of the Shivaganga matha (thirty-eight miles north of present-day Bangalore), and then to others.[29] While honors were intended to index privileged statuses, it cannot be assumed that such privileging was univocally ratified. A ruler could not afford to disregard mathas other than the Sringeri matha without potential damage to himself. In 1811–1812 the Mysore maharaja deftly preempted a confrontation between the Sringeri guru and Sumatheendra Swami of Nanjangud, near Mysore, who objected to the Sringeri guru's passing in front of his residence. The Mysore maharaja, having learned of this objection, invited the Nanjangud swami to stay at Mysore so that his stay in Mysore would coincide with the

Sringeri guru's visit to Nanjangud.[30] Speaking of the criteria that underlie the system of patronage and honors, Burton Stein notes, "Criteria may be socially denotative; they may also be spatially denotative; in all cases these criteria are viewed as morally valenced, that is possessing a dimension of appropriateness in *nature* and in *conduct*."[31]

Nicholas Dirks, documenting the vast areas of tax-free land donated to brahmans (brahmādēya) in Pudukottai in Tamil Nadu by seventeenth-century Tondaiman rulers, posits that royal gifts were a "principal element of statecraft," morally and symbolically binding recipients to the king through an elaborate system of honors, emblems, titles, and privileges. He says,

> While the gifts did not specify service in a contractual form, they were often given after services were performed and/or with the expectation that future services would be performed. Even Brahmans who were granted lands simply for their scholarly attainments signified their participation in the rule of particular kings and dynasties by accepting land grants. When persons were incorporated into the kingdom—into the sovereignty of the king—through gifts, they became, in a relational sense, obligated to the king.[32]

Whereas this may indeed be true of royal patronage in general, the Sringeri case presents certain complexities in the obligatory linkages that result from royal donations. Since brahmans in Sringeri were part of the religious and administrative infrastructure of the matha, donations to them became symbolic of gestures of support to the matha. Thus the management of reciprocity toward the donor king became the onus of the matha, and not so much of the brahman. Recipient brahmans were instead bound to the matha, and the matha on its part depended on these brahmans to carry out its functions and duties. A net of mutual dependencies was thus generated.

If, through endowments, the matha became affluent and gained in political authority, the kings who patronized it acquired in the matha a valuable resource for the dissemination of loyalty to the king.[33] Romila Thapar elaborates, "Each sectarian group [the guru and his disciples] maintained a network of links and controls over a large geographical area and thereby helped to build a political base [for the king] as well. If the sect was politically loyal to the king, the monasteries they controlled would act as focal points in the diffusion of loyalty, thus providing a further support for the administration."[34] The instance of the Vijayanagara king, Krishnadevaraya's grant of the village of Huyyaru in AD 1515, exemplifies royalty's expectation of returns for patronage. The inscription recording the donation to the matha notes that Krishnadevaraya's objective in making the grant "was threefold, viz. the destruction of his foes, unswerving attachment of his supporters and allies, and increase of his life, health and prosperity."[35]

The enduring configuration of temple as landowner is illustrated in the Sringeri practice of building a small private temple, around which a Sringeri home would then be built, and dedicating agricultural land to this temple. The expenses of the temple and financial support for its priest came from the revenue generated by this agricultural land. Quite interestingly, public festivity can temporally transform this private landowner-temple-priest equation into a public expression of that connection. For example, during Sringeri's Ramanavami celebrations the private Rameshwara temple of the Murthy household and the courtyard are transformed into a center of public festivity where the entire brahman community of the town of Sringeri gathers for the festive meal following the ritual coronation of Rama. While providing occasion for the family to locate their home and daily endeavors in the grace of a protective deity, this public festivity in a private space also enacts the larger system of royal patronage of a temple, a brahman community, and public festivity.[36]

The political leverage provided by the Sringeri matha made it clearly profitable for various rulers who succeeded the Vijayanagara kings to continue bestowing land-grants and other gifts to the matha and support it through administrative decrees. The diffusion of centers of power was signaled by the critical battle of Talikota in 1565, a culmination of the recurrent skirmishes between the Vijayanagara empire and the Muslim kingdoms along its northern borders. The decisive defeat of Vijayanagara in this battle subordinated the empire, breaking it into smaller states, and set the stage for the rise of Muslim power in south India.[37] Consequently, this period saw the spread of Islam, as well as the emergence of competing Hindu religious orders like the Virashaiva and Vaishṇava faiths of feudatory kings.[38] It was often political expedience, and not necessarily religious affiliation, that seems to have determined the patronage of the Sringeri matha by administrations of the Virashaiva Keladi Nayakas, the Sri Vaishnava Mysore Wodeyars, the Mysore Muslim ruler Hyder Ali and his son Tipu Sultan, and the British, all of whom purposefully cultivated "cordial relations" with the matha, even privileging it over other religious institutions.

Among the numerous instances supporting this argument, the involvement of Muslim rulers with the matha is most striking. In 1760, upon hearing that Raghunatha Rao, the Maratha ruler, had invited the Sringeri guru,

Hyder Ali, whose hostility to the Marathas is legendary, wrote to the guru, saying, "You are a great and holy personage. It is but meet that all should desire to pay respects to you, and I am happy you are responding to Raghunatha Rao's invitation."[39] Hyder Ali is further reported to have donated an escort for this journey comprising "one elephant, five horses, one palanquin and five camels, besides making him costly presents . . . and 10,500 rupees for his expenses."[40]

When a part of the Maratha contingent returning from defeat in the third Mysore war (1791) against Tipu Sultan plundered Sringeri and looted its temples, Tipu Sultan, commiserating with the matha, sponsored the restoration of the temples. In fact, it was for this war that Tipu Sultan requested that the Sringeri guru conduct elaborate rituals for ensuring his victory and arranged for the necessary supplies.[41] His 1793 letter to the guru reads: "You are the *jagadguru* [guru of the universe]. You are always performing penance in order that the whole world may prosper and the people may be happy. Please pray to God for the increase of our prosperity. In whatever country holy personages like yourself may reside, that country will flourish with good showers and crops."[42] Surendranath Sen, in his study of the Sringeri letters of Tipu Sultan, argues for Hyder Ali and Tipu Sultan's general religious tolerance, but speculates that Tipu Sultan's solicitations were politically expedient: "It may be argued that Tipu was at this time hard-pressed by his enemies and wanted, therefore, to conciliate his Hindu subjects and at the same time to bring about the discomfiture of his enemies [the Marathas] by means of these superstitious rites."[43]

The politics and patterns of patronage display different complications in the period following the fall of Vijayanagara. Records suggest that after the breakdown of the central authority of Vijayanagara that had been principally responsible for the matha's establishment as a samsthana the matha, in order to retain its holdings and its claim to religious authority, was confronted with the challenge of having to negotiate carefully with multiple kingships, which many times ruled concurrently and warred constantly with each other. The main sources of information about the administration of the matha and its diverse interactions with rulers and devotees during this period are its official records, copper plate and stone inscriptions found in Sringeri and in the relics of capitals of erstwhile kingdoms, and literary works eulogizing the lives of Sringeri gurus. According to A. K. Shastry, the matha's official records (kaditas) are grouped into "orders" (nirupas), "account books," and "letters of respectful communication and petition" (binnavattales).[44] While the kaditas, for the most part, have been taken at face value and interpreted as "evidence" for unconditional reverence of all rulers toward the Sringeri gurus,[45] the information they contain nevertheless sufficiently suggests that communication between the matha and other agencies was motivated by social and political considerations and by the desire to maintain power amidst conditions of turmoil.

In the vortex of political chaos after Vijayanagara, among the dynasties that rose and fell in rapid succession was the Nayaka dynasty of Keladi, a small state a few hundred miles south of Sringeri. The Keladi Nayakas took over the role of reinstituting the Sringeri matha, which had begun to see a decline in its control over the by now widely distributed properties.[46] Post-Vijayanagara rulers involved themselves directly in the local life of Sringeri through their patronage of the matha. The Keladi chieftains, as other rulers, frequently acted as intermediaries; at the local level, for instance, they often restored land to the matha that had been lost to tenants through illegal appropriation. In fact, Shivappa Nayaka, Keladi chieftain between 1645 and 1660, is famous in Sringeri for his siṣtu (land assessment) by which he reorganized the system of revenue settlement that existed between the matha and the tenants who cultivated its lands. A few centuries later, a similar situation occurred, and the Mysore Maharaja, at the request of the matha, had land records scrutinized to redress the misuse of lands that the matha had allotted to tenants in return for specific duties such as the conduct of worship in a temple. The investigation resulted in the Sringeri Jagir Inam Settlement Regulation of 1897 which boosted the matha's annual revenue from Rs. 60,000 to Rs. 130,000.[47] The Keladi queen and daughter-in-law of Shivappa Nayaka, Rani Channammaji, issued in 1691–1692 an order to her officers that no tax be levied on goods needed by the matha, an order that continued to be reiterated by succeeding administrators including the British even as late as the mid-nineteenth century.[48] Further, when the question arose whether the matha should submit annual accounts to the British government, L. B. Bowring, who became chief commissioner of Mysore in 1862, declared that the matha did not need to submit such returns, and that it was free to exercise its "time-honored privileges."[49]

A striking example of the manner in which the matha engaged in dialogue with the politics of its times is provided by the "letter of benediction," ashirvada patrike, that it often sent to various rulers and administrations. Although the scanty information available to us does not say much about the particular circumstances and texts of ashirvada patrike, it is obvious that while these letters were indeed used to convey blessing, their agenda was more wide-ranging. The gurus, for example, sent ashirvada patrike to seek assistance in regaining lost property, to request protection during their journeys, and to confirm good relations with recipients. To illustrate, Sachidananda Bharati I (1622–1663) wrote an ashirvada patrike to Shivappa Nayaka soliciting his help in recovering land revenues from defaulting tenants of the matha. It was in response to this letter that Śivappa Nayaka instituted his śiṣtu, investigating malpractices, and reorganizing Sringeri's revenue system[50]. An ashirvada patrike written by the mahajana, or "eminent persons," of the agrahara of Vidyaranyapura to Basavappa Nayaka II (1739–1755), informing him of the demise of the guru and the accession of the guru nominee to the Sringeri pitha (seat), suggests that such a communication was an obligatory responsibility—in the absence of the guru, the mahajana were bound to discharge the responsibility of upholding the relations of the matha. The Keladi administration, it is recorded, urged the guru in the mid-eighteenth century to send an ashirvada patrike to the Maratha ruler, Balaji Bajirao, believing that it would set right a misperception the Maratha ruler held of the matha. Given that the Keladi administration itself could have directly communicated with the Marathas as it did on other occasions, its mediation in this matter raises the question whether diplomatic propriety could have motivated this request. Although A. K. Shastry maintains that the request shows general Keladi "concern" for the matha's welfare,[51] it is possible to argue that the Keladi administration saw in the "misperception" of the matha's standing a challenge to its own reputation, being the high-profile, visible patron that it was. The colonial British government was also a recipient of ashirvada patrike. The guru sent an ashirvada patrike to Colonel Cubbon assuring him that the matha prayed "for the perpetual prosperity of the [British] government."[52]

The political motivations of acts of cordiality are more vividly discerned in the conferring and confiscating of territorial rights and religious insignia by rulers. For instance, rulers issued administrative decrees categorically subjugating other mathas in their conflicts with the Sringeri matha and granted the matha exclusive ownership of cultural icons using their royal prerogatives. Shastry reports from the Sringeri matha's kaditas that the branch matha at Kudli attempted to secure some villages belonging to the Sringeri matha by enlisting the help of officers in the administration of Bijapur, political rivals of the Nayakas of Keladi. Virabhadra Nayaka, we are told, wrote to the Bijapur officers that the matha's "possessions should not be disturbed,"[53] and further passed an order stating that "citizens of 32 villages [should] recognize the control of the Sringeri *swami* over all Dharmasthalas [places of pilgrimage] and other mathas," while informing the Sringeri guru that he had the "the privilege of receiving homage from other *sanyasis*."[54]

In addition to thus ensuring the protection of the physical territory of the matha, administrations also deemed certain religious emblems to be the exclusive property of the matha. The insignia possessed by an institution are important signifiers of its cultural authority and the Sringeri matha regally displayed its various insignia[55] during public festive events and processions. As Alessandro Falassi observes, public celebrations provide an opportunity for ruling groups to communicate the message that they are "guardians and keepers" of cultural icons, and "depositories of religious or secular power, authority, and military might."[56] Consequently, the appropriation of insignia that belonged to another institution amounted to the appropriation of cultural power, constituting a symbolic aggression on cultural territory.[57] Little wonder then that insignia became sites of contestation between the Sringeri matha and other religious institutions.

But subtexted in insignia were also statements about appropriate conduct. The adda pallakki, a palanquin carried sideways, was one such insignia that was the privilege of the gurus of Sringeri who used it during their religious tours. Since the adda pallakki occupied the entire street and prevented passing, only those whose honor and status could not be disputed were entitled to it. L. B. Bowring reports of the Sringeri guru: "It may be said that his influence is far greater than that of any spiritual guide in India, and I presume it is for this reason that he is regarded with such unlimited respect. He is the only guru in the province who is permitted to carry the Adda Pallakee, or cross palankeen, and he has in his possession *sunnuds*[58] of great antiquity from the Nizam, the Peshwas, the Mysore Rajah, Holkar, and others, all enjoining the utmost respect to him."[59] Given its association with honor, the gurus of the branch mathas of Tirthahalli and Kudli also wanted to use the adda pallakki and appealed in 1928 to the British Resident for this right. The British, in whose political and administrative interest it was to support the more prominent Sringeri matha, rejected the appeals.[60] More than a hundred years earlier, in 1807 Purnaiyya, the chief minister of Mysore, had "held that no other swami could be taken out in *adda pallaki* and sent through the *amildar* of Koppa a stern warning to a wealthy merchant Hecca Timmayya against instigating the swami of Hariharapura matha to be carried in *adda pallaki* or assume any insignia he was not entitled to."[61]

It was inevitable that this rich history of political endowments and honors eddy into the local communities of Sringeri and widen the network of obligatory linkages between the matha and royalty. The acquisition of lands and property, although it extended the spheres of influence of the matha, was essentially inappropriate to ascetic life and necessitated that the grihastha (householder), become part of the institution. Through oral accounts in Sringeri I learned that, soon after the Shringapura land grant to the matha in 1346, Vidyaranya invited about three hundred learned brahman families of Telugu, Tamil, and Kannada origin to live in Sringeri. These brahmans were known as the mahajana of Sringeri. One of the first descriptions of the mahajana that I heard was in a conversation with Murne mane Rambhattru. In his words, before the position of the matha's "Agent" (or as he is now known, "Administrator") was established

> (The mahajanas) ran the place.
>
> L: Really?
>
> There was hardly any role for the *Administrator* or *Agent* or anybody like that. There used be something like a *committee.*
>
> There were about three hundred families around here then.
>
> In Shringapura, a hundred and fifty people, Vidyaranyapura a hundred, then in Sachidanandapura, Narasimhapura some fifty each.
>
> Some twenty to thirty were selected from these to form the mahajana *committee.*
>
> Anything that happened in the matha had to be authorized by them, and people lived in accordance with their decisions.
>
> Although the guru was officially the "head," all affairs were managed by the mahajana.
>
> It was like that then.[62]

Burton Stein's observations about the mahajanas in tenth-century Uttaramerur in Chingleput district of Tamilnadu are relevant also to Sringeri: "Each of the mahajanas, or members of the great assembly, selected for membership of the committees had to meet rigorous qualifications and be free of specified disabilities. The qualifications were those of age (between thirty-seven and seventy years), Vedic learning and teaching experience, and minimum property expressed as a share of the lands possessed by the Brahmanas of the place."[63] Vidyaranya apportioned tax-free land to brahmans, who usually rented the land out to tenants for cultivation while they themselves focused on the religious and administrative duties of the matha. It became customary for rulers to honor the matha by establishing agraharas where brahmans could reside, and in this way the present-day agraharas in and around Sringeri came to be, shaping Sringeri's geographical identity.

Commenting on the interrelatedness of monastic institutions and surrounding settlements, Thapar concludes:

> In the early stages, the reach of the *vihara* [Buddhist monastery] or the matha into secular economic life was limited and was related at a simple level to redistribution and reciprocity. Redistribution was enforced by the lay community having to maintain the renouncer on alms and by the making of donations and endowments. For the ordinary householder, the feeding of monks was sufficient. For the rich householder, there was the providing of oil and clothing, the repairing and building of monasteries and, for even wealthier patrons, the endowment of land. Reciprocation lay in the tying of *dāna* [gifts] to *puṇya*, where, in exchange for alms and donations, the householder acquired merit. . . . Ultimately, the society of renouncers had to be supported by the lay community. The opposition inherent in the status of *grihasta* and *sannyāsa* remains, but the relationship is essentially dialectical, for the one cannot exist without the other. Changes within the lay community affected the community of renouncers and the lay community was, in turn, influenced by them.[64]

Indeed with autonomy in virtually all areas of government, the matha leased its vast holdings of land[65] to tenants who remitted annual taxes (kandāya). Until the liquidation of the matha's landed properties in the decades following 1958 when the first land reform act was introduced, the arrangements with tenants were many and complex: one, although the matha was the titular owner, its lands were endowed to its different temples like the Mallikarjuna or the Sharada temple. Tenants of the matha were essentially tenants of particular temples and had to give a portion of their crop (and/or cash) to the temple as revenue that was due to the matha. Further, there were landowners who were not tenants of the matha but were bound to the matha via the jagir tax. Then there were tenants who entered into simulated tenancy relationships with the matha by leasing the matha's lands and subleasing them to their own tenants who paid the stipulated revenue directly to the matha. Such intermediation facilitated, among other things, the mutual display of cordiality or goodwill between the landowner and the matha: the landowner granted the matha a favor by absolving it of the responsibility of managing lands and in return gained the social prestige associated with patrons of the matha. Each arrangement brought with it its own complexities of reciprocity.

Giridhara Shastry and Ajji

Within the very first weeks of my settling down in Sringeri, I was told often that I should meet "Shastrygalu." Indeed, not only did I quickly follow up on this valuable recommendation, but I also went back to Shastrygalu at each stage in the making of this book. Giridhara Shastry, an administrator of the matha during the tenure of Sri Abhinava Vidyatirtha, is now a lecturer in English at J.C.B.M. College. I first met Giridhara Shastry in 1994 when he was in his mid-forties in their home in Vidyaranyapura where he lived with his mother (who everybody in Sringeri calls "Ajji"). They now live in the college quarters overlooking a beautiful ravine in which the Tunga flows as it heads out from Sringeri. Their house is always full of visiting children and college students, and there is at least a visitor or two. Giridhara Shastry gives lessons in yoga and Sanskrit to children in the locality, teaches Sanskrit hymns set to music to groups of older residents, and conducts lessons in the *Bhagavad Gītā*. From others in Sringeri, I gathered that his father, a quiet, erudite scholar, who had passed away in a tragic boat accident in the 1970s, also had done such free-of-charge community work. Along with a team of other volunteers, and under the initiative of M. M. Subramaniam (a retired industrialist from Tamilnadu, now a Sringeri resident), Giridhara Shastry has set up a free homeopathy clinic.

Discussions with Giridhara Shastry—often in his book-lined study—helped me understand, and in fact reorient my questions about various subjects that I discuss in this book, such as the political history of the matha, social relations in Sringeri, and matha-community relations. His voice, most of all, has provided critical commentary on this book. Shastrygalu's formal education is in Sanskrit and English literature, but his knowledge goes far beyond such categories, and every time I have stopped to chat with him I returned home inspired to write, seek connections, more carefully articulate different perspectives, widen my analyses, and narrow my claims. When I enthusiastically rattled off some of the origin stories I had been encountering during my first few months in Sringeri, I remember Giridhara Shastry's gentle reminder to consider multiple historical sources for such stories, sources that might yield more complicated narratives of conflict, collaboration, or collusion (rather than only of the "tranquil past" genre).

The liveliness of children and youngsters streaming in and out of Giridhara Shastry's house (whether in Vidyaranyapura, in Sringeri town, or in the college quarters on the outskirts where they now live) is enhanced by Ajji's comforting presence—and tasty delicacies with which she lavishly pampers visitors. Once I visited them, suffering from a bad cough, and ten minutes into a conversation with Giridhara Shastry over drafts of this book, Ajji emerged with the traditional remedy of steaming kashaya or herbal decoction. Knowing that I typically waited till the hot drinks she gave me cooled, she returned every few minutes to ensure that I would drink the decoction while it was still hot, so that it would most effectively relieve the cough. As I began to spend more time with Ajji, I came to understand that the affectionate gestures were integral to her ethics. "What use is a ritual or a practice that hurts somebody?" she often remarked. This usually meant a very thoughtfully reasoned position on particular ways of "speaking" and "doing" that took into full consideration views that either challenged or contradicted her own ways. As I reflect on the paramount importance Ajji places on "not hurting anybody in any way" and the practical ways in which she—and Giridhara Shastry—practice this conviction, I also began to understand how their home always feels so spacious.

Responsibilities of managing the matha itself included the collection of annual dues, maintenance of records, supervision of repairs and construction of buildings, and the overseeing of agricultural activity. In addition, markets had to be managed for sandalwood and timber from the jagir's forests, and agricultural products like areca, paddy, cardamom, and betel leaves had to be processed and sold. For these it was inevitable that the matha draw on local populations. For Giridhara Shastry there was no doubt that these transactions made the matha central to everyday life in Sringeri: "In the jagirdari days the matha was the center because the matha wielded all powers—if one wanted to chop wood from the forest, one had to approach the matha; if a land matter came up, the matha decided; moreover, people were employees of the matha, tending the matha's many acres of land. Then the matha was always the 'natural' center of the area's religious activities; and people came to the matha for advice in spiritual matters. The matha was the center for day-to-day affairs."[66] What this means is that a milieu of interdependency developed between the matha and local communities and affected patterns of daily life.

Narratives in Sringeri, in fact, emphasize the personal dialogue that was possible with the matha "in the days of the jagirdari"—the seeming lack of it

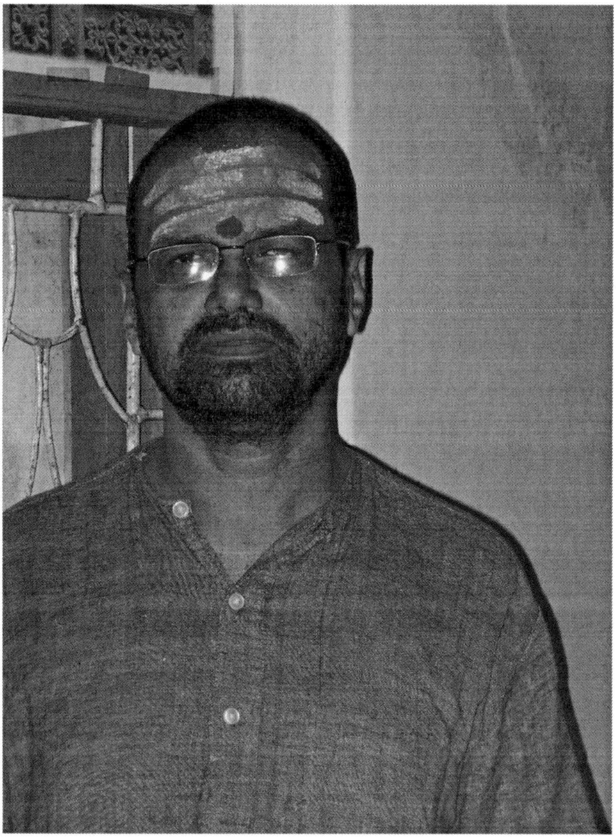

FIGURE 2.1. Giridhara Shastry in his study. *Photo by S. Shankar*

quite often feeds criticism of the matha in its postjagirdar phase. Just as the stories I heard about the gods and goddesses of the local temples had held up their Sringeri visages for me, recountings of experiences with "the matha"—with its gurus and its other custodians—held up the matha as a peopled institution with many voices. Dodda Murthy once told me how in the days of the jagirdari the matha's administrative office used to be down by the Gandhi maidan,[67] the sprawling open ground where the west-east flowing Tunga turns sharply to the north, encircling the ground on two sides. The office would keep time by ringing a big bell on the hour, and Dodda Murthy's father and other brahmans would hurry for their sandhyāvandana[68] by the river when the bell struck the evening hour. Putta Murthy recounted:[69]

FIGURE 2.2. Ajji near the Tulsi plants by their house. *Photo by S. Shankar*

PM: Many brahman families used to work in the matha in an *honorary capacity.* For instance, my father was the peshkar (superintendent).

If there was any event in the matha, my father would be asked to look after its *management.* And he used to go and help.

My older brother too worked as peshkar.

My other older brother (Dodda Murthy) also worked in the taluk office which was the matha's responsibility.

I too worked in the matha for a few years. So *honorary service*—

L: For free?

PM: that was what we had all resolved—

to work for the matha for a while before we took up any other job, seve (service).

We wanted to serve ammanavaru (the goddess Sharada). They used to give me twenty rupees as salary in the matha.

L: Only twenty!

PM: Twelve rupees—not even twenty, a salary of twelve rupees and an *allowance* of six rupees—totally eighteen rupees.

But this was plenty!
I didn't eat out, and there weren't other expenses.
Didn't eat in a hotel or smoke cigarettes, didn't have these habits.
So we used to do service for the matha.
In this way, we used to work for the matha.
Other groups did, too.

But, as I noted in the previous chapter, the brahman community in Sringeri consists of many subsects, a fact that acquires some salience when one notes that relations in the earlier half of the twentieth century existed not just between a homogenous "brahman community" and the matha, but between particular subsects and the matha. These were *differentially* expressed relations, with some subsects being more restricted than others in the capacities they could interact with the matha (for example, some brahman subsects were not allowed access to the matha's kitchen and granary or could not eat with other more privileged subsects). Reading a draft of this chapter, however, Giridhara Shastry pointed out to me that such privileging was not normatively derived: Another way of thinking about the question of who had access to what spaces of the matha, according to him, is to consider emigration-immigration patterns. The oldest communities (Babburkamme, Hoysala Karnataka, Andhras) who formed the oldest employees of matha traditionally held the responsibilities of cooking for and serving the guru, privileged forms of religious service. With emigration out of Sringeri in these older communities and immigration of other communities (Shivalli, Kota, for example) into Sringeri, it is possible that the practice of restricting access to the matha to newer communities was more of a strategy to retain generational hold on privileged duties, rather than a belief in innate subcaste superiority.

While in contemporary times, the matha does not maintain distinctions between brahman communities, these distinctions of the past are nevertheless *remembered* by descendants of families that were disprivileged. In some cases these memories are incorporated into "family traditions" that enact a deliberate distancing from the matha. For example, one such practice is that of a family that sends a kāṇike (contribution, gift) to the matha for a puja year after year, but chooses to do so in absentia or through proxy. In the 1890s, although the matha decided to "re-recognize" some ostracized communities, this recognition is as much subject to validation by the community being reincorporated. As Webb Keane observes, in an interactional context, recognition cannot be the prerogative of one party; unequally shared though this prerogative may be, recognition is essentially "dialectical and potentially power-laden."[70] Reciprocity is thus enmeshed in questions (that could illustrate ironies) such as: Who seeks recognition, and in what manner? Who grants it, and in what manner? Further, if the matha formally recognized some brahman families for the service they rendered to the matha, it simultaneously formally recognized others for their material patronage. Perhaps reciprocity, beyond the *act* of recognition itself, is about *kinds* of recognition—recognition of service, of economic strength, or of erudition, for instance.

As we try to nuance our understanding of the culture of interdependency that seems to have developed in the Sringeri region, it is critical to also note that there are some families in Sringeri that disclaim obligatory ties to the matha, since their lands have not come from the matha. The absence of a land-based economic connection affects how matha-family relations are described by individuals. One brahman agriculturist whose name I must keep anonymous said to me, "My grandfather came here and bought land from somebody, so where is the question of being obliged to the matha? We did not take anything and we did not receive anything." In fact, later in the conversation, he described a recent episode in which the matha came up for sharp critique for the manner in which it had acknowledged a donor. As others in Sringeri also recounted, the administration had hung a framed picture of the donor couple in the main temple, and a few local residents (whose families also had long-standing relations with the matha) objected. This agriculturalist said that he went up to the counter in the temple where one pays for the pujas one wants conducted and requested to pay for a puja to be conducted to the framed picture. When the clerk at the counter replied that such a puja was not possible, he asked that the picture then be removed. Others in Sringeri said they too had made similar facetious requests. The administration soon had this picture removed.

Intrigued by the mix of stories, especially romanticizing the jagirdari days, I once remarked to Giridhara Shastry in a conversation about Sringeri that I often had heard people say the days of the jagirdari had been better. I present below an edited version of his response, which I recorded on audiotape:[71]

GS: After all the farther the highest power people can appeal to, the less satisfied they are with the arrangement. It wasn't like that here.

For instance, there used to be revenue inspectors of the matha who would go to the farmer to collect taxes.

Let's suppose the farmer had to give ten quintals of paddy.

The revenue inspector would say, "You have to give the 10 quintals."

Now suppose the farmer said,

"No sir, I can only give eight,"

and the revenue inspector didn't budge, the farmer could appeal—appeal to the administrator.

If the administrator also didn't concede, the guru was always there.

The farmer could fall at the guru's feet, and the guru would just dismiss the case, saying,

"Don't bother to pay anything!" So what would you naturally prefer—this negotiable system, or today's government with its courts where your case will sit unresolved for years together?

Which do you think people will want?

The older families in Sringeri today—they were personally invited to come and settle here.

In those days Sringeri used to be *thinly populated.* Say a house needed to be built.

The matha would give them some land; the matha would, say, cut as much timber as you need from the forest. The matha would do all these things in the past.

Today such things won't work, right? None of that happens today.

In the past these older families were in the position to dictate to the matha.

If some of them came together, they were in a position to command the matha.

Who can they dictate to now?

The government?

What's happened is that the government has become *impersonal* now—it wasn't *impersonal* then.

And the guru, *he knew almost every family.* He knew what was going on in every family.

There were families—for many families, the matha was—what's the word?—the matha was *guardian.*

There used to be a person here, whose father passed away when he was still a boy.[72]

He left behind only young children.

At that time the matha stepped in, appointed a *guardian* to take care of the children. And then—there was another family—

L: So were they *literally guardians*?

GS: *Literally guardians*! The —— family?

The father, he passed away early.

Again it was the matha that appointed guardians.

The matha's appointees would market the family's areca, manage the fields, manage everything.

As soon as the boy became a major, they handed it over to him.

The matha also gave loans.

It was easy to take a loan from them. Everything took place right there in the matha.

When things were like that—

L: Were there only brahmans here then?

GS: Of course not, there were Vokkaligas too—

L: Other castes—did the matha look after *them* too?

GS: Oh yes! In fact, I've heard—the Vokkaligas in Tekkuru—were helped by the matha.

So you see, the matha's involvement in those days was totally different. *Relationships* with the matha were inevitable.

And as I said, it was for all these reasons.

There was dākṣinyā (obligation), you see.

For the Navaratri festival, and for marriages, you were expected to gift something to the matha.

The day tenancy was abolished and people became sole owners of the matha's lands—the generation changed.

This generation does not have that kind of contact with the matha.

It isn't possible.

The abolition of the jagirdari system and the transfer of land ownership to tenants severed the networks of reciprocity that, in Giridhara Shastry's view, characterized social relations in Sringeri in the jagirdari days. While the tenant was freed from the imposition of jagir tax and revenue payments to the matha, the sympathetic hearing the tenant was accustomed to in the matha was lost in the impersonal corridors of power in the state capital, Bangalore. Although the conversation highlights the negotiations possible with the matha, perhaps leverage was more a prerogative of older established landowners who were powerful enough to collectively command the matha. For these landowners then, the loss of the matha's jagirdar status implied a loss of their own bargaining power.

Despite its centrality in Sringeri life, the matha was not a monolithic construct of power, and oral histories bring out inner configurations of contestation. The challenge to the matha's sole claim to authority is seen, for example, in its conflicts with Sringeri's mahajana, especially after the creation of the position of an administrator in the early twentieth century. Holding perhaps the most powerful position in the nonrenunciate realm of the matha, the administrator supervises the extensive properties and public relations of the matha. A major dispute between one of the administrators and the mahajana came up in a conversation with an older resident whose ancestors belonged to the mahajana of Sringeri.[73] We had been talking at length about various gurus and the administrative structure of the matha in recent times. According to him:

R: This administrator[74] was very powerful—the guru had given him the full authority to decide all affairs of the matha. "Mane bēre alla, matha bēre alla," there was no difference between home and matha (for this administrator). He was that dedicated. That he caused hardship to others is a different issue.

L: They say the guru used to involve the townspeople in decision making . . .

R: Oh, yes—that was how it used to be.

Sanyasis were prohibited from getting involved in worldly affairs, and so we were invited, given land in inām (endowment), so that we could spend our time studying the Vedas, performing rituals, and looking after the matha's affairs.

Now, (this administrator) wanted to administer

L: Hunh?

R: independently—and the mahajana wouldn't let him.

If the mahajana opposed him together, he figured that he would not be able to run the place by himself.

So he wanted them to sign their lands to the matha and to revoke their land grants.

The mahajana naturally resisted.

They protested.

The dispute went up to the British.

One British revenue official called Grant was asked to conduct an inquiry. There were all these copper inscriptions, and he said,

"I would like to see them, bring them."

So they were given to him.

Grant asked—

now he didn't know Kannada, and the vaidikaru (orthodox brahmans), the mahajana didn't know English.

The intermediary translator was on the matha's side, on (the administrator's) side.

My father used to tell me the inscriptions clearly said that these lands were given to us in Vidyaranya's times so that we could be supported while we studied the Vedas and performed the pujas, and hence these lands belong to us.

But the translator said that the copper plates read,

"These lands belong to the matha, and should be in the matha's account."

Every plate was translated in the same way!

Grant got suspicious and thought,

"How is it that all of them read exactly the same? There is something else going on here."

L: He must have known!

R: So at the end (of his report), he added a clause that said that if a dispute took place again within twelve years, a re-inquiry would be ordered.

This was somewhat of a blow for (this administrator) because, if any complaint arose in twelve years, the matha stood to forego the land.

So he told the mahajana,

"If you lease the land to tenants, one year they will give you more (harvest as revenue) and another year less. Also, you will have to go to the villages and haggle with these farmers. Instead, let us (the matha) collect all the harvest on your behalf and bring it to your doorstep."

L: Hunh . . .

R: The mahajana reasoned, when somebody is actually offering to get the harvest to our doorstep, why should we go to the villages?

Later we learned that the "offer" was made simply to avoid dispute for twelve years.

So, accordingly, every year for twelve years the matha collected the paddy and the areca due to the mahajana and gave it to them dutifully.

The *thirteenth* year (the administrator) instructed that the harvest be brought directly to the matha.

L: Oh!

R: When the harvest didn't come home as usual, the mahajana approached the administrator:

"How is it we have not got any harvest this year? We haven't got our areca or anything."

L: Hanh!

R: (The administrator) replied:

"Naturally. The harvest from the matha's property will come to the matha. You had given statements saying this was the matha's property and that harvests could be given to the matha.

We're just following through with the order that was passed. There's nothing we can do about it. All these years, we've already done in excess of what was due to you."

L: That was cunning!

R: So the *entire* property of the mahajana became the matha's.

But you know what the land reforms finally did—

you see, when a rupee is changed to a hundred paise, it isn't noticeable,

but when it is unchanged, it catches people's eyes.

So the state government noticed and abolished the jagir.

"Land to the tiller," they said.

With that it was over.

"Namagū illa, avaragū illa" (nothing for us, nothing for them either).

The administrator in question provokes admiration from the older generation of Sringeri who respect him for his unparalleled dynamism in managing the public relations of the matha and his competence in ritual procedures, but interleaved is a certain reservation that comes from the feeling that he was also an astute politician. He is credited with making the role of the administrator powerful and prestigious—tipping the balance of power in favor of the matha and away from the mahajana. By this account the incident not only diminished the economic assets of the Sringeri mahajana but also introduced a change in moral topography: This raises the question whether the transfer of lands also indexed a transfer of moral authority, although the latter is less clearly mappable. What is clear, however, is that confiscating lands in order to reverse a power structure resulted in permanently disenfranchising the mahajana and affected the matha's relations with local residents. It is interesting that although the mahajana lost political power, *maryāde* (respect, honor) accorded to that status continues to be shown formally to their descendants.

Oral narrations indeed present undulated understandings of the relationship between "the matha" and "the local community." In another resident's perspective, which I present below, the conflict is seen less as a narrative of personal losses and gains, but as part of the broader history of land (mis)appropriations in Sringeri.

> These brahman families (who had been granted the lands by in Vidyaranya's time) were so immersed in the Vedas and their pujas that they had totally neglected their lands.
>
> Quite often, lands were appropriated by whosoever tilled them. The situation had got to the point where there was no accounting for whether tenants paid revenue or not.
>
> Then, during the reign of the Nayakas of Keladi, Shivappa Nayaka *reclaimed all* these lands and gave them back to the brahmans.
>
> L: Shishtu . . . ?
>
> R: That's the reason why "Shivappa Nayaka's shistu [assessment of revenue]" is famous in this region.
>
> So Shivappa Nayaka set in place an arrangement that continued for some time.
>
> But our folk lost everything yet again!
>
> L: Oh, no!
>
> R: This didn't mean they lost the *titles*—they had the *titles*, but the land was virtually useless to them.
>
> Everyone wanted to administer lands staying at home; nobody went to the fields to personally look after their lands. Eventually, their situation got somewhat worrisome.
>
> L: Hunh?
>
> R: And yet, they were not willing to let go their *control* over the matha—the matha was entirely *controlled* by them.
>
> L: Hanh!
>
> R: Even the guru had to follow their directions in whatever he did and said—every single matter had to be sanctioned by them.
>
> It got to a point where matters had to be remedied, you see.
>
> L: Oh!
>
> R: So at this point, what (the administrator) did was—
>
> he gave loans to whoever was in financial difficulty, got the lands signed as collateral, and *gradually* confiscated them for the matha.

> In this *gradual* manner, they say, he managed to bring the power back to the matha.[75]

Thus, although the collective presiding authority of the mahajana may have helped to counter a centralization of authority in the administrator, there is more than a hint that the allocation of power within the mahajana "committee" was not much more diffused. But, stripped of their lands and rendered *dependent* on the matha for livelihood, one could argue that now an obligatory logic bound the mahajana to the matha in a way that the matha was not bound to them. Thus, although the two understandings of this tussle for power differ in their emphases, they both tell us that land became an important instrument in the reallocation of moral authority.

Tenancy legislations passed by the Karnataka government after India's independence further impacted social relations in Sringeri. Motivated by the socialist agenda of the central government, tenancy legislation, essentialized in the slogan "land to the tiller," were intended to redress the inequities of a feudalistic system of land ownership. The first piece of legislation (passed in 1958 but implemented in the mid-sixties) ruled that no institution could govern or collect tax independent of the government. M. A. S. Rajan reports that "all over Karnataka the State had acquired sovereign rights over all land by virtue of the provisions of the national Constitution. In the field of land taxation it had abolished all tax intermediaries of all kinds."[76] As a result, Sringeri lost its status as a jagir and became part of the state of Karnataka, which was then called Mysore.[77] Then, in 1974, the second piece of legislation passed by the ruling Congress government of Devaraj Urs lowered land ownership limits further.[78] As the largest "landowner" in the region, the matha's holdings exceeded the land ceiling specified by the reforms, and the government confiscated the matha's endowed lands, reapportioning them among its tenants and new bidders. In Sringeri taluk itself the matha had to relinquish five thousand acres.[79]

Needless to say, the loss of the jagirdar status seriously compromised the economic hold of the matha, created breaks in the power dynamics that had existed until then, and, as can well be imagined, splintered the land-based social relationships between the matha and the people who lived in the jagir. It is important to note that narratives in Sringeri, while recounting what was lost and what was gained by owners and tenants, also emphasize the profound shifts in sociability that accompanied tenancy legislation. No longer obligated to each other by land tenancy, many former tenants and landlords in Sringeri who shared cordial relationships find themselves renegotiating their relationship so that their moral kinship or *bāndhavya* continues to be maintained.

In this complex arena of shifting configurations of power and economic ties, it is clear that relations between gurus, administrators, local priests and scholars, families, ascetics, rulers, landowners, and tenants registered changes. This chapter has tried to explore how these changes were expressed and negotiated in social relations that brokered memories of past reciprocities and distances, new statuses, and emerging directions. Upachara in Sringeri can narrowly be understood as the performance of hospitality, but more comprehensively as "conduct," a normative concept that demands historical and relational circumstances be factored into the aesthetic expression of propriety.

With the crystallization of the matha as a Dharmashastra-interpreting institution that, at different times, was empowered differently, the question arises as to how the notion of shastra—also about right conduct—manifests itself in the community around the matha. While this question's immediate locale is Sringeri, the importance of the idea of shastra in wider Hindu contexts makes this a discussion about the imagination of the normative in Hindu culture.

Vijaya Krishnamurthy and S. J. Krishnamurthy ("Meshtru")

"I've made raw jackfruit huḷi (a type of lentil soup) today, because I knew you were coming!" Vijaya called out from inside as soon as I stepped into their house for lunch. Knowing that the jackfruit season had ended, I knew that Vijaya must have made special effort to acquire the fruit. She had made jackfruit huḷi a tradition to follow when I visited Sringeri and had lunch with them. We had become good friends over the ten years since I attended a parayana in their house. I had felt extremely awkward about attending the event (and the lunch following it) since I had not been invited formally, but a common friend, knowing of my interest in cultural happenings around town, had insisted I go ("Really, they will love it"). We—Vijaya and Uma and Usha (her daughters, who were in their early twenties) and I—bonded instantly, developing the comfortable friendship that allows banter.

Through Vijaya, who is from the Maidan regions but has lived in Sringeri since she married S. J. Krishnamurthy ("Meshtru," or teacher, as he is known) in the 1970s, I gained a sense of the cultural distinctiveness of the Malnad—foodways, in modes of address, or in ritual practices. These were described non-judgmentally, often with self-deprecating humor. Perhaps it was this ability to suspend criticism that "explained" how Vijaya blended so easily with all generations, relating as a peer to Uma and Usha's friends with the same gusto as to her own friends and to Chayamma's generation. She once said, when Uma and Usha had completed their graduate education in mathematics and physics respectively and taken up jobs at the local college, "I tell them, "Why don't you girls just wear churidaars to work instead of saris?' but they won't listen to me. Usha says, 'We'd end up looking like college students ourselves!'" In another context, when I had asked, perhaps sounding skeptical, whether the young and suddenly widowed daughter of a common friend would find it hard to remarry, Vijaya chided, "Come, if people like you think this way, it won't do! Times are changing and she will find somebody." By the time I visited next, the girl had remarried, was well settled into a new home and a bank job she liked, and was raising a family.

I ran into Vijaya and Meshtru often in the temple. Meshtru invariably said, "When will you come home? This evening? Tomorrow, or day after?" and invariably I would show up at their house. Meshtru, who had retired as a schoolmaster and performed voluntary service at the matha, especially knew I valued conversations about Sringeri. In 1995 he had taken me to the temple of the goddess Banashankari, who, as her name suggests, ensured crops and vegetation. It was on that hour-long walk that he had told me how his father and his uncle had started the first bus service in Sringeri, a business that took most of the family money but ended in heavy losses because of the heavy rains and poor roads. Through Meshtru's stories I came to imagine Sringeri gurus in lively quotidian detail. For instance, illustrating how one needs to carry oneself with deference and humility in the presence of a guru, he told me a story. In the mid-nineteenth century a man, sporting a flowing handlebar mustache, went to seek the blessings of Ugra Narasimha Bharati. While giving him tīrtha (sacred water), the guru looked at him, and said, "Ēno mīse?" ("How are you, Mustache?" or "What is this mustache?"). Next morning, the hapless man discovered that one side of his mustache had turned white. "That is why you should take a plate of fruit when you visit the gurus," Meshtru concluded. As is well-known in Hindu practice, divine beings or dharmic persons are acknowledged to have an extraordinary gaze that is capable of transforming what it falls on. Meshtru's stories were short and brisk, but they made their points graphically. I remember them by their catch phrases, like "ēno mīse?" In another example a man who had been treating his mother badly at home, but had come to seek a guru's blessings, was greeted with "Illigū banda nīca?" So have you come here too, you base man?"

In 2004, looking back at how their children had been placed in life (their son was now an engineer with a multinational corporation; Uma and Usha had married and were enjoying academic careers in Bangalore) and at their modest new house (which they acquired after a long wait), both Vijaya and Meshtru had only one thing to say. Meshtru said, "It is all due to the anugraha (grace) of the guru," and Vijaya said, "Ammanavara kripe (the kindness of the goddess)," echoing what I had heard her say for years.

FIGURE 2.3. S. J. Krishnamurthy and Vijaya in their backyard. *Photo by S. Shankar*

3 *Shastra*

Divine Injunction and Earthly Custom

"Now that my daughters are married and have left home, I don't think I will do an elaborate display of dolls (for Navaratri), but, for the sake of shastra, I'll maybe arrange two dolls in the puja room," mused Vijaya Krishnamurthy, when I telephoned to greet her for the upcoming Navaratri festival. I agreed, remembering the many times I too had done things to conform to shastra at least minimally. For example, balancing the Hindu festive calendar with a workday calendar that did not recognize those festivals meant that sometimes we would cook just chitrānna and pāyasa[1] to mark the meal as auspicious and festive. One encounters the term *shastra* in countless contexts of everyday parlance in Hindu worlds in spirited phrases such as "It is said in the shastras" or "It goes against the shastras." Indeed, for over two thousand years the notion of shastra has had an astonishing presence in Hindu normative thought and culture, and shastras, as codifications of knowledge, have been composed in virtually every aspect of life from love and politics to thieving and horse rearing. The term *shastra* comes from the Sanskrit root *śās,* which means "to teach or instruct," and shastra is commonly translated into English as injunction, order, command, precept, rule or compendium of rules, religious or scientific treatise, and lawbook.[2] Just as often, shastra is translated imprecisely as "scripture."

While many times an individual may rhetorically invoke the phrase "the shastras say" to validate a moral position, justify an action, or to subvert and negate somebody else's position and actions, the enduring sense of the term is associated with the performance of correct action or duty (dharma), the creation of auspiciousness, and compliance with context-specific regulations on conduct. Indeed, the concept of shastra yokes precept and practice in a way that perhaps no other concept in Hindu life does, and indexes a complexity that is not fully conveyed by the dictionary meanings of the term.

How might we understand the so-called modifications (to what, indeed) individuals make between "knowing" and "doing" the "right" thing? What voices of authority are summoned by the term *shastra* and what visions of the past and future are created by it in everyday contexts? What subjects of life and living are imagined to be under the purview of shastra? Or, more broadly, what kinds of cultural knowledge are called shastra?

While the preceding chapter traced the growth of the matha into a powerful Dharmashastra-interpreting institution, emerging in the midst of, and contributing to, a distinctive ethos of social relations in the region, this chapter looks at shastra itself as a normative concept in Hindu thinking. Contemporary quotidian theorization in Sringeri about the normative (of which shastra is one aspect) makes striking conversation with conceptualizations of shastra in early and medieval India. In the sections that follow, I provide a brief review of how shastra was imagined in Vedic times, across post-Vedic schools of philosophy, in medieval bhakti traditions, and in colonial India. With this historical background, in the next chapter I consider a wide variety of Sringeri perspectives on shastra and locate the concept amid a field of multiple normative concepts. In this review I pay particular attention to the Dharmashastras—shastra texts that most prominently address everyday Hindu life—in whose interpretation the Sringeri matha has been considered an authority. So vivid are the Dharmashastras about injunctions for daily living and legal practice that they mesmerized many powerful British colonial administrators into believing that these texts were *exclusive* and fixed codes for Hindus across the breadth of India. British colonial policy, relying on a book-based understanding, subjected these highly context-driven codes to parochial deployment in the creation of an Anglo-Indian judicial system.

Theorizing Shastra in Early India

To one growing up in India, "shastra" often appears to be a stodgy inflexible set of ancient rules whose origin and clarity seem apparent only to the elders and the priests who invoke them. It was only when I self-consciously reflected on this concept, persuaded by my experiences in Sringeri, that I discovered that the term, dating back to Vedic and early post-Vedic times, was in fact profoundly multivalent and heterogeneous. Shastra and its cultural cognates reveal themselves to be intricate and even idiosyncratic in everyday contexts. Yet a history of the term shows remarkable parallels between the debates of a distant past and those of contemporary times, although we do not know enough about how the shastras played out in the actual life of the past. The diffused views on shastra reveal debate and deliberation on the nature and source of authority, competing jurisdictions of moral and practical knowledge, the efficacy of prescribed actions, permissibility and rigidity of injunctions, and the problem of textuality.[3]

In a wide-ranging study of shastra in early Indian thought, Sheldon Pollock finds that for over twenty-five hundred years the concept of shastra, indexing an impressive range of "cultural grammars" has been "invested with massive authority, ensuring what in many cases seems to have been a nearly unchallengeable claim to normative control of cultural practices."[4] Arguing that shastra is the equivalent of "theory" (if theory is understood as doctrinal and programmatic), Pollock takes up the intriguing question of how such a practice-oriented genre as shastra itself theorizes the relationship between "theory" and "practice." He concludes that "theory" in Sanskritic literary culture is posited as always preceding and regulating "practice" (*prayoga*) because all theory is hypothesized as originating in a divine, eternal, and omniscient source, often identified as the Vedas.[5] A text like the panoramic treatise on the theatrical arts, the *Nāṭyaśāstra* by Bharata (dated sometime between second century BCE and second century CE) imagines itself as a "shastra of *prayoga*," a theory of praxis. In fact, "the written text in the case of the [Nāṭya] *śāstra* could at best be a residual record or memory aid of a much deeper, more intense and pervasive oral discourse within the tradition."[6]

Although the word shastra first occurs in a Rigvedic verse to Indra,[7] its earliest signification is in the grammatical tradition of the third and second century BCE where shastra is defined as a rule that regulates grammatical usage. Early grammarians like Katyayana and Patanjali insisted that shastra regulates not only the province of language but human conduct itself for the achievement of spiritual and dharmic goals. By the third century BCE, compendia of dharma (duties) known as the Dharmasutras had already emerged in Indian sociophilosophical literature, and, soon, domains of life that come under the three life goals (puruṣārthas) of an individual—right conduct (dharma), material pursuit (artha), and aesthetically refined sexuality (kama)—saw codification.[8] There are shastras on every imaginable subject from grammar and architecture to statecraft and the fine arts. Although commentarial tradition and popular parlance occasionally describe the Vedas and the *Bhagavad Gītā* as moksha shastra, it is harder to find treatises on the fourth goal, moksha (liberation), perhaps because moksha is understood as being realized only through selfless action, devotion, a guru's guidance, and, above all, divine grace. Although absorbed with particular subjects, shastras assume that human realms resist invariable compartmentalization and thus see themselves as addressing all three types of human endeavor (dharma, artha, and kama). Under no circumstances, they argue, should any one of the life goals impede the other two.[9] For instance, Kautilya's *Arthaśāstra* and Vatsyayana's *Kāmasūtra* also grapple with the question of dharma within the contexts of their specific subjects of statecraft or sexuality respectively, even though dharma is the substantive concern of the Dharmashastras.[10]

If one considers the ways in which texts declare themselves shastric (keeping in mind that texts not explicitly called shastra bear features of the genre while others that do not bear generic traits may be designated as shastra),[11] shastra appears as a deeply self-reflexive genre. For example, shastra texts often justify themselves by arguing that they are necessary in an age of moral decline in the current era of Kali. The decline in human intelligence, the general need for a synoptic presentation of the imponderably vast literature of the subject, and the fact of human mortality are offered as reasons for composing shastras.[12] For example, in the manner of many shastric texts, after tracing a complex genealogy of divine transmission for the *Kāmasūtra*, Vatsyayana tells us that the process of abridgement that had taken place prior to his work had rendered the "original" text available either in too vast a form or in too specialized a form so that he is compelled to codify the knowledge into the manageable text of the *Kāmasūtra*.[13] Madhva, the thirteenth-century philosopher-saint and founder of the Dvaita ("dualist") school of Vedanta philosophy, cites the corruption of the pristine text of the *Mahabharata* and the proliferation of regional versions as reasons for his commentary.[14]

Other shastras, especially relating to the performing arts, where we see a well-articulated tension between individual talent and a governing rule book, also tackle the question of why a shastra is indispensable. In the encyclopedic *Nāṭyaśāstra*, Bharata declares that we need shastras because, unlike divine creation, the human creative act calls for regulation.[15] An interesting story is told about a lost shastra on dance authored by Tandu. We learn that Tandu's shastra existed from Bharata's *Nāṭyaśāstra* into which it was incorporated, and from a commentary on Tandu's work by the tenth-century critic, Abhinavagupta.[16] The *Nāṭyaśāstra* tells us that Lord Shiva, the perfect cosmic dancer, asked his disciple, Tandu, to instruct Bharata on Shiva's distinctive dance known as the *nṛtta*. This divine command led to Tandu's formulation, which figures in the fourth chapter of Bharata's *Nāṭyaśāstra*. Mukund Lath concludes that this reflects Bharata's attempt "to proclaim an immanent relation between his own *śāstra* and that of Tandu, which was an obviously earlier *śāstra*."[17] Such embedding and entextualization of texts illustrates the supple intertextuality that is characteristic of shastric literature.[18]

Shastra and Schools of Philosophy

The *Pūrva Mīmāṃsā* school, which flourished from the second century CE onward, argued that ritual injunctions in the Vedas were the *only* means by which dharma could be known.[19] Yet, how does one know that acting according to an injunction produces the result it promises, and how does one interpret the nonachievement of a result? To answer these questions, the seventh-century commentator Kumarila Bhatta and later scholars pointed to the world of the imperceptible: results *do* ensue from following injunctions, but some results can be "seen" (drishtha) and others "unseen" (adrishtha).[20] Vedanta schools of philosophy from the eighth century shifted their attention from the ritual-oriented Brahmana portions to the Upanishads, the more philosophical part of the Vedas. In his *Vivekacūḍāmaṇi* the Advaita philosopher Shankara says, "Acceptance, with firm conviction, of śāstra and the words of the Guru as conveying the Truth is called faith by the wise. By this does reality become apprehended."[21] At the same time, the *Vivekacūḍāmaṇi* unequivocally cautions against shastra *vāsanā* (becoming too attached to shastra), which can impede wisdom.[22] Thus, says Shankara, "individuals may read and recite the *śāstras*, sacrifice to the gods, perform rituals, worship deities. Still, liberation will not occur, even after hundreds of millions of years, without a personal experience of one's identity with the Self [Brahman]."[23]

In *Śrī Bhāṣya*, the renowned exponent of Vishishthadvaita ("qualified nondualism"), Ramanuja (CE 1056–1137) argues that shastra is relevant only to the world of sentient beings who are capable of action and agency and who desire to realize Brahman. Devotion is the means of attaining Brahman, but devotion itself is to be *learned* through shastra. Madhva, the eminent Dvaita ("dualism") philosopher, also posits that the shastras are the only mode of knowing Vishnu's attributes and his "authorship of the universe."[24] The program for liberation is spelled out in a wide spectrum of texts that Madhva identifies as agamas (canonical texts), a term he frequently interchanges with shastra. The agamas or "true shastras" (sadāgama) are of two types. The nonhuman (apaurusheya) shastras are the eternal Vedas and Upanishads, while the human-authored (paurusheya) are the Pancharatra treatises (Vaishnava ritual texts), the epics of the Mahabharata and the Ramayana, the Puranas, and "whatever else is in conformity with their teachings."[25] Madhva tells us that there are also divinely composed shastras whose purpose is to delude; these are mohashastras, shastras of delusion, composed to trick evil forces into darkness. The mohashastras illustrate the potency of a shastra, for, despite being ontologically false, they are seen as capable of securing their objective when their pragmatic program is followed.

When a body of literature such as the poetry of the Alvar saints (sixth–ninth centuries CE) is conferred Vedic status, or when a text like Bharata's *Nāṭyaśāstra* calls itself a "fifth Veda," it takes on the Vedic attributes of transhuman knowledge and doctrinal authority.[26] R. C. Dwivedi argues that, thus, a "marginal, occasional, symbolic, mythical, and dialectical relationship has always existed between the Vedas and subsequent development of *śāstras*."[27] Brian Smith elaborates that many texts and practices that call themselves "Vedic" express this relationship through strategies of "reflection (this *is* the Veda), restatement (this is *based* on the Veda), reduction (this is the *simplified* Veda), reproduction (this *enlarges* the Veda), recapitulation (this is *condensed essence* of the Veda), and even reversal (the Veda is *based on this*)."[28]

Bhakti and Shastra

Although Vedantic schools readily acknowledged bhakti (devotion) as a precondition for higher knowledge, it is in the bhakti traditions of the centuries after the Alvars that one finds a range of attitudes from bold critique of shastra to conformity with it. For example, in the colloquial poetic form known as vacana (lit. "thing said") adopted by Virashaiva poets of the tenth to fourteenth centuries, one finds a powerful critique of shastra both as specific injunction and as normative socioreligious code. For many Virashaiva poets shastra is a distraction in the search for Shiva, who is the one and only reality. As Basava (twelfth century) declares: "They plunge / wherever they see water. / They circumambulate / every tree they see. / How can they know you / O Lord / who adore / waters that run dry / trees that wither?"[29] Allama Prabhu's repudiation of convention is similarly illustrative: "The Vedas are a matter of recitation, *śāstras* a chatter of the marketplace, *purāṇas* are only a meeting of goons."[30] At the same time, the crucial relationship between "knowledge" and "practice" debated by centuries of shastric literature is identified as central to existence itself by the vacanas. As the vacana of Dasimayya (AD tenth century) puts it: "Fire can burn / but cannot move. / Wind can move / but cannot burn. / Till fire joins wind / it cannot take a step. / Do men know / it's like that / with knowing and doing?"[31] Efficacy is understood in the vacana as *movement*, as "taking a step," affirming the Virashaiva ideal of the wandering ascetic (*jaṅgama*).

However, the uninhibited critique of brahmanical customs that one generally finds in the vacanas has tended to overshadow the fact that there were Virashaiva thinkers whose response to Vedic tradition and its allied shastras was more complicated than outright rejection. The thirteenth-century Telugu Virashaiva poet, Pālkuriki Somanātha, who was staunchly antibrahmanical asserts in his *Basava Purāṇa* that he was a "scholar of the 'four Vedas'" and that Virashaivism fully conformed to the Vedas and the shastras.[32] As Narayana Rao observes, the precondition for engaging the shastras, at least in the *Basava Purāṇa*, is the disacknowledgement of the custodial hold of brahmans and brahmanism over the Vedas and the shastras.

The tension between censuring mechanical or pretentious enactments of shastra, on the one hand, and overt allegiance to shastric norms on the other, is vividly brought out in the poetry and hagiographies of many Vaishnava bhakti saints. The *Chaitanya Charitāmṛta*, a well-known sixteenth-century biography of the saint Chaitanya who inspired a popular Krishna-bhakti movement in the Braj region, depicts him as a keen adherent of varṇa (caste) and aśrama (life stage) stipulations specified by the Dharmashastras. Just as many times, however, Chaitanya seems to transgress varnāśrama dharma in the ecstasy of devotion.[33] This dual response to shastric stipulation, Graham Schweig argues, is rooted in the *Bhāgavata Purāṇa*, which validates socially structured existence, but ultimately subjugates it to the service of Krishna; the latter being the highest dharma (parodharma).[34] Hagiographies of Mirabai, the most famous devotee of Krishna in sixteenth-century Rajasthan point out that although she rejected the social role of *pativratā* (lit. worship toward the husband) described by the shastras as incumbent on a married woman, that rejection was only relevant to the human sphere. For, as stories go, Mira believed, in the manner of the *gōpī* tradition (the cowherding girls who loved Krishna), that she was already and eternally married to Krishna, and in this relationship, she indeed was a *pativratā*.

The autobiography and abhangas (eight-lined poems) of the Marathi brahman saint Bahinabai (1628–1700) testify to her intense effort to reconcile the demands made by the shastras of a woman with her desire for a life of unfettered devotion to Lord Vitthala and to her guru, the poet-saint Tukaram.[35] Her attempts to seek Tukaram, who was of a so-called lower caste, incited tremendous opposition and physical abuse from her husband, who was a vaidika, a professional reciter of the Vedas. While Bahinabai's everyday struggles challenged her spiritual aspirations, she was also frustrated by misogynist characterizations in the shastras that prohibited her from following shastric prescriptions that had salvific power.[36] Yet her later poetry shows that she came to the understanding that the shastric path liberates only in the living out of the root significance of injunctions and not through their mechanical observance.[37]

The Dharmasutras and the Dharmashastras

Most relevant to the Sringeri context where historically the matha has been an interpreter of the Dharmashastras are the Dharmasutra and the Dharmashastra texts.[38] Perhaps no other group of shastra-texts recorded and codified everyday life, especially as it pertained to the upper castes as these treatises did. Compiled by various authors approximately between 500 BCE and CE 400, they broadly cover four topics spanning personal conduct (achara), expiation (prayaschitta), business (vyavahara), and governance (raja dharma).[39] The Dharmasutras, written in aphoristic style, are part of early ritual texts called the Kalpasutras that are one of the six ancillary Vedic texts.[40] While most Dharmasutras are lost to us now, or known only through extracts alluded to in other texts, four Dharmasutras, whose authorship is attributed to Gautama, Apastamba, Baudhayana, and Vasishtha respectively, have been translated into English.[41] The Gautama Dharmasutra is regarded by some to be the oldest; some others consider Apastamba the oldest. The Dharmashastras, composed later than the Dharmasutras, are in verse but show a general similarity with the Dharmasutras in content. They are less easily traceable to specific Vedic schools. The only preserved Dharmashastras are those of Manu, Yajnavalkya, Narada, and Parashara, with consensus in scholarship being that Manu is possibly the oldest.[42] Dharma, according to these texts, "includes all aspects of proper individual and social behaviour as demanded by one's role in society and in keeping with one's social identity according to age, gender, caste, marital status, and order of life."[43] Extraordinary in their imagination of everyday and ceremonial contexts and social categories, the sutras and shastras enumerate, among other things, the dharma appropriate to kings, householders, renouncers, and students, ritual procedures, dietary practices, holy pursuits, sins and their expiation, and women's roles. Aware of the ever present possibility of breaches, these texts also specify preventive and reparatory measures.

The antiquity, sequence, the actual location in the Vedic corpus, certainty of authorship, and textual completeness of Dharmasutra and Dharmashastra texts continue to be indeterminate and perplex modern scholarship. Yet commentaries on these texts from the seventh to the eighteenth century do not doubt their authoritativeness, associating them with the Vedas and with sages whose knowledge was considered transcendent and irrefutable. These texts on dharma, however, have proved challenging to interpret. They are terse and cryptic, with critical junctures marked by elision, and often different texts voice varying opinion on dharma. Over the centuries vast and erudite commentaries (ṭīka) and digests (nibandha) were written addressing problems such as consistency, ambiguity, variation, adaptability, and the general question of application. The writers of these deeply intertextual digests were often experienced ministers or royal councillors who drew on systems of grammar, exegesis, and logic to interpret the Dharmashastras (systems that also helped them to strengthen the theoretical link with the Vedas).[44]

The texts recognize that while dharma itself is a binding principle from which no one is exempt, rules are in fact knowable through particular idioms: the dharma of a region (deśadharma), the dharma of a group (jātidharma), or the dharma of the family (kuladharma). In an important observation increasingly shared by modern scholars of Dharmashastras, Patrick Olivelle notes most of the rules of behavior specified in these texts are custom derived, and "cannot be traced to the Vedic texts. There is, then, a dissonance between the theologically correct definition and epistemology of dharma and the reality of the rules of dharma encoded in the *Dharmasūtras*."[45] Thus, it is the more immediate worlds of achara, or exemplary conduct from the lived context, and not so much the distant and awe-inspiring Vedas that provide these texts with their normative detail.[46]

But it is critical to note here that the English translation of achara as "custom" obscures the moral clause included in the Dharmashastric use of the term. Not all customs were indiscriminately sponged up by the Dharmashastras for formulating the basis of dharma(s). For example, Apastamba says that the authorities (pramāṇa) for his Dharmasutras are twofold: 1. the agreement (samaya) of those who know the dharmas and 2. the Vedas. As P. V. Kane puts it, "just as the revealed books (Veda) and the smṛtis authoritatively lay down what dharma is, so also in our quest to find out what dharma is in the varying circumstances of life, the practices of those who may be called śiṣṭas[47] [the virtuous; eminent] furnish us with the necessary criterion or norm, i.e., śiṣṭācāra [conduct of the virtuous] is the touchstone for judging whether an act in consonance with what the *śāstras* require us to do."[48]

So, we may well ask, who are these shishthas (exemplars) from whom emanates so much moral authority? Exemplars are, according to Baudhayana, "those who are free from envy and pride, possess a jarful of grain, and are free from covetousness, hypocrisy, arrogance, greed, folly, and anger. As it is said, 'Cultured people are those who have studied the Veda together with its supplements (A 2.8.lo–11), in accordance with the Law [dharma], know how to draw inferences from them, and are able to adduce as proofs express Vedic texts (G 3.36 n).'"[49] Again, a further qualification is made: not all actions of a shishtha are exemplary—acts that have clearly visible motives or done to secure pleasure do not qualify as authoritative means of instruction.[50]

The sense contained in the key term *samayācāra* (practice or conduct that is conventionally agreed to be good) is also radiated in other terms such as *śīla* (good character) used by Gautama and Manu, *āgama* (practices/tradition) by Baudhāyana, *sistācāra* (virtuous conduct) by Vaśiṣṭha, and *vṛtta* (practice) by Apastamba.[51] This recognition of custom and convention that are ratified by learned individuals of good character is suggestive of the shastras' adaptability to, and reliance on, local environments and exigencies, but it is an adaptability that does not overturn the universal premise that dharma had to be followed in *all* cases. Several Dharmashastras additionally posit the notion of sāmānya dharma, "common code of conduct," which enjoins all Hindus to observe nonviolence, truthfulness, nonstealing, purity of mind and action, and restraint and control over the senses.[52]

The Dharmashastras: European Observations and Colonial Interventions

With the advent of British colonial rule, the Dharmashastras witnessed dramatic adaptation and deployment in a newly evolving judicial system.

The question whether, and to what extent, inscribed rules were followed in practice is a complicated one for which we do not have clear and definite answers and about which there has been continuing debate. According to Ludo Rocher, it is extremely unlikely that the Dharmashastras were ever *uniformly* understood as the law of the land by Hindus or accepted and applied by *all* Hindu groups in practical jurisprudence. He argues that when the Dharmashastras were in fact consulted it is likely that "in actual dispute settlement, each region or each group knew exactly the set of customs that applied to them, and they applied them consistently."[53] Richard Lariviere, on the other hand, sees the "aphorisms, guidelines, and advice" found in Dharmashastra texts as having had practical application in that the Dharmashastras functioned as authoritative resource in the administration of law.[54]

However, the ethnographic observations of two seventeenth-century Jesuit missionaries suggest something important in the context of legal practice: precolonial Hindu legal systems drew upon plural and multiple sources that included not only inscribed sources of dharma (the Dharmashastras, palm leaf records, and so on) but also orally circulating, memorized customs that adapted "knowledge" to "situation." In his protoethnographic essay about Madurai society in CE 1613, the Italian Jesuit missionary, Roberto de Nobili notes that the administration of justice across different caste bodies was based on a fluid collage of convention, actual practice, and textual prescription.[55] Jean Venant Bouchet, a French Jesuit missionary resident in Pondicherry was more vocal in his observations. In a letter of CE 1714 to a well-known jurist in Paris, Bouchet wrote:

> They have neither codes nor digests, nor do they have any books in which are written down the laws to which they have to conform to solve the disputes that arise in their families. . . . The equity of all their verdicts is entirely founded on a number of customs which they consider inviolable, and on certain usages which are handed down from father to son. They regard these usages as definite and infallible rules, to maintain peace in the family and to end the suits that arise, not only among private individuals, but also among royal princes. . . . I have asked them occasionally why they did not collect these customs in books which one might consult if needed. Their answer is that, if those customs were entered into books, only the learned would be able to read them, whereas, if they are handed down from generation to generation through the channel of tradition, everyone is fully informed.[56]

Bouchet's remarkable letter, which also presents translations of "maxims" and "quatrains" employed by locals during adjudication, reveals an oral system that referenced customs accepted by a caste, customs accepted in variant forms across caste groups, and customs accepted by all castes. Justice was sought and rendered in caste and village assemblies through experts and authority figures such as community elders, village headmen, chiefs and kings rather than through written compendia. Bouchet was informed that there were, at one time, copper plates with inscriptions about laws, but that they were largely lost when the temples that stored them were destroyed during conquests. These inscribed sources were known to learned brahmans in "Caungibouram" (Kanchipuram)[57] who were consulted when specialized legal information or historical data became necessary in deciding cases.

Indeed, examining legal practice between the fourteenth and the eighteenth centuries in Kerala, Donald Davis persuasively demonstrates that legal practice was founded on the concept of regionally based boundaries of propriety, deśamaryāda (also understood as ācāra, exemplary conduct, "community standard"). *Deśamaryāda* was itself a combination of 1. "dharmashastra literature, whether or not it was consciously appropriated as such," 2. legal practices possibly external to this literature but prevalent in the region having been established perhaps through "community interaction" and "political intervention," and 3. customs particular to those patronized in the "semi-autonomous political territory" called Trikkandiyur sanketam whose legal locus was a prominent Nambudiri brahman family.[58]

Yet, early British colonial administrators did not see or comprehend what may have been vibrant and viable, even if multiple, indigenous judicial systems that were already in place, and much less did they perceive the complex context-sensitivity of those systems. Lacking fluency in Sanskrit and other Indian languages (at least initially), lacking familiarity with the deeper cultural mechanics of Indian society, and confronted by startling diversity of practice, they attempted to fashion a legal system that would combine Dharmashastric norms and Chancery principles of justice, equity, and good conscience.[59] By the mid-seventeenth century the East India Company had established a secure trading foothold in Bengal. It operated courts initially for its own needs. Following the battle of Buxar in 1764, and the company's acquisition of the right to collect revenue and administer civil justice in Bengal, Bihar, and Orissa, an English-type court system was established to attend to both Company and Indian disputes.[60] The Regulating Act of 1773 passed by the British parliament (to salvage the corrupt East India Company from the disasters it had created and brooked) established a Supreme Court in each presidency, and appointed Warren Hastings as the first governor general of Bengal (1773–1784).[61]

Hastings is widely cited as pioneering the formulation of a shastra-based judicial system. In his 1772 *Plan for the Administration of Justice*, Hastings declared that in matters of "inheritance, marriage, caste and other religious usages or institutions, the laws of the Koran with respect to the Mohamedans and those of the Shaster with respect to the Gentoos shall invariably be adhered to."[62] This pronouncement, whose principal intention was to administer Indian laws to Indians and simultaneously convince the East India Company's directors that India had a pedigree civilization with "laws," ironically took for its model the ecclesiastical court system in England. Not only did this approach severely abridge the encyclopedic scope of the shastras, but it also undercut the fact that dharma governed all of life in Hindu society and not merely a handful of topics.[63] Toward jurisprudence, the British sponsored the publication of handy digests that saw application in various courts of law. The production of these digests was a vast and complicated project that involved translation across at least Sanskrit and Persian and collation of diverse shastric literatures by commissioned pandits, assisting scholars, and English orientalists.[64]

Although prominent scholars of Sanskrit literature in eighteenth century like William Jones (a judge of the Supreme Court, Calcutta) and Henry Colebrooke (an official in the East India Company's revenue department) persuaded the colonial administration that the Dharmashastra texts provided uniform law for Hindus,[65] there were also strong dissenting voices. For example, in 1877 John H. Nelson, a civil servant and judge in the Madras High Court, protested that Dharmashastric law, based on brahmanical customs, was being imposed on nonbrahmanical populations. He bleakly concluded that the High Court had taken on "the self-imposed duty of civilizing the 'lower castes' of Madras, that is to say, the great bulk of its population, by gradually destroying their local usages and customs."[66] John D. Mayne reported that pandits whose opinions did not corroborate shastric texts were liable to be dismissed as ignorant and corrupt. He observed that the consequence of the inability of British colonial judges to recognize where social practices parted company with the shastras "was a state of arrested progress in which no voices were heard unless they came from the tomb. It was as if a German were to administer English law from the resources of a library furnished with Fleta, Glanville, and Bracton, and terminating with Lord Coke."[67] Tracing the peculiar colonial career of the Manu *Dharmaśāstra*,

Nicholas Dirks shows how such brahmanical texts were endowed with a pan-Hindu status and an "anthropological significance" that persisted until more contemporary times.[68]

"Contradictions" in shastric texts were ostensibly resolved by consulting "custom" to arrive at an authoritative common Hindu law, a process that disastrously misunderstood the contextually filtered character of shastra and edited out other normative discourses that guided lived experience. The project of codification that resulted in the passage of numerous acts and codes after 1833 would seem to seductively indicate that the "new" Anglo-Indian law was grounded in local custom if one only considered how it painstakingly utilized survey after survey on the customs of regions, castes, and provinces.[69] The practice of relying on pandits as law officers in Supreme Courts to translate passages from the shastras and assist with case settlement was discontinued in 1864.[70] Customs were then admitted into the evolving canon of "Hindu Law" only when they had "clear proof of usage," were "ancient, certain and reasonable,"[71] and did not violate English understandings of equity, good conscience, and progress. Dinshah F. Mulla and many Indian lawyers protested in vain, knowing the difficulties of establishing proof of usage, and, as Mulla put it, "Some ancient texts and injunctions favoured by the commentators which had not been accepted as part of current law and virtually abandoned in practice were in some cases received as binding law and given inflexible interpretation."[72]

Summing up the transformations effected on the relationship of shastra and Hindu society during colonial rule, Rajeev Dhavan observes that the custodianship over shastra gradually shifted from diffused structures of local authority to the state, and the attention of commentators shifted from interpreting the shastras themselves to how *Anglo-Indian courts* would interpret the shastras (making shastra more litigation centered, and sidestepping traditional methods of regulating the interpretation of shastras through Mimamsa hermeneutics and sadācāra, for example).[73] What is clear for the substantive scholarship on the fate of the Dharmashastras during colonial rule is that 1. a fluid and plural normative "system" underwent parochial textualization, 2. despite ambiguity about their usage in social life, the Dharmashastras became iconic of Hindu practiced law, and 3. contemporary contexts of social life suggest that, while colonial intervention was significantly disruptive to formal jurisprudence, it failed to unsettle the more day-to-day beliefs and practices that engage the notion of shastra in Hindu social and ritual life.

The Sringeri Matha and the Dharmashastras

Historically, the Sringeri matha has been an influential interpreter of the Dharmashastras, especially before the abolition of the jagirdari (land-grant state) in 1958, when it used to function as an independent judiciary with its own court (cāvaḍi).[74] Numerous cases documented in the kaditas (ledgers) of the matha show that individuals from a wide variety of castes consulted the matha about matters such as marriage alliances, adoption, ostracization, property settlement, and daily Hindu ritual. Many times village-level forums comprising elders worked closely with the matha in resolving disputes.[75]

Giridhara Shastry explained that until 1997, the matha used to have a shastra-interpreting department called *Achara Vichara*.

> Learned scholars, like Shesha Shastry, who was regarded an expert in the Dharmashastras, were appointed to head this department. The position was called *Ācāra Vicāra dharmadhikāra sthāna* (the position of the dharmadhikari to adjudicate in matters of conduct). But it was not enough for the dharmadhikari (official interpreter of the shastras) to be learned in the shastras and be competent in Mimamsa techniques of interpretation. The scholar was required to bring a *humane understanding* to the interpretation of the Dharmashastras, of being able to interpret them in *the context of the times.* Basically, the interpreter had to ask: What difficulties does that person (whose case is being considered) face? What shastric decisions can that person abide by? For instance, while elaborating on certain rules of conduct, or while recommending certain reparations, the interpreter would have to consider the character and capabilities of the person. . . . The dharmadhikari also often cleared doubts (about customs or conduct) that people brought to him. There were times when matters could not be resolved by the dharmadhikari—for example, when two parties were in dispute, and one party felt that the dharmadhikari's resolution was unsatisfactory, they would take it to the guru. Then debates would follow . . . different pandits and experts would be called in—it was virtually a court. Then a decision would be reached. In Sringeri, most of the time, however, these matters would be sorted out by the dharmadhikari.[76]

Such contextual interpretation by the dharmadhikari would seem to be at odds with the position taken by the spiritual heads of the matha who maintained that their duty was *not* to adjust the shastras to changing times but to inform people about what the shastras say. Sri Abhinava Vidyatirtha Swami, the spiritual head of the matha from 1954 to 1989, explains carefully that the shastras *themselves* offer alternatives when their injunctions cannot be observed and make provisions for extenuating circumstances. However, shastras also set limits on how flexible they can be.[77] The dharmadhikari's interpretations are set within these bounds and additionally take into account regional, caste, and family based tradition.

The dharmadhikari's duties went beyond the resolution of doubts and disputes; when the guru was unable at times to undertake journeys (yātras) to the North and South Kanara regions, the dharmadhikari would go on his behalf and look after the welfare of the matha's disciples. The matha saw the maintaining of this samparka (connection) as part of its dharma. The dharmadhikari used to appoint representatives in different communities, especially in the South Kanara region, who would settle disputes within their own communities. And thus, "most disputes used to be settled by a group of elders after due hearing of the parties concerned. This was a regular feature mainly because the court was far away and people wanted quick and fair settlements."[78] The department of Achara Vichara also had dharmapracārakas (propagators of dharma) whose duty was to ensure that proper conduct was observed in the samsthana and to prevent "irreligious activities" in the families of the disciples of the matha.[79]

Numerous documented cases show that individuals and groups (of castes as wide-ranging as Āreru, Bēḍara, brahman, Gauḍa Sāraswat, and Vālmīki) wrote to the matha, among other things, about the appropriateness of particular marital alliances, adoption, problems of ostracization and excommunication, property settlement, professional choices, and daily observances and practical routines. Disputes of a social or economic nature were first taken to the panchayat, the local body of village elders and elites, while caste matters were handled by a jāti or caste panchayat.[80] K. Gnanambal finds in her study of various mathas in south India that generally mathas specified adjudicatory procedures for panchayats (village councils), and the panchayats deferred to the decisions of the matha. Case records reveal complex and varied negotiations between individuals, panchayat authorities, and matha authorities. For instance, in a 1940–1941 case, a woman accused of conceiving after her husband's death and of killing the infant child had been excommunicated by the panchayat. She appealed to the matha for reversal of this decision, arguing that she had in fact been molested with the molester absconding, and that the sessions court had declared her innocent. She requested the matha to prescribe appropriate "expiation." At the end of a most interesting exchange of letters between the matha, the panchayat, other elders, and the woman herself, the dharmadhikari, concurring with the woman's claim, ruled, "It is the direction of the Shastras to excommunicate a person only when no other mode is prescribed for that particular transgression and not in cases where expiation for sins has been prescribed." Although I saw no confession of guilt in the woman's own letter—rather an exasperated willingness to pay a fine and get on with life—the dharmadhikari prescribed prayaschitta (expiatory ceremonies) for her "defilement," and the matter was settled. Very interestingly, two decades later, Gnanambal visited the woman and her family and learned that she had been reincorporated into her community and had been able to arrange the marriage of her daughters.[81]

Today shastric counsel is given by a matha-appointed pandit who is selected for his erudition in the Dharmashastras, his sensitivity, and his worldly wisdom. Vinayaka Udupa, the current appointee who lives in Mangar (just outside the town of Sringeri), said that letters seeking advice continue to pour in from Hindus of all groups. After he studies each case, he occasionally consults other pandits, and formulates his advice. The decision is forwarded to the guru before it is conveyed to the inquirer. The problems are categorized (grammar, logic, astrology, Vedanta, and so on) and questions are forwarded to appropriate experts. Intrigued, I asked Giridhara Shastry, given the many Dharmashastras and the numerous communities whose customs varied, how shastric recommendations were actually arrived at. The matha consults the Dharmashastra appropriate to communities: for instance, *Āśvalāyana gṛhya sūtra* for Rigvedis, *Āpastamba* for Yajurvedis, or *Hiraṇyakēṣi* for Chitpavan brahmans.[82] For questions relevant to all Hindus—for example, on which day ought one to observe a fast when *ekādaśī*[83] fell on two consecutive days—the matha consults digests (for example, Kashinatha's *Dharmasindhu* (1790–1791), Kamalakara's *Nirṇayasindhu* (1612), or Vaidyanatha's *Dīkṣitīyam* (seventeenth century), which are based on smriti texts. Even here the interpretation is contextual. The matha gives considerable weight to the customs and the contextual particularities of family and region. For instance, a letter in its records advises an inquirer that a particular marriage alliance be decided based on *deśācāra* (custom of the region).[84]

The adjudicating reach of the matha, however, became circumscribed with the introduction of colonial institutions and processes such as Anglo-Indian court systems and litigation, the involvement of the princely state of Mysore in the matha's administrative structure (for instance, deputing an officer-in-charge who supervised the administrative operations of the matha),[85] and the loss of the status of a land-grant state by the matha in 1958. While the colonial administration itself does not seem to have directly interfered in the matha's role as Dharmashastra-interpreting entity, or question its moral stature in the region, largely content with keeping a watchful eye on its revenues, Giridhara Shastry pointed out that nevertheless, "colonial policy is one of the major causes for the decline in the influence of the matha in 'secular' matters."[86] That is, today, problems relating to land, property, divorce and so on are necessarily taken to court systems, while, in the past, these would have fallen within the matha's jurisdiction.[87] The introduction of new systems of education, the spread of English literacy, and the establishment of bodies such as cooperative societies and municipal councils eroded the judicial centrality of the matha in *all* matters. It is ironic, added Giridhara Shastry, that the matha itself took the lead in establishing these schools, hospital, banks, and the cooperative society.

Oral accounts in Sringeri of the matha's normative authority seriously unsettle the assumption that the matha's normative voice is monologic and unified, an assumption that one could make if one heard only the adjudicating voice of case records. Dodda Murthy recounted the following episode (probably from the 1920s or 1930s when the Agent was the administrator of the matha) when I asked how shastric matters were decided *within* the matha:

DM: The ritual of upakarma (annual rite of changing the sacred thread by brahman males)—
have you seen it take place here?

L: No, I went home . . .

DM: It used to be conducted regularly in the matha.
The ritual is different for Yajurvedis and Rigvedis.

L: Yes.

DM: We too used to attend the ceremony.
There used to be a priest who would conduct the ritual.
We used go in the morning—a three-hour event—with our janivara (sacred thread).
It used to be mandatory to attend, and the matha was strict about the observance of this ritual—

L: Oh!

DM: the prayaschitta was elaborate (if we did not attend),
so we used to *compulsorily* go.

It's all gone now.

There was this man, a Rigvedi who used to live here.

L: Hanh! (*interested, sensing a story is beginning*).

DM: There had been some problem with him; he had committed some apacara (improper conduct) of some sort—

L: Oh!

DM: taken a second wife or something of that sort, and he had been ostracized.

They said they would not allow him to join the others (for the upakarma event).

He was worried that he would end up forgoing this mandatory rite and lose his status.

He went to the priest and told him that he would attend the upakarma ceremony.

But the priest was adamant about not admitting him—he said,

"Go do it elsewhere."

So this man approached the administrator and pleaded his case.

The administrator said,

"OK, go ahead and join the group. Tell them I had said so."

L: Hah!

DM: So this man showed up on the day with his mogaṭa (traditional clothes), his plate and materials for the ritual,

and sat in line with the others.

The priest saw him. He called him.

He said,

"Sir, I see you are joining the others. I will not start the ceremony as long as you sit here."

The man replied,

"No, I have asked the administrator. I have his permission."

But the priest was adamant:

"Perhaps. The administrator may well have agreed.

But—no matter whose permission you have—the authority here is mine.

The matha may be theirs.

However, *this* space you see here, this *sthāṇḍila* (ritual space) is under my authority until the karma (ritual) is completed.

I will not permit you.

The place can become the matha's once again after the ritual is done.

You are free to tell the administrator this if you like."

The man quickly went to the administrator and reported this conversation.

L: Hanh!

DM: The administrator thought for a while and said,

"Just go home and put on a new janivara yourself."

The administrator or agent in this anecdote was a long-term powerful appointee from outside Sringeri, much respected for his shastric erudition and pragmatic dynamism, but also controversial for his dominating administrative savvy. Oral folklore about this stentorian-voiced figure is well-known in Sringeri, and virtually any conversation about Sringeri's affairs in the twentieth century includes an anecdote or two about his personality and times. Although the administrator had attempted to use his discretionary powers to permit the ostracized man to participate in the upakarma ceremony, it is clear both he and the priest knew that there were spatial and temporal limits on the former's authority. The priest fully exercised his priestly jurisdiction to disallow leeway. That the administrator quietly yielded to the priest was probably his acknowledgement of the impossibility of dislodging social opposition when it is "enclosed" in ritual space and in ritual time—over which a priest (and not an administrator) has final say. Given the ambivalent feelings locals bore toward this administrator, one might also wonder if the priest's inflexibility was some measure and expression of his resistance toward the administrator's authority, resistance that was not possible to express in other contexts. Shastra—which makes it possible for the priest to have complete authority over the ritual space—becomes a strategic tool for dissent.

4 *"The Shastras Say . . . "*

Idioms of Legitimacy and the "Imagined Text"

Conversational narratives in Sringeri reveal that, although historically traced to millennia-old Sanskrit texts and manipulated to a great degree by colonial administrations, shastra is in everyday life a nebulous but dynamic and open-ended cultural background that influences conceptualizations of conduct and is in turn influenced by them. Sringeri stories and conversations argue that a phenomenology of shastra requires that we extend the widened understanding of text and textuality to recognize "shastric texts" also in the world of material and oral practices that are animated by human agency and function as vibrant forms of moral guidance for Hindus. In understanding the visage and the vocabulary of normative authority, it is important therefore to ask, along the lines of Ludwig Wittgenstein: What are the patterns of use that constitute the "grammar of our concepts" that relate to shastra? What "family resemblances"[1] are uncovered through an ethnographic study of the notion of shastra? This chapter demonstrates that a lived grammar of the normative includes a wide sociosemantic field of discourse and praxis, one that is marked by vivacious interplay between shastra and other normative concepts like sampradaya (tradition), niyama (rule), achara (practice), and paddhati (custom), concepts that make competing claims to authority. Contexts of usage and practice reveal that subtle, if not consistent, differences are made among these terms.

I argue that underlying ethical practice is a dynamically constituted "text" that draws on and weaves together various sources of the normative—a sacred book, an exemplar, a tradition, a principle, and so on. Such a text is essentially an *imagined text.* It is a fluid "text" that engages precept and practice and, in a sense, always intermediary. In this imagined text the normative manifests as emergent, situated in the local and the larger-than-local, the historical, and the interpersonal.[2]

Sringeri Conversations and Expressions of the Normative

It was May of 1995, and I was visiting Halanduru (yet another of Sringeri's characteristic single-home villages), about five miles northeast of Sringeri town. Friends in Sringeri considered Halanduru Nagabhusana Bhattru's 250-year old house one of the must-see homes of the region. I had visited Halanduru many times after Dodda Murthy had introduced me to eighty-five-year-old Nagabhusana Bhattru, his close friend from their school days together. As on earlier visits, the bus from Sringeri dropped me off in a clearing in the forest after a twenty-minute ride. As I plodded along on the lonely mud path to Halanduru through the forest for nearly forty-five minutes, cursing my baggage—camera, recorder, cassettes, clothes, notebook—the usual thought that something might happen to me (falling prey to hungry tigers or drunken men or both) crossed my overimaginative mind, and, quickening my step, I struggled to focus instead on the verdant comfort of the Malnad forest around me. On my first visit, Nagalakshmi,[3] Nagabhusana Bhattru's daughter-in-law, and her seventeen year-old daughter, Bhargavi, had shown me around the house. Nagalakshmi, in her late thirties when I got to know her, had married Laxminarasimha Bhattru (L. N. Bhattru) when she was sixteen, from within the extended family. As we chatted about our families (I was in my mid-twenties, married, and without children then), she pointed out that although she felt she had married too early and would rather Bhargavi wait for a while, the small age gap made them "relate like friends."

I had come to know the house and the household through mother and daughter: they had shown me, among other things, the deep, closed dry shelves that ran along the walls just below the ceiling for storing provisions like cardamom, happaḷa, pickles, and tamarind during the monsoons, and the

FIGURE 4.1. Halanduru Nagabhusana Bhattru's house. *Photo by Leela Prasad*

huge wooden tub for oil baths. The family's areca and paddy fields spread out in front of the house. A small Ishwara temple where puja was done every day graced the front yard. Behind the house, down a flight of about thirty steps, flowed the gurgling Tunga, in which stood huge boulders. As a place legend narrates it, the mighty Bhima used one of the concave boulders as a stove for his famed cooking during the Pandavas' exile. Another boulder looked like a shivalinga, yet another a human face, and each had its story.

L. N. Bhattru was busy with work in their fields, and their nineteen-year-old son, Ananda, was away playing a cricket match. I joined Nagalakshmi in the kitchen where she was preparing lunch. As we rolled out chapattis together, our conversation gradually turned to everyday, festive, and seasonal Malnad cuisine. Nagalakshmi laughed when I turned on my small tape recorder, amused that I wanted to record such everyday conversation. I too laughed self-consciously, knowing that my recording habits were becoming known as another of my oddities. "Do they make this where you're from?" she asked often between descriptions of food dishes. Initially flustered that I could hardly match her repertoire of intricate region-distinctive foods or her fluency in narration, I fell back on a childhood association with Pune and the Marathi-speaking world, which saved me as I described something like the popular *sābudāṇyaci khicadi*, a spiced cooked sago dish, unknown in the Malnad. "We make *meṇassāru* (pepper-soup) when it gets cold around here in the rainy season," she explained. "The pepper doesn't grind well in the electric grinder, but the stone grinder keeps it *rough* and gives the right *taste*."

"Isn't this what they made at the lunch at the parayana (votive recitation) the other day?" I was looking at the creamy white kāyi-rasa (a coconut milk preparation) she had just finished making.

"Had they? This kāyi-rasa—with it, one also needs to make sāru (soup). It's a must for *functions,* and cooks make sure to make it. If it is the mango season, they make raw mango gojju (sweet-sour concentrate). There's always sāru, then tovve (lentils), then two types of paliya (vegetable curries)—this is standard. Then some folks make kāyi-rasa, some make the gojju, either from okra, or from mango (depending on the season). I think what they made that day (of the parayana we had both attended) was the okra one. It was sweetish—but it isn't the mango season yet. Then majjige huḷi (buttermilk soup). At least four to five *items* must be made. . . . Oh! To learn our aḍige paddhati (ways of cooking), a whole year is what you need. Stay here for one year. This coming in the morning, leaving in the evening, won't do!"

Nagalakshmi was right, and I felt embarrassed, for although I stayed overnight or for a few days every time I visited Halanduru, I always returned to my small rented apartment in the town of Sringeri. I had earlier that morning asked her for Malnad recipes so that I could show off Malnad meals for visiting family. She had suggested a few items, but had also added gently, "But you can't merely listen and then go and cook that dish! You learn paddhati only when you observe somebody make that dish."

So I asked her how she had learned to cook.

"By observing! One learns by observing others. There's no such thing as formal teaching. Sometimes a mother may instruct her daughter, now do this, or do that. Or we also watch while helping somebody make this or that. Or when there's some *function,* one gets to observe adige bhattru (cooks)—and watch how they cook."

"I wonder where *they* learn?" I was thinking of the adige bhattru, the male brahman cooks who typically cater during festive or ritual occasions in homes and in temples. But my question went astray as Nagalakshmi continued, "Some have the *knack.* Not everybody is able to bring out the taste and ruchi (flavor). And there are some, who, no matter how much they observe, are stuck in one *type* of cooking, in their own thing. They just don't have it."

I described how my mother had learned Maharashtrian recipes during her long stay in Pune and how Andhra cuisine included much regional variety. Perhaps I had voiced a cookbook-style approach, the sort that picked up recipes from here and there and promised a dazzling combination of regional varieties that speak of a "national cuisine," to use Arjun Appadurai's phrase.[4] "Around here, we don't travel much outside, so we don't learn other kinds of cooking, but *our* region's paddhati, we get to know well. But even within our extended family there are differences. So we ask one another, 'How do you make this? How do you make that?'"

As we talked, she scraped water out of the stone grinder, made different spice-pastes, and cut vegetables. I watched the preparation processes. Food talk, ubiquitous in Indian life, was not new to me, but Malnad foodways (Malnāḍina aḍige paddhati) were new to me. Other local friendships taught me also that there could be pangada (subcaste) variations in foods and in styles of cooking, differences that were subtly contained in the popular category of Malnad foodways, but sometimes accentuated in demarcations of "us" and "them," such as in seating arrangements during ceremonial occasions. There were instances when Karnataka brahmans and Shivalli brahmans, who otherwise shared congenial relationships, would not be invited to each other's "functions"; the former imagining itself a higher pangada.[5]

Food and its social life is a long-favored subject of Indian thinking. From the *Rigveda* onward, prescriptive, taxonomic, and narrative texts abound with theorization about the moral qualities, sacred potential, and the medicinal properties of foods.[6] One hears of the legendary culinary skills of Nala and Bhima of the *Mahabharata,* and one also encounters scores of folktales and stories from the Puranas that play with food motifs. The term *pākaśāstra* (or *sūpaśāstra*) tells us that there may have been treatises on cooking, but an actual text that informs daily practice remains elusive.[7] Even though written texts may well be lost, we can still ask what the absence of an exclusive codified written textual tradition about cooking tells us. One can speculate that food, acknowledged as important, was nevertheless considered secondary to the recognized this-worldly goals of life (dharma, artha, kama), but this is improbable considering the pivotal role of food in the Hindu experience of the sacred. It is more likely that, because the subject of food is so important, it was incorporated into a wide array of shastric texts that dealt with other domains of life (such as the Dharmashastras or Ayurvedic compendia). The regionality of food traditions may also have contributed to the lack of pan-regional shastric discourse on foodways.

My conversation with Nagalakshmi showed that, despite all the existing cookbooks of past and present, to learn a paddhati or mode of cooking, one has to rely on a wide range of seeing-and-doing orientations concerning food that are integrated into daily living.[8] I had never imagined when I recorded this conversation that it would say something to me years later about the imperceptible and deeply dialogic ways in which shastric discourse manifests itself not only in everyday Sringeri life but also in Hindu life in general. Put in terms of a question, how does one learn what one learns about "rules" and "ways" of being Hindu in all its varieties? Distinctly injunctive in parts, normative in import, and grounded in a flexibly understood local (regional, seasonal, familial, and so on) that was connected to the translocal (auspiciousness, well-being), the knowledge that Nagalakshmi shared with me could well be called *shastric,* but we did not use that term. Instead, the word that Nagalakshmi and I used throughout our conversation was *paddhati,* way or custom. How do these terms engage with each other?

In fact, three other terms, *sampradaya, achara,* and *niyama,* also entered such conversations, and these five terms (*shastra, sampradaya, paddhati, achara,* and *niyama*) frequently strolled into each other's realms. The seemingly synonymous use of these terms in conversation makes it tempting to conclude that *shastra* is simply the same as these other terms. And indeed, the overlap in the denotations is not merely a sleight of translation across languages but is often confirmed by usage. The sibling nature of these words is apparent if we look up Kittel's Kannada-English dictionary:

1. shastra = (also in Sanskrit) "order," "command," "precept," "rule or compendium of rules," "religious or scientific treatise," "law-book."
2. paddhati = "way," "path," "manner," "usage," and "custom." Monier-Williams's Sanskrit-English dictionary glosses paddhati as "way," "path," and additionally as "guidebooks or manuals for particular rites and ceremonies."
3. sampradaya = "giving, bestowing," "tradition, established doctrine transmitted from one teacher to another," "traditional belief," "custom, usage." (Monier-Williams lists the same meaning for this term drawing from the fourteenth-century encyclopedic manual on assorted subjects, *Sāraṅgadhara Paddhati*, addressed to royalty.)
4. achara = "conduct," "manner of action," "good behavior," "custom, usage, practice."

5. niyama = "restraining, restriction," "fixed rule," "agreement, contract," "any self-imposed restraint or religious observance voluntarily practiced, as fasting, watching [?], pilgrimage, praying, etc."

Nagalakshmi and I had talked about what foods were or were not auspicious for which ritual occasions, methods of cooking that were appropriate for specific foods, regional variations, ingredients that worked as "substitutes," reparations, combinations for nutritious foods, season-oriented menus, and medicinal foods, such as those for pregnant women. It was clear why it would take a full year, indeed even many, to acquire such knowledge, founded as it was on observation, experience, informal modes of transmission, and a capacity to grasp and innovate, a *knack,* to use Nagalakshmi's term. As I consider how I processed the general idiom of this conversation (and other similar ones), returning often to the question of what it means to define oneself as "Hindu" in so many variant ways, I find insightful A. K. Ramanujan's ruminations about the context-sensitivity of Hindu life. He writes,

> Such a pervasive emphasis on context is, I think, related to the Hindu concern with *jāti*—the logic of classes, of genra and species, of which human *jātis* [classes] are only an instance. Various taxonomies of season, landscape, times, guṇas or qualities (and their material bases), tastes, characters, emotions, essences (*rasa*), etc., are basic to the thought-work of Hindu medicine and poetry, cooking and religion, erotics and magic. Each *jāti* or class defines a context, a structure of relevance, a rule of permissible combination, a frame of reference, a meta-communication of what is and can be done.[9]

Thinking about the conversation with Nagalakshmi as I sat with Chayamma on the wide swing on the veranda of their house, I brought up the question of shastra. In her typical way, Chayamma at first responded to my shastra question saying, "I don't know much about stuff like that; why don't you ask her [referring to Lakshmidevamma, Putta Murthy's wife]?" They were co-sisters and inseparable companions of four decades. But I had learned to persist with Chayamma. "So we have all these Dharmashastras. . . . But I've been thinking about what we end up doing with shastra in our everyday lives. You know, what does shastra really mean?" Remembering that Vinayaka Udupa, dharmadhikari of the matha and a scholar of the Puranas, had remarked to me that "shastra principally means 'Veda,'" I trailed off as she began, "What we've come doing from the past. . . . Now, your mother does something and you later remember that she used to do things this way, and you do it the same way, thinking this itself is my shastra, my sampradaya. If somebody tells you, 'This is not the way to do it,' you say, 'This is how my mother used to do it. This is what *she* said was the shastra, the sampradaya.' Won't you say this? Although you live in America, I'm sure you do things the way your mother does in Hyderabad, don't you?" It was easy to agree; nostalgia, two young daughters, e-mail, and the telephone had even strengthened the connections and conformities I tried to make between my mother's ways and mine.

The term *sampradaya* enjoys a high place in Hindu life, from schools of philosophy to music and the fine arts where it refers to a specific "teaching tradition" (a philosophical orientation or a mode of practice) orally passed down from teacher to student.[10] Upon reading this section, Giridhara Shastry brought my attention to Shankara's words in *Bhagavadgīta Bhāśya* 13–2:

> *Asampradāvit sarvaśāstravidapi mūrkhavadeva upēkṣaniyah*
>
> "One who is ignorant of tradition has to be ignored like a fool, even though versatile in all shastras."

Giridhara Shastry added his explanation, "Tradition is the education obtained from any experienced teacher. Interpreting the text based only on one's intelligence is asampradaya—non-tradition. Any anubhava shastra—shastra related to experience—gives special prominence to tradition."[11] According to Shankara, the "correct tradition" has as much authority as the written shastra because it too takes root in the Vedas—specifically Vedanta—which can be interpreted and transmitted by a guru.[12] The teacher becomes the embodiment of knowledge that is considered sacrosanct, and thus sampradaya, "tradition," bears the authority to clarify and provide direction in the application of knowledge.

As we shall soon see, this understanding of sampradaya implies that the individual and the community relate to each other in temporal ways and weigh the past against the contingencies of the contemporary. In this context, it is useful to recall T. S. Eliot, although we might substitute the gender, location, and lineage he calls up with our own:

> Tradition is a matter of much wider significance. It cannot be inherited, and if you want it you must obtain it by great labour. It involves, in the

> first place, the historical sense, which we may call nearly indispensable to anyone who would continue to be a poet beyond his twenty-fifth year; and the historical sense involves a perception, not only of the pastness of the past, but of its presence; the historical sense compels a man to write not merely with his own generation in his bones, but with a feeling that the whole of the literature of Europe from Homer and within it the whole of the literature of his own country has a simultaneous existence and composes a simultaneous order. This historical sense, which is a sense of the timeless as well as of the temporal and of the timeless and of the temporal together, is what makes a writer traditional. And it is at the same time what makes a writer most acutely conscious of his place in time, of his contemporaneity.[13]

In the realm of performative arts, as far back as the thirteenth century, Sarangadeva asserted that sampradaya was as authoritative as shastra.[14] The *Nāṭyaśāstra* itself, often, after laying out elaborate rules and principles of dramaturgy, adds, "these can be changed according to the needs of time and place."[15] The fifteen-century commentator Kallinatha clarifies that sampradaya authorizes the teacher to deviate from the stipulated gesture in the shastra, as long as the improvisation can be justified as coming from *some other part* of that shastra.[16] In the contemporary male martial arts practice of Kerala called *Kalarippayaṭṭu*, Phillip Zarrilli finds that a student's knowledge can be considered complete only when he has fully engaged with the art: has received guidance from a living guru, has mastered lineage-maintained manuals of practice, and has come to embody the art itself. It seems that shastra is understood here not as a singular manual with an end point but as a physical and spiritual *continuum*. The process of transmission from teacher to student secures for this continuum a perpetual reverence in the community.[17]

But the larger question remains, why indeed is it important to recognize the connection between generations—tradition—to nourish it, and to do enough to see it takes seed in the next generation? The more I dwell on this question, beyond the detail of whether one uses the *parijāta* flower for a puja or whether one wears the auspicious green sari for an event, the more I realize that nourishing the connection in whatever way one can clarifies the deeper question "Who am I?" And the "who I am" becomes meaningful in relation to the presences before, around, and after. Actions or words of elders (or of members of a community), acts of remembering, and enactments constitute sampradaya, and so strong is the generationally transmitted sampradaya (the giving, the given, a tradition) that it is possible to defend what one does with the statement "this itself is my shastra, my sampradaya."

The deeper relationships of self, other, and community that underlie shastra also make shastra the site of conflict and anxiety. For example, friction in marriage alliances across boundaries of caste, race, gender, or religion frequently centers on constructs of shastra—or, more broadly, on a normative stage that is also crowded with material and social inequities. The moral leverage of shastra also hovers over the day-to-day jostling for personal spaces and expression. For many women especially, self-expression and familial identifications are recurrently challenged at the crossroads of the in-law home and the mother's home. How do normative persuasions make, mar, or ambiguate familial ties and affect a woman's subjectivity and her physical being? What is her agency in norm-centric practice and resistance? Pervasively across Indian situations, differences in paddhati are often used to convey insider-outsiderness and to engage in domestic power play.[18] Giridhara Shastry's eighty-four-year-old mother, whom we all called Ajji (Kannada for "Grandmother") observed,

> Shastra and paddhati are basically the same (*ella onde*). But we make up differences, and arrogantly use those over daughters-in-law and over children. Isn't this true? And if there are many daughters-in-law in the family, then there are more opportunities for domineering ("jōr māḍakke avakāśa"): "This one has not done *madi* right,[19] that one touched clothes reserved for madi, and so on." Differences are invented only to enforce rules.

As my friendships in Sringeri deepened, women shared with me quotidian experiences of tensions with in-laws in which shastra or paddhati or one of their cultural cognates formed a fault line. Yet these episodes cannot be brought to the public pages of this book if I am to honor the requests and unstated understandings that I not reproduce those narratives in any shape or form. Kirin Narayan, reflecting similarly on the struggle to represent voiced, unvoiced, and unvoiceable self-articulations, finds that in the Himalayan foothills of the Kangra region where she recorded women's life stories, among upper-caste women, family honor was critical to the cultural validation of silence regarding domestic conflict. For two women from a "smaller caste," however, personal honor impelled the *tellings* of their life stories as well as the women's mandate that these stories not be made public in Kangra but recounted instead to a wider global audience.[20] Family honor or respectability perhaps partially explains why my Sringeri friends too, who came from various caste backgrounds, asked that I not document their experiences of in-law discrimination. But, without minimizing the heinousness of domestic abuse anywhere, more than family or personal honor, the women who shared their stories were reluctant to characterize their lives as proceeding around ill-treatment or to characterize the instances they narrated as symptoms of patterns of abuse. By committing such stories to writing, they feared, relational contexts would be frozen or even lost, personal activism obscured, and a misleading static quality imposed on relationships and family structures that in reality are continually evolving. In many of the in-law stories that women shared with me, the notion of shastra was strategically used to allege incompetence, "excessive" attachment to the maternal family's sampradayas, or to fabricate one family's superiority over another. Since pseudonyms and disguised contexts do not mitigate my obligations toward my Sringeri friends or toward my ethnographic ethics, I present examples from other settings in India that mirror the experiences narrated by my Sringeri friends—a deflection made possible by the pervasive politics of shastra in domestic life across Hindu society that ensures a ready inventory of illustrations.[21]

Thus, my friend in Sringeri will empathize with my friend elsewhere who recounted to me in tears her experience of her first Varalakshmi puja at her in-laws. In the absence of her mother-in-law, she had sincerely and carefully conducted the puja after consulting the family elders on its procedure. To her shock, however, she discovered that her unmarried sister-in-law was performing the puja all over again, offering the cold justification that my friend's puja had been out of step with the family's sampradaya. Some of my Sringeri friends living in joint family situations will also identify with the friend who said that every time she expressed a desire to visit her mother's house her father-in-law would cite some family paddhati that prohibited a visit at that time. It is common—and infamous—knowledge that inevitable differences in sampradayas in wedding ceremonies create minefields between the two families, usually set by the extended networks of relatives.

Yet, looking closely, the day-to-day lives of women also speak eloquently to the ways in which women creatively plait paddhatis that they draw from maternal and in-law homes as well from their local settings. I asked Vijaya Krishnamurthy, the friend with whose words I began this chapter, how she figured out "what the shastras said" after she got married and came to live in Sringeri from the bayalū sīmē (plains) region. "My mother's paddhati(s)!" she matter-of-factly said, adding, "My daughters, like you, think, 'Oh Amma used to do things this way.'" "But did the sampradaya of your husband's family change this?" I wondered. "No, it is mostly my mother's; shastra is usually what our parents pass on to us, isn't it? When I saw that things were done a little differently around here, I asked people, and started following Sringeri's paddhatis." She cited the Tulsi puje (worship of the basil plant) popular among Hindus and especially in the Sringeri-Malnad region but not quite practiced in her family. Vijaya's "asking around" about local ways of life conveys many things: an attempt to understand cultural difference, a willingness to incorporate into one's habitual practices something that is external, and the desire to belong—all greatly enabled by knowing that worshipping the sacred plant could only promote well-being.

For Ajji, too, worship of the Tulsi had become a necessary part of her daily life. When I asked her who had taught her this paddhati or that, Ajji's surprised answer was, "What is there to teach? It's all there in the family." Hers had been a childhood especially vivified by a large joint family, but her response nonetheless reminds us of the osmotic ways in which one, growing up in a Hindu family, learns traditions, practices, and ways of being that are saturated with the sense of "this is auspicious, this is correct, this is ethical." I am also reminded of A. K. Ramanujan's apt observation that in India one never hears the *Ramayana* for "the first time"; one simply encounters it continually and episodically,[22] and so one's empathies, possibly changing, with the moral characterizations in the story are spread over and stretched across a lifetime, in many domains. The subliminal imbibing of shastric knowledge similarly is continuous: "All my daughters do this everyday—they should have a bath, wear clean washed clothes, do the Tulsi puje right away and then do other things; this is what I taught them. To be physically and spiritually clean. I did not tell them all 'this is shastra'; I said this was 'niyama' (voluntary restraint)." While some of the practices Ajji taught her daughters are in fact Dharmashastra-endorsed (i.e., the exhortation to be physically and spiritually clean), her choice to frame these practices as voluntary observances confers upon them a moral immediacy that is perhaps even more persuasive than when it is mandated by a distant shastra.

As Ajji and I talked about various challenges that one faced in the modern world with the choices one makes or has to make, she was critical of an application of shastra that was immune to humane considerations. Using achara and shastra synonymously, she said, "When girls have their monthly periods, to isolate them in other rooms is basically torturing them.[23] Is that achara (shastric practice)? We don't do that in our family. That doesn't mean that they can go everywhere in the house; they cannot enter the kitchen or the puja room. What can you do when you live in cities or even in America like you do? Can you cloister yourself in a room? Do the best you can." She continued, "Shall I tell you something else that I have come to understand? Madi should not be made impossible for others; follow stipulations without hassling others. Don't tell people you can't eat this or you can't eat that or can do or cannot do something because of your madi. Just say, 'It does not suit me.' You won't hurt others this way. If you don't hurt people, you've followed achara." Thus even the concept of madi that anthropological and Indological research for long imagined as the bastion of brahmanical ritual life becomes elastic under the commitment "to not impose on others or hurt them."

An idea I encountered often in Sringeri, and in other contexts of my life, was that the yardstick for correct performance of shastric expectations was the sense of fulfillment (manas trupti). Echoing Ajji, Vijaya also said, "One does what one's capacity allows one to do, to keep up the achara (shastric practice) you've learned from your parents in whatever measure, and the satisfaction comes from the knowledge that you've done your best. One shouldn't let it go altogether."

Does shastra then largely designate the impersonal realm of the stipulated, the grand imperative, while observances (vows and fasts) and duties fill the space of the personalized, the voluntary, the everyday? Notwithstanding that actual shastric codification often includes detail that one could classify as "observances," Ajji voiced a perception I had heard from others that shastra concerns broad principles: "Treat everybody alike; do not disparage anyone; do not say 'Don't come here, don't touch this or that.'" I was beginning to see how Ajji's understanding of shastra blended into her sense of duty, the broad guideline finding expression in specific daily acts that she identified as her duties and observances—which ranged from washing the doorstep early in the morning, drawing rangoli (floor design from colored rice powder), fetching flowers, to maintaining physical and spiritual cleanliness and being considerate toward others.

Although Ajji saw the essence of shastric teaching as affirming humanistic values, she also recognized shastra as legislating specific ritual activity like shraaddha (annual rite of "feeding" ancestors, *pitṛ*). So, for example, she argued that during shraaddha not everyone who was close to the departed person could be invited to the meal. "As per shastric stipulation," she said, "only kin have the authority to partake of the shraaddha meal." Giridhara Shastry however, noted, "The shastra says that on the day of a shraaddha the hosts must feed a brahman. The shastra does not specify that one must only feed a Kamme brahman or a Shivalli brahman, and yet family sampradayas insist on maintaining and implementing such nonshastric clauses." Indeed, "there are times when sampradaya is prabala (predominant)."

And yet human discretion holds up spaces in which negotiations can occur: "In the puja place and the kitchen, *we* have freedom (namma svatantra). Once the daily puje and the naivedya are done, I don't object to whoever comes into these rooms," Ajji said.[24] It is indeed hard for me to see any boundaries or closed doors in Ajji's house, which seemed always full of people dropping in for a chat or for music lessons, medicines, yoga, and recitation classes, although only Ajji and Giridhara Shastry lived there. But her emphasis on *our* freedom also identifies the agency one could activate to draw up rules and obligations that are centered around family, event, or activity.

As I took my shastra question around Putta Murthy's family, I had a long conversation with Panduranga, whose observations elicit several nuances in the usage of the terms *shastra* and *sampradaya*:

P: What it comes down to is *rule* versus *act.* The Constitution (of India)—**rules**—may say one thing, but in procedure, we could *act* differently.

Let's take wearing the kacche sīre [25] in the Iyer community,
there's no **rule** about it, it's a sampradaya.
Or that lunch should be cooked before one has eaten anything, say, breakfast.
There's no rule about this,
some family's sampradaya will allow eating before cooking the main meal and some other family's sampradaya will not.
But at some level people are not able to distinguish between *rules* and *acts,* so they say everything is shastra.
"That's said in the shastras,"
they say.
Shastras only give us *broad* guidelines, they tell us how to live.
What broad directions should you follow in your life?
That's the question that shastra addresses.
"Follow dharma"is a stipulation that shastra makes.
And what does dharma tell you?

L: Hanh?

P: "Be a good student,"
"Take good care of your parents."[26]
Now sampradaya can modify this, add details.

L: So sampradaya allows one to negotiate? (*Listening to my tape now, I am not sure I meant "negotiate with the shastra" or "itself be negotiated."*)

P: Sure. When you modify shastra for a *context,* it becomes sampradaya. Let me tell you a kathe (story) about a paddhati.

L: Hanh!

P: In this area, there was a household where daily pujas would take place.

A bowl of milk would be set for use in the puja.

But the house cat would inevitably drink up the milk.

(*Leela is amused*)

P: So it became a pattern that everyday this man who sat down for the puja would ask the person who brought the milk to tie up the cat.

Time went by, and in the next *generation* it came to be that the daily puja was given up. Still, they invented the paddhati of tying up a cat when they went to do the namaskara.

Then it happened that some successive generation did not have a cat at all.

Do you know what they did?

L: No!

P: They started to *maintain* a pillar to which a cat could be tied.

L: (*laughing*) Oh no!

P: So today if you ask what is in their paddhati or in their sampradaya, a pillar has to be built when they construct a house.

If you ask why, the answer you get is, it's the cat-tying-pillar.

This has become a sampradaya![27]

(*everyone who overhears this story laughs*)

P: When the younger generations ask what is the meaning of this or that, it's hard to explain.

The meaning is hidden, in the past.

Often when we are unable to give a reason for doing something the way we do it, we say this is shastra.

L: In order to *cite authority*?

P: Where shastra does come into the *picture* is, when some ācaraṇe (ritual practices) has to be performed, then shastra tells us who should do it and how it should be done.

But in our day-to-day life—take the mangala gouri vrata or the giving of tāmbula, these have come from compulsions of the past (anivāryavāgi bandirōdu) when a girl used to be married young.

Until she went to her husband's house (after puberty), she had to be taught the *lifestyle* that was probably observed in the husband's family—so each family kept modifying and *adding* (to traditions like the mangala gouri vrata).

This, they called, our family's sampradaya.

The shastra doesn't say "do the mangala gouri vrata" or "this other vrata in this exact way" and so on.

There is no (shastric) rule about this.

All this comes from family sampradaya. There is no relevance today.

For instance, in those days a girl who had matured but was unmarried was not permitted to cook and do other things in madi in the house.

There were many others in the house who would do the work, and the girl was too young to have understood the *concept* of madi, or some such reason.

So they probably *started it.*

But today there isn't any relevance to this.

L: Right, there isn't any relevance, and yet one must follow them (rules), and then this becomes a pain.

But what do people do when they get doubts (about procedures)?

P: In the past they used to resolve it in the family by asking elders.

Now, if *a doubt comes,* they just *drop it,* right? (i.e., drop the sampradaya or the aspect of it in question). Ultimately, *all the rules, all the laws, the acts, are created to facilitate the people to live happily, that's all.*

But in the end, *rigidity* comes in because people begin to believe that they should live for the rules.

And then rebellions happen.

In the past people used to act in ways appropriate to those times.

And if they could not give a reason for a particular act, they would tell themselves it was a rule.

If you understand it this way, then there is no "reason" for most of ritual.

L: Hmmm . . . *how often do people consult the matha to resolve a doubt*?

P: In achara vichara there was really no question of consulting (the matha). In the past, there used be the joint family, so one would just consult elders and follow their advice.

Now breaking *ācaraṇe* itself has become a thing to do, so there is no scope for doubts! So today it is more likely that you will hear the older woman say,

"Oh all those (precise procedures) were for those times, for those generations, kaṇe.

Now just do as you judge best!"

Nobody goes to anybody and clarifies anything.

I found Panduranga's thinking in remarkable conversation with Wittgenstein's later writing,[28] agreeing with it and complicating it, with the crucial difference being in the dharmic tenor of Panduranga's vocabulary. Wittgenstein argues that it is *practice*, or *usage*, that reveals how individuals conceptualize a word or a rule, and usage reflects the ability to participate in "a form of life," the extended network of extralinguistic cultural "activities" shared by a community.[29] Acquiring this ability enables an individual to engage in a variety of "language games" that range from translation and storytelling to practical mathematics.[30] A philosophy of language begins, then, not with a systematized body of rules about syntax and semantics but in the unraveling of a "lived" grammar that underlies our concepts and one that yields a sense of the connections, expressible and inexpressible, that individuals make: what patterns of language use can be gleaned from the ways in which individuals extrapolate, verify, contextually apply, explicitly instruct, or illustrate a rule?

From this perspective, the complication in unraveling a grammar of the concept of shastra, is that shastra, a normative body (that Panduranga identifies as "rules") that claims divine origin, sinuously interacts with sampradaya, also a normative, loosely defined body characterized by practices ("acts"). In Panduranga's view, exemplified by Chayamma, Vijaya, and Ajji's observations, this sinuous interaction makes it difficult—even redundant—to differentiate between shastra and sampradaya. But, differing from Chayamma and Vijaya, Panduranga preliminarily finds it useful to distinguish between shastra and sampradaya as "rule" and "act," a distinction that helps him accentuate their contours and some of the ways in which they relate to each other. First, like Ajji, Panduranga notes that "shastras only give us broad guidelines" for life that can be modified by sampradaya, the field of enactment. If shastra advises, "Take care of one's parents," then a family sampradaya could regulate *ways* to express this care. But Panduranga's comment that "at some level, people are not able to distinguish between *rules* and *acts*, so they say everything is shastra" provokes us to ask *how* it is that one could confuse a rule with an action. It seems to me that the "confusion" in fact requires that we reconsider normative sources for actions.

While shastra is recognized as a body of conceptual rules—what Pollock calls theory—that presents itself as orienting our ways of being and doing, sampradaya too functions as a body of rules, except in the crucial detail that rules of sampradaya are engendered through practice (and therefore bring with them a dynamism characteristic of lived situations) and bear the imprint of region, family, profession, and so on. Rules are thus derived from rule bodies (shastra) as well as from rule following (sampradaya), and *both* attempt to uphold dharma. The unbounded interplay of interpretation, contexts, and discernment, and the inarticulated sense ("intuition") that underlies the observance of shastric rules make it impossible to situate precisely a shastric stipulation in the world of practice. It is not a "blind" observance of rules; on the contrary, following rules is justified by "agreement" that is expressed not merely in opinions but "in form of life."[31]

For Panduranga, as for Wittgenstein, the continuity between rules, whether derived from shastra or sampradaya, and seemingly related acts is a continuity that can be interrupted, meandering, or, as Panduranga especially underscores, even hypothetical.[32] In day-to-day contexts it is useful to come back to Chayamma's statement, "this is my shastra, this is my sampradaya," to understand both, how, from observing or performing an action, it is extremely difficult to say whether the action is impelled by shastra or by sampradaya—a combination of both or indeed neither. Despite the fact that a rule may be defined with some precision in the shastras or in the sampradaya (or any normative body), "its" meaning emerges in the practice itself; indeed, the connection of an enactment to a rule that governs it is at times enunciated primarily in the rhetoric that argues for it as in the often-invoked phrase "The shastras say." That we can justify a practice, or seek exemption altogether from explanation for an act, by citing "shastra" (that is, we do something simply because the shastra requires it) indicates, however, that intrinsic unquestionable authority is attached to the notion of shastra.

Despite this, specific as the codified shastras may be in their imagination of potential circumstances, the limitlessly manifesting complexities of human life ultimately outpace shastric breadth and specificity. Individuals, aware of this, constantly assess, extrapolate, disregard, or improvise shastric rules according to their relevance and resources, engaging in an intriguing process that does not disturb *theoretically* the intrinsic immutability associated with shastric knowledge (considered to be of divine origin), but witnesses continually the adaptation of shastra in practice.

Shastric prescriptions, explains Panduranga, are especially applicable to achara vichara (matters of ritual conduct), but he situates the mangala gouri vrata[33] in the province of sampradaya. The mangala gouri vrata is prescribed in the *Bhaviṣya Purāṇa*,[34] a Purana that is thematically synchronous with the Dharmashastras. Despite this textual location, Panduranga makes the important point that the primary location of the mangala gouri vrata is in the sampradaya local to the Malnad region. This location, at least for Panduranga, acknowledges the social and historical contexts of the tradition—a record, however tentative, of the community's past—reminding me of a conversation with Nagalakshmi in Halanduru in which she held up the immediate, familial face of another Gouri vrata tradition—a more certain record, one could say, of important present-day relationships. Talking about the Gouri puje performed by women and girls at the time of the Ganapati festival, Nagalakshmi had shown me the gejje vastra ("anklets and clothes" artistically made of cotton, paper, and sequin) that she had received from her mother's place. In the Malnad the gejje vastra that have been used to adorn the goddess Gouri during the festival are sent to a married daughter from her mother's home after the festival has concluded—something that I was only dimly aware of even though this puja tradition exists in my Telugu-speaking family, living in Hyderabad. This, Nagalakshmi had told me, was a Malnad sampradaya. "Even if there is a flood, we make it a point to send these across to my sisters-in-law," she said, emphasizing, "Not to send them is amaṅgaḷa (inauspicious)."

I find myself wondering, outside these conversations, along the lines of Kunal Chakrabarti's work, which finds that medieval Bengal Puranas adapted themselves to existing vrata traditions, whether the Puranic impetus and location of the mangala gouri vrata is one of the factors that makes the vrata's performance malleable as well as optional.[35] Interestingly, the genre of the vrata is a prime example of the ways in which shastric prescriptions are particularized by sociohistorical circumstances, family exigencies, and regional mores. Differences in ways of performing "common" ritual acts or in observing customs can be the cause of embarrassment. My fieldnotes from April 18, 1995, record an episode that occurred during the collectively performed Satyanārāyaṇa vrata that takes place in Sringeri immediately after the Ramanavami festival. Prasad (my husband) was visiting from Philadelphia, and, as usual, I roped him into my activities:[36]

> Ramachandra Bhattru asked me while we were watching Prasad perform the puja, "Does Prasad do nitya puje [daily puja]?" I thought he meant the sandhyavandane, and nodded vigorously, yes, yes. But he meant regular puja like the one being performed there, with all the sāmagri (items

used in worship) and puja vidhi(procedure), and I think he asked me because he must have known that Prasad did not do puja everyday. Worse still, Panduranga (who was sitting next to Prasad) kept telling Prasad what he was supposed to be doing next, so it must have been kind of obvious that we did not know the puja vidhāna(procedures) too well. To complicate matters, Prasad bungled pretty badly by putting his mouth to the cup in which *pānaka* (sweet drink from jaggery) was given, while all the others were drinking without touching their cups to their lips. I glared at him, and he went quickly to the tap to wash the cup. But I never stopped wondering if the sharp eyes of those bhattrus missed what he had done and his cover-up.

To return to the conversation with Panduranga, his cat story kept us all laughing but it also highlighted that a paddhati, with no shastric precedent, initiated by a person of suitable authority like an elder in the family, could develop into a family's sampradaya. The story also has a facetious edge to it, both in its content and in its telling: Its ironic content suggests that not all practices, even if they are part of sampradaya, are shastric, while the telling gently drew my attention to the point that if I tried too hard to exhume chronologies and "meanings" for every norm (as I must have come across as wanting to do), I could end up with anticlimactic origins-of-norms stories.

Yet the citing of shastra as an "explanation" for an act evokes the vast sense of the adrishtha (the unseen) that infuses our lives, a sense that the Mimamsa philosophers argued gave Vedic injunctions their transcendent authority. The phrase "the shastras say" may be treated as a variant on Wittgenstein: "If I have exhausted the justifications, I have reached bedrock, and my spade is turned. Then I am inclined to say, 'This is simply what I do.'"[37] Or, as Chayamma said, "this is how my mother did it." The phrase seems to call an end to the project of meaning seeking.

Nevertheless, the interpretive process can be fraught with doubt, misunderstanding, or incomprehension. For, after all, says Wittgenstein, "A rule stands there like a sign-post.—Does the sign-post leave no doubt open about the way I have to go? Does it shew which direction I am to take when I have passed it; whether along the road or the footpath or cross-country? . . . Or rather: [the rule] sometimes leaves room for doubt and sometimes not."[38] Panduranga's answer to my question about how one proceeds in the midst of doubt (Wittgenstein's "how to go on") locates the problem of knowledge and action in a historical framework: "In the past, they used to ask elders . . . people used to act in ways appropriate to those times." It is also telling that Panduranga spontaneously delineated the process of resolving a doubt as it unfolded in a conversation between two women ("Oh all those [precise procedures] were for those times, for those generations, kaṇe. Now just do as you judge best!")—kaṇe (girl) is a popular familiar form of address to a female in Kannada.[39] When we looked over this transcript together, Panduranga agreed with my impression that the hypothetical scenario of sharing advice between women that he had mentioned unconsciously reflected not only the central agency of women in the enactment of rules but also the particularities of the Murthy household in which Chayamma, Lakshmidevamma, Indira, and Radha actively interpreted the customs of their family.

My question about how often people turned to the matha to resolve a doubt betrays my assumption that the matha, as Dharmashastric authority, would moderate the daily lives of Sringeri residents, but I am directed rather to a local agency in determining paths of action. The past practice of consulting elders to resolve doubts is now partly replaced by acts that are inspired by the feeling that a particular rule has lost its relevance or that modernity is expressed in nonconformity to the rule.[40]

Even within the matha, however, all roads do not always lead to shastric recommendations on conduct. The normative power of sampradaya is illustrated by the following anecdote that Dodda Murthy narrated to my father, S. Nagarajan, who was visiting me during the Navaratri festival in 1994. They had been musing about Sringeri's past and the arrival of the motorcar to Sringeri in the early 1900s.

DM: Pandit Madan Mohan Malaviya,
SN: the founder of Banaras Hindu University,
DM: Hanh.
He once invited the thirty-third guru Shivabhinava Narasimha Bharati (1879—1912) to Varanasi
with a two-week notice of an event.
When the guru responded that the pallakki (palanquin) would take much longer to get to Varanasi,
SN: In those days--
DM: Malaviya assured him that, instead of a pallakki, he would arrange a car to take the guru to Varanasi and bring him back.
The guru replied,
"It is all very fine, but this car . . .

> I do not know of a sampradaya in which previous gurus have traveled by car.
>
> I am not saying that it contradicts our shastra, but we simply don't have the sampradaya.
>
> I do not wish to start a sampradaya that has not existed before . . .
>
> I will send my blessings from Sringeri."
>
> In the end, his pāduka (wooden sandals) were sent to Varanasi.

The anecdote took me by surprise because it toppled my uncomplicated understanding that for the guru of the matha the shastric word would be final *in every case.* I wondered if the mere two-week notice had also not gone down too well. Less facetiously, however, for a practice to be permissible, the sanction of shastra, specifically the Dharmashastras, is not enough; the greater ratification must come from sampradaya. The Dharmashastras, while regulating modes of transportation for sannyasis, itself may permit some leeway, so why did the guru not want to start a sampradaya? Was the guru's decision not to travel by car a negation of innovation? Perhaps. But if one turns to the many other episodes associated with the same guru, it is evident that he was reputed to be one the most path-breaking gurus of the Sringeri parampara (lineage).

One episode narrated to me concerns a brahman subsect that had been for many generations disallowed by other brahman subsects to be seated in the same pankti (row) during meal events. The disenfranchised community brought the matter of this ostracization to the attention of this guru, arguing that they were being unfairly denied the recognition appropriate to their status. The guru considered the matter in all its social subtlety (*sūkśmavāgi vicāra māḍi*), taking into account the position of the Dharmashastras, and delivered the matha's decision. He declared that the community had the same seating rights as other brahmans, overturning a long-held sampradaya that had led to the discrimination. In another instance, he similarly mandated that the ostracization meted out to another group of brahmans be discontinued, arguing that it had been founded on a historical conflict between Shaivas and Madhvas many centuries ago and was not supported by shastric reckoning. So the refusal of the car to Varanasi may not have been because of a reluctance to start or halt a sampradaya. The reluctance may have come from the fact that the use of a car would have signaled the admittance of a personal luxury, anthithetical to the very institution of sanyasa, and also countered the ideal of shishtha, an exemplar. Not only was the car an index of luxury, but it was also at that time a "foreign" item, alien to Indian ways.

Jonathan Parry reports an interesting parallel in the performance of *śrāddha* rites in Varanasi. A priest who had been performing death rites according to the customarily followed printed paddhati manuals on one occasion changed the ritual procedure to "conform" to those laid down in a shastric treatise. When Parry discussed this, the priest's brother, also a priest, repudiated the shastric procedure as unnecessary "innovation" in the customary practice, saying, "'In my whole life, I have only performed two or three *shraddhs* according to the *Shastras.* I emphasize *lokachar* [the popular tradition]. What the women of the family say, that's the truth. Blowing our conch shells, we Brahmans throw dust in people's eyes.'"[41] Although it is not certain that lokachar is exactly the same as sampradaya, the two views suggest that normative authority is not *uniformly* accepted as being contained either in the realm of shastra or in the realm of lokachar or sampradaya. Despite the priest's brother's prioritization of "popular tradition," Parry states that his "informants" assert that shastric stipulations are considered "unquestionably authentic" (in another place, "unquestionably authoritative") and inviolable, while laukika (popular) is of "dubious validity" ("to be discarded if it offends against contemporary canons of good sense").[42]

The dharmic depth of sampradaya that sometimes allows it to override shastra is illustrated by an episode involving the guru of the matha from 1912–1954, Shri Chandrashekara Bharati, who succeeded the guru in the above anecdote. The guru, a great yogi, was so inward-oriented (antarmukhi) and meditative that he often became too aloof from the affairs of the matha. The agent, Srikantha Shastry, urged him to appoint a successor who would be able to involve himself more in the matha's matters. I had heard from many in Sringeri that the relationship between the world-savvy Srikantha Shastry, who brought an unparalleled commitment to the matha's management, and the deeply introspective and detached guru was often tense. Their callings diverged. On the day of the ceremony of initiating and appointing the disciple as the junior guru, the traditional palanquins of gold and silver were made ready for the procession. Instead of following the sampradaya of seating himself in the gold palanquin as the senior guru, Shri Chandrashekara Bharati moved toward the silver palanquin meant for his disciple. Srikantha Shastry quickly reminded him of the sampradaya. The guru replied, "You know the circumstances and background relating to today's installation ceremony. Please recall [*them*] and remember [*them*] always. From now on, he is the Jagadguru, not I. . . . I wish to withdraw from all worldly dealings."[43] The guru's remarks to Srikantha Shastry were a reminder of the "worldly" concerns that had necessitated the appointment of a disciple. Playing on the word *Jagadguru,* "guru of the world," Shri Chandrashekara Bharati indicated that he had abdicated the world, and, thus, if the sampradaya was to be truly followed, the gold palanquin was more appropriate for the disciple who was now the Jagadguru, and not for him, the world renouncer.

Text and Moral Authority in Hindu Sacred Literature

Authorship, orality, locatedness in cultures and languages, and occurrence across multiple media (art, architecture) are some variables that tangle the concept of "text" in Hindu contexts. Centuries could separate the composition of a text and its appearance in written forms, and manuscripts of purportedly the "same" text could be geographically dispersed.[44] Performance and patronage keep textual production in flux, tracing varying routes to history, social life, community ownership, and poetic vision. Thus "text" asks to be understood as positioned at an eternal intersection, in the midst of the traffic of human life, amid crisscrossings of written/recorded, oral/performed, and received/transmitted texts.[45] The many ways in which texts are conceptualized in Hindu worlds helps us understand why it is also possible to envision and experience the normative in plural terms.[46] What are some of the ways in which texts claim moral authority, and how is the textuality of a text interwoven with that claim? In this section I will allude to some directions in which scholars have explored this vast and complicated question.

At the level of authorship, there are texts whose moral authority lies in their having divine or transcendental authors (apauruṣeya) like the Vedas. Then, another kind of authorship is that associated with "Vyāsa" of the *Mahabharata,* a text that calls itself the "fifth Veda," most appropriate for providing moral direction in the confused age of Kaliyuga. Vyāsa has been thought of as a "symbolic" author who indexes an accretion of authors and therefore embodies the moral authority of tradition. Vyāsa has been imagined by Hindu epic and Puranic traditions also as "mythical" author (a ṛṣi or seer whose scribe is none other than the god Gaṇeśa), and he has been understood as a mimetic author who "performs among humans the role that Brahma performs in mythology."[47] In many Hindu narrative traditions Brahma is recognized as the creator of the Vedas and the universe. A third way by which authorship bespeaks moral authority is seen in the signatures of bhakti poet-saints who address the divine with a personally chosen name such as *Kūḍalasangamadeva* ("Lord of the Meeting Rivers") or *Giridhara* ("hill bearer"). The personally chosen name of course conveys the poet's identity, but it also points to an authorship that is united in poetry with the divine. As Jack Hawley notes, such a compounded signature "anchors a poem to a life, a personality, even a divinity that gives the poem its proper weight and tone; and it connects it to a network of associations that makes the poem not just a fleeting flash of truth—not just new and lovely—but something that has been heard before and respected, something familiar and beloved . . . [lending poems] authority and conviction."[48]

In terms of oral/aural textuality, the Vedas, conceived in sound, preserve their normative authority in sound. Sound is scrupulously regulated and protected for in it are embodied the rhythms of the universe and a language of communication with the gods—despite David Carpenter's speculation that parts of the Vedas have remained relatively unchanged because of the "extreme conservatism of those entrusted with their preservation."[49] In fact, some Hindus consider reciting the Vedas from a book as against dharma—the Shankaracharya of the Kanchipuram matha maintains that the normative status of the Vedas is lost when it is read out of a book (or heard from an audiocassette?).[50] The genre of the vrata katha is a more ubiquitous expression of how moral meaning is wrapped up in the oral/aural experience.[51] A vrata is a Hindu votive practice in honor of a specific deity, and is performed for auspiciousness, well-being, or a specific desire. Especially popular among women, vratas are marked by fasting, worship, religious gathering, recitation, and storytelling. But a crucial part in the performance of the vrata is the telling and hearing of the story (katha) associated with it. Typically, vrata kathas recount the procedure of the vrata through the experiences and actions of an exemplar and describe the benefits to be gained by the correct performance of the vrata. Although the moral content of a vrata katha is explicit, holding up as it does the life of an exemplar (usually a virtuous woman), the act of narrating (kathana) and listening (śravaṇa) at the end of the vrata provides the satisfaction of proper closure and the assurance of fruition. It is this overall oral/aural context that amplifies the dharmic ambience and the normative intent of the vrata.

The connection between text and normativity is also secured through processes of transcription, transcreation, or written composition. As Narayana Rao argues in the case of the Puranas, the "recorded" text is often only *part* of the story. The *paurāṇika*, or oral storyteller, who draws on his knowledge of, and training in, the Puranas, imparts "fullness" to the text in performance, and thus the *paurāṇika*'s knowledge shapes the "received" text.[52] To understand how texts travel across categories, acquiring possibly different shades of moral authority, one could turn to the well-known classification of texts into shruti ("heard") and smriti ("remembered"). Pollock finds that the term *smriti* (which originated in *Pūrva Mīmāṃsa*) refers to a Vedic text that is no longer available to be heard in recitation but exists as "remembered." The lost Veda surfaces in a new form through memory, and a shruti text comes to inhabit the world of smriti[53]—bringing with it the imprint of authority of the Vedas (as in the *Mahabharata*, the *Nāṭyaśāstra*, and the *Tiruvāymoḻi* claiming to be the "fifth Veda.") Apastamba, the author of one of the oldest Dharmasutras, uses the "lost Veda" strategy to argue that all rules of dharma, whether or not traceable to extant Vedas, are ultimately derived from them. In the view of the Shankaracharya of the Kanchipuram matha, Vedic association makes the Dharmashastras unmodifiable: "It is important to realise that if we are to remain true to the *śāstras* it is not because they represent the views of the seers but because they contain the rules founded on the Vedas which are nothing but what Īśvara has ordained. That is the reason why we must follow them. It is my duty to see that the *śāstras* are preserved as they are. I have no authority to change them."[54]

Shastra as an Imagined Text

Sringeri perspectives remind us that moral praxis, while girded by transcendent arguments (of bhakti, Vedic origins, Advaita, for example) is in fact quite thoroughly situated in local (and larger-than-local) structures and cycles (such as kinship, agricultural seasons), often historically envisaged ("this [practice] is traced to the Vijayanagara times") and interpersonally developed (between parent and child, neighbors, or teacher and student). The unraveling of a lived grammar of the normative through ethnography uncovered for me a wide sociosemantic field of normative discourse and praxis that is characterized by a fluid movement between shastra, sampradaya, niyama, achara, and paddhati. Contexts of usage and narration hold up the synonymity of these terms, but also hold up differences between them; differences in intention, in the nature and source of normative authority, in jurisdictions of moral and practical knowledge, in the efficacy of action, and in the flexibility associated with them. As individuals contextually sift the meanings and associations of these idioms seeking for legitimacy, "the normative" manifests itself as an emergent phenomenon located in, and drawing on, a wide range of sources—oral, visual, written and practiced—spread across codebooks, exemplars, and practices—all of which bear intertextual relationships with each other. The boundaries of this sociosemantic field of shastra continually shift, and, as I suggest elsewhere, the poetics of social life preempt the drawing up of an exhaustive list of moral concepts that determine practice.

What keeps the normative from being fossilized or relegated to one set of codebooks is not only this range of normative sources of which shastra is but one, but also the desire to work out a dharmically accountable life and to create a clearing of auspiciousness in the jungle of ambiguity and uncertainty. Continuous reflection on what is binding, on the limits of innovation, and on what constitutes conformity and "sense of fulfillment" (manas trupti) in addition ensure that normative authority and concomitant power are kept in circulation and diffused.

But conceptualizing an ethics in practice also means that we need to understand—to use Edward Said's phrase to describe the interplay between Quranic text and circumstantiality—the "constitutive interaction"[55] between injunction and action. The constitutive interaction, I suggest, can perhaps be understood in terms of an *imagined text* that each individual puts together commingling memory with implicit learning and teaching. A sense of pervading adrishtha consequences and an awareness of the provisionality of injunctive knowledge systems thread the imagined "text."[56] As Said says, "texts have ways of existing that even in the most rarefied form are always enmeshed in circumstance, time, place, and society—in short, they are in the world, and hence worldly."[57] Chayamma and Vijaya Krishnamurty reminded me matter-of-factly that mothers, more generally elders, have a special agency in articulating the injunctive, and memory works in powerful ways to foster the connection between "what one's elders did or taught" and "what one does." The do's and don'ts that Nagalakshmi spontaneously outlined for me about Malnad foodways (adige paddhati) came from the seeing-and-doing orientations of daily life that highlight Ajji's remark, "What is there to teach (explicitly)?"

Ajji's perception that shastra and paddhati "are the same" in day-to-day conduct, differing during certain rituals, implies that the imagined text is contingent. This contingent, intertextual, imagined text also seems to underlie the dispersed interpretation of shastra that master architects and sculptors hold in Tamilnadu. Samuel Parker observes, "In everyday speech *śāstra* is typically used by Tamil architects and sculptors, not in reference to books, but to *bodies of knowledge*" "objectified" in three interlinked ways: 1.

in the person of the *sthāpati* (the master architect), 2. in temples and their sacred images, and 3. in written texts (the *silpaśāstras*). The priority of each of these understandings of shastra is enunciated contextually; thus, "the living *sthāpati*, as a human incarnation of *śāstra*, is supreme in the context of production. The temple or image is supreme in the context of devotion. The text is supreme in the social negotiation of authority."[58] In a similar fashion, David Reck notes that in the context of Karnatic music, shastra exists as an "invisible 'book' . . . in the collective minds of all musicians practicing within the tradition. . . . There is a vast core of shared knowledge and agreement, the solid and tangible (though unwritten) common ground of tradition."[59] But Reck also notes that the "tradition is only partially conveyed by the guru to the disciple. The rest the *śiṣya* [disciple] and aspiring musician picks up simply by existing within the tradition 'like a fish swimming in water.'"[60]

Shastric textuality, Pollock notes, is marked by "systematicity, stability, and repetition" and is a constitutive feature of the genre of shastra.[61] One might ask what distinguishes the textuality of the imagined texts of moral praxis? Like the sacred subterranean river Sarasvati, the imagined text is both elusive and present in Hindu life, and, like the river, it too has a presence that is defined by the perennial confluence and divergence of streams, oral and written, seen and done, regional and transregional, and lost and recovered pasts. While the precise textuality of imagined texts does not derive from any one particular text, imagined texts, born out of and lending themselves to powerful interpretative agency, are marked by an intermediacy and a compositeness that comes from the collation of various rule systems. The text can be firm (drawing on authoritative rule systems) or fragile (open to vacillation, especially about "procedures" and "benefits"), or it can be flexible (supple bodies of rules adapting to situations) but bounded (limits relativism and interpretation).

What is interesting in Sringeri is that in this normative compass the word *shastra* occupies a particularly important place. Panduranga's insight that when individuals cannot identify the "reason" for a rule they ascribe it to shastra, or Chayamma's assertion that, when challenged, one is likely to respond with "this is my shastra, this is my sampradaya," alerts us to the metaphorical potential in the term *shastra*. When the word *shastra* is invoked in conversation—"I did this for the sake of shastra" or "this is what the shastra says"—it only *sometimes* alludes to an actual body of rules like the Dharmashastras. More often than not, the word *shastra* is used to bestow theoretically the immutability and authority associated with shastra to imagined texts. The vast, continuously updating pool of normative resources and expressions and the constant putting together of imagined texts by each individual and community remind me of Ramanujan's wonderful observation about the endemic presence of the Ramayana story in texts that appear as phrases, songs, folktales, curses, or even as arithmetic problems: "These various texts not only relate to prior texts directly, to borrow or refute, but they relate to each other through this common code or pool. Every author, if one may hazard a metaphor, dips into it and brings out a unique crystallization, a new text with a unique texture and a fresh context. . . . In this sense, no text is original, yet no telling is a mere retelling—and the story has no closure, although it may be enclosed in a text."[62] In the end I am inclined to argue that shastra is ultimately, as George Lakoff and Mark Johnson would say, a "metaphor we live by."[63]

Cat Lessons on Shastra

Oddly enough, in this search for shastra I encountered cats again in a conversation with Ramachandra Bhattru (RB) that I recorded. Often, after he and his wife, Amrutamba, who was also a schoolteacher, came home from school, we would meet for a chat in their house. During brisk winter evenings our conversations were accompanied by cups of steaming *kasāya*, a spicy decoction of herbs.

RB: If a cat shows up,
at a shraaddha
it is inauspicious.
So how does one prevent a cat from showing up?
Well, one could do things like build barriers. But what if it was a housepet?
So this priest who went to somebody's house for a shraaddha,
He saw that they had a cat, and that for that day the cat had been shut in a basket.
And, a stone hoisted on top of the lid.
So that until the shraaddha was done, the cat would remain in the basket, and not show up inauspiciously in the middle of the ceremony.
So he (the priest) saw this. He who had gone to be fed as a brahman at the shraaddha.
"Oh ho, I see.

To perform a shraaddha in the most authentic manner, a cat must be placed in a basket—

And he decided to do the right thing at his own father's shraaddha! But he didn't have a cat.

So, somehow capturing a cat, he shut it in a basket,

L: (*laughing*) What attention to procedure!

RB: And exactly when the priests arrived, he brought it out and placed it *right in front of them!*

Absolutely inauspicious!

And he said to the priests,

"In our family, you see,

we perform a shraaddha only with a cat *shut* in a basket!"[64]

5 *In the Courtyard of Dharma, Not at the Village Square*

Delivering Ashirvada in Sringeri

Ashirvada, a Sanskrit term for "blessing,"[1] refers in Sringeri in particular to a ceremony of blessing that occurs at the conclusion of a religious event such as a parayana (votive reading) or a wedding that is hosted by a family in a home, a temple, or a rented space. Irrespective of the caste of the family that is conducting the religious event, an ashirvada performance toward the end of the event is integral to it. It includes the following parts: 1. a formal request made by the host family to the assembled purohitas (priests) for blessing, 2. the recitation of Vedic mantras of blessing by purohitas as members of the host family do the namaskara (obeisance), 3. an extempore ashirvada narrative delivered in Kannada by a priest or a learned brahman that begins with upachara vakya (statement of praise and good conduct), and words of appreciation to the hosts and guests. The ashirvada then develops into an exegesis of the ritual event just concluded. The entire ashirvada ceremony takes twenty to a maximum of thirty minutes. What is interesting is that when people in Sringeri use the term *ashirvada* in this context, they could refer to the *entire* blessing ceremony or exclusively to the narrative. Thus an ashirvada could be "done" (māḍodu), "delivered" (koḍodu), or "said" (heḷodu).

Ashirvada narratives, which are display events for local erudition, reveal a spectacular interplay of voice, textual allusion, and poetic mood. The result is an emergent oral text that is rarely duplicated because of its performative qualities. Occupying a space somewhere between shastra and sampradaya, between individual talent and tradition, between ritual occasion and everyday routine, the narrative stands out as an eclectic instance of ethical instruction: it cites the Vedas and the Upanishads, the Dharmashastras, alludes to stories from the epics and the Puranas, and subtly weaves social commentary to create a layered ethical text.

The ashirvada tradition is cited widely by residents as a "unique" tradition among Sringeri smarta brahmans, often as a rejoinder to the accusation of inhospitality made by tourists and pilgrims who come expecting lavish material attention from local residents.[2] Initially I was puzzled that a speech-oriented performance tradition was constructed as a demonstration of hospitality. However, the many ashirvada performances I attended made me recognize the deeper ways in which ashirvada sustains the guest-host paradigm.[3] While upachara is the colloquial Kannada word for "hospitality," etymologically it means to "come near, approach" indicating attentive service, as in "waited on, served, honoured, adored."[4] Ashirvada performances are expressions of upachara because they formally enunciate and celebrate idealized guest-host relations. After feeding and personally attending to guests (tasks taken very seriously by the host family), the hosts formally apologize for any unintended lapses in hospitality, and seek forgiveness and blessings from those assembled. The purohitas, who speak on behalf of all the guests, express their satisfaction (manas trupti) at a well-done event and, in the narrative, they continue in the idiom of "high conduct" by elaborating on the "meaning" of the ritual. At the same time, the performance becomes a broader occasion for enunciating "right" conduct.

As aware as the ashirvada performer is of the specific context of the event—the identity of the hosts, the scale of the ritual, the manner in which the ritual was performed, for example—the "text" of the ashirvada narrative and its delivery are of the greatest importance. Scholars and priests who perform ashirvada pointed out the importance placed on the emergent text—on what one says and how one says it. Unlike storytelling performances in small settings in which audience interaction with the narrator or other members of the listening audience implicitly affects the delivery and the delivered text itself,[5] in ashirvada the audience does not shape the text of the ashirvada narrative. Instead, it is the ritual event (the particular karma that has been performed) that determines the ashirvada narrative.[6] At most, the lineage of the host—whether the hosts are followers of the *Rigveda* or the *Yajurveda*, for instance—determines the specific Sanskrit shlokas (verses) selected for the blessing. In homes where the hosts are not brahmans, Vedic shlokas are replaced by generic shlokas of blessing from texts other than the Vedas.

During the decade of the making of this book, I attended many ashirvadas at numerous ritual events in brahman homes of varying subcastes in Sringeri. I also attended some in the homes of my Bunt and Vokkaliga friends, where I learned interestingly that ashirvada is not considered by these communities to be significant in *their* repertoires of performance genres. The "doing" or "giving" of ashirvada is associated primarily with the brahman community of Sringeri by both brahmans and nonbrahmans alike. The text and the contexts of the ashirvada performance that I present here and the metacommentary about ashirvada need to be understood as being within the bounds of the brahman "folklore community" (which shares general knowledge of an expressive tradition and the rules governing its performance) and the "folklore group" (comprising performers and audiences at a particular performance), to borrow Flueckiger's elastic terminology.[7]

Durga Dipa Namaskara Ashirvada

In early June 2004, when the auspicious festive season was drawing to a close, Nagaraja, Ramchandra Bhattru's son, told me about the Durga dipa namaskara puja (also referred to as Durgārādhane and Durga puje) he had been asked to perform in Gochanhalli, just outside the town. "It's rarely performed around here—more popular in South Kanara—and the many lamps they will light in the evening will make the whole thing quite beautiful. Why don't you come?" he suggested. I knew that to attend such events uninvited was accepted, even welcomed, and I amusedly thought to myself that in Sringeri I must have made a perfect fit for the cultural category of atithi, the word for "guest" whose etymology in Sanskrit means "one who comes without prior date or appointment."

Being among the first to arrive, after introductions and a warm welcome, I settled down to watch the family's friend, Suryanarayana Bhattru of nearby Vaikunthapura, and Nagaraja make an exquisite Chandika mandala[8] using rangoli in the central room of the house. As they filled the beautiful eight-petalled lotus design with flaming red, green, yellow, and white powders and bordered the design with full-blossomed marigolds, I began to anticipate how the puja to Durga would soon invoke, invite, seat, and worship her amidst hundreds of lamps and words of praise. The family was preoccupied with serving coffee to guests who had begun to arrive and with other preparations for the puja. Lamps, incense, camphor, coconuts, and several silver, brass, and copper containers with sandal paste, turmeric, kumkuma, water, and flowers, soon surrounded the mandala. The silver kalasha[9] that would represent Durga was placed in the center of the mandala. Nagaraja, who had introduced me to the host family, asked them whether I could videotape the puja, and they enthusiastically agreed. The house was now filling up, and people stood conversing in groups under the large chappara (tent made from areca and coconut fronds) that had been set up outside the house.

I fell into conversation with one of the daughters-in-law who was trying hard to restrain her young son from scampering over the mandala. The Durga dipa puja was being performed, I learned, for the welfare of the family's contracting business and to mark the occasion of ninety-four-year-old Menase Ganeshaiyya becoming a great grandfather. It had become a four-generation family. Ganeshaiyya had served for many years in the matha, supervising its public meal arrangements. The Durga puja was being performed in the house of his son, Subramanya Ghanapati, who was a public works contractor.

The puja commenced abruptly with the ringing of bells and the chanting of invocatory shlokas. A large open window allowed me to conveniently record the puja and the later ashirvada from the verandah where many of the guests stood and watched. After the puja, for which the *Durgā Saptaśatī* was recited, the family performed the pledged 108 circumambulations and namaskaras.

Since it was past 9 PM when all this concluded, there was some discussion between the purohitas and the family about advancing the ashirvada to before dinner instead of making it the usual postmeal performance. Nagaraja announced that the ashirvada was going to commence, and guests and family crowded into the two rooms. Although Nagaraja had conducted the puja, he had been informally guided by Suryanarayana Bhattru and an elderly priest, who I later learned was Prabhakar Devdhar Bhattru (or, Prabhakar Bhattru), the priest at the Kanyakumari temple in Menase. Prabhakar Bhattru, being the eldest of purohitas present, was requested to bless the family with mantrakshate (turmeric-dipped rice grains). Beginning with the oldest, one by one, members of the family paid their obeisance to him while all the other purohitas joined in reciting ashirvada mantras from the *Rig* and *Yajur Vedas*, and the *Durga Saptaśatī*. Following this, Suryanarayana

FIGURE 5.1. Nagaraja conducting Devi puja in Thorehadlu. *Photo by Leela Prasad*

Bhattru requested Ganeshaiyya, as the eldest of the host family, to approach the purohitas.

(*As members of the host family, beginning with the eldest, prostrated individually before the purohitas, Prabhakar Bhattru, Nagaraja, Suryanarayana Bhattru, and a few other guests who were purohitas recited "ashirvada mantras" collated from the Taittirīya Brāhmaṇa [of the Yajurveda], the Rig samhita, and the Devī Māhātmya. This procedure lasted ten minutes.*)[10]

SURYANARAYANA BHATTRU: (*prompts the formal request by the host for the blessing*)

I have conducted—[11]

GANESHAIYYA: (*haltingly*)

I have conducted this Durga puja to the best of my ability.

I am not sure how it went.

PRABHAKAR BHATTRU: (*indicating me*)

If you say "I don't know how it went," she's going to *record* it! (*laughter*).

GANESHAIYYA: (*continuing, more emphatically*)

Forgive me for any shortcomings and give your blessings too all of us.

OTHER PUROHITAS AND PRABHAKAR BHATTRU: (*back and forth between them*)

You do the ashirvada—

—No, you do it.

—No, no, you!

WOMAN: (*to a child*) Sit down here!

(*people talking*)

SOMEBODY: Quiet! *Other folks, please, quiet!*

PRABHAKAR BHATTRU: (*softly, very deliberately, a brief upachara vakya*)

You have performed a very rare and important act of worship (*devata kārya*).

SOMEBODY: (*to others in the room*) *Shhh!*

PB: (*beginning the ashirvada exegesis*)

If one asks what this puja is called,

"Durga namaskara puja."

That is what they say it is called.

If one asks who this *Durga* is

(*shifting to a singsong style, much like a recitation*)

Extreme misfortune-causing

sort of evil powers

that envelop a man

and keep ruining his life

(*returning to the earlier prosaic style and saying in one breath*)

The dispelling of such powers

By this shakti (power) called Durga

And the granting of our desires and wishes

That is what the ārādhane of this Durga shakti earns us

This

is not a power that is *ordinary.*

The instant this universe was created,

the māyā that emanated from Vishnu, not visible to anybody,

extraordinary,

such a power it is.

It is not meant to be used for everyday things.

It is very gambhīra (deep), very gauptya (esoteric).

The *gods* too

were troubled by evil powers—that is, by rakshasas (demons)

Like *great* ascetics, they (the demons) too were worshippers of Ishvara.

Performing austerities,
pleasing different gods,
they would ask for boons.
For what?
They
(*in one breath*)
were full of evil, seeking not to benefit the world, or enrich it.
(*resuming normal pace*)
Desiring to win the whole world, desiring themselves to be all-powerful, to be kings of the world,
such boons they sought of the gods.
Even so,
when they were pleased with the austerities of the rakshasas,
the gods were *obliged* to grant boons to those who asked.
And they unfailingly granted whatever was asked.
In this way,
many rākśasas like Mahishasura and others,
winning even the world of the gods,
winning the three worlds,
making *themselves* known as the "most powerful in the universe,"
they began to harass the gods.
In such circumstances,
when the gods, left without any recourse, went to Brahma for help,
he led them all to Vishnu
and asked Vishnu (for help).
Then,
(Vishnu says)
"There is no way out. However, there exists one other power.
If we pray to it and obtain it,
we can overcome our troubles,
regain our rightful authority and live in the world of gods."
Thus saying they make a resolve.
Then *all together*, they pray to that shakti.
When that shakti appeared,
each of the gods and goddesses surrendering their weapons and powers to her, say,
"*You* are our only hope. You must protect us by vanquishing these demons," they pray to her.

Then,
destroying Mahishasura and all the other demons,
and fulfilling the desire of the gods and goddesses, she asks—
(*breaks the thought for a moment*)
The gods sing her praises in *many* ways.
At that point,
Durga asks again,
"What *else* do you need me to do for you? Ask!"
Then the gods and goddesses say,
(*chanting musically from the Devī Māhātmya*)
"Na kiñcidavaśiṣyate" (Nothing remains to be done).[12]

"Now that you have destroyed Mahishasura and restored our authority, after this, we have no greater expectation.

However—
if you wish to grant us a boon—"
Do you know what they ask for?
(*Prabhakar Bhattru says the line "Na kiñcidavaśiṣyate" rapidly, cuing himself, then recites*):
yadi cāpi varo deyastvayāsmākaṁ maheśvari
saṁsmṛtā saṁsmṛtā tvaṁ no hiṁsethāḥ paramāpadaḥ[13]
Devī! If you still desire to grant us a boon,
saṁsmṛtā saṁsmṛtā tvaṁ no hiṁsethāḥ paramāpadaḥ
yaśca martyaḥ stavairbhistvāṁ stoṣyatyamalānane
tasya vittarddhi vibhavairdhanadārādisampadām
vṛddhaye'smatprasannā tvaṁ bhavethāḥ sarvadāmbike
This is what they ask:
"You have protected us this time.

But we desire that whenever evil forces like these become powerful in this world and harass others,

even on the earth,
not just in heaven, on earth, the world of mortals,
whoever sings your praises—
but also those who do *not* sing your praises—
(*in one breath*)
everybody, we desire that you free them from such evil forces and protect them. Become the goddess who grants them the wealth and progeny they desire."
(*pausing*)
That is what they pray to the Devi.

Thus, we—

Although they were gods—*even gods*, they need *another* power.

What then humans?

Humans of course need it.

The gods will always need a power that is greater than their own.

Vishnu prays to Shiva, Shiva prays to Vishnu.

In this way, not in one, but in twos, the world must proceed.

(*in one breath*)

In the future, too, in whatever circumstance, whether on the earth or in heaven, she (Devi) agrees to protect the world from harm from demons. It is said that once upon a time

there was one Aruna, a powerful rakshasa.

If you ask what boon he had obtained through his penance, it was

(*reeling this list off*)

not through a four-legged animal, not through a two-legged animal,

not by man or animal,

not even by gods,

not by any of these should death come to me,

not from birds that traverse the skies,

not from animals *without* legs,

from none of these should death come,

This was the boon he had obtained, it is said.

Aruna was his name.

yadāruṇākhyastrailokye mahābādhāṁ kariṣyati||

tadāhaṁ bhrāmaraṁ rūpaṁ kṛtvāsaṅkhyeyaṣatpadam|[14]

"We—there is nothing more than this to win. We have vanquished all. Now we are the greatest of all."

In this manner (of Aruna), should *anybody* ever think,

There is another power that surpasses, that is far more gauptya,

(that is) endowed with *extraordinary* strength

That God *most certainly* keeps hidden,

One seed of poison.

So what happened to such a demon (as Aruna)?

Not able to withstand his tyranny, all the gods prayed to Devi:

"He has been granted the boon that he cannot be killed by anything."

Then they come up with a new strategy.

(*this stanza is narrated especially dramatically*)

As soon as he held the rock like this
(*Prabhakar Bhattru demonstrates by grabbing an imaginary rock with his right hand*),
asaṅkhyeyaṣatpadam—becoming *six-legged bees,*
out of the rock she (Durga) came and came and came,
and—*asaṅkhyeya*, meaning, *"without count"*—
They (the bees) stung and stung and stung, and killed him, so they say (*antaha heḷuttāre*)
(*pauses*)
In this way, *always,*
this worship that is called *Durgārādhane*
is like what is called a *brahmāstra* (a divine, infallible weapon),
it is so *powerful* and so *sacred* a force.
That is why in the *Durgāsūkta*, it is declared in the manner of the Vedas,
"*Nāveva sindhu duritātyagniḥ*"[15]
Meaning, whatever troubles we encounter,
if we pray to Durga and worship this Durgi (*addressing Durga affectionately*),
when this *wide river* or this ocean seems impossible to cross,
A *nāva*—*nāva* means *doṇi*—
like in a boat we easily cross from one side of the river or the ocean to the other,
like that, when this Durga shakti is pleased with us,
it will take us across the *kaḍalu* (sea) of all troubles
to the other shore safely,
and protect us, it is said.
(*now makes more elaborate the upachara vakya that he initiated at the beginning of the performance and combines it with the actual blessing*)
Such an incomparable and powerful force
this day, in this sacred tirtha
(*phone rings in the background*)
(*Ganeshaiyya*) being born a *ghanapāṭi*[16]
in this sacred site,
having served many years at the feet of the guru,
blessed with a son,
Subramanya Ghanapati,
to whom a grandson has been born—
(*turning to Ganeshaiyya's family standing nearby*)

Ganeshaiyya has *invoked* such a goddess today
    and prayed that all of you be blessed by Durga's grace.
    Following his request,
    in the same *complete* way (as he did the puja)
    we pray that whatever the evil forces that trouble you,
    may they all be warded off,
    and may Durga's grace *always*
    be like an *armor* around you,
    and bestow you with happiness, wealth, progeny.
    So praying, we bless you.
(*closure*)

ALL THE PUROHITAS JOINING PRABHAKAR BHATTRU: *Tathāsthu*!
(So be it!)
(*concluding mantras are recited by the purohitas*)

The ashirvada begins with ninety-four-year old Ganeshaiyya making the customary statement of apology for any oversight that may have inadvertently occurred and presents a formal request for ashirvada. Perhaps because of his age, or because of the lateness of the event, this becomes a perfunctory exercise with some banter included. Prabhakar Bhattru begins the ashirvada with a brief statement of praise for the hosts and moves swiftly into the exegetical mode. The fifteen-minute ashirvada was delivered with great dramatic variation, with shifts in tone, pace, and narrative style (including recitation, chanting, and melodic narration). As the ashirvada unfolds, it becomes evident that its intent is to provide the host family with an understanding of the cosmic underpinnings of the puja they had performed. The elucidation draws on the *Devī Māhātmya*, the most celebrated text of goddess theology and worship that is part of the *Mārkaṇḍeya Purāṇa*.[17] The *Devī Māhātmya* envisions the universe as emanating from, sustained by, and withdrawing into Durga. The text establishes the goddess as immanent and transcendent. Prabhakar Bhattru's opening question of "who Durga is" is one that the *Devī Māhātmya* tradition itself reflexively asks and answers through her various names and deeds, but he focuses on explicating the meaning of her shakti, her power. This, Prabhakar Bhattru describes as an extraordinary power, "deep" (*gambhīra*), and "esoteric" (*gauptya*).

Adhering to the progression of the *Devī Māhātmya*, Prabhakar Bhattru alludes to the first episode in it, which personifies Durga as the deep sleep, or *yoganidrā* [yoga of sleep] that has overcome Vishnu. Two *rākśasas*, Madhu and Kaitabha, taking advantage of Vishnu's slumber, assault Brahma, who is seated in a lotus that issues from Vishnu's navel. Unable to awaken Vishnu, Brahma desperately prays to Durga, who responds by leaving Vishnu's body, and Vishnu, now awake, slays the *rākśasas*. Durga is thus illusion (*māyā*), but she is also the remover of *māyā*. This initial segment of the ashirvada ends on a cautionary note: "It is not meant to be used for everyday things." The remark, however, suggested to me that the family's reasons for performing the puja were commensurate with the power being invoked.

Again, following the sequence of events in the *Devī Māhātmya*, Prabhakar Bhattru next outlines the story of Durga's victorious battle against the buffalo-demon, Mahisha. Prabhakar Bhattru uses the story to signal a theme that he develops in the rest of the ashirvada: the ethics of praying, asking, and bestowing (already hinted at in Brahma's appeal to Durga for protection and in her acquiescence). First, the gods, we are told, *must* give, even at their own peril, when they are prayed to appropriately. This inviolable obligation makes power vulnerable and fragile and subject to imbalances in the distribution of power between gods, humans, and rakshasas. Durga, in whose power it is to restore balance, is in fact bound to do so by the ethic that requires her to grant to the gods what they desire—for, they have prayed and appealed to her. Indeed, her task is not complete until they declare, "Na kiñcidavaśiṣyate [Nothing remains to be done]."

Second, just as those who are prayed to are obliged to give, those who need help are obliged to pray and please. Durga will not volunteer her help to the gods or to humans unless she is prayed to. The seeking of help is necessary for it takes two, a bestower and a supplicant, for the functioning of the universe. If the gods themselves live within this equation, how much more so is it required for humans? (Here, Prabhakar Bhattru adds something that is not said in the *Devī Māhātmya*: that the gods, in their magnanimity, secure the grace of the goddess even for those humans who neglect to pray).

Then, deviating from the *Devī Māhātmya*, which narrates the story of Durga's battle with Shumbha and Nishumbha after the Mahisha episode, Prabhakar Bhattru proceeds to the story of the rakshasa Aruna.[18] The ashirvada now emphasizes a third aspect of the ethics of asking and receiving; the question of what happens *after* a desire has been fulfilled by the gods. The demon Aruna, intoxicated by his apparent invincibility, oversteps the boon that has been granted to him when he begins to harass the world and consequently invites his destruction. Prabhakara Bhattru concludes from the Aruna story that should anybody claim to be the most powerful, there is in divine reserve a mysterious, hidden power ("one seed of poison") that God can deploy to contain unbridled and anarchic power. Humility, and remembrance of the divine source of one's empowerment, must accompany the asking, the receiving, *and* the living out of boons, a moral that implies that these are not one-time acts, but continual processes with responsibilities. The *Devī Māhātmya* portrays the gods as obeisant and full of praise for Durga even after she has fulfilled their desires. In closing, Prabhakar Bhattru likens the Durga puja to the *brahmāstra*, the most powerful of weapons, that which is given by Brahma and has no counterweapon. If the Durga puja has the effect of the *brahmāstra* on a worshipper's troubles, it is a sheltering boat (*dōṇi* in Kannada) that ensures safe passage for the worshipper across a sea of troubles.

The traditional upachara vakya (remarks on their good conduct) about the hosts marks the formal closure of the ashirvada. Using praise language, it shifts from the cosmic to the here and now—the sacred site of Sringeri, the goddess Sharada, Ganeshaiyya's family, and the puja that has just been concluded—and places the hosts in the protective realm of Durga. The upachara vakya signals to the other purohitas and elders who pronounce the definitive "*Tathāstu!* [So be it]" at the appropriate moment.

FIGURE 5.2. Prabhakara Bhattru delivering the Durga Dipa ashirvada. Leela standing in the doorway. *Photo by Baba Prasad*

FIGURE 5.3. Prabhakara Bhattru and his wife. *Photo by Leela Prasad*

The next morning I was on my way to Prabhakar Bhattru's house in Kunchebayalu to talk to him about the ashirvada he had delivered. I hoped also to gain a sense of the place of ashirvada in the broader contexts of his life as priest. With some trepidation, I peered out of the speeding autorickshaw at the first clouds of the southwest monsoon that were gathering into a thick, dark canopy, but the rains were to hold back for a few more days. Prabhakar Bhattru had just finished the morning puja at the Kanyakumari temple a few yards from his house. The house and the temple were secluded, set amidst a clearing in a thick grove. The temple especially impressed me as something out of a storybook—except, as I soon found out, that it had all the traces of daily worship. It of course quickly came alive as we took darshana of Kanyakumari, the deity, and as I heard Prabhakar Bhattru describe how the once old abandoned temple had become increasingly popular in recent years. While he downplayed his role in the restoration of the temple, I had heard the night before at the Durga puja that Prabhakar Bhattru had been instrumental in raising funds and conducting large-scale puja(s) that had popularized the temple. "He is very learned, but you will not find a more humble man," the person had said.

As Prabhakar Bhattru chewed betel nut and I sipped hot coffee (which his wife brought out within minutes of my arrival), my tape recorder sat in front of us, its small lights flickering as it recorded our voices. I asked him if he had been delivering ashirvada for many years. Light-eyed, seventy-five year-old Prabhakar Bhattru is a Chitpavan brahman (a community that traces back to Ratnagiri in Maharashtra) of the *Yajurveda* branch. "I am not a greatly learned man," he started, and I squirmed at how overly to-the-point my question had been.

> We were a poor family. My father (Ananta Bhattadevdhar) was a priest at the Kuthugodu family temple and had also cultivated a small field. My upanayana was done when I was fourteen, and he taught me some priestly duties. When I was sixteen, he passed away and we were left with a large family. Although I was the third oldest in the family, I was the one more familiar with devara puje (rituals of worship) and all that. So puja was the only source of livelihood. I therefore did not have opportunities to go out and study. I used to go here and there to learn at night. And occasionally at the matha, and on my own, I would research various grantha(s) (books) and understand them. We moved out of Kuthugodu. Gradually, I picked up on my own through study and never gave up my anuṣṭhāna (personal daily religious practice), and did the Gayatri japa[19] thrice a day. I have had the opportunity to perform the Chandi homa (fire ritual) and the Gayatri homa.

For many weeks I wondered why in response to my interview-like question about how long he had been delivering ashirvada, Prabhakar Bhattru chose to elaborate on his many years of research (*samṣodhana*) of various texts and on his personal daily religious practice (*anuṣṭhāna*). I gradually came to understand that shastric knowledge is a basic requirement for ashirvada performance. I realized that my initial question had unintentionally pegged the issue of authority, which I felt Prabhakar Bhattru had addressed by bringing up his study of texts and his everyday and professional practice. The authority to deliver an ashirvada is recognized by the community as belonging to a knowledgeable person who has the ability to speak persuasively.

I spent the morning talking to Prabhakar Bhattru about various aspects of ashirvada: who is called on to deliver it, what makes a "good" ashirvada, what sources does a ashirvada draw on? Drawing on similar conversations with many other experts and with people in the Sringeri community who form the audiences for ashirvada performances, and also drawing on my own observations of the ashirvada events I attended over the years, I have been able to construct for ashirvada, what Alan Dundes calls "oral literary criticism,"[20] a theoretical framework that builds on the interpretative and evaluative commentary on a performance tradition by performers and audiences.

Ashirvada: Continuities

Among the questions I asked and explored was whether the ashirvada tradition of Sringeri has any connections to the concept of *ashis* that is treated in the Vedas. Ashis is the necessary concluding act of a Vedic sacrifice, and many rules, depending upon the sacrifice being performed, are prescribed for its correct performance. Jan Gonda, in his detailed study of the role of prayer and blessing in Vedic ritual, says that ashis is a "*mantra* (traditional text or occasional formula) which is expected to fulfill all desires. . . . It is uttered for the benefit of the patron of a sacrifice who, it is hoped, is to profit from the rite to which it belongs, and of which it is a means of securing its fruits. If an *ashis*—in our sources as a rule the repetition of a fixed text—is invoked in accordance with the prescribed ritual, within which it is in the relevant Vedic literature always found, a supernatural result is expected to ensue so that it acquires a more or less sacramental character. Once pronounced it is real and effective by itself."[21] All the same, scholars find certain features common to Vedic ashis: a salutation to Agni, the fire god (who carries the prayer to the invoked deity), an assertion of the power of the ashis to strengthen the deity and to fulfill the desires of the worshipper, and the requirement that the ritual be performed correctly to make the ashis effective.[22]

In Sringeri, however, despite similarities between Vedic ashis and the ashirvada tradition, no conscious connection was made between the two. At most, since I asked explicitly, Sesha Bhattru said that one could think of the ashirvada tradition as a "smarta prayoga" (practice) of the Rigvedic ashis. "In the Rig Veda," he explained, "after the brahmans have been fed, they must give their ashirvada, and only then is the purpose of ritual considered complete. The utterance of the ashis by the brahmans also gives the host peace of mind." He added that a more plausible continuity with the past could be found in the "sampradaya of *this* place, going back maybe eight hundred years."

Others also pointed to the tradition of upachara vakya that is publicly recited during celebrations organized by the matha and the community,

FIGURE 5.4. Sesha Bhattru delivering an ashirvada. *Photo by S. Chandramouli*

such as the chariot festival at the Sharada temple during February-March in which the goddess rides out into the streets of Sringeri in a bedecked chariot. Befitting the festivity is a grand enactment of an invitation delivered in formal courtly-style Kannada. The public procession begins with the guru going to the Durga temple and performing the puja and arati. Meanwhile, the smaller image of the goddess that is reserved for taking out in processions (utsava murti) is made ready and installed in the chariot. Then arati to this image is performed by priests, and then, in an elaborate ritual, the Sringeri mahajana gather to collectively invite the guru who is in the main temple to join the procession. The sampradaya is that the guru does not see the deity being seated in the chariot. Many in the community savor the rhythm and stylized idiom of the courtly invitation known as the ahvana[23] that is announced by the mahajana.

I was asked to make sure I did not miss recording this invitation, especially as recited by S. K. Ramaswamy, who in 2004 was in his early nineties and had retired as principal of the Sanskrit college. Soon I found myself enjoying the invitation's magnanimous phrasing and its grandeur as I listened to S. K. Ramaswamy in his house, having caught him just before he left for his brisk evening walk "that ends in a chat with friends round the corner" as he put it. The invitation began by locating the present guru in the guru parampara (guru lineage) of Sringeri. Then Durga is praised in lavish language as "the most auspicious one who takes many forms (Kali, Durga, Saraswati), the one who protects all devotees and living beings and dispels fear." She is described as being seated on the procession chariot "at this most appropriate moment (sumuhurta)" amid Vedic chants and music and appearing to have verily manifested herself. Into such a presence the invitation on behalf of Sringeri's community requests the guru to join the procession and bless the event. The invitation can be understood as an enactment of "protocol" by the mahajana who "invite" the guru (even though the function is sponsored by the matha). After S. K. Ramaswamy finished reciting the invitation, he added, "I'm old now, but in the presence of an enthusiastic crowd there is an excitement in the delivery." Although the invitation (ahvana) does not have the exegetical intent of the ashirvada, and they are two distinct "cultural performances," to use Milton Singer's term,[24] they are part of an environment of discourse that is celebratory, idealized, and normative. In this environment one finds other forms of honorific expression such as the letter of blessing or benediction (ashirvada patrike) sent by the matha to its patrons with a gift.[25]

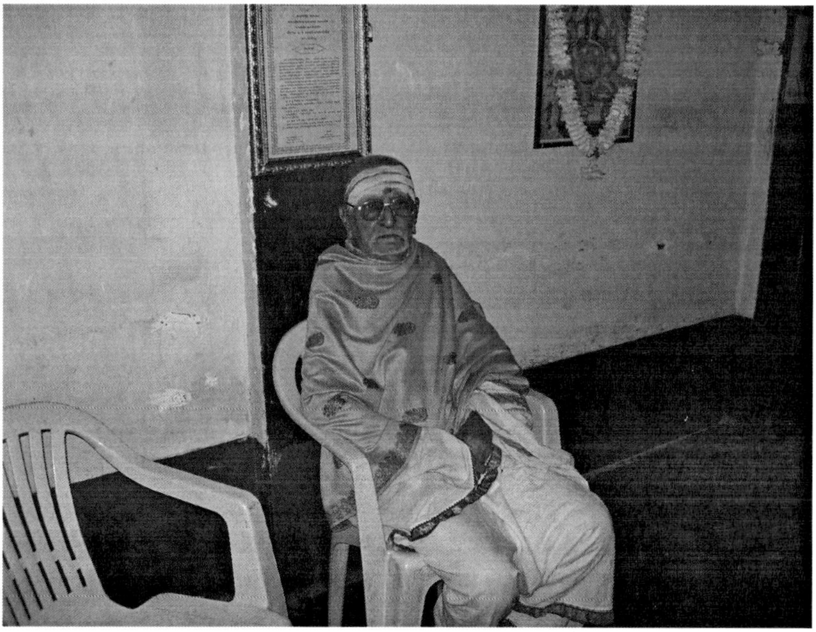

FIGURE 5.5. S. K. Ramaswamy in his house. *Photo by S. Shankar*

The Moral Poetics of Ashirvada

An ashirvada performance typically takes place after the first set of guests (including the purohitas) has finished the festive meal. The performance includes the following acts: the family's namaskaras to the purohitas as the purohitas sprinkle mantrakshate on the family reciting mantras (from the Vedas in brahman homes and from the Puranas and the *Bhagavad Gītā* in nonbrahman homes), the host's "apology" for unintended shortcomings in hospitality and a request for ashirvada, the upachara vakya (praise statement for the hosts and the event), the exegetical narrative itself, and finally the blessing (the actual ashirvada). Some variations occur in this broad structure to accommodate circumstances and the preferences of hosts and purohitas, although I have never seen the mantras and the namaskaras deferred. For instance, in the Durga dipa ashirvada, owing to the lateness of the hour, Ganeshaiyya's statement of apology and request was minimal, and Prabhakara Bhattru deferred most of the upachara vakya to the end when he combined it with the blessing. When it is said expansively, the host statement is something like this: "We have invited you and possibly caused you inconvenience. If there were shortcomings in our hospitality or in the performance of the ritual, we ask you to forgive us. We hope you are satisfied and pleased despite our failings. We seek the blessings of the learned elders and purohitas who have gathered here today."[26]

Over several months I spoke to various people about the ashirvada tradition.[27] As the views of scholars and participants unfolded, it was exciting to discover a well-developed poetics of ashirvada that inspires the comment: "avaru tumba channāge hēḷuttāre! (He says it [the ashirvada] very well indeed)." One of the first things I had to correct myself in, as I began to observe various ashirvadas, is that it is not always the priest who has conducted the ritual who is asked to speak, nor is it the eldest male among those gathered, but as Prabhakara Bhattru said, "somebody who has both the knowledge and *vāk cāturya* (verbal skill)."[28] The central question that the Sringeri metacommentary on ashirvada asks and answers is: What is a "good" ashirvada, and what characterizes the capability of a competent ashirvada speaker?[29]

Vinayaka Udupa, the current dharmadhikari of the matha who had taught the Puranas at the matha's Sanskrit school for thirty years, is considered an accomplished ashirvada speaker. During my conversation with him in his house in Mangar, just outside Sringeri, he pointed out that the mantras, far from being rote, are crucial to the ashirvada. The matha school's curriculum includes training in prayoga (application), which teaches ashirvada mantras for ritual occasions. These mantras are gathered from various sources: Some are culled from the Vedas and remain standard no matter the ritual or the hosts, others vary with the ritual event being performed, and some others are specific to the host family's Vedic affiliation. Sesha Bhattru, a noted *Alaṅkāra śāstra* ("science of the figures of speech") scholar and accomplished ashirvada speaker, who retired after teaching Sanskrit in the Girls High School for thirty-four years, explained, "When a Rigvedi purohita visits a Yajurvedi home, unless he is really competent, he will not be able to deliver the ashirvada because the mantras will have to come from the *Yajurveda*." However, Vinayaka Udupa added, "If a purohita trained in the Veda of the host family is not available, then a Rigvedi purohita can perform the ashirvada. In a Rigvedi home only a Rigvedi purohita can perform the ashirvada." To a lay observer many of these conditionalities are not obvious. The subtle proprieties are tactfully observed among purohitas and learned members when calling on a speaker to deliver the ashirvada.

Local scholars argue that Vedic mantras—considered permanent and infallible—preface the ashirvada, giving it sanctity and setting it apart from "ordinary speech" that registers the fluctuations and ambiguities of daily life. The ashirvada becomes empowered to make the ritual event accomplish its goals. "Even if you have not done the ritual perfectly, the ashirvada helps to secure the fruit (phala)," said Vinayaka Udupa. Sesha Bhattru elaborated, "'You have performed this karma without any faults, following the procedure stipulated in the shastras. From this, you will be sure to benefit.' Only when such a statement comes from the purohitas, does the host feel satisfied. The ashirvada is a mirror image (pratirūpa) of that statement."

As I dwelt on the "texts" of many upachara vakyas and statements of blessing, which are at many times combined, it became evident that the ashirvada does not concern itself primarily with how the ritual event was actually performed or with how the actual hospitalities were offered by the hosts. Describing occasions when a host who is a nonpracticer requests the purohita to perform on his behalf actions that the host should perform, Sesha Bhattru said, "However inept the performance of a ritual may have been, it should not affect how one delivers the ashirvada. Mistakes in ritual performance are brought to the attention of the host later, privately, if at all."[30] Speaking of ashirvadas at weddings, S. K. Ramaswamy noted that since contemporary marriage alliances and styles of ceremonies vary widely, and different members of the family bring diverging expectations to the marriage, it is improper for the upachara vakya to favor any one perspective.

S. K. Ramaswamy added, "Therefore, I would be inclined to say, 'You are very fortunate people. You have chosen a fitting groom for your daughter and conducted this auspicious event in a propitious muhurta, following the shastras. May the newly married couple live happily with unbroken love and trust forever along with their family, under the full grace of the goddess Sharada, mother of the universe, and of the Jagadguru, Shri Shankaracarya—this is the blessing of the mahajana.'" Ramaswamy provided another example to illustrate more emphatically the generalized moral tenor of the event: "You have performed this event with sadhana (discipline), shraddhe (faith), and bhakti (devotion). May Narayana (Vishnu), who is fond of such karmas (rituals), become pleased with this and remove all obstacles to your achieving your desires and bestow upon you lifelong auspiciousness and the best of worlds. May the married couple live as if they were in brahmaloka (the world of Brahma) without earthly troubles. May the rest of you too be blessed with long life, good health, prosperity, and fame for all time."

Such aloofness from verisimilitude is what allows ashirvada speeches to serve not as realistic annotations of conduct but as idealized ones, which emphasize the "ought" over the "is." The ashirvada's injunctiveness is based on abstraction. The disinclination to comment in particular terms on the enacted ritual also reveals further that, in the ashirvada tradition, such an engagement with situational detail would be considered a breach of propriety from the point of view of the poetics of the tradition.

However, situational detail is not omitted altogether. The delineation of a symbolically resonant world is not entirely unresponsive to the social and material particularities of the host families or to the influence of different audiences. In addition to knowing what mantras to recite when, given a family's Vedic identity, ashirvada speakers maintain a subtle and important balance between contingencies they are aware of and the moral recommendations they make—but how they perceive and express this balance depends largely on individual talent. I had not noticed until it was brought to my attention that the ashirvada delivered at an upanayana ceremony for a speech-impaired young boy did not dwell on the importance of articulating the Gayatri mantra correctly, a point that is quite elaborately made at other upanayana events. This ashirvada focused, instead, on "clarity of intention" and on the "necessity of daily practice" of the sandhyavandana that is expected of a boy for whom the upanayana had been conducted. The purohita who had delivered the ashirvada said, "By going on about 'articulation,' (uccāraṇe, in Kannada) I would have hurt the feelings of the parents and the boy and brought unnecessary public attention to their situation. It would not have been right on my part, so I concentrated on other aspects of the life of a brahmachari (celibate bachelor)." A younger purohita, in training, said, "If you know about any strife in the family, such as disagreement between brothers, you could gently address this in very general terms of 'family harmony' that is important to maintain and so on." Others I spoke to were less sure that the ashirvada was an appropriate forum for such moralization.

Some speakers noted that an interested audience—which never verbally expresses its engagement—makes the difference between "an inspired ashirvada" and a jaded one. Mahabala Bhattru, an experienced priest and ashirvada speaker, whose ashirvada I had heard at an upanayana, said that "occasionally there are gatherings where guests simply want to get on with other things and convey the sense 'let-the-priest-blab-on-while-I-go-finish-lunch' or something—such settings obviously see very quick ashirvada explanations. So there *are* times when just the mantras and the blessing are delivered; the *speech* is not performed at all." In sum, the ashirvada is an exercise in articulating the right fit between particularization and generalization in order to maximize normative effect.

Many scholars concurred that the upachara vakya had to be kept to the minimum, especially when it concerned life-cycle rites that are considered obligatory such as shraaddha for deceased parents and upanayana for one's son. One scholar, overhearing my ambling conversation about ashirvada with a young priest, remarked sharply, "These are *duties;* what is there to praise the host for? Such praise should be limited to events in which hosts make large donations or feed hundreds of people without the shastras requiring them to do so. That's all there is to it." Indeed, as Sesha Bhattru more humorously put it, "One shouldn't make statements like 'The jilēbi (a popular deep fried sweet) you made today was really good' and forget that it is the *ritual event* (kārya) that has to be praised: what is its history, its philosophical significance, the phala (result), and the procedures relevant to it. The host can be praised, but the praise has to be within limits."

Giridhara Shastry voiced a view shared by nearly everybody I spoke with in Sringeri when he said that competent speakers are "those who know Sanskrit, who know the shastra, and have *a natural fluency in elaborating the significance of that event, its uniqueness.* There are some who are not pandits of the shastra, but know the mantras well. They dwell on the significance of the mantras that are recited, and do not delve into the shastric treatment of the subject at hand (marriage, naming, and so on)." Mentioning the names of a past generation, notably Ramachandra Bhattru's paternal uncle, Samaka Ganesha Shastry, he said, "When it is well done, an ashirvada is considered an *education.*" The analogy to education was quite specifically echoed by Vijaya Krishnamurthy. She compared a good ashirvada speaker to a "good teacher in a school"; somebody who enunciates clearly (biḍsi biḍsi heḷuttāre), and explains concepts in simple and clear language (viṣayagaḷanna saraḷavāgi heḷuttāre). "The best ashirvadas succeed in helping listeners *relate* to the content," she added, comparing the styles of local speakers.

In practice, Giridhara Shastry observed, "When the speech is being given by a speaker known for his scholarship, then, even if his *oratorical skills* are not that impressive, people still pay attention to his words with the intention of learning from him." Yet, those who deliver and listen to ashirvadas agree that melodic and intonational variations make the ashirvada an aesthetically satisfying experience, an aspect that is crucial to the effectiveness of the ashirvada. Sesha Bhattru commented that even the mantras that precede the ashirvada can help set the melodic tone for the ashirvada exegesis: "The larger the assembly of purohitas, the more beautiful an ashirvada can be to hear. In such cases, we make two groups, and divide the mantras; one group recites one line and the other another line, the recitation varying according to pitch, mandra (low pitch), madhyama tāra (middle pitch), and so on."

In Mahabala Bhattru's view, a capacity to elicit empathy and a commitment to practice makes a good ashirvada speaker a mārga dāyaka, an exemplar. According to Vinayaka Udupa, "Only those people who have studied the Vedas and maintain anuṣṭhāna (personal religious practice)] should deliver an ashirvada, just as only a disciplined vaidya (traditional doctor) should administer medicine." Although strictly speaking, the ashirvada is addressed to the hosts, its "message" reaches everyone present. In Prabhakar Bhattru's words, the ashirvada is like a full-blossomed Sampige (Champaka) tree, whose flowers can perhaps be restricted to some people, but its fragrance cannot. While, of course, Sringeri residents bring different levels of engagement to an ashirvada performance, and take away different things from it, one woman said, the explanation makes the practice "meaningful and beautiful," so much so that the desire to continue traditions is cultivated through exposure to such performances.

Speaking to a fourteen-year-old girl in 2004, and watching children attentively listen to what appears as fairly serious moralism, it seems that the ashirvada is both "storytime" entertainment and also a forum for explicit learning about traditions. To quote Tejaswini, Ramachandra Bhattru's school-age daughter, "It's kind of nice (ondu taraha chanda)] to know why we do something." In the moral poetics of ashirvada, thus, the content of an ashirvada and its delivery are as important as the "character" of the person who delivers it, although such judgments are left to "tacit knowledge." Moral persuasiveness is intimately tied to the art and the act of narration and to the actor.

Proficient ashirvada speakers are adept at weaving illustrative stories from various sources into the exegesis—but an unwavering principle is that these stories must be precisely *appropriate* to the context. Often, stories from the Puranas or the epics animate in the ashirvada the normative idiom of the Dharmashastras, although sometimes, as in the ashirvada of a Rudra homa (worship of a form of Shiva) that I attended, stories are substituted by a network of allusions that spans across various Hindu sacred literatures. Typically, the speaker tries to draw out the essence of the benefits of performing the ritual by tracing its adrishtha effects. (Illustrative examples, however, must remain within a circumscribing framework.) According to Vinayaka Udupa, whatever the examples, "They have to be *100 percent* relevant and natural to the context." It is misleading to assume, as I initially had, that a well-done ashirvada explicitly displays its references to literature. On the contrary, it carries its locatedness in literature in a subtle way through allusion, by being conceptually or thematically synchronized with ideas expressed across various scriptural domains. To illustrate, the Durga dipa ashirvada that Prabhakar Bhattru delivered was networked to the many stories in the Upanishads, the Puranas, and the epics that recount how powers that result from penance may be misused to upset dharmic equilibrium.[31] Although most listeners are unable to trace immediately all allusions made in an ashirvada to their textual sources, it is not uncommon for individuals to ask a speaker later about the textual location for an allusion. Innovation in the ashirvada tradition is generally not conceptual innovation; instead, the innovation is pressed into the service of a well-endorsed moral vision that provides the ashirvada its normative force.

Mahabala Bhattru qualified that mundane or worldly (laukika) examples are best kept minimal because "they do not really carry the weight that dharmic examples do," by which he meant examples from Sanskrit sources. "After all," Nagabhushana Rao, in whose house I had been chatting with Mahabala Bhattru the day after we attended an upanayana at which Mahabala Bhattru had delivered the ashirvada, said, "this is an occasion for speech that should be respected." Despite his fluency in English, Mahabala Bhattru added that he did not like to admit "even one English word into the ashirvada, which should be entirely in Kannada, with maybe some Sanskrit."

Such perspectives indexed the importance of linguistic appropriateness in the poetics of ashirvada.

Stylistically, brevity is considered crucial for a persuasive ashirvada. Practical considerations make it necessary to keep the speech "short and sweet," given that often ashirvadas take place immediately after the first batch of guests has eaten and that hosts and volunteers (who are quite tired from the activities and preparations) will not have had their meals yet. But brevity is also a stylistic requirement for a successful ashirvada. "Long ashirvadas," said S. K. Ramaswamy, "will make guests want to read the newspaper or go about sundry jobs, just as most of us do when politicians make long speeches which are written by other people." The older generation of ashirvada speakers I spoke to strongly disapproved of ashirvadas that expansively talked about "dharmic matters," but a few of the younger priests felt such occasions were ideal opportunities to conduct quick tutorials on dharma. In one ashirvada that I attended a speaker in his mid-twenties enthusiastically spent thirty-five minutes explaining "why Hinduism is a sanatana dharma (eternal religion)" and comparing it to other religious traditions before briefly dwelling on the ritual that had been conducted. When I later talked to him about ashirvada, I learned that although he was training as a Rigvedic purohita, his sources for that ashirvada were primarily pamphlets issued by twentieth-century religious orders whose literature responded mostly to colonial critiques of Hinduism. Although he did not attribute his own style of ashirvada to political influences, he wondered whether contemporary interest in ashirvada among the younger generation is a renewal stimulated by right-wing political organizations.[32]

The value placed on appropriateness came home to me vividly on one occasion when I attended what was later described to me as a "failed" ashirvada. The customary ashirvada was performed after the ceremonial lunch at the death anniversary (shraaddha) of a renowned scholar, whom I shall call "Hiri Shastry." A scholar, probably in his mid-forties, was called on by other well-reputed, elderly scholars in the gathering to deliver the ashirvada on account of his having been a former student of Hiri Shastry and a respected faculty member in the matha's Sanskrit school. In a room that was packed with Hiri Shastry's family, who now lived outside but had grown up in Sringeri, and with many townspeople who had been close to Hiri Shastry, the speaker began the ashirvada after the chatter had subsided, and all attention turned to him.

The speaker began loftily by praising the hosts for their hospitality, but a little too explicitly added, "you have also given handsome dakshine (gifts of money) to the brahmans who have come today." A few people embarrassedly laughed. Then he traced the family history of Hiri Shastry, but made a glaring error about the family's history that even I, an outsider, recognized. At this point—in the only time in dozens of ashirvadas I have attended—several members of the audience interjected to correct him. Making the correction, the speaker then proceeded to outline the symbolic significance of the shraaddha ritual. However, as he seemed to be about to move on from the topic of "ancestors" (pitṛ) to another topic, one of the older scholars in the audience interrupted—again, the only time I have seen this happen—and recited an illustrative Sanskrit shloka, ending it with "antaha heḷuttāre (so they say)." The intervention conveyed that the speaker had not utilized an appropriate shastric verse that would have made the point *in shastric terms*, not merely in terms of the speaker's opinion. Also, the phrase "antaha heḷuttāre" came across as loaded: the "they" in *so they say* may have meant the "past" in the sense of the formulaic phrase conventionally used in ashirvada speaking to bring the weight of the past into the present (and this speaker had omitted the phrase entirely); the "they" also may have been a reference to other ashirvada speakers who treat that same point differently (using the illustrative shloka, for instance); finally, the "they" may have meant the sages who "authored" the shastra from which the shloka was drawn. On the whole, however, the interruption had the effect of a corrective. But the signal came to me that the ashirvada had really failed when, even as the speaker was winding up, a group of elders prematurely uttered *tathāstu*, the traditional closure of an ashirvada, bringing the ashirvada to a hasty conclusion.

After the ashirvada was over, a jaunty discussion about it immediately ensued. A very well-respected scholar and elderly colleague of Hiri Shastry said, laughing, "Oh, when you said, 'Many of the people of his age are *still* here' I thought you were going to send us to join him up there!" The ashirvada speaker had probably intended "The praise I am giving can be verified by people of his age who are here in this audience," but an inappropriate choice of words had created a tactless cultural subtext (referring to the *ripe* old age of Hiri Shastry's contemporaries). The speaker's defensive response, "Just because I said so, does it mean it will happen?" was washed away in the general laughter in the already dispersing group. In retrospect, a misaligned and poor aesthetic sense, factual errors, and a marked paucity of shastric sources had frittered away the moral potential of the ashirvada.

But sources cannot be used indiscriminately. Ramaswamy was emphatic that an ashirvada cannot become an occasion for general storytelling: "I refuse to elaborate on such things (digressions). When giving an ashirvada for Rama Navami,[33] it is inappropriate to go on about Kumbhakarna's sleep or about Rama's battle against Ravana. Instead, the ashirvada should focus on subjects like Rama's character, his obedience to his father, the love between Rama and Sita, how brothers should relate, or the devotion of Hanuman." While other Ramayana tellings may interpret the epic story differently, Ramaswamy's point was that an ashirvada's purpose was to synthesize ideals, not merely present interesting plots or intrigue, and that these ideals must emerge from the ritual event in question. And thus it is that Sesha Bhattru's memorable summation finds itself making the title of this chapter: "One's speech must stay within the quadrangle of that ritual, within the courtyard of dharma. The ashirvada is not a political speech to be shouted out from the village square."

Dramaturgical Propriety (Auchitya) in Sanskrit Poetics

The poetics of ashirvada calls for the harmonization of the moral and the aesthetic, a condition possible through the observance of propriety. In this, ashirvada finds itself in remarkable conversation with the notion of dramatic propriety (auchitya), developed about a thousand years ago in Sanskrit poetics. Understood as the fitting adaptation of poetic means to the poetic end, the concept of auchitya was systematized by the eleventh-century literary critic Kshemendra in his *Aucityavicāra carca* (Inquiry into deliberations on propriety).

To understand the place of auchitya in Sanskrit literary theory, it is necessary to briefly review the long and complex debate regarding what element of poetry most significantly evokes poetic emotion or rasa (lit. "juice," essence). Rasa is understood as distilled aesthetic emotion that arises when "feelings" are depersonalized and transcend their historical contexts. Sanskrit poeticians singled out eight stable feelings (sthāyibhāva) from the multitude of human feelings (love, joy, grief, anger, fear, energy, disgust, and wonder) for the dramatic representation of life. Through a rigorously specified compositional process (that different poetic theories describe differently), these feelings are metamorphosed into corresponding dominant moods or emotions (rasas), namely, the erotic (śṛṅgāra), the comic (hāsya), the tragic (karuṇa), the furious (raudra), the fearsome (bhayānaka), the heroic (vīra), the disgusting (bībhatsā), and the wondrous (adbhuta) respectively. Later scholars like Anandavardhana add a ninth rasa, śānta rasa (peace).[34]

The rasa becomes "an imaginative system of relations"[35] produced by the harmonious coming together of enabling constituent elements: the preconditions (vibhāvas), the consequent emotions (anubhāvas), and the transitory emotions (vyabhicāribhāvas). The preconditions of evoking rasa can include scene, background, characterization—factors that abet but do not of themselves cause the dominant emotion. The consequent emotions are signs that suggest the dominant emotion—sighs and tears signifying grief, for instance. Transitory emotions, while passing, highlight the dominant emotion and help to sustain it, as when appreciation of a flower in full blossom (i.e., of beauty) supports the mood of love.[36] But, as Ramanujan clarifies, "The *rasa* and all its constituents are not in an effect-cause relationship. . . . Nor is the relationship one of experience and memory. *Rasa* comes into being with the *experiencing*" (emphasis mine).[37]

Historians of Sanskrit poetics distinguish four schools of criticism between the eighth century CE and the fifteenth century CE. The Alaṅkāra school argued that figures of speech (alaṅkāras) constitute the central feature of poetry that primarily evokes rasa, while the Rīti school considered style, or the arrangement of words, to be the crucial element of poetry. The school that is historically prominent because it integrated the "experience" of poetry with its "ornamentation" in a unified theory of poetics is called the Rasa-dhvani school. It argued that the soul of poetry is in its power of suggestion (dhvani). Thus, while undisputedly the poetic end was the evocation of rasa, the aesthetic experience of emotion, the question of how rasa could be evoked was debated for centuries.[38] While Sanskrit critics differed on the importance to be assigned to auchitya or propriety in relation to other criteria in evaluating a poetic work, they agreed that auchitya was a regulatory principle that influenced the overall poetic merit of a work of art.[39]

Kshemendra contributed to this debate by arguing that only when every feature of artistic representation—figurative speech, style, intent, and so on—is deployed in the manner most befitting the whole, can a work of art convey rasa. While Kshemendra was the first to devote an entire treatise to the subject of propriety in poetic representation, he developed the notion from the epochal *Dhvanyāloka* (Light on poetic suggestion) by Anandavardhana, an acclaimed critic of ninth-century Kashmir. Centuries before Kshemendra systematized the concept of auchitya, Bharata's *Nāṭyaśāstra* had spelt out in astonishing detail the modes of production, speech, gesture, music, dress, ornamentation, makeup, and so on that were appropriate for specific kinds of dramatic representation. For example, in the section on "Modes of Address and Intonation," Bharata stipulates terms of address, differentiating speakers and addressees on the basis of caste, class, rank, age, and gender. He recommends, "By a superior woman, a handmaid is to be accosted with the word 'Hey child.' . . . Brahmins may address the kings at their pleasure, by their names. This should be tolerated, for the brahmins are to be adored by the kings. . . . The term *lady* should be applied to the chief queen by her servants as well as by the king. The remaining [wives of the king] may be addressed [simply] as 'madam.'" Bharata also prescribes naming conventions to be observed for dramatic characters: "To warriors should be given names indicating much valour. . . . Hand-maids should be given the names of various flowers. . . . To superior persons should be given names of deep significance so that their deeds may be in harmony with such names."[40]

The rasa-prayoga (elicitation of rasa) of each section assiduously reiterates that improper representation constitutes the most serious literary flaw; the entire *Nāṭyaśāstra*, can in fact, at one level, be regarded as having engendered the idea of compatibility of form and content in artistic representation—although Bharata did not explicitly employ the term *auchitya*. In fact, the first explicit reference to auchitya may be traced to the early eighth century, in the prologue for the play *Rāmābhyudaya* by King Yashovarman of the north Indian province of Kanauj.[41] Yashovarman refers to two kinds of propriety: that of expression ("speech which is in accord with the nature and rank of the characters"), and that of rasa ("delineation of characters in their proper moods with an eye to developing the Rasa in the proper place").[42] The first writer on poetics to insist on appropriateness as a critical consideration in literary composition was Rudrata (a near contemporary of Anandavardhana) in his *Kāvyālaṅkāra* (Poetic figures of speech; CE 880).[43] Rudrata—like Bharata—cautioned that figurative speech could be successfully introduced into a work of art only after its appropriateness to the theme had been evaluated and that action, appearance, and speech, in a literary work must necessarily be adapted to the country, caste, class, wealth, age, and position of the characters being depicted. Rudrata defined a set of styles (rīti) of composition based on the degree of compounding and identified these styles as being most appropriate to particular rasas. Auchitya, in Rudrata's view, was the appropriateness of the style employed in the poem to its content.[44]

Under the influence of the *Dhvanyāloka* of Anandavardhana and the influential dhvani school, the concept of auchitya became fully integrated into the critical vocabulary of Sanskrit poetics. According to Anandavardhana, rasa, the supreme goal of poetry, can never be directly expressed but can only be evoked through dhvani, suggestion. The *Dhvanyāloka* argues that a work of art that succeeds in suggesting rasa presupposes that all the various formal elements have been delineated and combined in the most appropriate manner, be it through sound, words, collocation, or theme. In Anandavardhana's words, "If one describes the energy or the life of a god or the like as belonging to a mere human, or that of a mere human as belonging to a god, the emotion will be inappropriate. For example, in a passage dealing with a king who is a mere human, if one describes activities in which he leaps across the seven seas, one's description, even if beautiful in itself, will, as a rule, be without *rasa* and tasteless. The reason for this would be its inappropriateness."[45]

Critiquing what he felt was the inflated characterization of King Satavahana in the *Mahabharata*, Anandavardhana says:

> We do not say that descriptions of the extraordinary power of kings are inappropriate; rather, that in a narrative which has been invented and is based on purely human characters, matters that are appropriate to gods are unfitting. If the character in a narrative is partly divine and partly human, there is no contradiction in introducing matters appropriate to both, as in the narrative of Pāṇḍu and his sons [the Pandavas of the *Mahabharata*]. As for the heroic deeds traditionally ascribed to Sātavāhana and others like him, if we treat of their deeds within the traditional limits, our description will be proper. But anything other than that . . . will be improper. The heart of the matter may be put thus: "For the spoiling of *rasa*, there is no cause other than impropriety. On the other hand, composing a work within recognized proprieties is the very Upanishad [that is, essence] of *rasa*."[46]

Thus by the time Kshemendra wrote the *Aucitya vicāra carca*, poetic propriety had been acknowledged as indispensable to composition, although its place had been perceived as secondary to the principal means of eliciting rasa. Kshemendra's treatise, regarded by modern Sanskrit critics as belonging to that genre of critical works composed for the training of a poet, is indeed a practical guide, and begins by rhetorically asking whether there is any point in critically assessing the decorative aspects and other merits of a poem in which auchitya, the very soul of poetry, is indiscernible.[47] Kshemendra categorically states that that it is auchitya, and not style, imagery, or suggestion that is the life element of rasa (rasa jīvitabhūta) and foundational to aesthetic pleasure (camatkāra). Referring to numerous examples drawn from Sanskrit literature to illustrate both the observance and the breach of literary proprieties, Kshemendra discusses twenty-seven places in a poetic work where it is essential to observe propriety. Every single feature of poetic representation—prosody, syntax, diction, tense, figurative speech, sentiment, circumstance, intent, social status of characters, time (kāla) and place (deśa) of poetic action, every possible feature—derives its merit in an artistic work, Kshemendra argued, only by being appropriately deployed and being well-aligned to each other. As Abhinavagupta had posited, "One cannot indiscreetly use the word, '*aucitya*' by itself; *aucitya* is un-understandable without something else in relation to which things are uchita [appropriate]. *Auchitya* is a relation, and that to which things are or should be in that relation must first be grasped."[48] For Kshemendra, auchitya is no longer a criterion to be adhered to by a poet; it has become the "abiding life of poetry, full of flavour."[49]

Sanskrit literary discourse on propriety reminds us that the aesthetic order is grounded in a social order, and that the effectiveness of, and the play within, a composition is accomplished by establishing consonant correspondences between the literary and the social. Thus the social "text" is replete with denotative and connotative references to conventions (the wearing of an anklet, for example), cultural symbolism (a swan, for instance), "religious" acts (a pilgrimage to Varanasi), and so on. The reader's understanding and enjoyment of the literary text is dependent on knowing and recognizing the subtexted social world, an idea that becomes crucial in the next chapter as we try to understand how stories carry moral meaning. Without further simplifying the highly complex literary theories of early and medieval India, I wish to make the point that literary vision was in fact quite thoroughly a literary-social vision, much like the ashirvada tradition that unites the aesthetic and the moral in a single framework. From the conversationally derived oral poetics of ashirvada, it is clear that appropriateness, auchitya—in choice of speaker, idiom of delivery, selection and range of illustrations, content and length of the ashirvada exegesis—is the overall criterion that defines an ethically persuasive and aesthetically pleasing ashirvada. This view is highlighted by phrases such as ucitavāgira bēku (should be fitting) sērira bēku (should be in harmony). As Ramanujan aptly observes, "in Indian traditions, whether they be legal, medical, literary or whatever, we have 'context-sensitive' multiple systems" that are "elicited appropriately in well-defined contexts" and so "explanations are not judged by standards of consistency but of fit [aucitya]."[50] Thus, in the failed ashirvada delivered at Hiri Shastry's death anniversary, one could say that a number of inappropriate words and details had not only wasted the ashirvada's moral intent but had also resulted in rasābhāsa (clash of rasas).

Interestingly, in Western poetics, decorum, as a poetic principle, has enjoyed a distinguished career from classical antiquity to the eighteenth century. Emerging as a critical aspect of genre criticism, but also merging ethics and aesthetics, auchitya is comparable to conceptualizations of decorum in Western poetics.[51] For Aristotle and Cicero decorum was a governing principle in literary composition. It was necessary that oratorical genre, occasion and circumstances, subject matter, diction, and style be most fittingly aligned to one another for ethically grounded persuasive oratory.[52] Decorum is at the core of Horatian poetics (*Ars Poetica*) also, which aimed principally to achieve verisimilitude in artistic representation. Thus, for Horace, decorum guided everything from the choice of genre, which had to be appropriate to the capacities of the poet, to diction, dramatic characterization, meter, poetic invention, and the intended effect. Horace argued that there must be unity and harmony—a perfect fit—between content and form, between parts and the whole, between linguistic innovation and traditional usage, between scene and sentiment, and so on.[53] These ideas had a lasting impact, and in seventeenth-century England found expression in writers like Milton. According to Milton, poetics is "that sublime art" (beyond prosody)—illustrated best by Aristotle, Horace, and Italian commentators like Castelvetro, Tasso, and Mazzoni—that teaches a poet the laws for composing a "true" epic, drama, or lyric, or satire. But it also teaches the poet decorum, "which is the grand master piece to observe."[54] Wesley Trimpi makes a point about the notion of decorum that highlights the shared focus of both "decorum" and auchitya:

> Decorum is an activity rather than a set of specific characteristics of style or content to be discovered, preserved, and reproduced. It is a fluid corrective process which must achieve and maintain instant by instant, the delicate balance between the formal, cognitive, and judicative intentions of literary discourse. . . . As soon as they reduce it to a doctrine concerning either a given kind of subject or a given kind of style or a fixed relation of the one to the other, decorum ceases to exist, because its activity is a continuous negotiation between the two.[55]

The connections that ashirvada participants make between a literary-social aesthetic and a moral aesthetic argue that these are not hermetically bounded from one another and encourage one to see dialogue between Sanskrit poetics and the poetics of ashirvada.[56] However, they raise questions about possibly differing poetic goals. If, in Sanskrit poetics, propriety, according to Kshemendra, is the principal means to evoke the experience of rasa, the ultimate goal of poetry, what analogous experience is sought by the principle of appropriateness in the ashirvada tradition? In rasa/auchitya terms, it seems that the poetics of ashirvada, in demanding that various poetic and extrapoetic elements be appropriately chosen and aligned in the delivery of an ashirvada, also seeks to create a "dominant mood." Could we understand this mood as a "moral mood" that stirs in listeners and viewers a dharma-bhakti, devotion to a dharmic way of life? If so, the structure of the ashirvada performance lends itself to the articulation of this feeling, with its emphasis on the largely depersonalized speech, the movement between the particular and the general, the elevated moral idiom, the visual and sensory impact of the ritual background, and the occurrence of the ashirvada at the end of a dharmic event. In the words of Vasanthi, Nagabhushana Rao's wife, whom I accompanied to a puja and an ashirvada, "When we listen to ashirvada, we feel motivated to continue practices (māḍa bēku anusatte). One gets peace of mind (nemmadi)." Her view represented the popularly expressed opinion that experiencing a good ashirvada performances sparks the desire to continue dharmic traditions. At an ashirvada event one goes through the experience of dharma-bhakti. And yet, one must also ask, surely everybody does not respond in the same way to ashirvada, given that, while most people are attentive, some are bored, some are distracted, and some others are just not interested?

This question takes us to another interesting parallel between Sanskrit and ashirvada poetics: What repertoires of knowledge (conditioned by gender, age, status, and so on) must one possess—and in what social domains—to be endowed with the authority to assess appropriateness in everyday conduct? Sanskrit critics believed that dramatic propriety could be evaluated only by a sahridaya ("like-hearted"), a rasika, one with a "cultivated" literary sensibility. Abhinavagupta, a leading critic of the tenth century, defined a sahridaya as a connoisseur who "participates in the consensus of minds and . . . who has perceived the natural appropriateness of what is represented. His mind has become lucidly receptive like a mirror, through effort and constant practice of poetry."[57] Drawing from the Vaishnava view on bhakti-rasa (aesthetic emotion of devotion), one can say that the sahridaya at an ashirvada is akin to both the literary critic as well as the bhakta, the devotee.[58] Interestingly, on a note of closure to this preliminary exploration, while Sanskrit critics were able to specify the process of rendering appropriate a poetic impropriety, and there was an instructive debate on rasābhāsa (inharmonious rasa) in kāvya (poetry), the essentially performative nature of ashirvada makes it harder to implement "reparation" to an ashirvada that has been performed (without it sliding into a failed one, as happened on Hiri Shastry's death anniversary).

6 *Edifying Lives, Discerning Proprieties*

Conversational Stories and Moral Being

"Who? Papanaiyya, the freedom fighter?"[1] Ramachandra Bhattru asked, when I mentioned to him a name I had often encountered. "You could call it our history (itihasa), one that many of us in Sringeri are beginning to forget," he began, as, in the summer of 2004, he recounted to me his memories of Papanaiyya's life. Papanaiyya, whose formal name was Phaniappa, was a brahmachari who had lived in Sringeri all his life, save for the time he had spent in Gandhiji's ashram in Gujarat and had participated in India's freedom struggle.[2] It had been a period, however, that had given him his mission in life: to be self-reliant and serve the community. "His day began with yoga and a bath in the river. He then took the bus to neighboring villages on his daily tour selling bangles—would you believe he had a junior college degree?" Ramachandra Bhattru said. I tried to imagine the opportunities that would have been available to Papanaiyya in those times with that degree. Yet, at least four other things—not his college degree—marked the image of Papanaiyya in Sringeri's folklore about its people, all of which were in one way or another inspired by his belief in jana samparka (contact with, or connectedness to people). First, there is the image of him as a nontraditional bangle seller ("He sold plain bangles, but people liked to buy whatever he had," added Amrutamba). Although Papanaiyya lived with his brother and his family, money from the sale of bangles met his few needs. In fact, he always paid for the vegetables used in his brother's household. Second, Papanaiyya is remembered for his services at the Durga temple just outside town. Through the week he would collect donations of cash, coconuts, and fruit that Sringeri residents wished to make at the Durga temple but could not themselves do because of busy schedules; on Fridays, after the puja at the temple was done, he would distribute the prasada, going from house to house, to whomever he met on the way. Third, Papanaiyya invariably was the first to arrive when somebody died. He would take upon himself the task of preparing the bier and be one of the carriers of the corpse to the cremation grounds. Finally, Papanaiyya had worked out an arrangement with the local branch of the Indian Bank that allowed him to collect worn-out currency bills that people wanted to exchange for fresh ones. "Often people forgot about these *notes,*" remarked Ramachandra Bhattru, "but Papanaiyya never would, even if it was a few months before he came back with a new *note.*" While these reminiscences brought to life a person I was never to meet (Papanaiyya had passed away just before I moved into Sringeri for my research), Ramachandra Bhattru reflected, "one could write a whole book on Papanaiyya." After a pause, he added, "And you know the other Gandhian in town . . . N. S. Lakshminarasimha Murthy . . . " The conversation turned to Dodda Murthy.

It was this sense of the unfolding of a universe of implicit and explicit meanings, time and again, during my interactions with people in Sringeri that convinced me that conversationally shared stories powerfully illustrate the moral process by which individuals perceive and engage with their histories, their surroundings, their visions, and their realities. Stories illustrate the multifarious ways in which the "moral life" is experienced, imagined, and constituted. There is something profound about what seems an ordinary encounter: someone recounts a story, someone listens to it, possibly initiating (or continuing) other narrations.[3] In contrast to the formal idiom of the ashirvada tradition that at least theoretically seeks to present and affirm a shastric model of conduct, conversational stories bring with them the dynamic, improvisational quality, the ambiguity, the struggle, and the individual agency that mark the quotidian world. As experiences are selected, synthesized, organized into narratives, and expressed in dialogue, the question of "moral meaning" becomes a zone of exploration for both the narrator and the listener(s) in different ways.

The question "who was Papanaiyya?" became also "what values did Papanaiyya represent?" Further, there was no mistaking Ramachandra Bhattru's endorsement of those values, and there was no doubt that I had been moved by Papanaiyya's story, even though I had an eclipsed understanding of Papanaiyya's life at best. We both brought to the narration our own experiences and expectations of "a life worth admiring" and we had influenced the narration itself, each in a separate way. Why was I moved by his story, moved enough to want to emulate something of his humility and selflessness? What is it that makes a narrative morally persuasive?

Paul Ricoeur, drawing on the Greek tradition, builds on the process of mimesis to consider how a possibly "pre-narrative structure of experience" is transformed into narrative form that in turn could lead to a transformation in our perception of the world.[4] For Ricoeur the question is, "In what way is the ordinary experience of time, borne by daily acting and suffering [enduring], refashioned by its passage through the grid of narrative?"[5] Using Aristotle's concept of mimesis (creative imitation that "*produces* what it imitates")[6] to trace this imaginative transformation, Ricoeur suggests three interrelated processes; the first, mimesis$_1$ (or prefiguration of action) is the preunderstanding of what the world means and "what human action is, its semantics, its symbolism, its temporality."[7] This preunderstanding is processed into narrative in a second stage that Ricoeur calls mimesis$_2$ (configuration). Here a narrator, through emplotment, brings together various conceptions of time ("felt like ages," "today," "in the past," and "once upon a time") to restructure an interpretation of experience and action, however tentative and complex.[8] Emplotment implies a narrator's knowledge of paradigms and his or her relationship with them. Thus one could write a novel that goes against the grain of the novelistic genre, but the divergence nevertheless proves the historicity of that imaginative effort and of its engagement with *tradition(s)*. The emplotted world of narrative, through all its complex interaction with tradition, makes possible a third kind of mimesis, mimesis$_3$, in which the "world of text" intersects with the "world of the reader."[9] By this process of refiguration, individuals integrate the imaginative endeavor into lived contexts, and narrative thus enters the arena of social action.

The experience of sympathetic emoting and imagination are central to the process of refiguration. However, in orally shared narrative (as compared to written) processes of mimesis interact in far more complex ways. They occur simultaneously, are blurred, and often, in one is the other. For instance, when a story is narrated, this configuration by the teller could mark the imperceptible birth of the prefiguration of a specific sort (of, say, upachara, shastric stipulation, sampradaya's expectations, other normative traces) for the hearer. At the same time, in different ways and at different times, it could mark a refiguration for *both* teller and hearer, as they engage with the narrated story in their own lives.

While Ricoeur's framework explains the process by which preunderstandings find artistic form and then artistic form finds contexts in personal lives, it leaves open the question *why* narratives place themselves and refigure in the lives of listeners. The answer could be explored through rasa poetics, a poetics that makes one of the most sustained contemplations on the primacy of the experience of emotion in the aesthetic enjoyment of drama and poetry and on the nature of the connection between the world of narration and the world of the listener. Bharata's *Nāṭyaśāstra* states that "drama is a reproduction of the mental states, action and conduct of the people,"[10] and early commentators like Lollata and Shankuka argued that drama produces an illusory cognition that becomes the basis for the experience of rasa in the viewer.[11] However, for Sanskrit poetics beginning with Bharata, the aim of poetic representation was seen as the elicitation of emotion, not mimesis.[12] As reviewed in chapter 5, Sanskrit literary criticism posits that the soul of poetry is rasa ("juice," essence). Rasa is experienced when personal feeling is metamorphosed into aesthetic emotion, making it possible for the listener or viewer to vicariously inhabit the emotional space of the poetic depiction—rasa is not something out there, but is to be found in the experiencing. Abhinavagupta, the prominent tenth-century critic, argued that the sahridaya, the literary connoisseur, is able to experience the rasa because his or her mind ("heart") has been trained by everyday inferences so that, when presented with preconditions (vibhāva) that give rise to an emotion, the sahridaya ("the like-hearted") is able to sympathize and to identify with these preconditions. This sympathetic identification is "a process that forms the seedling for the full relishing of *rasa* about to ensue."[13] Edwin Gerow's synopsis of Abhinavagupta's interpretation of the rasa experience helps us understand *why* conversationally shared stories can become powerful vehicles of moral communication:

> All that seems to happen—in the theatre—is that the play permits the spectator to clarify the implicitude of his emotional propensities—propensities which he brought to the theatre with him and which he will take away again; for these emotional dispositions are the very ground of his sentimental or worldly life—they are what make it possible to feel

> such-and-such in the context of this or that determinate situation. Of course these propensities are present in everyday life as well—in this sense the play does not seem to differ radically from the world we live in—and the peculiar character of art resides only in the manner of determination; from this derives the uniqueness and the clarifying strength of the play.[14]

From this we can speculate that in oral stories about life experiences the narrator often reimagines a moral moment in her life, but the reimagining also initiates, in the listener, a moral recognition or a stirring, however tacit and embedded. Even if the listener has not undergone the narrated experience itself, the *possibility* of its occurrence is intimated and thus a "sharing" of emotion takes place between tellers and listeners. The quality of the telling (or more specifically, the *bhāvānukīrtana*, the narration of emotion) itself enhances—or detracts from—the instress of the narrative.[15]

In a way quite different from the theatrical and poetic experience that rasa poeticians theorized, in exchanged narratives, the dialogic sharing is explicit, constructed within the ambit of relationships to people, to situational contexts, and to histories. The dialogue that shapes expression not only takes place between speakers and listeners, but could occur between individual and community, between pasts and presents (and futures), between expectations and realizations, between multiple discourses. As Bakhtin says,

> the word in language is half someone else's. It becomes "one's own" only when the speaker populates it with his own intention, his own accent, when he appropriates the word, adapting it to his own semantic and expressive intention. Prior to this moment of appropriation, the word does not exist in a neutral and impersonal language . . . but rather it exists in other people's mouths, in other people's contexts, serving other people's intentions: it is from there that one must take the word, and make it one's own.[16]

The unceasing polyphony of life inevitably affects the "ideological becoming" of an individual, the "process of selectively assimilating the words of others" in order to form one's system of ideas or the basis of one's behavior.[17] Narratives often hold up or comment on the (necessary) struggle that underlies this process of moral being—or becoming.

The premise that narrative is particularly appropriate for moral deliberation has given form to the divergently conceptualized field in Western ethics that has come to be called "narrative ethics." Alasdair Macintyre has argued, for example, that "storytelling" is intrinsic to human nature and that narrative helps cultivate the sense of historical continuity crucial to personhood.[18] For narrative theologians in Christian ethics a moral life is constituted by stories shared by the faith community, stories that ultimately shape a *Christian* character.[19] In a literary and philosophical context, Martha Nussbaum considers selective literature (especially the novel) to be a powerful moral resource whose advantage over abstract moral philosophy is a particularization of life through character and plot that makes individual moral education possible.[20] The reader/moral agent, through discerning, emotionally engaged reading of certain literary texts, acquires a literary and moral sensibility, a "perceptive equilibrium . . . in which concrete perceptions 'hang beautifully together,' both with one another and with the agent's general principles; an equilibrium that is always ready to reconstitute itself in response to the new."[21] Although Nussbaum does not draw on Indian narrative traditions or theory, the equilibrium she talks about is akin to the experience of rasa so searchingly explored in Sanskrit poetics for two millennia.

Proposing a newer reading of narrative ethics that avoids an allegorical or doctrinaire turn, Adam Newton argues that the moral value of literature is not just in the ethical education it offers through characterization, plot, and so on, but rather, more fundamentally, through the narrative act itself. The very act of reading narrative prose fiction is an ethical act that entails a profoundly contingent, intersubjective experience: "One faces a text as one might face a person, having to confront the claims raised by that very immediacy, an immediacy of contact, not of meaning."[22] Drawing on Emmanuel Levinas, Mikhail Bakhtin, and Stanley Cavell, Newton says that author, reader, character, and "invisible others" make "reciprocal claims" on each other in incommensurate terms that have to be negotiated by the reader, often in solitude. That is, the act of reading narrative fiction binds author, character, and reader in an intimate ethical transaction whose terms unfold during the process of interpretation. Indeed, one is taken back to Ricoeur's observation that the significance of narrative "wells up from the intersection of the world of text and the world of the reader."[23] At the same time, Newton recognizes that the "limits bounding the ethics of fiction, in other words, are ones posed by reading and responding to fiction—to be reckoned as one performs and interprets a text—and not facilely breached in order to apply "lessons for life."[24]

These observations, important as they are, nevertheless demonstrate to us that narrative ethics has rarely ventured beyond examining written narrative, and it has, for the most part, limited itself to the Anglo-Christian world. Perhaps more critically, one is left looking for the human voices and faces and the lived cultural contexts that seem to be the promise of this field. If Nussbaum and Newton turn to narrative because it encompasses particularity and a directness of contact, what insights indeed can one draw for narrative ethics from the dynamic particularity that characterizes conversational narrative and oral narrative in general? In his essay "What Is a Text?" Ricoeur observes, "When the text takes the place of speech, something important occurs. In speech, the interlocutors are present not only to one another, but also to the situation, the surroundings, and the circumstantial milieu of discourse. It is in relation to this circumstantial milieu that discourse is fully meaningful; the return to reality is ultimately a return to this reality, which can be indicated 'around' the speakers, 'around,' if we may say so, the instance of discourse itself."[25] The situatedness of narrative is critical, in fact, in the "narrative approach" to the study of moral development, which posits that "moral experience issues not from the cogito of independent actors, but from the linguistically informed and storied design of the relationships in which persons, as dialogical selves, are always situated."[26]

As linguistic anthropologists note, the sense of drama underlying conversationally shared narrative lends to "ordinary language" a remarkably context-sensitive compositional quality that differentiates it from "literary" language.[27] In fact, these scholars, drawing on folklore, phenomenology, and developmental psychology, discuss "everyday stories" along "dimensions" such as "tellership" (who narrates), "tellability" (what is selected for narration), "embeddedness" (discourse context), "linearity" (ordering of narrative time), and "moral stance" (perspective on experience).[28] Interactional "frames," emphases and elisions, topical detours and repetitions uncover the individuated poetics of speaking.[29] Drawing on these approaches, one can ask how relationships between listener and teller (even beyond the immediate setting), and their location in a particular spatial-temporal context, affect their moral agencies, which are to some degree mutually constructed.[30] While everyday stories are part of conversations and not imagined as "performances," they do nevertheless carry the unconscious artistry of our daily lives. The artistry is inspired by the emotional resonance of our memories and experiences and the narrative style and competence of the individual storyteller. Tellers and listeners engage in a process of *articulation*—"the structure of significances that the storyteller imparts"[31]—that uncovers moral agency, indicating distances or affinities felt toward the subject and the degree and kind of engagement sought with the conversational setting. The on-the-spot decisions of what to say or what to omit, what is central and what is marginal, whether and when to shift between multiple narrative points of view, for example—first, second or third person—and when and how to vary the tone, all point out that it is essential to recognize the moral self and the artistic self are continuous with and shape each other, providing ironic commentary on each other. Moral agency and persuasiveness thus become intimately tied to the aesthetics of narration.

Stories, as well as acts of narration, can also be understood as expressions of a struggle to align or reflect upon the relationships between experience, intention, and language, which, while not partitioned, often exhibit asymmetries and create gaps in "meaning." We might turn to the work of sociolinguistic phenomenologist Ragnar Rommetveit for understanding the daily humdrum of experience and communication. According to Rommetveit, natural speech is elliptic, but understanding occurs because individuals share a "complete complementarity [of social knowledge] in an intersubjectively established, temporarily shared social world."[32] Acknowledging, however, that such "complete complementarity" does not exist in everyday interaction, he posits that the "meaning" of utterances amidst ellipses relies on "contracts" between speakers about how things are to be understood, on who has control over the "temporarily shared social world," on public endorsement of private understandings, and so on.[33] Ellipses then are "bridges" that link specific utterances to the shared a priori knowledge that persons already have or jointly generate about their social universe.

While understanding the nature of ellipsis helps to disambiguate referential relations, the place of ellipsis seems more complicated in the profoundly suggestive and speculative arena of "silential relations" (i.e., "the relations of the said to the unsaid and the unsayable") that we often face in everyday situations.[34] For us to recognize the intimate collaborations between "the said" and "the unsaid" or "the unsayable" in the expression of intent, the notion of linguistic ellipsis would need to be broadened to include the "blank spots" that literary phenomenologist Roman Ingarden defines as the inevitable unstated aspects of any discourse.[35] Blank spots, Ingarden argues, emerge from the disparity between "actual" [literal] and "potential stocks of meanings" of utterances. "Readily potential meaning" refers not so much to the multiple layering of meaning generated by an utterance as to a meaning that foregrounds itself from a vortex of alternatives by virtue of its contiguity within the discourse.[36] Ingarden also discusses how (literary) interpretation proceeds from varying "acts of consciousness" on the part of "authors" and "readers" that are not always reducible to their intentions.[37] Given the vast possibility of communication to generate gradients of "meanings" and "blank spots" (which are *not* the more readily identifiable linguistic ellipses), what do the "blank spots" index? William Hanks suggests, "The blank spots point to the intersubjective context, linking verbal form to the extralinguistic horizon of social knowledge. When this knowledge is available in the perceptual fields of the two parties, then reference proceeds on the basis of *recognition*."[38]

Yet, as insightful as phenomenological approaches are to understanding the process of meaning making and unraveling—discussing the messy but tremendous roles played by linguistic ellipsis, blank spots, consciousness, recognition, and so on—they leave untouched the area of communication that occurs beyond "sociolinguistic" worlds, connecting them to the metaphysical. As many stories from Sringeri—and indeed from broader Hindu worlds—vigorously demonstrate, what one could call "visionary," "divine," or "dream" communication swirls through the this-worldly, enriching it temporally and spatially. Individuals often think about the philosophical and pragmatic implications of such communication, and two stories that I present in this chapter in which a guru deciphers (*Aviveka*) or a priest seems to foretell ("It's only when misfortune strikes") explicitly illustrate the pervasive engagement with divine signage in Hindu moral worlds.

With these remarks, I now turn to six conversationally shared narratives from Sringeri. For each narrative I provide a few details of the contexts in which the narratives were shared. However, the stories must ultimately be understood within the relationships that I have with the individual narrators. Interactional circumstances have no doubt shaped the narrations, but these circumstances are located in relationships and speak in complex ways to the memory and self-understandings of narrators, and therefore the contextualizations I provide have to be read alongside the biographical vignettes dispersed throughout the book.

In the situations described in these stories, appropriate conduct is more about accountability, subtlety, discernment, and humility than an explicit engagement with the concept of dharma. Dharma remains implicit in these narratives, figuring in the sense of "right conduct." In dealing with familial environments, ritual actions, encounters with exemplars or itinerant sanyasis, multicaste eating, these stories provide insights into the versatile moral universes of individuals. While some of the subjects are treated to a considerable extent in the Dharmashastras, these stories challenge the rigidity of social categories and, above all, suggest that the interpretation of the "normative" is diffuse and at times contested, but, most interestingly, is aesthetically rendered in dramatic reenactments of experience.

Ricoeur leaves us with something to think about:

> Without leaving the sphere of everyday experience, are we not inclined to see in a given chain of episodes in our own life something like *stories that have not yet been told*, stories that demand to be told, stories that offer points of anchorage for the narrative? Once again, are not stories recounted by definition? This is indisputable when we are speaking of actual stories. But is the notion of a potential story unacceptable?[39]

I am reminded of a story about a potential story from Indian folk narrative. In a Telugu folktale called "A Story in Search of an Audience," a number of individuals who are too busy to listen to an old woman's story about Sūrya, the sun god, are punished with ill fortune.[40] The old woman's story, whose telling and hearing are considered auspicious (and mandatory) on a Sunday in the month of Māgha (January-February), finally finds an eager audience in an unborn girl child of a pregnant woman. For having heard the story, she is blessed with magical powers and great fortune by Sūrya, who himself comes to revive her dead husband, the king. The story eventually becomes a permanent tradition with tellers and hearers.

Murne mane Rambhattru: *Aviveka* (Indiscrimination)

When Murne mane Rambhattru knocked on my door one early evening, bringing with him his three-year old grandson, I was elated. Visitors dropping in for a chat made me feel that I belonged to the community—even today, Chayamma tells me on the phone that she passes by "my" apartment that I had rented ten years ago—but Murne mane Rambhattru's visit was special in view of his age and erudition and the recentness of our connection. As he settled down on the mat on the floor, I mentioned some places I had visited recently. "Kigga" started him off on the story of the sage Rishyshringa, and as he went on to describe Ugra Narasimha Bharati's association with the hill in Kigga, I brought out my tape recorder. "You want to record this?" he asked, somewhat baffled. "If you don't mind," I said. He said he did not mind, and I turned on the recorder. As we spoke, his grandson occasionally poked at the recorder, attracted by the small red lights flickering with our voices. The story, which I translate below from Kannada, is one of the many "guru stories" he shared with me that evening.

MRB: There was once a Timmanna Bhatta in the Vidyashankara temple here.

Of Tamil origin I think—

His family had been chief priests in the temple since the time of Vidyaranya.

L: Oh, way back then!

MRB: At the shrine of Ugra Narasimha Bharati (the matha's spiritual head from 1817–1879),[41]

as you know, the abhisheka (ritual anointing of the image) is concluded by cleaning the image with kaḍale hiṭṭu (chickpea flour). It removes the grease.

One day, after Timmanna Bhatta had performed the ritual—

the regular priest had been promoted to another temple—

and Timmanna Bhatta had been asked to do the puja here.

After the puja had concluded—you know how the image is cleaned, right? (rubbed with soft chickpea flour)

At the ugrān,a (the granary and store),

they did not have the chickpea flour he needed.

So, using the rough husk of a coconut, he scrubbed the vigraha (image of deity) till it was clean.

That done, he went home.

That night, the guru of the matha (from 1912–1954),

Chandrashekara Bharati, had a dream.

In his dream, Ugra Narasimha Bharati appeared, crying out,

"Uri, uri! (burning, burning!)

burning, my body is burning!"

The guru was disturbed.

He rose before dawn,

meditating on the dream.

That morning

After his bath, he enquired,

"Who did the puja at the Ugra Narasimha Bharati shrine yesterday?

What aviveka (indiscrimination; error) could have happened?"

When he learned that this priest had performed the puja, he sent for him.

Timmanna Bhatta went.

"Did you do the puja (at the shrine) yesterday?"

"Yes, gurugale (guru), I did."

"What did you do?"

"Nothing special. Usually the store gives some chickpea flour or some other flour to clean the grease. They didn't have it yesterday.

So, I just used coconut husk and *scrubbed* the image well. And the grease came off."

"Aha! This is the aviveka you have committed.

Well, you had better go right away and do the rudrabhisheka[42]—

and the offering *must* include dadhyanna (yogurt mixed with rice)—

Do the oil abhisheka and offer curds and rice."

That was what he said to Timmanna, we are told.

It was only after all this had been done that things were set right.

How it must have been for such a great sage as Ugra Narasimha Bharati to have been driven to appear in a dream, crying,

"Burning, my body is burning . . . "

It was not long afterwards that I learned that Murne mane Rambhattru was living in the very house in which Chandrashekara Bharati had been raised. It was also another coincidence that, as I reflected on this story months later, in my father's library I came across a slim, rare copy of a self-published booklet titled *Pilgrimage to Sringeri* by M. S. M. Sharma, a disciple of Chandrashekara Bharati and sometime editor of the erstwhile Patna newspaper, *Searchlight*. In faded ink, on the cover, appears my grandfather's name: "Presented by the author to S. Srinivasan, June 1955." The booklet recounts several vignettes about the matha, but my attention was immediately drawn to episodes that concerned Ugra Narasimha Bharati and Chandrashekara Bharati. I began to understand more fully the significance of the dream communication in Murne mane Rambhattru's story and the nature of the impropriety that had apparently taken place.

In the Sringeri matha and temple complex, each of the previous gurus is enshrined and worshipped in the form of a stone shivalinga, the central symbol of Shiva's generative potential. A silver casing with the likeness of the guru is fitted over the linga after the worship. The worship of the shivalinga involves a daily abhisheka that is performed by a priest. Since there are several shrines, one for each past guru of the matha, duties for these shrines are allocated to various priests, and Timmanna Bhatta had been assigned to conduct worship at the shrine of Ugra Narasimha Bharati.

Ugra ("fiery") Narasimha Bharati is known in Sringeri for his rigorous asceticism. He had lived for twelve years on a hill in Kigga, subsisting only on raw bitter gourd while engaged in penance, a practice he observed all his life. The hill is today called the Narasimha Hill after him. Reinforcing what I had heard in Sringeri, Sharma writes: "It used to be said of him that while his body had been reduced to skin and bones and it looked like a parrot cage, his face was remarkable for its yogic splendour. This Guru, in his time, had traveled all over India, from the Himalayas to Kanya Kumari."[43] He was believed to have been endowed with great mystic powers, and his long hours of meditation on Narasimha, the fierce man-lion incarnation of Vishnu, they say, had given him also a leonine appearance. His power of healing was such that a mere glance or nod from him was believed to cure physical ailments.

Among the many stories that are told about him, one narrates how, on a visit to Gujarat, he had been requested to stay in an abandoned house by its owner. In the midst of his worship he apprehended a brahmarakshasi[44] who had appeared in the guise of a traditionally dressed brahman. Recognizing the real identity of the "brahman," Urga Narasimha Bharati sprinkled a few drops of the sanctified water he had been using for his worship onto the "brahman." Instantly, the imposter fled the house, screaming, "Fire, fire!" A splash was heard at the well, and the abandoned house became fit to be inhabited again.[45]

Chandrashekara Bharati, the thirty-fourth guru,[46] about whom I had heard the most from my own family and from people in Sringeri, was also known as jīvan mukta, one "liberated" even while living. He would spend nearly seven to eight months as antara mukhi, immersed in a yogic state of sustained spiritual introspection.[47] Although remaining secluded in an inner room thus, seemingly oblivious to the world, he could clearly see what was happening in the outside world. There were times when he would come out of his seclusion, not wishing to disappoint a particular disciple who he knew had come to see him. Many of Chandrashekara Bharati's devotees note the compassionate responses he made across great distances from Sringeri when devotees were in distress. Most of the time the problems did not need to be articulated to him at all; he intuited them. When darshan was sought of him, through mere sight, he knew the predicaments and the wishes of his disciples and advised them accordingly, indicated solutions to dilemmas, or comforted with spiritual guidance.

M. S. M. Sharma narrates that when his daughter was burned severely in a fire accident in Delhi, even as he learned of the accident while he was in Calcutta (Kolkata), he received a telegram from Sringeri informing him that the guru had asked him to perform agni homa (fire ritual) to Lord Narasimha and assuring him that everything would be all right. The doctors in

Delhi asked the family to take the girl home because she had less than twenty-four hours to live. Writing five years after the episode, Sharma says that his daughter recovered completely.[48] This ability of Chandrashekara Bharati to see and know beyond the visible world suggests that there may be another way of understanding Murne mane Rambhattru's term *dream.* What was Chandrashekara Bharati's state of consciousness when he perceived the transgression that had taken place at Ugra Narasimha Bharati's shrine? The "dream," it seems to me, is more likely to have been a yogic state of supreme consciousness known as turiya that underlies, but transcends the states of "waking," "dreaming," and "sleeping." Such a state is marked by a crystal-like awareness of the world, past, present, and future, even when not immersed in the everyday.[49] It is well-known that Chandrashekara Bharati continually lived in this state of total awareness, and the dream communication he received from Ugra Narasimha Bharati may have been on such a plane of consciousness.

The narrative also builds on the common recognition that worship, or puja, is a way of effecting communication between the human and the divine. This communication is structured around the guest-host paradigm in which the deity is guest exemplar and is honored through elaborate ritual acts or services, which the shastras delineate as sixteen, although often, in practice, a shorter sequence of acts is performed.[50] The shastras specify what kinds of substances are to be used, what substitutes are permissible; they indicate consequences of improprieties and, in some cases, suggest reparations. Abhisheka, ritual bathing of the image, involves the anointing of the image with five substances considered "ambrosial"—milk, curds, ghee, butter, honey, and sugar[51]—after which the image is washed. The procedure for washing the image is also specified in the shastras. It allows for a certain range in methods, many of which depend on the image being anointed and subsequently washed.

That the improperly conducted rite of cleaning after the usual rites of worship could inflict bodily pain on even such a formidable ascetic as Ugra Narasimha Bharati underscores the belief that improprieties in ritual procedure could have consequences that extend beyond the tangible, phenomenal world. Even he who was perceived as possessing a fierce penetrating radiance because of his tapas or penance felt he had been set on fire. Murne mane Rambhattru used the Kannada (or Sanskrit) word aviveka, indiscrimination, to describe the impropriety. While the shastras may allow for some flexibility in interpreting the stipulations for the cleaning procedure, had Timmanna Bhatta used discrimination in substituting chickpea flour with coconut husk?

What could be made of the fact that Timmanna Bhatta admitted substances and actions that were unfit for use in cleaning? Second, and more important, the cleaning procedure is also intended to be a cooling one. A great heat is believed to be concentrated in the shivalinga, heat that is produced by the rigors of asceticism, for Shiva is the paradigmatic ascetic (mahāyogi, the great yogi).[52] Above each shivalinga is a copper, brass, or silver pot from which water falls in a steady stream over the shivalinga, keeping it cool symbolizing the sacred waters of the Ganga.

Drawing on Rambhattru's evaluation of the impropriety that had occurred, it would seem the unfortunate priest had violated, to use Wittgenstein's term, the "constitutive rules" that define the actions they govern (as opposed to "regulative rules" that merely stipulate action). However, as Veena Das points out, even constitutive rules cannot cover *all* situations in real life—or, here, all possible enactments of worship—because possibilities are unpredictable and unmappable and consequently there is "always a gap between the rule and its execution."[53] In the absence of specific rules discretion may well be one's guide.

In choosing husk, the priest's real error may have been the failure to recognize the image as both an emblematic shivalinga, needing cooling substances, and as a representation of Ugra Narasimha Bharati. Instead, the choice of husk to clean the linga implied that the priest considered the shivalinga a mere stone image.[54] Soft chickpea flour is indeed a traditional cleaning and cooling substance commonly used by people to clean their bodies, but the abrasive husk is reserved for objects such as cooking pots and pans. It is interesting that Ugra Narasimha Bharati had subsisted on bitter gourd, which Ayurvedic medicine considers to be a cooling and an antipyretic substance. Was the "dream communication" also intended to teach the priest to be mindful of the presence of Ugra Narasimha Bharati in the shivalinga and of the mode of worship appropriate for a shivalinga as well? M. S. M. Sharma's booklet tells us that so powerful was the shivalinga in the Ugra Narasimha Bharati shrine that water poured over it during worship was believed to have healing properties.[55] Chandrashekara Bharati's advice that Timmanna Bhatta offer cooling substances in reparatory worship, especially *dadhyanna*, is in keeping with the understanding that the image is both a shivalinga, with a tendency to heat, and the fiery ascetic Ugra Narasimha Bharati, who must be cooled.

Interestingly, despite the burning impact of the breach, the fact that it was inadvertently committed allows for remedial action. Moral accountability for an act appears to be commensurate with intention. When "gaps" between intention, interpretation, and act occur, who has the authority to first *recognize* and then address them? Perhaps an answer to this question is in the priest not being directly made aware of the breach save through the guru. Appropriate retribution for the aviveka has to be mediated through the *viveka* (discrimination) of somebody with the spiritual stature of Chandrashekara Bharati.

Ramachandra Bhattru: *Sukshma* (Subtlety)[56]

Once, when electricity supply was down in April 1995, Prasad and I visited Ramachandra Bhattru. As we talked about the ongoing construction of his house—he was in the process of adding another floor so that he could rent it at a subsidy to students who came from outside to study in Sringeri's Sanskrit College—the talk drifted to his childhood reminiscences. He recounted how his father and his uncle, eminent Vedic scholars at the matha, had rigorously observed "shastric regulations" in their everyday routines. This adherence to "what the shastras say" is particularly illustrated by the manner in which Ramachandra Bhattru's father passed away. Ailing, he had known that death was imminent and instructed Ramachandra Bhattru that on no account should he allowed to pass away on the cot. Death on a raised surface that had no direct contact with the ground would be comparable to the miserable existence of Trishanku, the king who was trapped between heaven and earth (because of his insistence on passage into heaven in his mortal body defying his guru's prohibition), doomed forever to remain neither here nor there.[57] Ramachandra Bhattru's father had wanted to be put on the floor at the moment of his death. On the new moon night just before the Navaratri ("nine nights") festival commenced, he asked Ramachandra Bhattru for a sip of holy Ganga water (considered sin-removing) stored in a little container in the house.[58] Ramachandra Bhattru feared the end was near, but his father said "Not yet." Then, on the ninth day of Navaratri, when the rest of the town was as usual in the midst of celebrating the goddess in all her forms, he pointed urgently to the floor. Ramachandra Bhattru did as his father had instructed and moved him to the floor. The minute he was placed on the floor, he died. "Such a death is an icchāmaraṇe (death when desired)," Ramachandra Bhattru said, "He *wanted* to die on *navami* (ninth day of the lunar calendar) for which he had carried on for nine days."

In the context of illustrating his father's interactions with itinerant swamis (renunciates), Ramachandra Bhattru narrated some stories about swamis who used to visit Sringeri regularly in the course of their wanderings. The following is one such story:

RB: In our childhood,[59]
visits by swamis meant that my parents would lock us up.
P: All of you—?
RB: This practice—now, why would they lock us up?
L: Because you'd go and touch things, and do something like that?
RB: No.
When a sanyasi (renunciate) comes seeking bhiksha (alms)
and there was a (mutually agreed upon) date on which he was supposed to visit us—
on that date,
my parents would sanctify themselves ritually—you know,
They'd lock us children in a room downstairs.
One day it so happened (*chuckling*),
I thought,
What do they do with the swami?
Why shouldn't we know?
I had to see! *Arre*!
What was it they did that we children had to be locked up (*laughing*)?
How could you expect us to understand their reasoning?
L: Right (*laughing*)!
RB: I must have been in the sixth or seventh grade then, in *middle school.*
On that day around that time,
I managed to slip away!
You know, the time when we would have been locked up,
L: Oh, you must have learned to anticipate that moment well, what with all the previous "lockings!"
RB: So at the time we would have been locked up—
P: You escaped!
RB: At noon, the swami arrived.
The moment I saw him ascend the stairs I showed up.
"Hari! Hari!"(the swami comes in saying God's name)
He arrived, and through this window here, that old one,
I peeked: "What do they do?"
Of course, *they don't do anything* (*laughing*).

A wooden plank (*for a seat*) is put out for him,
and he stands on it.
It's easy for me to understand this today.
So he stands on the plank,
and for his hands—
They give him water to wash his hands,
They serve cooked rice from a plate,
serve him some curds (yogurt), and *that's it.*
There's nothing more to this.
(*pause*)
But *curiosity* at that age, you know.
I had to show them that I was an important person, right?
I wanted my father and my mother to know that *I had seen,*
and I wanted the swami to know that too.
Boyhood back then!

L: That's right, all mischief!

RB: Bhikshe (alms) had been served.
He had come here after obtaining bhikshe from two other homes.
Bhikshe, meaning, his rice.
The third home he had come to was ours.
Would it suffice to announce merely that I had seen?
No!
I remember exactly the way it happened:
I went right up to him,
And prostrated at his feet (*RB thumps his hand on the floor*).
I was thrilled! *Hah*!
What an achievement!
(*pause*)
And what was the achievement?

P: That you had prostrated?

RB: *That I had seen!* (*laughing*)
That I had seen what these people did behind closed doors!
(pause)
My faa-ath-er (*voice gradually rising in crescendo*)
his head bursting with r-a-g-e (*rapidly, laughter subsiding quickly, voice lowered*).
I did not know then.
But today I understand.
The swami said,

"The boy has acted innocently, sir,
Don't punish him.
I must now leave."
Saying this, he left (without eating).
Barely had he reached the last step—
Well—
in those days we had little tufts on our heads—

L: Oh, no!

RB: My father held me by it—
Right there, you know how firewood is stacked for the rainy season—
it must have been a piece this thick,
he walloped me as if I were *an ox.*

L: Abhaa . . . (*ouch*)

RB: And why? Why was such a furor made?
That whole day I was not given any food.
When, finally, I asked my father, he said,
"A yati (renouncer) was so unjustly denied food today,
because you fell at his feet,
at the feet of a sanyasi in a grihasta's (householder's) home today,
you denied him his food for the day."
I'm sure you understand what that means—
If you prostrate before a sanyasi to whom you have offered alms,
he will probably not tell you this,
but he will throw away that offering of rice and forego food for the day.

L: Oh no . . .

RB: But how was I to know this?

L: True. A child, after all—

RB: But look at the way the swami had responded to my father,
The sukshma (subtlety) in his saying,
"The boy could not have known, don't punish him, sir."
My father had known,
the swami had also known.
But that the swami ended up having to *starve* that day, was anguish my father could not bear.
After *I* became a householder,
I too began to lock up my son!
(*laughing at his facetious remark*)

To contextualize the narrative, the matha and the temple—or perhaps the quiet seclusion of the Sringeri region—used to attract itinerant renouncers, some of whom, with their regular visits, began to associate closely with a few Sringeri families. Residents like Ramachandra Bhattru are nostalgic about the times when such visits by sanyasis to their homes were part of their weekly lives and regret the dwindling number of these visits in recent years. These wandering ascetics, without "habitation or name," seem to have acquired some permanence in the folklore of Sringeri, and I grew to enjoy hearing the stories about them. There was the "Bhavani swami" who would ask for elaborate meals to be prepared on the day he came for alms only to eat merely yogurt and rice, having requested the elaborate meal so that children in the host's family would get a festive meal on that day. Then there was the sanyasi who went around the shrines in the matha, asking the priests for bananas and other fruits that had been offered to the deities by devotees so that he could then sit under a tree and give these away to children after he had them recite a sacred verse (shloka) or two. These visiting ascetics were usually nicknamed by some personal characteristic or by the place where they had last stopped before coming to Sringeri. Thus I heard about the"Banana swami" (bālehaṇṇu swāmi) who distributed all the bananas he got among children and the"Kāshi swami" of this narrative who had come to Sringeri from Kashi (Varanasi) and was known for his austerities.

As Kirin Narayan's ethnography shows,[60] itinerant renouncers and holy persons are important figures of religious teaching in Hindu life, imparting knowledge about particular scriptural texts or divine orders, but, perhaps even more influentially, about how to lead a spiritual day-to-day life. Sanyasis in Sringeri have often played this role, if indirectly. Implicit in Ramachandra Bhattru's narrative is a pedagogical discourse that comments on conduct that is appropriate to sanyasi-householder interactions. Central to these interactions is the giving and the receiving of bhiksha (food given to a sanyasi). The awkwardness of Ramachandra Bhattru's prostration to the Kashi swami comes not from the act itself but from the timing of the act: When blessings are sought of the Kashi swami when he is himself seeking bhiksha—that is, in fact, an *impersonal* seeking of food—he is forced to enter into a worldly transaction (food in exchange for blessing) that demands reciprocal transaction. The food then becomes unfit for consumption, tainted by a certain worldly quality, precisely the characteristic a renouncer has vowed to eschew. Sringeri families perceive it to be their duty to feed renouncers and go to considerable length to fulfill this duty.

One learns from this story that, despite the detailed attention to the merits gained by householders when they offer alms to a renouncer, the actual mode and manner of bhiksha is ultimately defined by the renouncer, not by the householder, and these particular preferences may receive no direct treatment in any of the *Saṃnāyasa Upaniṣads* or other texts that comment on the institution of renunciation and ascetic life.[61]

In sharing many narratives from his repertoire of stories about sanyasis, of which I have provided only one here, Ramachandra Bhattru seemed to construct simultaneously a metanarrative that commented on how the stories must in fact be interpreted. His directives, such as "This is about the human will," "This is about faith," "This is about subtlety," which interspersed his sanyasi narratives—in fact, index, as Richard Bauman and Charles Briggs would say, "not only features of the ongoing social interaction but also the structure and significance of the narrative and the way it is linked to other events."[62] In the narrative presented in this chapter Ramachandra Bhattru drew attention to what he considered noteworthy, and abstractable, from the experience: the notion of sukshma, or subtlety, in speech or gesture. That the Kashi swami did not even mention the breach of conduct that had occurred through the young Ramachandra Bhattru's act, much less reproach him or his father, leaving the matter instead to the tacit knowledge that the adults shared about social norms, is, in Ramachandra Bhattru's retrospective view, an act of sukshma on the sanyasi's part. The fact that the sanyasi had then chosen to *excuse* the breach, and anticipated the repercussions it had for Ramachandra Bhattru, all comes through in his statement "The boy does not know, don't punish him, sir." Sukshma then is a quality that privileges the maintenance of cordiality even when there are unwitting breaches of hospitality and interpersonal conduct. While Ramachandra Bhattru ended this little story saying he too "locks up his son," that comment was in fact facetious, for, of course, he does not. At the same time, the narrative leaves the question open whether, and to what extent, children are expected to acquire knowledge of injunctions or proprieties through nonexplicit, or sūkṣmavāda upāya, subtle means.

Giridhara Shastry: "Dress, the Right Fit"

In 1984 the matha conducted a kumbhabhisheka (ritual consecration) of the Mallikarjuna (Shiva) temple on the hill in the town. The renovation of the temple had taken an entire year, and the upcoming consecration was eagerly awaited by Sringeri residents. Giridhara Shastry, as the administrator of the matha, had been in charge of organizing the event. He recounted how the arrangements of "free meals" provided by the matha became a complicated issue involving caste.[63] When we discussed this narrative later, and I asked whether I could reproduce it in this book, Giridhara Shastry responded, "Sure, as long you don't want to argue that it reflects polarization of society or use it to create differences." I elaborated that what I saw in the narrative was caste awareness, but, even more, the shared sense that amicable solutions had to be arrived at through debate and consensus.

GS: At the previous kumbhabhisheka, which the matha had conducted in 1963, the meal arrangements had been made so that individuals were seated according to their caste.

Brahmans in one area, Vaishyas in another—

Separate seating areas were designated.

But in the 1984 kumbhabhisheka we faced the dilemma of what to do for meal arrangements.

Between 1963 and '84 *circumstances* had changed *a lot,*

so we couldn't obviously *duplicate* the 1963 arrangements.

But—at the same time—if we declared that people were free to eat anywhere, who could say what *reactions* that would produce?

We thought *really* hard about what to do.

But couldn't come up with *any* *solution.*

So,

in the end, we reasoned,

"No-o, this is not going to be *resolved* without there being a *galāṭe* [noisy disagreement and argument],"

so instead of trying to implement a "formula" that we had come up with,

and having a fight break out *after* all the arrangements had been worked out, it would be better,

if there was to be a fight over this issue,

better that we have the fight before, and get a *solution* that we could *follow,*

rather than have a fight during the event or after.

That's what we reasoned.

L: Uh-huh.

GS: So we organized a *meeting,* and invited representatives of all groups for the *meeting.*

And, in the *meeting*, the question—what meal arrangements should be made?—was thrown open for discussion.

We said to the group, "Let us know what you decide should be done."

L: How *interesting*! So what happened?

GS: I also added, "I will not be able to stay for the *discussion.*"

Because had *I* remained in the room (during the discussion)

they would have felt constrained.

They wouldn't have felt *free* to talk about the matha.

And I felt that they should have the freedom to even *criticize* the matha if they wanted to.

So I planned beforehand to leave the room and requested a couple of friends to make sure the *discussion* did not end in *trading blows!*

And the *discussion* took place—

bisi bisi charche (a raging discussion)!

Finally, after a long *debate,* the communities came up with this *solution.*

What was that?

The vaidikas, they agreed, it wouldn't be right to mandate that they eat with the rest of us.

The vaidikas, and those brahmans who strictly observe the shastras—madi and achara—

they would be served meals *inside* the matha.

And in the Gandhi maidan (grounds) across

they proposed a huge chappara (tent) be set up.

And that's where everybody else would be served—sārvajanika (for all people) meals.

But sārvajanika meals didn't mean that anyone could sit anywhere.

Those who would come wearing panche-shalya (the traditional dhoti and upper garment),

they would be served in half the chappara that would be clearly separated from the other half.

In the other half—

AJJI: Clearly separated—like different *rooms*—

GS: People who came dressed in *pants* and *shirt,* or whatever else—could eat—it wouldn't matter.

That's it: just these two *divisions.*

Then the question of who would serve whom.

L: Hanh!

GS: Where the people dressed in panche-shalya would be seated, only those who were similarly dressed would be allowed to serve.

As far as possible, brahmans would serve there.

And where people wearing *pants* and *shirts*—here anybody who wanted to could serve.

L: Oh!

GS: Oh! Apparently there was much *discussion* about these *points*!

For the initial two or three days of the kumbhabhisheka people were guided to appropriate areas as they came in for their meals.

And then, you know, something interesting began to happen.

L: Hunh?

GS: Curiously, the brahmans and the nonbrahmans began to sit separately of their own accord.

Nobody had instructed them, nobody had objected, nothing of the kind.

It just happened that way.

Those dressed in panche-shalya, they were mostly brahmans.

Those who wore *pants* and the like—they'd themselves go and sit in the area other than that occupied by the brahmans.

And then, of course, there were those (orthodox persons) who ate in the matha.

One principle we followed very strictly—

whatever the menu in the matha, the same would be provided in the maidan—

(*speaking rapidly*) if there was bean curry in the matha, there would be bean curry in the maidan. If it was cabbage sāmbār in the matha, then that's what it would be in the maidan.

The program went on for twenty-one days. And, for twenty-one days, that was one principle we did not compromise on.

There would be no differentiation between the matha and the maidan.

That's how it was.

There wasn't *even a single* disturbing episode to report during this time.

Women who attended could go to the area where the panche-draped people were seated.

You see, with women, one couldn't tell (what community they belonged to). Whoever felt a sense of social standing went to the panche side.

> Not even on a *single day* was there any kind of *friction.*
> The event went off very *peacefully.*

The narrative poses the interesting question of how moral authority, seemingly freed from the institutional authority of the matha on the Dharmashastras, is deployed at a critical moment by a committee drawn from diverse castes on a matter that is elaborately regulated by the shastras. Caught between its roles as institutional host in a democratized setting that frowned upon caste discrimination, on the one hand, and as upholder of the Dharmashastras and sampradayas, on the other, the matha faced the challenge of conducting itself appropriately toward a diverse community of patrons. This challenge did not exist, we learn, in 1963, when the matha had organized a similar event. To understand why meal arrangements should constitute a "new" challenge to the matha's conduct, one needs to recall the matha's historical role as mediator: the matha had acquired a position of power by being a key player in the negotiations between administrations and local communities amid volatile political times between the fourteenth and eighteenth centuries. With the loss of its status as jagirdar, its political visibility and centrality in local life was diluted. A diversified community of patrons, loss of power arising from losing patrons to other mathas, a disempowered status in local governance, and a general climate of democratization seem to make, in Giridhara Shastry's recounting, a greater sense of accountability necessary on the part of the matha in the second hosting of the event. That is, the matha could not afford to ignore either local politics or the preferences of its "orthodox" brahman followers (who remain important to its own traditional structure and function).

It must be remembered that the matha, although divested of its former political and economic standing, remains a religious interpreter of the Dharmashastras, and hence felt obliged to honor commensal stipulations of shastric texts. Appropriate conduct, interestingly, is constructed in the narrative as the product of a democratic process that is signaled by vocabulary such as "mixed-caste meeting," "forum," "debate," "consensus." The solution that was arrived at through debate and consensus similarly equated propriety with the secularization of seating arrangements, but in a way this proved more problematic. The point that all guests—except the vaidikas (strict observers of the Vedas and the Dharmashastras)—be fed under a single/common chappara (itself a metaphor?), the reliance on a dress code, and not on caste, to separate people, and the provision of the same menu for all guests, underscore the fact that, for the matha, appropriate conduct meant that, given the times, caste-based divisions of guests could not be made. As is often the case in such events, eating areas were separate for men and women, but other lines of demarcation (vaidikas, "those who wear panche-shalya," and "those who wear pants and shirts") were blurred.

Or *were* they really blurred at all? The vaidikas, being strict adherents of "tradition," were accorded an inner space of the matha. By the same logic, for the committee the dress code in general reflected the statement that the panche-shalya was appropriate to the occasion and to the host (the matha), both symbolizing "tradition." Those who came in panche-shalya, then, acknowledged this point even if they did not practice madi and achara. (It may be recalled here that men who seek darshan of the guru have to be either dressed in panche-shalya or are asked to remove their shirts, while women, mostly wear saris).

But Giridhara Shastry's observation that "brahmans" and "non-brahmans" ended up sitting separately raises questions that go beyond the rationale that might have been envisaged by the committee for the three categories of seating. First, are there any codes really freely available? Second, what markers does the dress itself include? That is, did the quotidian fact that the panche-shalya is worn in such a way that one's "sacred thread," (janivara in Kannada), is visible make also visible a rite of passage associated with "upper castes"? Were people reluctant to overturn traditional demarcations of caste and subcaste mixing, given the religious nature of the event, even though other social contexts had undergone change?

It is critical to note that a dress-based division was not drawn up for women by the committee. Perhaps the committee reasoned that women had to be exempted from the dress code because, otherwise, a caste-based division that had been deemed inappropriate would have been made necessary. The process of discerning propriety from multiple perspectives, Giridhara Shastry suggested, highlights the cultural importance placed on propriety: propriety had to be considered first by Giridhara Shastry, who deferred his authority as administrator of the matha to the authority of a representative committee, second by the committee (which had to gain community acceptance), and finally, to the people who attended the twenty-one-day event and decided which seating area was most appropriate for them.

This narrative also belongs to a particular phase in the matha's history. When I visited Sringeri in 2001, I ate at in the newly constructed single dining hall in which three thousand persons—irrespective of background—are served together. At the same time, I was told that old-time vaidika brahmans who expressed a desire to partake of the prasada would be served in a small, private room in the temple complex.

Vijaya Krishnamurthy: "It's only when misfortune strikes . . ."

Vijaya and I had been talking about astrological predictions, and especially about what an astrologer may and may not reveal in a consultation. She had just finished recounting how a young astrologer who had foreseen the accidental death of a newly married young man had told him and his bride to their faces that such a disaster was coming their way. After the death had taken place as foretold, the bride had been inconsolable, remembering this prediction. She regretted that she had not been "vigilant enough" to prevent the death. The astrologer too—who was in fact a friend of the couple—had been distraught, and was reprehended by other friends about having inappropriately revealed his inauspicious (ashubha) prediction. We then moved on from this episode to another context in which a prediction was pronounced:

V: You know, ultimately, we cannot *neglect* astrological predictions. *It's when misfortune strikes, that you remember . . .*

L: that "somebody had cautioned you."

V: If misfortune doesn't fall on us, we don't think much about it (the prediction), do we?

L: Yes, this happens quite often, and we remember later that somebody had warned us.

V: Just the other day—take this small example. The other afternoon, Savitramma, because somebody was coming to their house for lunch—you know my friend, Savitramma, right?—was going to the market to buy some bananas.

Near the Kandaswami temple, where the vegetable shop is, right next to the lane. Somehow she didn't see some stones and she *fell, dhapp*, like that.

L: Ay-ya!

V: The stones on the pavement are loose out there—

She fell and badly hurt herself. Poor thing, she tore her sari and she hurt her legs.

Then—that's why she did not come to the Rama bhajane the day we sponsored it (*voice dropping*)—

so I went over to check and asked, "What happened, why didn't you come?"

And she said,

"This is what happened, kaṇe.

Today being Monday, I had gone to the hill (Mallikarjuna Temple)."

(*explaining to me*)

She gives *durve* (sacred grass) to Ganapati on the hill temple—

L: Oh, I see . . .

V: (*resuming Savitramma's first-person narration*)

"So I gave some durve to Ganapati and I kept the remainder to give to the Ganapati temple in the matha,"

she said.

She had picked a lot of durve that day.

But the bhattru (priest) took all the durve and put it in another place.

She later noticed the durve in that other spot.

"What happened? I had left some durve there. How did it come here?"

And she reached out to take it.

The bhattru said,

"This is for the Ganapati temple."

"No, no, I have already given the durve to Ganapati at this temple. I have kept this other bunch to give to Ganapati at the matha's temple."

Saying this, she took the bunch.

At that

(*speaking in a stern voice, imitating the bhattru*),

"If you take this away, something (bad) will happen to you today!" he said.

(*sounding quite shocked*)

That's what he apparently said!

L: Oh-o.

V: *And that very afternoon, she fell and she hurt her legs!*

You know, I kept thinking, *why on earth* did he say—but that's when it *flashed* on her.

She said to me,

"I kept wondering, why did he say that? Why did he say that? Now see, I have hurt myself . . . "

Both legs had these really large red bruises. She could barely walk.

(*S. J. Krishnamurthy, Vijaya's husband, who has been listening, interjects here*)

SJK: But how did it matter which Ganapati temple—

She could have given all the durve at the hill temple itself!

V: See? Only when misfortune strikes, does it *flash* on you!

"That has been gnawing at my mind ever since,"

Savitramma said to me.

So I told her,

"It's OK, let it go. Next week, when you go to the hill, you could just give a quarter or a one-rupee kāṇike (donation) to Ganapati. Don't dwell on it . . . "

(*all of us agree; Vijaya raises her voice above all our assents*)

We console others in this way (by suggesting reparations), but when it happens to us, we go through the same regret.

It's only when you get hurt, that it **flashes* . . .

When I narrated this story back to Vijaya many years later, she could not recall it, but she said, "But things like that do happen all the time, don't they?" It is precisely this everydayness of the experience recounted in the narrative that prompted me to think about the problem of action and its consequences in daily life and how it is "resolved," without always being taken to a spiritual teacher or an astrologer. Vijaya's empathetic identification with Savitramma comes through in her assuming Savitramma's story, her voice, and her perception of the priest's voice and actions. Although she "marks" her own identity though shifts in narrative point of view—especially underscored when she narrates her role as counselor—she reminds us that one slips into Savitramma's situation all too easily and all too often. The view that it is only in retrospect that "meaning" and "intention" flash on us is something to which I found myself connecting readily.

Savitramma's unfortunate experience and Vijaya's suggestion of a remedial measure lucidly articulate questions many Hindus ask themselves, albeit in different ways: Why was such an inauspicious pronouncement made? Was it made unintentionally, impelled by an impersonal destiny that simply looks for spokespersons and chooses somebody because of some coming together of moment, place, and person? How is "this" action connected to "that" experience? When and how does one "pay heed" to a prediction? When and how does one recognize a "sign"? These questions—indeed, many others—belong to a vast moral field that unfolds around the pivotal concept of karma in Hindu life, in which "cause" and "consequence" are seen as interlinked.[64]

Although the word *karma* itself did not enter our conversation, these questions suffuse the experience described in Vijaya's narrative. Clearly, Savitramma and Vijaya saw the problem not in terms of a long-term karmic residue but more as the immediate phala (result) of an inappropriate act. As I thought about this narrative I recalled the saying that in Kaliyuga[65] the consequences of one's karma are immediately experienced: "Perform an act with one hand, experience its karma with the other." The priest at the hill temple played a crucial part in the process by which Savitramma came to "see" the connection between her refusal (to give all the durve to the Ganapati at the hill-temple) and her accident.

What exactly was Savitramma's error? Whom had she displeased? What was the agency of the priest? And why was reparation seen as still necessary even after she had experienced the "punishment" by falling down? Since she had a large fresh bunch of durve, Savitramma had made up her mind to offer some at the Ganapati temple in the matha. The priest's "ordinary" action of taking the remaining durve for the hill Ganapati acquired a special significance in the light of his sudden, dramatic prediction of "consequences." His prediction is preceded by his statement that the durve was for the hill temple—and perhaps Savitramma simply interpreted his statement as the expression of an insistent priest, as a contest of intentions. It is only in retrospect that she—and we—realize what she had not "seen" was that the claim for the durve was probably being made by a transpersonal agent far greater than the human priest. That she—and Vijaya—came to this conclusion is evident because they did not hold the priest responsible for her mishap, and the reparation that Vijaya suggested was toward the *deity*. The priest is not seen to have uttered a curse (śāpa), but to have made a prediction.

As I struggled to understand why Savitramma's act was so egregious, I turned to the offering itself that was at the center of this episode: the durva.[66] Along with kusha grass (*Poa cynosuroides*), durva (*agrostis linearis*) is the most sacred grass of all Hindu mythology, with worship discussed in detail in the *Skanda Purāṇa*. Self-born and seedless, this two-bladed grass is extremely difficult to grow, and yet, when it does, it becomes firmly implanted, so much so that it is compared to our *vāsanas*, the strong impressions that carry over from previous lives. Its toughness makes it a symbol of longevity. Born in water, durva is a favorite food of elephants—hence also of Ganapati, the remover of obstacles.[67] Had Savitramma unwittingly made a partial offering of durve or, worse, withdrawn the offering even when the priest had indicated its "rightful" recipient (i.e., the Ganapati at the hill temple)?

In doing so, she had angered, by the narrative's assessment, the deity, Ganapati, himself, while the priest had only functioned as a *sign*, whose utterance in Hindu astrology would probably be called a *nimitta*. As the Kanchi Kamakoti swami explains, "A *nimitta* does not produce any result on its own. It points to the result that has already been ordained by some other factor."[68] Vijaya's remedial measure seemed to me to be an attempt to redirect Savitramma's regret for not having recognized and paid heed to the sign (of Ganapati's anger) to prevent further repercussions—and seek forgiveness of Ganapati.

Interestingly, Meshtru Krishnamurthy asks a question that one usually asks oneself when reflecting on the larger-than-local designs of our life: what does it matter which god one prays to? How is this Ganapati different from that one, after all? What is human will against divine will anyway? As Vijaya echoes throughout her narration, knowledge of such sort often comes as a *flash*, making the connection between an act, a sign, and a consequence apparent in a sudden, luminous moment.

Lakshmidevamma: "Pickling"

Browsing through the University of Pennsylvania's library for anything on Sringeri as I prepared for fieldwork, I came across a list of the names of municipal councillors of Sringeri in the *Chikmagalur District Gazetteer*. As I took notes, little did I know that Lakshmidevamma, listed as the only "lady councillor," was in fact a family friend. By the time I became acquainted with her, Lakshmidevamma had retired from political and social welfare activities, but it was a past that I was fascinated with, and often spoke to her about it. It was, strangely enough, many years after I met her that I enquired about her growing up in Sringeri; she was among the few women I knew whose natal home was Sringeri. One afternoon, as we all sat chatting in Indira and Nagaraja's part of the house, I pointedly asked her what it was like to grow up in the house right across from the home she married into. Before she recounted the narrative I present below, she had been describing her mother-in-law as a soft-spoken, noninterfering, spiritually absorbed person who rarely insisted that her daughters-in-law follow her somewhat more orthodox ways.

LAK: Even though I did not know much, my mother-in-law kind of used to *adjust* a lot and carry on (*laughs*).

"Poor thing, she has grown up coddled all along, her folks—"

(*quoting her mother-in-law*)

You see, they knew everybody in my family pretty well, there was a lot of coming and going between our homes.

My grandmother used to visit this house often—she was related to (S. K.) Ramaswamy's family, and there was much *contact* between them.

So she (mother-in-law) used to say,

"Oh, she's been brought up in a family that is skilled in artistic work." (*laughs*)

Decorating dolls and all that—my mother and grandmother used to do these things.

And at home they used to braid girls' hair with jasmine buds that used to grow in the yard, and girls from this house used to come to my house to have their hair done up in "jasmine braids."

So she used to say,

"Now that's a family that is skilled in artistic work . . . "

(*laughs again, and I join her, warming up to her recollection*).

"She (Lakshmidevamma) too knows all that,"

she would say that.

Drawing rangoli outside the front door every morning.

M-e-e—

I couldn't trace a line holding the powder in my hands!

Had never done it, didn't know how to!

L: (*enthusiastically*) Oh, it's comforting to hear this!

(*I say this recalling how my own rangolis are the target of my family's humor*)

LAK: My sister-in-law used to stand there by the door, watching and laughing at my short, crooked lines!

I'd trace and retrace and wipe the design off. *I just couldn't draw those long lines!*

I would feel terribly humiliated!

(*cracks up laughing; taking the voice of her sister-in-law*)

"Amma, you keep saying 'She's from a family that is skilled in artistic work,' and she can't even trace a rangoli!"

(*taking the voice of her mother-in-law, and speaking fast*)

"Ayyo, she's only not used to it, kaṇe. You just wait and see, she'll do better than everybody else soon!"

You see, my mother-in-law had that much confidence (*bharavase*) in me . . .

L: Exactly . . .

LAK: And then of course I came to draw many designs, and when I used to fill the front yard with rangoli, she used to be very happy. She used to like it.

Once it happened—Chayamma had gone out of town, to her mother's house.

(*narrative shifts into a slower pace and lowered tone*)

This, uh, this raw mango had been soaked in salt for pickling.

A tall jar with heaps of cut raw mango.

What one does with this is to strain the salted juice out, and boil the juice— the mango pieces are wiped dry, put into the boiled juice with all the spices and allowed to pickle.

In my house, too, my grandmother and mother used to do this too—but *I had never watched them do it and I didn't know!*

(*Nagaraja, who was getting ready to leave for Kadavadi, began to chuckle.*)

So, once my mother-in-law told me just before lunch, "The mango has been soaked enough, go strain the juice . . . "

You know where we had our breakfast today—(a small second kitchen).

L: Uh huh.

LAK: that was where the jar was.

You know how they drain the water out of boiled rice (where the water is all poured out and cooked rice retained)? In the same way, I drained the juice into the wash area!

NAGARAJA: Oh no, all the salted juice was lost!

L: Aww!

(*peals of laughter from all of us*)

LAK: Yes, the salted juice was all lost. I had no *idea* whatsoever!

(*clapping her hands once*).

After lunch was over, my mother-in-law said,

"The salted juice that you strained, bring that, let's set it for boiling."

Where is the salted juice to bring? It has flowed down the drain!

I-did-not-know-what-to-say.

Scared!

So I just stood quietly.

"Why, what happened?" my mother-in-law asked.

So I told her.

"Um, I, I did not know, I poured it into the wash area."

"Ayy-ayy-yo! You poured it down the drain?

You didn't know, and I too didn't tell you!

That's OK, forget about it . . .

You know, if it had been someone else—because, you know, the sour essence that is in that juice, from the raw mango.

So, saying "let it be," she boiled salt water separately and made the pickle with that.

Had it been some other mother-in-law, she would have broadcast this deed to everybody and made an issue of it.

L: So she didn't tell anybody?

LAK: No, to this day, nobody else knew what I had done.

When this event took place, Lakshmidevamma was around seventeen years old. More than fifty years later, the memory of it was fresh and still called up the newness and nervousness felt by a young daughter-in-law getting used to the mores and ways of the in-law house. Nagaraja later told me this had been the first time he had heard of the incident. I wondered if the manner in which I had phrased my question ("marrying into the house across the street") had unlocked the memory of having trod the border between being familiar with the Murthy household and being unfamiliar with it as a daughter-in-law.

The poignancy of the narrative is in the manner in which it explores the experience of vulnerability with humor and grace. As she struggled to find her feet in her new home, Lakshmidevamma found herself inadequate to perform tasks that were not only expected of a daughter-in-law in those times but especially of one who came from an artistically talented family. The sister-in-law's gaze is symbolic of the public scrutiny Lakshmidevamma felt herself under, but as the conversation unfolded it was clear that for her this was a time of heightened self-consciousness as well. In fact, Lakshmidevamma mentioned later that in those early days she had not known even how to warm coffee on a wood firestove: "I used to stand with the vessel in my hand for ages, wondering how to place it on the fire without burning my hand, and my sisters-in-law would laugh at the sight." The narrative conveys the tremendous sense of fragility that marked familiar situations that Lakshmidevamma found herself in.

And yet Lakshmidevamma's mother-in-law, occupying a position of power in the domestic set-up, refused, time and again, to exploit her situation or even to arrive at a final assessment of her daughter-in-law's capabilities. With Chayamma, her peer and constant companion, away, the entire annual supply of pickle in question (raw mango not being available for a whole year until next summer), and her total unfamiliarity with the pickling process, and without experience to back her, for Lakshmidevamma the pickling incident was probably her most vulnerable moment in her in-law's home. Against the image of a young girl standing speechless with fear and guilt are the reassuring words of the experienced mother-in-law, "You didn't know, and I too didn't tell you."

The mother-in-law's refusal to blame her young daughter-in-law, preferring instead to share responsibility for the fiasco, and her natural forgiving of an innocent mistake made the memory of the episode immortal for Lakshmidevamma, imbuing it with moral meaning that resonates across five decades. That the experience remained a "potential" story for all this time perhaps says something about its depth as well as about the ultimate inexpressibility of its value in her life. While such everyday incidents and reparations may seem ordinary gestures and ordinary events, it is the narrative of the ordinary that shapes and fires one's clay. As I imagined a yard filled with *rangoli* designs, as I came to perceive the sophistication and boldness of Lakshmidevamma's political and social welfare work, and as I enjoyed the wonders of her kitchen, I came to see what an immeasurable difference her mother-in-law had made in those tender years, when her self-worth and talent could have been damaged for life.

Dodda Murthy: "Two Weeks at Sevagram Ashram"

In June 2004, with rains in the offing, Dodda Murthy and I sat in an inner room poring over back issues of almanacs of nearly seventy years and invitations to matha programs dating to the 1920s. This was an activity I relished on every visit to Sringeri, marveling at how Dodda Murthy's inexhaustible archive always had something I had not seen before. He read out some of his notes about the days of Mahatma Gandhi's Quit India Movement (1942) from his diary. I remarked that he had once told me about his experiences at Mahatma Gandhi's Sevagram Ashram (which Dodda Murthy also calls

Sevashram) near Wardha in Maharashtra. "Yes, that was a significant meeting," he said. He started to recount that experience again, and my tape recorder, as usual, stayed on. I realized too, as he recounted the experience, that I had forgotten some of the details.

DM: When I was studying in Shimoga in the high school, through all my reading I became very interested in Gandhi.

And there were some teachers who used to praise Gandhi a lot. And I became even more interested. So, friends, teachers, books, all these—in those days there was a lot of Gandhi activism. The Independence movement was in full swing, you see. I used to be *v-e-r-y* interested in the Independence movement.

And this interest rose and rose and rose, and it became a burning desire to go and see Gandhi.

In those days we were young, so how was it possible to go (to see Gandhi)?

If I had one rupee from pocket money that was a treasure!

After I started earning, I went. I decided to go, and I went.

Travel was also very difficult in those days. In 1944—

L: Was your father alive then?

DM: My father and mother were both alive.

L: And they didn't say anything?

DM: They were not very keen on all this. I didn't tell them I was going to see Gandhi at all

(*grins mischievously; I laugh*).

L: They wouldn't have let you go?

DM: They did not have much *interest* in Gandhi.

I was there for fifteen or twenty days (in Sevagram).

I worked there—

L: Oh!!

DM: Because there would be vegetables to cut.

And,

not only was there the cutting—every morning there would be heaps of vegetables to be cut and chopped, fresh vegetables, beautiful vegetables. Even Dasappa[69] used to come. Dasappa and his wife, Yashodamma,[70] they all used to come.

After the vegetables were cut, there was another task to do.

Something that we weren't used to—cleaning latrines.

L: Oh, yes! I have read that Gandhiji used to clean the latrines himself.

DM: He used to. But when I went, he wasn't well. So he didn't do it, but the rest of us used to. We would have to scrub and wash and do all that. Since I wasn't used to this, it was difficult. Dasappa used to do a fine job. I wasn't in Dasappa's group. There were a couple of others with me, of my own age. We used to do the task somewhat insincerely—(aśraddhavāgi).).

Noticing this, one day, the man in charge said to us,

"Look! If Gandhi had seen the kind of job you are doing, he would have punished you!"

"*He will punish you!*" he said.

Hearing this, I was promptly angry. I told myself,

"I have not come here to live permanently. I have come here for a few days. It may be best to leave."

I came to this decision.

"Who is going to put up with this punishment?" I thought.

Then, *next* he said—

(*voice drops*)

I felt a little scared also.

"What could the punishment be?" I wondered.

The man said,

"You know what he (Gandhiji) would have done to punish you?

He would have *fasted* for *one day.*"

L: Ayyo!

DM: "Because you are working without faith, he would have *fasted* for *one day* and experience the punishment himself," he said.

As soon as he said that, my hair stood on end (romāñca vāg biḍuttu).

Ahimsa works so wondrously! If Gandhi was to fast for an hour (on account of us), how miserable we would be! Thinking like this, I was immediately *converted.* Instantly, my anger disappeared, and I thought,

"No, no, I have to work properly. If Gandhi sees my work, what will he think?"

Then, from the next day, I started working at the lavatories very assiduously.

I remember this even today. Ahimsa works so powerfully!

Well, in the afternoon, there would be lunch. Wonderful food![71]

I wrote about my experience at Sevagram in six or seven articles for the *Tāyināḍu.*[72]

L: Oh, really? Can I get a copy?

DM: Do you want to see? It is in Kannada.

L: That's not a problem, I would love to.

DM: OK—I will pull out the papers and give them when you next come home.

The articles have many more details. I have forgotten many incidents—it's been over fifty years, you see!

(*resumes recollection of Sevagram*).

OK. After the lunch, we used to take some rest. Nobody worked in the afternoon in the ashram. Then, in the evening, he (Gandhiji) would go for a walk and we would accompany him e-v-e-r-y d-a-y.

About ten or fifteen of us following him.

Then, there was the evening prayer. The prayer used to be a wonderful experience. About an hour. Hindu, Muslim, all religions—a shloka from each religion, and at the end, shlokas from the *Bhagavad Gītā*.

Then, an accounting of how much yarn each ashram member had spun that day.

A girl would announce the names. *First*

"Bapuji!"

How much has Bapuji spun today? Somebody would announce on his behalf how much he had spun that day.

This way, everybody—Dasappa, also: "Dasappaji!."

Each person had to announce how much yarn he or she had spun that day.

L: What would they call you?

DM: I was still a young man. Also, I was only a visitor, and (Dodda Murthy guesses my intention) this accounting was not for me.

This was only for *permanent* residents of the ashrama.

The prayer for an hour—it used to be so silent. There used to be a small light, and it was a large stone-paved courtyard. Gandhi would sit in the center. We would all sit on the cool stone slabs. One hour. It used to be wonderful.

This used to be after the evening meal. The evening meal was at 6 PM everyday.

I remember even today—

One day, I started, I thought I would visit nearby Wardha to do some sight seeing. It was not very far, about *five miles.* But the *road* was not very good.

So I started.

After I finished seeing everything in Wardha, I reasoned,

"By the time I get back to the ashram, it will be past dinner time."

So I bought and ate some oranges, and maybe I drank some milk.

By the time I got back to the ashram, it was about 8 PM. Somewhere between 7:30 and 8:00 PM.

I went to Dasappa and was sitting there chatting with him.

Just then—there was a manager—what a satpurusha (noble person) he was!

What kind of people there were (in that place)!

The manager—he came there by chance. As soon as he saw me, he said,

"Narasimha Murthy! I don't think you were at tonight's dinner, right?"

I was taken aback!

When there were forty-five to fifty people at the dinner, how did he notice my absence?

And after all I was just a young man, nobody important.

"Yes, I did not come. I had gone to Wardha and got delayed."

"I have packed your dinner and kept it aside.

Please go to the kitchen and take it."

I went to the kitchen. There was this large covered plate. The cook gave it, and when I looked inside there were about eight to ten small cups with various dishes—everything that must have been served at the dinner!

And chappatis!

I was amazed—who was I but a small person?

Despite this, they had noticed my absence and kept this meal ready for me.

I remember this even today.

So I spent some time like this. Then a couple of young men from Nanjangud (near Mysore) came and we got to know each other.

L: So you went there *alone?*

DM: Yes! *Alone!*

I used to see Gandhi everyday.

I didn't speak to him—after all, I was not—

L: Seeing Gandhiji, with your own eyes!

DM: Saw him, stayed with him.

Everyday, when he used to go for his bath, along the path he took, there was a verandah. I used to sit there and watch him go by. Everyday, around 10 AM.

He used to have long baths, in a big brass tub. He used to walk slowly to his bath and chat quite a bit with children along the way.

On his way in and his way out, I used to see him.

It was only this seeing, never felt worthy enough to talk to him.

(*laughs self-deprecatingly*)

I was young in age. And what fitting topic would I have to *discuss* with him?

(*long pause, during which my tape is filled only with the hammering sound from the construction that is going on in the house and with the honking of vehicles outside; I turn toward the door, hearing something.*)

DM: Who is it?

L: Chayamma. Come, Chayamma!

(*Chayamma comes in with fresh jackfruit fries* (muḷaka) *and coffee.* She quietly listens to our conversation for a while and leaves.)

DM: So. Once there was a prayer meeting. And Gandhi never spoke to anybody during those times (*demonstrates through a still posture*).

There was this little girl he was very fond of.

Maybe a four or five year old. She came running into this prayer meeting, and I picked her up and carried her.

Hmm, how old do you think she would be now?

L: Sixty-four, sixty-five?

DM: Possibly. I remember even *today.*

(*a longish pause*)

Then, on the l-a-s-t day, a few of us, the two boys from Nanjangud and I—the three of us—were ready to leave.

Evening. We were supposed to halt at Wardha for the night. Stay at the Commerce College hostel with a friend.

It was evening, exactly around this time

(*looks at the clock hanging on the wall*).

Then

(*voice lowered*)

Gandhi, at that time, was coming back to the ashrama from his *walk.*

At that time we were in the *gāḍi* (the buggy cart).

The three of us got off and reached down and touched his feet in namaskara.

(*explains to me*)

That's the way one did namaskara to Gandhi. Not by joining palms.
"Hanh, bas! (That'll do)" he said.
Who?
Gandhi.
Then, Dasappa who was there, H. C. Dasappa,
he said,
(*almost inaudible tone*)
"These three boys are about to leave now. They have assured me that they will live according to *your teaching*. This is what they have assured me."
This he said in English to Gandhi.
(*in a quick and assertive tone*)
"*Let us see!*" (*Gandhi said*)
(*Dodda Murthy laughs in remembered awe.*)
He said nothing more.
Let us see.
He said, smiling.

L: That was all?

DM: *Nodaṇṇa*! (*Let us see!*)
That's what was said to us.
(*slaps the desk beside him*)
That was the l-a-s-t sight of him that I had.
His words. Just these three *words.* **Let us see.**
He said these to Dasappa, smiling.
These exact three *words.* I remember them to this day.
(*then, with a finality in tone*)
That was the *last sight.*
Those were the *last words.*
Then he went away.

Dodda Murthy went on to muse that he had gone to Sevagram at the "*correct time.*" If he had not gone in 1944, he would never have been able to see Gandhi. The previous year, Gandhi had been imprisoned, and the following year World War II ended in May, bringing the release of jailed leaders like Jawaharlal Nehru, Sardar Patel, and Rajendra Prasad. Political activity became intense with Independence becoming imminent, and Gandhi became very preoccupied traveling to Delhi, Bengal, and other places. Dodda Murthy ended the account by speculating that Gandhi perhaps never came back to Sevagram again.

Once I was back in the U.S., I went back to my earlier recording of Dodda Murthy's recollection, dated May 7, 1995. I was astonished by the similarity between the two narrations—they reflected each other *almost* word for word, even in spoken emphasis. The rise and fall of tones, the self-deprecating laughter, and the long pauses that constitute the moral cadence of the reminiscence, whose theme is humility—they were the same.

But there were also small differences between the two narrations, differences that made them speak to each other, enlivening each other. I questioned whether I could rely on one telling to comment about another telling, but when I brought this up with Dodda Murthy he simply said, "Fifty-sixty years is a long time to remember everything, you know." At the heart of both narrations is a sense of a self-transformation, as if the young brahmana from Sringeri had passed through an ethical sieve at Sevagram. A third narration of the experience comes to us in the form of the essay that Dodda Murthy wrote for the regionally acclaimed nationalist daily, *Tāyināḍu* (Motherland), eight years after the stay at Sevagram.

Running through both narrations are variations of the remarks, "I remember this even today" and "After all, who was I?" Sevagram, for Dodda Murthy, was a humbling experience through a series of "lessons." Although Dodda Murthy was already predisposed toward Gandhiji, it was a fiery nationalist sentiment fueled by reading, classmates, teachers, and the then prevailing mood of India that motivated him to undertake the arduous journey from a small town in the Malnad to another distant village in what is now Maharashtra, many hundred of miles away. In his 1952 two-part newspaper article, "My Experiences at Sevagram," Dodda Murthy describes the physical journey and then goes on to write, "I was amazed upon seeing a small village called Shegaon near Sevagram. I had not seen such a backward village ever, although I myself am from a small village in remote Malnad and I have seen many villages in my life. Perhaps the Mahatma selected this location for Sevagram so that so that he could transform this most backward region in India."[73]

The series of humbling experiences that Dodda Murthy undergoes at Sevagram begins with the cleaning of public toilets: Dodda Murthy must first learn to accept the idea of cleaning public toilets; second, he must learn how to clean them; third, he must clean them well; fourth, he must clean them with shraddha (faith), without disgust. In the 1995 recording, Dodda Murthy reports Dasappa's comment when he was doing a bad job of cleaning the lavatories. Dasappa (who was a Vokkaliga) remarked, "You brahmanas cannot bring yourselves to do this kind of work! You are only fit to lecture. You lecture well in colleges, that's about it!" Dodda Murthy realizes that cleaning of public latinres must also become a cleansing of the ego, this being the core of the ethics of service followed at Sevagram. Dodda Murthy's "conversion" is so complete, it seems, that decades later he is able to appreciate that "Dasappa used to do a fine job" (of cleaning toilets). The experience simultaneously gives Dodda Murthy a personal glimpse into the power of ahimsa, nonviolence, whose ethical force comes from the moral change it creates in the "opponent" through self-directed action.[74]

The prayer meetings and the postprayer accounting of yarn spinning activity at Sevagram made another permanent moral impression on Dodda Murthy. Still, reposeful, meditative, and, above all, deliberately pluralistic (the prayers themselves and the teamwork indicate a mixed community based on coexistence and collaborations), they redraw for Dodda Murthy the image of the "Indian nation." Such a nation uses indigenous modes of production through which it critiques foreign goods.

The manager's act of saving the meal for Dodda Murthy despite the lateness of the hour is something that Dodda Murthy recalls "even today" as a lesson in the ethics of other-consideration. So moved is he by the fact that a nonentity and a visitor such as himself is "remembered" that he describes the manager with a Sanskrit term not commonly used in everyday Kannada; a satpurusha (a noble person). No one, Dodda Murthy seems to realize, is small or insignificant at Sevagram.

Although I expressed my awe that Dodda Murthy had "actually seen" Gandhi, Dodda Murthy's "Gandhi" is one who has been internalized through a quiet process—not through conversation with him but by silently following him on his walks, by waiting to see him, by observing his interactions with others, by noting that Gandhiji calls himself to account first, before everybody else, even in yarn spinning. In the 1995 recording, Dodda Murthy had said, "Just to see Gandhi was puṇyā (religious merit)." The value of the silent imbibing of Gandhi's presence was in fact underscored for me by the climactic one-on-one encounter with Gandhiji, in which all Gandhiji said was "Let us see" to Dasappa (and, through him, to the three young men). When I asked Dodda Murthy after the June 2004 narration why this made such an impression on him, all he said in his typically understated way was, "It was a significant meeting." I turned to the earlier recording again. There, Dodda Murthy closes the narrative with the remark, "Gandhi was a stubborn man. He must have seen hundreds of persons like me." "Which of these," Gandhi's single remark seems to suggest, "will *practice* what they say? Only time will tell." For Dodda Murthy the two weeks at Sevagram had provided, indeed, a rich harvest for life.

Ethics, an Imagined Life

"It will be good to read this when the rains come," said Dodda Murthy as I gave him a copy of this book's chapters in draft as June approached, the month when the monsoon usually set in. Already rainwater was pouring down the roof of the Rameshwara temple in the courtyard and splashing noisily on the soaking earth. I liked to imagine Dodda Murthy sitting in his armchair on the veranda and reading about himself and people he knew—what would he think? So intrigued by the past, so meticulous about preserving documents about it, so fastidious in "telling things as they are," which pasts would he recognize in this book, and which tellings? He was amused and moved by my choice to retell his reminiscences of his "Sevagram" days, but added, "Those days were like that."

In this book, I have tried to explore, in one South Indian town, the connections between oral narrative, moral identity, and the poetics of everyday language and ceremonial speech. My central question has been: What relationships do individuals envisage between generalized moral imperatives, moral reflection, and acts in everyday life? Stylized narratives of ashirvada and stories from conversations illustrate how experience-centered approaches can vivify and challenge the study of ethics, which usually overlooks the crucial role of oral narrative and everyday practice in shaping moral being. Such a perspective would privilege how people engage with precepts and tell us something about the dynamic ways in which individuals not only imagine and live out their ethical worlds, but convey this imagination to others through narrative. Texts leave their times and enter ours to become new texts, *our* texts, and the ethical process is one of gathering and unfolding manifold impressions—that are enlivened through emotional engagement.

Studies of Hindu ethics over the decades have brought to light the complexity of moral precepts in texts like the various Dharmashastras, the Upanishads, the Puranas, and the Sanskrit epics. More recently, such studies have explored how some of these texts address topical issues like abortion, euthanasia, vegetarianism, and the environment.[1] Epic narrative, nationalist moral tracts, sectarian codebooks, and devotional literatures further show us that prescriptive discourse is itself significantly differentiated and can generate a vibrant moral tension amid its variety.[2] Oral traditions of course endorse, refuse, alter, or even pointedly ignore the Valmiki *Ramayana*, the Vyasa *Mahabharata*, or other panregional written texts that are generally considered repositories of ethical models, and thus indicate that the normative center of written texts is best imagined as diffused in everyday life.[3] Underlying and complicating this diffusion are intertwined relationships between the "oral," the "written," and the "practiced."[4]

Ethnographic studies of Hindu life seek to make us hear the many cadences in which Hindus interpret and practice pilgrimage, gift giving, religious storytelling, renunciation, and ritual and priesthood.[5] How do men and women in different cultural settings arrive at such culturally salient ideas? How do different caste groups claim cultural genres, and how do individual performers express variation and dissent through their repertoires? How do political "ideologues" cultivate religious symbolism to generate political community? Asking questions such as these, ethnographic approaches can yield images that refuse flattened perceptions of Hinduism, holding up for scrutiny both imported canons and indigenous categories of interpretation. Lived perspectives of religious practice also perform the useful task of returning us to vocabularies and values that are often shared by Hindus worldwide and show us how connections are made to and across transnational forces and a global world.[6] As the critique of anthropology cautions, one must recognize that such knowledge passes through many sieves and is provisional and partial.

In this attempt to understand the "normative ambience" in the smarta brahman community of the small pilgrimage town of Sringeri, with its Dharmashastra-endorsing matha, I hope to leave readers with impressions of normative discourses that are strictly circumscribed, playfully teased out, but always imaginatively and plurally lived out. Important to this lived environment, for example, are the terms upachara, shastra, and sampradaya that come with long regional and panregional histories and are deployed variously and creatively in everyday parlance. The relational emphases of these terms argue that moral authority is most fruitfully understood as something that accommodates variant, dynamic, and symbiotic constructs of self, text, and community.[7] Moral articulations take place in the ethos of Sringeri, but, like that of every place, it is an ethos that is hardly static or singular; it is distinctively and differently characterized in regional consciousness, in festival celebrations, or in town histories and architectural expressions. Shaping these various configurations of Sringeri's ethos is the important historically developed theme of upachara, broadly understood as appropriateness in conduct and specifically as traditions of hospitality. One way to read Sringeri's history is to see it as wrapped around the history of the matha, which is marked by networks, linkages, and exchanges between kings and ascetics, agricultural landlords and tenants, gurus and townspeople, or even deities and devotees. It is an ethos of interrelationships that has maintained Sringeri as a significant religious, economic, and politically empowered site through gifting, expressions of honor and status, and acts of inclusion and exclusion. The culture of upachara is articulated in a past in which rina (debt) and dana (gifting) have bound the historical, the administrative, and the political to each other.

If upachara occupies a special place in the fluid normative imagination of Sringeri, so also do shastra and sampradaya, concepts that indeed can be seen to resonate far afield in other Hindu societies. But the centrality of these terms needs to be understood contextually. Shastra, for example, has witnessed great exposition in written literature—extending across virtually all realms of life—over two millennia—and this early literature is suggestive of shastra's rootedness in context. Yet the colonial period attempted to produce a pan-Hindu indigenous, although English-bred, judicial system, which resulted in a decontextualized uniform application of the Dharmashastras. With the establishment of the Anglo-Indian judiciary system, and the passage of land reform acts by the late-twentieth century, the Sringeri matha's jurisdiction had become restricted to "religious" spheres (in which it continues to be considered a shastric authority) and its economic holdings had considerably shrunk. However, the theological authority associated with the concept of shastra remained powerful, aloof from this turbulence—as everyday Sringeri discourse in the smarta community indeed testifies. The notion of shastra is associated with the performance of dharma, the creation of auspiciousness, and compliance with context-specific regulations on conduct.

Yet, normative authority is distributed. Sampradaya, paddhati, niyama, achara, and so on engage in spirited and creative interplay in everyday situations. The terms of moral authority embedded in these concepts vary across social contexts, and also across power symmetries. What is important to recognize as one follows the supple meanings of these concepts is that normative discourse is imbibed in imperceptible and profoundly dialogic ways, in many seeing-and-doing orientations. The normative is kept from being petrified or relegated to one set of codebooks not only by a wide range of sources (exemplars, traditions, sacred books, principles), of which shastra is but one, but also by a desire for a dharmically accountable and auspicious life. Continuous reflection on the obligatory, on the bounds of innovation, and on what gives a "sense of fulfillment" (manas trupti) also keep normative authority and concomitant power challengeable and in flux. Conceptualizing an ethics-in-practice means that we need to understand how "injunction" and "action" come together to constitute what I have suggested to be an *imagined* normative text. This imagined text is constructed by each individual—or by a community—commingling memory and experience with learning and teaching.

The carefully articulated, communally shared moral poetics of performance of Sringeri's ashirvada display and celebrate shastra in a manner that privileges textual bodies like the Dharmashastras or the Puranas. A fascinating overlap emerges between the oral poetics of ashirvada and Sanskrit poetics in the concept of auchitya, dramaturgical propriety, but the overlap is all the more exciting when we consider the pervasiveness of propriety in everyday life. Conversational stories claim their own poetics, one that is located in the experiences of individuals and dialogic environments. The continuities between literary aesthetics and social aesthetics might suggest new ways to imagine our pasts and to imagine ourselves in renewed ways in the present.

Just as rasa poetics argues that the rasa experience provides an immersion in the *possibility* of an experience, a similar intimation of emotion occurs between tellers and listeners in conversationally shared stories about life experiences. Stories like the ones presented in this book embody values such as discernment (viveka) or subtlety (sukshma), humility (nigarva) or service (seve), but the terms could vary according to individual experiences. The creativity of normative imagination dissuades one from divining an *exhaustive* cultural list of moral keywords or codes, but it does point to the imbibing of a culture of ethics. An individual's engagement in ethical thinking and morally appropriate conduct is deeply diglossic, but to try to trace a stable map of this diglossia is like tracing an eddy. An individual's "moral" knowledge seems cumulative, crisscrossing, processual, episodic, and narratives are like "luminous details" of an always only partially visible moral map. Oral narration and moral life and living demand that dharma—the ethical—be understood as an ongoing process, one that produces, and is produced by, the imagined texts of daily life.

Notes

Introduction

1. Each state in India is divided into districts, and districts into taluks. The town of Sringeri is the headquarters of Sringeri Taluk, which is in Chikmagalur District in the state of Karnataka.

2. Sharada is also Sarasvati, the goddess of learning. The word *pīṭha* (seat or throne) is generally understood to include the temples, the matha itself, the Vedic school, and the library.

3. The Sringeri Vidya Bharati Foundation in the Pocono Mountains of Pennsylvania is the first extension of the Sringeri Shankara matha outside India. See http://www.svbf.org.

4. Today the town of Sringeri is governed by an elected municipal council that reports to the district and state governments.

5. See Marriott, *Village India*; Redfield, *Little Community*; Singer, "The Great Tradition"; Srinivas, *Religion and Society*. For how the folk/classical schema was problematized in relation to indigenous analogous categorizations of cultural forms, see, for example, Coomaraswamy, "Nature of "Folklore""; Vatsyayan, "Cultural Patterns," on *mārga* and *deśi*; also see Ramanujan, "Relevance of South Asian Folklore," for *akam* and *puṛam*. For a fuller critique of this debate, see Prasad, *Scripture and Strategy*.

6. Blackburn and Ramanujan, *Another Harmony*, pp. 19–20.

7. Ramanujan, "Where Mirrors Are Windows," p. 189.

8. In this context I recall the following episode that occurred early in my stay in Sringeri. When a friend suggested that I record the rare songs of the then eighty-year-old Padmavatamma, who lived about five miles outside of Sringeri, I went to her house with my tape recorder. Padmavatamma's first question to me was, "Do you want short songs or long songs, arati songs, or what kind of songs do you want?" When I fumbled and asked her if she knew "folksongs," using the Kannada term, *janapada gīte*, she replied, "illa, illa, janapada gītegaḷu ella īcege bandirodu alva?" ("No, no, folksongs and the like are a recent thing, aren't they?"). Such "recentness" of "janapada" as a category of "folk" tradition is also evident in the changing claims made by practitioners for their art form to be classified in one or another particular category. Kathryn Hansen finds this true of the North Indian musical theater called Nauṭankī where state patronage and competition for economic resources have played a substantial role in the futile efforts of Nauṭankī to claim a "classical" status. See Hansen, *Grounds for Play*, p. 45. It is hence difficult to disinvest these terms of their political histories and economic implications and sift out their aesthetic content when describing cultural material.

9. Abrahams, "Rhetoric of Everyday Life"; Hymes, "Ethnography of Speaking."

10. The nuanced insider-outsider crossdisciplinary debate, especially sharpened after Clifford, *Writing Culture*, would seem relevant here, but I treat the premises of "self" and "other" (which are continuously expressed) in the contexts of relationships and narratives that appear throughout this book. However, for critiques of the concept of "native researcher," see Abu-Lughod, "Fieldwork of a Dutiful Daughter"; Aguilar, "Insider Research"; Appadurai, "Putting Hierarchy"; Brettel, *When They Read*; Nakhleh, "On Being a Native Anthropologist"; Srinivas, "Some Thoughts," for example. For a view of the native/non-native divide as a flexible configuration of "shifting identifications," see Narayan, "How Native Is a 'Native' Anthropologist?" and Herndon, "Insiders, Outsiders."

11. Strictly speaking, smarta brahmans, in addition, worship the five deities Shiva, Vishnu, Ganesha, Surya, and Devi. In practice, however, there is great variation. For an excellent overview of the smarta tradition in Sringeri, see Sawai, *The Faith of Ascetics.*

12. Ricoeur, *Time and Narrative*, and *From Text to Action*; also see Bakhtin, *Dialogic Imagination.*

13. Dundes, "Metafolklore"; also see Narayan, "The Practice of Oral Literary Criticism."

14. See Narayan, *Mondays*, especially p. xii.

15. Mills, "Feminist Theory," p. 174.

16. Laidlaw, *Riches and Renunciation*, p. 21.

17. Pollock, "The Theory of Practice," p. 499.

18. Laidlaw, *Riches and Renunciation*, p. 9.

19. Abrahams, *Everyday Life*, p. 1.

20. Khare similarly finds that a study of Hindu kinship in practice cannot admit a strict separation between "normative" categories of kinship as expressed in Sanskrit

texts and "pragmatic" kinship (as practiced) since they reflect each other in complex ways. See Khare, *Normative Culture.*

21. See Paniker for a succinct review and analysis of a wide variety of Indian narrative genres. See Paniker, *Indian Narratology.*

22. Narayan, *Storytellers.*

23. Blackburn, *Moral Fictions*, p. 278.

24. Ibid., p. 307.

25. See Bose, *Ramayana Revisited*; Hindery, "Hindu Ethics"; also Bhattacharya, *Dharma-Adharma.*

26. See the essays in Schomer and McLeod, *Sants.*

27. Patil, "Panchatantra."

28. I will elaborate on these insights in chapter 6, where I present and discuss a set of conversationally narrated stories. Some key articulations toward a narrativist ethics are by Hauerwas, "The Self as Story"; MacIntyre, *After Virtue*, Nussbaum, *Love's Knowledge*, and Newton, *Narrative Ethics.*

29. However, narrative ethics has seen considerable application in the field of bioethics, particularly in physician-patient interaction. See, for example, Nelson, *Stories and Their Limits.*

30. See, for example, Rosenwald and Ochberg, *Storied Lives*; Stahl, *Literary Folkloristics.*

31. Performance-centered analyses were influenced by developments in sociolinguistics in the 1960s. See, especially, Goffman, *Presentation of Self*; Gumperz and Hymes, *Ethnography of Communication;* for its fuller formulation in the 1970s and 1980s, see Abrahams, *Man-of-Words*; Bauman, *Verbal Art*; and Bauman, *Story, Performance, Event.* For a thorough historiography of the performance-centered approach in folklore and sociolinguistics, see Bauman and Briggs, "Poetics and Performance."

32. Ochs and Capps, *Living Narrative*, pp.1–58.

33. See, especially, Ben-Amos, "'Context'"; Georges, "Timeliness"; Bauman, *Story, Performance, Event.*

34. Norrick, *Conversational Narrative*; Hymes, *In Vain.*

35. See, especially, the insightful work of Cruikshank, *Life Lived Like a Story*, and also *Social Life of Stories.*

36. Pollock, "Theory of Practice."

1. Sringeri: Place and Placeness

1. A common mistake, one that I also initially made, is to think *malnad* comes from *maḷe* (rain).

2. Das, *Census of India.*

3. Liddell and Scott, *A Greek-English Lexicon*, s.v. *ethos* 1 and 2. I am grateful to my colleagues Micaela Janan and Melvin H. Peters at Duke University for leading me through Greek concepts and references. Thanks also to S. Nagarajan.

4. Halloran, "Aristotle's Concept," p. 60.

5. See note 3.

6. Reynolds, "*Ethos* as Location," p. 327.

7. On the broader genre of puranas, see Rocher, *The Purāṇas*; see also Narayana Rao, "Purāṇa."

8. I have retained the tense shifts in Ganapati Avadhani's narration.

9. This female initiative is absent in the Rishyashringa episodes of the Valmiki *Ramayana* in which Romapada's advisers *send* courtesans to attract Rishyashringa. For female orientations expressed in other oral Ramayana traditions, see Narayana Rao, "A Ramayana of Their Own," especially for a narrative song called "Śāntagovindanāmālu" sung by coastal Andhra women. Also see note 11.

10. A Vedic fire sacrifice performed to obtain sons.

11. The courting of Rishyashringa, his journey to, and his stay in Romapada's kingdom, his marriage to Shanta, and his officiating at the *putrakāmeṣṭi* sacrifice are recounted in sections 8–16 of the first book of Valmiki's *Ramayana*, the Balakanda. See Goldman's translation, pp. 139–158. In the Valmiki *Ramayana*, Shanta is Romapada's daughter, but I have heard versions in which she is either Dasaratha's adoptive daughter or Dasaratha's daughter given in adoption to Romapada.

12. Such connections between temples or sacred places are typical of sthala puranas, as Anne Feldhaus notes in *Connected Places*. In Tirupati, for example, a pilgrimage to the Venkateshwara temple on Tirumala Hill is considered "complete" only after the visit to the Padmavati temple in Tirupati.

13. See vignette on Putta Murthy and Lakshmidevamma's family.

14. Conversation recorded on January 22, 1995.

15. The school is characterized by its adherence to Vedic ritual and sacrifice. The debate is one of the well-known stories about Shankara's philosophical victories. The belief in the smarta tradition is that the debate was refereed by Mandana Mishra 's wife, Ubhayabharati, herself a learned scholar and an incarnation of Goddess Sarasvati.

16. However, the *Guruvamṣakāvya*, a Sanskrit work, which details the history of successive gurus of the Sringeri matha from the times of Shankara to 1734, states otherwise. According to this text, written by Kashi Lakshmanashastri, a Vedic scholar in the matha sometime between 1735 and 1739, it was Vidyaranya, the fourteenth-century guru and administrator, who established these temples. Sawai, *Faith of Ascetics*.

17. Aiyar Balasubrahmanya, *Greatness of Sringeri*, p. 6.

18. Rao, *Sringeri Revisited*; Aiyar Balasubrahmanya, *Greatness of Sringeri*, for example.

19. Kamath, *Historiography of Karnataka*, p. 25.

20. Thapar, *Ancient Indian Social History*, p. 75.

21. Mahavira (orginally King Vardhamana), who founded the Jain religion, is dated around 550 BC. See Rice, *Mysore Inscriptions*.

22. Ramesam, *Sri Śaṅkarācārya;* Sawai, *Faith of Ascetics*.

23. Venkataraman, *Throne of Transcendental Wisdom*.

24. The *Śaṅkara Digvijaya* texts are also known as *Śaṅkaravijaya*. The precise date and authorship of these variant biographies, composed between the fifteenth

and the nineteenth centuries, remains speculative. But the most binding, especially for adherents of the Sringeri tradition, is the *Mādhavīya Digvijaya*, an account ascribed to Madhava (who is generally identified as Vidyaranya, the famous twelfth guru of the matha in the fourteenth century). See Swami Tapasyananda, *Sankara-dig-vijaya;* and Padmanaban, *Srimad Sankara Dig-vijayam*. For a succinct overview of various extant biographies of Shankara, see Vidyashankar Sundaresan's essay at http://www.advaita-vedanta.org/avhp/sankara-vijayam.html.

25. See Ayyangar, *Studies in South Indian Jainism*.

26. Karnataka 2001 census data accessed at: http://www.bangaloreit.com/html/govtinformation/censuspaper2/Paper-2%20Chapter-9.pdf.

27. For how residents of Arampur in Bihar negotiate and express intercommunal relations in shared space, see Gottschalk, *Beyond Hindu and Muslim*.

28. The two main streets in Sringeri, Bharati Street and Harihara Street, bear the names of the personages involved in the Shringapura grant—Bharatikrishna Tirtha, the matha's guru at that time, and Harihara I, the Vijayanagara emperor.

29. Venkataraman, *Throne of Transcendental Wisdom*.

30. Oral communication, Murne mane Rambhattru, Giridhara Shastry, N. Lakshmidevamma, Sringeri, 1994–1995.

31. Oral communication, Giridhara Shastry, May 2004.

32. Strings of beads ("rosaries") made of basil stem, crystal, or the *rudrākṣa* seed.

33. Census of India, 2001.

34. Information provided by Giridhara Shastry, October 5, 2005.

35. Such a conception does not of course prevent property-based litigation, which exists in Sringeri.

36. Oral communication, Putta Murthy, 1996.

37. Conversation with Dodda Murthy, 1995.

38. Conversation with Dodda Murthy, January 26, 1995.

39. See Bowring, *Eastern Experiences,* for his detailed observations of the economic politics of areca nut cultivation in the Malnad and the former Bombay presidency in the 1870s.

40. Ibid., p. 128.

41. See Prasad, "Celebrating Allegiances," for a more detailed exploration of how senses of community vary in Sringeri in relation to "place" and "public festivity."

42. Flueckiger, *Gender and Genre*, p. 177.

43. On the ninth day of Navaratri is "Ayudha puja" when vehicles, instruments, and implements are worshipped because tools are believed to embody the goddess on that day. I attended this puja at the Choudeshwari temple with my close friend, Uma, whose family owns a transportation business. The goddess Choudeshwari is also their family deity. I became the unofficial photographer as the family performed a simple puja to their glistening lorries, which were decked brilliantly with garlands of marigold and jasmine.

44. Bauman, "Differential Identity"; Flueckiger, *Gender and Genre*.

45. Shuman, "Dismantling Local Culture."

46. The question how social and political processes mediate the elusive and concrete expression of collective identity has been widely explored in the social sciences

and humanities. For recent explorations, see Anderson, *Imagined Communities;* Herzfeld, *Poetics of Manhood*; and Ramaswamy, *Passions of the Tongue.* However, the fields of folklore, ethnography of communication, and symbolic anthropology have been centrally interested in the ways in which expressive traditions reflect and manifest "group identity"; for example, see Abrahams, "Phantoms of Romantic Nationalism." For earlier theorization about collectivity that emerges from a common morality or subscription to a sacred order, see Durkheim, *Elementary Forms*; but for a discussion of how ceremonial events, rather than only reaffirm solidarity, contain immense "antistructural" potential, see Turner, *Ritual Process.* Place-oriented "belonging" is also treated in literature on pilgrimage (Feldhaus, *Water and Womanhood*), nationalism (Van der Veer, *Religious Nationalism*), and diaspora (Gupta and Ferguson, *Anthropological Locations*, and Prasad, "*Live Like the Banyan Tree*"). For how the carnivalesque and the marketplace could index alternative community identity formation, see Bakhtin, *Rabelais;* Kapchan, *Gender on the Market;* and Falassi, *Time Out of Time.*

47. Malnad upachara is a popular motif in regional literature, beautifully explored in Kannada fiction such as Kuvempu's *Malenāḍa Chitragaḷu* (Sketches of the Malnad), 1933, Gorur Ramaswamy Iyengar's *Haḷḷiya bāḷu* (Life in the village), 1948, and Chandrasekhara Kambar's *Singarevva and the Palace* (English translation by Laxmi Chandrasekhara, 2002).

48. While Malnad traditions of hospitality express their distinctive idiom, the notion of hospitality itself in fact is accorded a high place in the normative literatures, the narrative traditions, and the everyday and ritual practices of various South Asian cultures. In the Hindu context the Sanskrit and Kannada term for hospitality is *ātithya,* which comes from *a,* meaning "without," and *tithi*, meaning "specific date." Thus atithi, a guest, is one who comes without prior notice. The Hindu saying from the *Taittirīya Upaniṣad, atithi dēvō bhava* (guests are like gods) indicates the exalted status of hospitality in Hindu social and ritual practice. According to the *Manu Dharmaśāstra*, hospitality is one of five daily sacrifices a Hindu householder must perform (in Buhler, *Laws of Manu*). The *Rig Veda* states, "A person becomes the protector, and a friend of one who offers him hospitality in the right way" (trans. in O'Flaherty, *Rig Veda*). The *Kaṭhōpaniṣad* narrates the famous story of how even Yama, the god of death, had to grant three boons to Nachiketas, a young boy, for having neglected his duties as a host for three days when Nachiketas visited him. Post-Vedic literature also specifies in great detail the rules of conduct to be observed by hosts and guests, discusses breaches of hospitality, and recommends reparations. For example, the *Āpastamba Dharmasūtra,* a Sanskrit treatise on conduct, says, "If a brahmana that has not studied the Veda comes to the house of a brahmana, the latter should offer him a seat, water and food, but need not rise to receive him" (cited in Kane, *History of Dharmaśāstra* 2.2:753). The annual shraaddha ritual, in which ancestors are "invited" and "fed," is an example of how rites and responsibilities of hospitality apply to other worlds as well. Many Hindu stories, especially in bhakti literature, illustrate that the intertwined relationships between guests and hosts are seldom straightforward, complicated as they are by caste injunctions, ritual

mechanics, and moral stipulations (see Aklujkar, "Sharing the Divine Feast"). For more on hospitality, see Khare, "Indian Hospitality."

49. Das, *Census of India*, p. 20.

50. Conversation with Putta Murthy recorded on May 5, 1992, Sringeri.

51. Conversation with Putta Murthy, December 24, 1994, Sringeri. My husband, Prasad, was visiting during Christmas break.

52. PM: Putta Murthy, PR: Panduranga, P: Prasad, L: Leela.

53. In Kittell, *Kannada-English Dictionary;* Monier-Williams, *Sanskrit-English Dictionary*; and Apte, *Student's Sanskrit-English Dictionary*, the meanings of the word upachara include "service," "attendance," "conduct," "behavior," and "acts of civility." The close link between athithya and upachara is exemplified in Dharmashastric elucidations of puja (worship of deities), which comprises sixteen acts of service called the *sōdaṣōpacāra* (*sōdaṣa* = sixteen + *upacāra* = acts of service). These acts derive from a model of hospitality in which deities are supreme guests. Deities, as guests, are invited, welcomed, seated, offered water to wash and bathe, given clothes, incense, and ornaments, fed lavishly, paid regal homage, treated to music and dance, and bidden farewell.

54. Putta Murthy passed away in January 2003 of throat cancer.

55. Kittel, *Kannada-English Dictionary*, p. 232

56. See Gold, *Fruitful Journeys*, for a lively account of her experience and study of the "darshan bus tour" in Rajasthan.

2. *Connectedness and Reciprocity: Historicizing Sringeri Upachara*

1. Bunts are a nonbrahman, agricultural community.

2. Also transliterated in literature as ṛṇa.

3. *Rina* + *anubandha*; *anubandha* = bond.

4. *Āpastamba Dharmasūtra* II.4.9.5–6, quoted in Nath, *Dana*. See also Hiriyanna, *Outlines of Indian Philosophy*, pp. 45–46, for his note on *ṛṇa-traya*, or the "triad of obligations."

5. *Śatapaṭha Brāhmaṇa*, I.7.2.1–5, translated and cited in Pannikkar, *Vedic Experience*, 393. See also Heesterman, *Broken World;* Madan, "Ideology of the Householder"; and Malamoud, *Cooking the World*, for more on obligatory indebtedness.

6. See Khare, *Normative Culture and Kinship*, p. 125. Other coordinates in Khare's fourfold classification are karma (effort), kartavya (duty), and daiva (fate).

7. But there are also many subhashitas, popular Sanskrit verses, that stress the negative consequences of accumulating rinas. For example, one such verse reads, "Of redemption from debt or sin, it is better to be free of debts: so it has been said; the sin may torment one in the next world, but the fire of debt burns one here as well as there"; translation in Sternbach, *Maha-Subhashita-Sangraha*, p. 1840.

8. The origins of the two brothers, Harihara (commonly known as Hakka) and Bukka, is a matter of speculation among historians. While some scholars argue that the brothers were from neighboring Andhra Pradesh (Venkataramanayya, *Studies in*

the Third Dynasty, for instance), others claim that Harihara and Bukka were of local origin and were ministers in the erstwhile Hoysala kingdom. See Nilakanta Sastri, *History of South India*.

9. See Thapar, *A History of India*. Not much is known about Sringeri in the years between the arrival of Shankara in the eighth century, when he instituted the hermitage and Sharada temple, and the emergence of the Vijayanagara kingdom in the fourteenth century. There were three successive Vijayanagara dynasties after its establishment in the early fourteenth century, until the combined Muslim forces of Bijapur, Golkonda and Ahmednagar, Bidar and Berar, in northern Deccan, overthrew the last Vijayanagar king, Sadashiva Raya, in the battle of Talikota in 1565 and destroyed the capital, Hampi. The rule of Krishnadevaraya (1509–1529) is considered the pinnacle of Vijayanagara glory during which the Sringeri matha was able to consolidate its vast holdings and acquire a high profile.

10. Stein, *Peasant State*, Devi, *Religion in Vijayanagara Empire;* Shastry, *History of Śṛingēri*.

11. The Shri chakra is a complex, powerful Tantric diagram uniting the male and female energies of Shiva and Shakti through nine enclosed triangles. The centerpoint (bindu) represents the eternal union of the two. The Shri chakra symbolizes the universe and infinity. Shankara is believed to have placed a Shri chakra (that he had etched on stone) below the image of the goddess Sharada in Sringeri.

12. Devi, *Religion in Vijayanagara Empire*, p. 11. Ever since, the gurus of the matha have been known as "Karnāṭaka Simhāsana pratiṣṭāpanācarya," or the sanyasis who are founders of the throne of Karnataka (Nagaraja, Sringeri, oral communication, 1995; also Shastry, *History of Śṛingēri*, p. 21. Sawai notes the variant title of "Karnāṭasimhāsanasthāpakācārya," or the preceptor of the supporters of the Karnataka dynasty, *Faith of Ascetics*, p. 32fn.

13. The obligatory fee a disciple offers to his or her guru in return for the teaching. Conventionally, as Kane notes, there was no agreement about the fee a student paid the teacher. The Dharmashastras recommend variously in this matter: the student could offer what was affordable or could ask the guru to specify the fees. Token fees or none were also acceptable, and Kane notes that very rarely do stories depict teachers making unreasonable demands (*History of Dharmaśāstra*, 3:958). Yet Hindu narrative also explores the ethical implications of unjust demands such as Drona's demand for Ekalavya's thumb to prevent Ekalavya from being a possible competitor to Arjuna.

14. Thapar, *A History of India*.

15. Kulke, "Mahajanas, Mahants."

16. Conversation recorded September 16, 1994. Sringeri.

17. Gonda, *The Ritual Sutras*. p. 140.

18. Row, *Selections*; Shastry, *History of Śṛingēri*; Devi, *Religion in Vijayanagara*; Venkataraman, *Throne of Transcendental Wisdom*.

19. Kulke, "Mahajanas, Mahants," p. 132.

20. By the eighteenth century Sringeri begins to be referred to as a jagir (land endowment with tax income). A Persian term, it gained currency during the Sultanate

period. A jagirdar is the entity that has been given a jagir, and jagirdari is the system in which jagirs are gifted.

21. Venkataraman, *Throne of Transcendental Wisdom*, p. 57.

22. Kulke, "Mahajanas, Mahants."

23. A gold coin of that time with the figure of a pagoda on one side. While most recent texts refer to pagodas, studies of Vijayanagara coinage use the more general term of varaha, which is a gold coin weighing 52 grams. Various figures of gods and goddesses are imprinted on them, and the term *pagoda* refers to one such coin, which has the figure of a pagoda on it. A gram of gold was worth about Rs. 400 in 1996, and in contemporary reckoning a pagoda would be about Rs. 21,000. In 1818 a pagoda was worth three and a half rupees. Dirks, *Hollow Crown*.

24. There is substantial writing on how redistributive processes connected temple rituals and patrons in medieval south India. See Nilakanta Sastri, *A History of South India*; Appadurai and Breckenridge, "The South Indian Temple"; and Stein, *Peasant State*, for patterns of patronage pertaining to south India. Appadurai, in *Worship and Conflict*, provides a detailed case study of the Śrī Pārtasāratī Svāmi Temple in Madras City. For studies of temple patronage in particular kingdoms, see Talbot, *Precolonial India in Practice*, for Kakatiya Andhra (especially chapter 3); and Dirks, *Hollow Crown*, for Pudukottai, Tamilnadu (especially chapter 9). Also see pp. 79–81 in Fuller, *Camphor Flame*, for a critique of Dirks and Appadurai and observations of contemporary patterns of patronage.

25. Although symbolically it is the deity who "allocates" honors, the process of allocation, controlled by temple authorities, could be political in itself. However, as Dirks points out, the king is still king and in "an a priori sense first devotee, and first to be honored in any state temple"; *Hollow Crown*, p. 288.

26. Shastry, *History of Śṛingēri.*

27. Part of puja, arati is the ceremonial waving of oil lamps, or a camphor flame, at the conclusion of a ritual after which the sanctified flame is taken around among all devotees present.

28. Oral communication, Murne mane Rambhattru, 1995. *Mane* is pronounced "maney."

29. Shastry, *History of Śṛingēri.*

30. Row, *Selections*, p. lxxxii.

31. Stein, *Peasant State*, p. 455.

32. Dirks, *Hollow Crown*, p. 136.

33. Interestingly, Dirks finds in his study of Pudukottai that brahmans "were among the first to speak of their loyalty and obligation [to the king]. The royal gift of land, rather than creating danger and dependence per se, preserved the relative autonomy of the Brahman at the same time that it displayed the moral excellence of the king"; *Hollow Crown*, p. 136fn.

34. Thapar, *From Lineage to State*, Pp. 91–92.

35. Row, Selections, p. lxx.

36. While land grants undoubtedly made brahmans and the matha more visible and powerful it has been noted that land grants are less "an indication of traditional

Brahman power or peasant subordination than a reflection of alliance-building by aspiring agrarian elites who used ritual ranking to lift themselves over competitors and institutionalised their status by patronising gods and Brahmans"; Ludden, *Agrarian History of South Asia*, p. 82.

37. Thapar, *History of India*.

38. Shastry, *History of Sringeri*.

39. Quoted in Venkataraman, *Throne of Transcendental Wisdom*, p. 96.

40. Row, *Selections*, p. lxxviii.

41. Venkataraman, *Throne of Transcendental Wisdom*; Shastry, *History of Sringeri*; Sen, *Studies in Indian History*.

42. Quoted in Sen, *Studies in Indian History*, p. 165.

43. Ibid.

44. Kaditas are long scrolls of cloth coated with black areca or charcoal paste to make thick paper-like material that is folded in the form of books. The material used to write the two- to three-hundred-page books is white soapstone. Shastry, *History of Sringeri*.

45. Row, *Selections*; Shastry, *History of Sringeri*; Venkataraman, *Throne of Transcendental Wisdom*; Sastry, *Sri Sringeri Jagadguru*.

46. Venkataraman, *Throne of Transcendental Wisdom*.

47. Ibid.

48. Shastry, *History of Sringeri*.

49. Quoted in Row, *Selections*, p. lxxxiv.

50. Row, *Selections*; Shastry, *History of Sringeri*.

51. Shastry, *History of Sringeri*, p. 31.

52. Ibid., p. 54.

53. The Bijapur officers apparently complied with this, but given the rivalry between the Bijapur Adil Shahi rulers and the Nayakas, it is unclear why the Nayaka request was heeded.

54. Shastry, *History of Sringeri*, p. 29.

55. These include ornaments like the heavy gem-studded gold crown given by the Nizam of Hyderabad, the *makara kānti* (makara = crocodile; kānti = necklace), a crocodile-shaped necklace with diamonds and emeralds presented by Tipu Sultan, a diamond necklace presented by the raja of Jamakhandi, and a seven stringed necklace of pearls and diamonds. Other traditional insignia are the *svetachatra*, the brocaded white silk umbrella, and the silver throne (also given by Tipu Sultan) to be used by the guru only in ceremonial occasions. The now discontinued adda pallakki—the horizontally carried palanquin—was exclusive to the Sringeri matha.

56. Falassi, *Time Out of Time*, p. 4.

57. See Eaton, *Essays on Islam*, for how various rulers made statements of power by patronizing, desecrating, or plundering temples and sacred images.

58. *Sunnuds* (also called *sanads*) are legal documents such as patents or property titles.

59. Quoted in A. K. Shastry, *History of Sringeri*, p. 54. Interestingly, Dodda Murthy narrated a story (February 3, 1995) about Bowring's personal encounter with the

Sringeri guru, Ugra Narasimha Bharati. I reproduce here this story for the interesting light it sheds on "local knowledge" about colonial interaction with Sringeri:

> The guru had been camping in Bangalore. While he was camping—this was before the Maharaja's times—this was during the rule of the British resident who ruled for forty years. He heard about Shri Narasimha Bharati's austerities, and he said, "I must see this for myself! They say he worships for *twenty hours* a day—does he really?" He got very curious, this British Resident. So, "Let's see," he thought, and set out for the camp at night. In the dead of night, it must have been 1 AM or 2. And he set out. Very soon, he arrived at the matha (in Bangalore). When he reached the matha, he stood there. As he stood there, he saw a curtain had been drawn across the doorway. The door was open, he could see the light inside—but a curtain had been drawn—and as he stood there, he thought, "O, the swami is doing his puja." It wasn't locked or anything, just—an attendant was standing there. "Can you part the curtain just a bit?" the Resident asked. The attendant thought, "This foreigner looks like somebody important, somebody in power," and parted the curtain a little—he wouldn't have done it for others. You could see the guru. And when the attendant drew the curtain, the resident saw that the guru was seated, performing the abhisheka (ritual anointing of deity), and immersed in puja. He saw this, and thought, "Oh, so what I've heard is true then." He doffed his hat and left! He didn't say anything, just doffed his hat and went away.

60. Until recently, Sringeri celebrated a festival (utsava) called the adda pallakki utsava twice or thrice a year, when the guru would be carried in the palanquin down one of the main streets in Sringeri. Other streets in Sringeri could only accommodate udda pallakki, the "length-wise" palanquin; Dodda Murthy and Chayamma, oral communication, 1996.

61. Venkataraman, *Throne of Transcendental Wisdom*, p. 103.

62. Recorded conversation, May 7, 1995, Sringeri.

63. Stein, *Peasant State*, p. 146–147.

64. Thapar, *Ancient Indian Social History*, pp. 91, 98. The case of Bommayya of Muginādu who, in 1674, was allotted an areca grove and in return had to assume charge of worship at a temple in nearby Anigunda is one of numerous such arrangements. Shastry, *History of Śṛiṅgēri*.

65. By the time Sringeri lost its jagirdari status in 1958, the Sringeri Jagir comprised 47 villages, 23 in Sringeri Taluk and 24 in other taluks. Its total area was 47,442 acres, of which 16,636 acres were cultivated, and 3,217 acres of cultivated land given away in minor inam. Venkataraman, *Throne of Transcendental Wisdom*, p. 206.

66. Conversation with Giridhara Shastry. Recorded in Vidyaranyapura on January 9, 1996.

67. The matha's office is now in the precincts of the matha/temple complex.

68. Prayers incumbent upon initiated brahman males.

69. Conversation recorded on December 24, 1994.

70. Keane, *Signs of Recognition*, p. 15.

71. January 9, 1996, Vidyaranyapura.

72. I have had to omit the names here both for reasons of confidentiality.

73. Conversation recorded May 1995.

74. R: Resident. At the request of the resident, I have reproduced this conversation without names of specific individuals.

75. Conversation recorded May 1995, Sringeri.

76. Rajan, *Land Reforms*, p. 56.

77. "Mysore" today refers to the town and district of Mysore, the former capital of the kingdom of Mysore. Along with the former state of Coorg (Kodagu), the Kannada-speaking parts of former Bombay and Madras Presidencies, and parts of the Nizam's Hyderabad, the Mysore kingdom became part of Karnataka in 1956.

78. With respect to the 1958 act, it was generally felt among political experts in the government of India that "the ceilings allowed by the many state governments were too high, that the exemptions allowed were too generous, and that not enough was being done to safeguard the tenant"; Rajan, *Land Reforms*, p. 24. For a detailed presentation of the complex macro- and microlevel political events and policies that led to both acts, see Rajan, *Land Reforms.* For a general overview of land-related legislation and the vast literature on it, see Ludden, *Agrarian History.*

79. Giridhara Shastry, oral communication, 1995.

3. *Shastra: Divine Injunction and Earthly Custom*

1. Spiced rice (*chitrānna*) and milk-based sweet dish (*pāyasa*).

2. Monier-Williams, *Sanskrit-English Dictionary.*

3. Although I shall discuss the problem of shastric textuality in some detail later in this chapter, I shall briefly note here one broad traditional classification of texts—shruti ("the heard tradition") and smriti ("the remembered tradition")—as articulated by post-Vedic exegetical schools. The genre of shruti, which encompasses the Vedas, considered to have been revealed to primeval sages (rishis), seers of truth, is eternal, authorless, and nonhuman (apaurusheya). Utterance being paramount, the intonation of shruti texts is fixed; indeed, the metaphysical power of the Vedas is in their precise recitation and ritual enactment, and the guardians of this literature held commensurate power in society. On the other hand is the genre of smriti, which admits human composition and witnesses extension and improvisation in a way that shruti literature does not. Smriti includes codes on conduct known as the Dharmashastras and the Dharmasutras, the Itihasas (histories, epics), the Puranas ("ancient lore"), and the Tantras (ritual manuals).

4. Pollock, "Theory of Practice", pp. 500–501. For a comprehensive overview of the phenomenon of shastra in early India, also see Pollock, "Idea of Śāstra" and "Playing by the Rules." Much of my summation of the historical traces of shastra comes from Pollock's analyses.

5. Daya Krishna notes that, interestingly, the term "Veda" has also been deployed to designate practical disciplines such as in the medical branch of Ayurveda (knowledge of longevity) and in Dhanurveda (knowledge of archery). Yet it seems that

Indian intellectual traditions have more prolifically prefixed or suffixed *shastra* to bodies of knowledge deemed practice oriented, as in *Arthaśāstra* (politics or statecraft), *Rasāyana śāstra* (chemistry), or *Kāmaśāstra* (love and sexuality); *Indian Philosophy*, p. 23.

6. Vatsyayan, *Bharata*, p. 163.

7. Ṛgveda 8.33.16.

8. See Dwivedi, "Concept of Śāstra"; Pollock, "Idea of Śāstra in Traditional India"; and Vatsyayan, "Inaugural Address."

9. Rocher, "The Kāmasūtra," p. 521.

10. Rangarajan, "Introduction," p. 15.

11. Pollock, "Theory of Practice."

12. Dwivedi, "Concept of Śāstra."

13. Keith, "The Science of Love," p. 468.

14. Titled *Mahābhāratatātparyanirṇaya* (The conclusive essence of the Mahabharata), 2.6–2.8. Accessed at http://www.sub.unigoettingen.de/ebene_1/fiindolo/gretil/1_sanskr/6_shastra/3_phil/Vedānta/m_mbhtnu.htm.

15. Vatsyayan, *Bharata*.

16. Lath, "Tandu," pp. 173–186.

17. Lath, "Ancient Dance."

18. For example, Olivelle argues that some passages in Manu's *Dharmaśāstra* seem to have quite consciously adopted vocabulary and concepts from Kautilya's *Arthaśāstra*. See Olivelle, "*Manu and the Arthaśāstra*."

19. See Jaimini, *Mīmāṃsa Sūtra*, 1.1.5–24 and 1.3, in Agarwal, *Six Systems of Indian Philosophy*.

20. Interestingly, in Kannada and Telugu, *adṛṣṭa* or *adṛṣṭamu* is used to refer to unanticipated good fortune.

21. No. 26, in Grimes, *Vivekacūdāmani*, p. 72.

22. Ibid., p. 177.

23. Ibid., pp. 61–62.

24. Sharma, *The Brahmasūtras*, 1: 80. See also chapter 15.

25. Ibid., p. 80; also see Stoker, "Conceiving the Canon," for a detailed consideration of canonicity in Madhva's doctrines; and Sarma, *An Introduction to Madhva Vedānta*.

26. See also Pollock, "Theory of Practice."

27. Dwivedi, "Concept of Śāstra," p. 46.

28. Smith, *Reflections on Resemblance*, p. 29; see also Stoker, "Conceiving the Canon."

29. Basava, vacana no. 581, in Ramanujan, *Speaking of Siva*, p. 85.

30. Allama Prabhu, vacana no. 465, quoted in Nagaraj, "Tensions in Kannada Literary Culture," p. 362.

31. Dēvara Dāsimayya, vacana no. 127, in Ramanujan, *Speaking of Siva*, p. 108.

32. Narayana Rao, *Śiva's Warriors*, p. 7.

33. Krsnadasa Kaviraja Gosvami, *Caitanya Caritāmṛta*.

34. Schweig, "Humility and Passion."

35. For fuller biographical analyses, see Bahadur, *Bahinabai;* Feldhaus, "Bahina Bai;" McGee, "Bahina Bai."

36. Abbott, *Bahiṇa Bāi*, abhanga 63.1, 2. I have modified Abbott's translation.

37. Ibid., abhanga 103, for example.

38. The term "Dharmashastra" commonly refers to both the Dharmashastras and the Dharmasutras.

39. Kane, *History of Dharmaśāstra,* 1:1.

40. The Dharmasutras and the Dharmashastras are part of the smriti tradition of sacred literature in contradistinction to shruti literature; i.e., the Vedas.

41. Buhler, *Laws of Manu*, Olivelle, *Dharmasūtras.*

42. L. Rocher, "Dharmaśāstras."

43. Olivelle, *Dharmasūtras*, p. xxi

44. Kane, *History of Dharmaśāstra*, vol. 5; Lingat, *Classical Law*, especially chapter 6. Two examples among the scores of well-known commentaries and digests are the ninth-century Medhatithi's *Bhāṣya* on Manu's Dharmashastra and the eleventh-century Vijnaneswara's *Mitākṣarā* on the Yagnavalkya smriti.

45. Olivelle, *Dharmasūtras* (n. 11), p. xxxix.

46. The sources of dharmic knowledge—shruti (i.e., the Vedas), smriti, and achara (practice; standards certified by good people)—are prioritized somewhat differently by Dharmashastra authors. See Kane, *History of Dharmaśāstra*, vol. 3, chapter 32, and Olivelle "Introduction," in *Dharmasūtras.*

47. Shishtha is the past passive participle of *śās,* which means "to teach, instruct." I am grateful to Professor Ludo Rocher for reminding me of this etymology.

48. Kane, *History of Dharmaśāstra*, 3:826.

49. Baudhāyana *Dharmasūtra*, 1.1.5–6, See Olivelle, *Dharmasūtras*, p. 132. "A 2.8.10–11" is Apastamba and "G 3.36 n" refers to Gautama.

50. See Manu 2.17–18. Reference from Kane, *History of Dharmaśāstra*, vol. 3, chapter 32.

51. Kane, *History of Dharmaśāstra*, 3:826–827.

52. Manu X.63 and Gautama 8.23, in Olivelle, *Manu's Code* and *Dharmasūtras.*

53. L. Rocher, "Law Books in an Oral Culture," p. 267.

54. Lariviere, "Dharmaśāstra, Custom, 'Real Law.'"

55. De Nobili, *Preaching Wisdom to the Wise*, p. 166.

56. L. Rocher, "Father's Bouchet's Letter," pp. 18-20. For a detailed analysis of Bouchet's letter (and of observations on practiced law in South India in the seventeenth and eighteenth centuries made by other Westerners), see. J. H. Nelson, "Hindu Law at Madras," especially pp. 221-230.

56. Possibly the Shankara matha at Kanchipuram?

57. Davis, *Boundaries of Hindu Law.*

58. Dhavan, "Dharmasastra and Modern Indian Society"; see also Derrett, *Religion, Law, and the State in India*; Lariviere, "Justices and Panditas"; and L.Rocher, "Law Books in an Oral Culture."

59. Skuy, "Macaulay," provides a lucid summary of landmarks in the development of Anglo-Indian law.

60. Ibid., p. 522.

61. In Forrest, *Selections*, pp. 295–296.

62. Lariviere notes that ecclesiastical courts in England dealt with "1. Administration of deceased persons' estates, 2. Matrimonial causes, 3. Probate of wills, 4. Matters of ecclesiastical status"; "Justices and Panditas", p. 759.

63. For the ambitious and checkered histories and juridical careers of landmark digests such as the *Vivādārṇava Setu* (Bridge across the sea of litigation) commissioned by Hastings in 1773, Nathaniel Halhed's, *A Code of Gentoo Laws, or, Ordinations of the Pundits* (1776; based on a Persian translation), and Colebrooke's 1797 *A Digest of Hindu Law* (based on Pandit Jagannatha Tarkapancanana's 1795 *Vivāda Bhaṅgārṇava* [Break against the sea of litigation]); see Derrett, *Religion, Law, and the State*; Lingat, *Classical Law*. For a discussion of the complex motives that shaped such ventures, see, for example, R. Rocher, *Orientalism, Poetry, and the Millennium*, on Halhed.

64. The case of sati starkly illustrates how political ideology and excessive textualism shaped the interpretation of Dharmashastric literature during the colonial period, marking a development in the Anglo-Indian judicial system that became permanent: the use of brahmanic texts for pan-Hindu legal policy and the overall devaluation of practiced custom in the constitution of legality. See Mani, *Contentious Traditions*.

65. Nelson, *Indian Usage*, p. 7, Quoted in Rudolph and Rudolph, *The Modernity of Tradition*, p. 276.

66. Mayne, *Treatise*, p. 44. See also Maine, *Village Communities*; Petheram, "English Judges."

67. Dirks, *Castes of Mind*, p. 36.

68. See for example, Steele, *Summary of the Law*.

69. An escalating distrust in pandits, inability of the Anglo-Indian legal system to cope with the pandits' frequent prioritization of local custom, and the acquisition of first-hand knowledge of the shastras by the British themselves led to the discontinuation of this practice. See Derrett, *Religion, Law, and the State*.

70. Mulla, *Principles of Hindu Law*, p. 66.

71. Ibid., p. 67.

72. Dhavan, "Dharmashastra." For the impact on modern Indian judiciary, see also Lariviere, "Justices and Panditas."

73. Shastry, *History of Śṛiṅgēri*, pp. 67–68.

74. Gnanambal, *Religious Institutions*.

75. Conversation recorded in Sringeri, May 2004.

76. *Divine Discourses*.

77. Giridhara Shastry, via e-mail to me, February 2005.

78. Shastry, *History of Śṛiṅgēri*, p 72.

79. Gnanambal finds that this is true of a wide spectrum of mathas across Smarta, Shrivaishnava, Shaiva, and Virashaiva orientations in south India. *Religious Institutions*.

80. Ibid., pp. 17–24.

81. The terms Rigvedi, Yajurvedi, Samavedi, and Atharvavedi refer to families that trace their ancestry to one of the seers associated with the Veda in question.

82. Eleventh day of the lunar fortnight, considered auspicious for fasting and prayer.

83. Gnanambal, *Religious Institutions*, p. 59.

84. From 1936–1959 the government of Mysore directly managed the affairs of the matha; Shastry, *History of Śṛingēri*, p. 70.

85. Giridhara Shastry, via e-mail, February 2005.

86. For a detailed religio-legal history of the Sringeri matha, see Gnanambal, *Religious Institutions*.

4. *"The Shastras Say . . . ": Idioms of Legitimacy and the "Imagined Text"*

1. Wittgenstein, *Philosophical Investigations*, no. 67.

2. For how categories of kinship expressed in Sanskrit texts and "pragmatic" kinship reflect each other in complex ways, see Khare, *Normative Culture*.

3. Following the custom in Kannada, I would add *avare*, the honorific suffix when I referred to her by name, i.e., "Nagalakshmi-avare."

4. Appadurai, "National Cuisine."

5. For early research on social ranking indexed by food in India, see Marriott, "Caste Ranking."

6. Food has been acknowledged as a coded activity by anthropologists and cultural historians. For an excellent, thorough overview article on food in Hindu thinking, see Khare, "Anna." Early anthropological studies emphasized connections of food to taboo, totemism, and sacrifice; see Frazer, *Golden Bough*. Early functionalist readings are Radcliffe-Brown, *Andaman Islanders*; Richards, *Land, Labor, and Diet*. Following the classic structuralist analysis by Levi-Strauss, *Raw and the Cooked*, Douglas's work, *Implicit Meanings*, provided a paradigm for more recent anthropological and folkloristic investigations of culturally situated food habits and eating patterns. For how foodways enable and reflect the persistence of ethnicity, regional and ecological consciousness, see Brown and Mussell, *Ethnic and Regional Foodways;* and Belasco, *Appetite for Change*; for food as a political tool as in hunger strikes, see O'Malley, *Irish Hunger Strikes*. For important analyses of food, wider social history, and gender relations, see Bynum, *Holy Feast;* and Sanday, *Women at the Center*.

In the South Asian context as well, food-related literature is vast and includes perspectives from religion, nutrition, medicine, ritual, production, aesthetics, and politics: for example, see essays in Khare and Rao, *Food, Society, and Culture;* and Achaya, *Indian Food*. See Khare, *Hindu Hearth and Home* and also *Culture and Reality* for ethnographic and metaphysical aspects of Hindu food systems; for how religious traditions regard food as divine and as a metaphor for human-divine relations, see Khare, *Eternal Food*; Toomey, *Food from the Mouth of Krishna*; for the politics of food production and consumption, see Appadurai, "Gastro-Politics"; for food in Vedic and early Indian culture, see Prakash, *Food and Drinks in Ancient India*; and Zimmermann, *Jungle and the Aroma of Meats*.

7. See Bhattacharya and Tripathi, trans. *Maharaja Nala's Pākadarpanam*. A few nineteenth- and early twentieth-century books bear "paka shastra" in their titles.

See, for example, *Pākaśāstra, otherwise called Soopaśāstra, or the Modern Culinary Receipts of the Hindoos, compiled in Teloogoo by Saraswate Boy*, trans. C.V. Ramaswamy (Christian Mission: Madras, 1836). Also interesting is an 1891 book by Ramachandra Rau titled *Maharashtra, Karnataka, Andhra, and Dravida Pākaśāstra: A Treatise on Hindu Vegetarian Cookery in Tamil*. See S. Muthiah's write-up on this book in *The Hindu*, January 5, 2004. Also valuable is Jyotsna Kamat's excellent study of the eleventh-century *Lokōpākara* by Chavundaraya of pre-Vijayanagara Karnataka, which contains detailed recipes and procedures about seasoning, juices, synthetic foods, and preservation specific to the Kannada-speaking region and the Sanskrit *Mānasollāsa* of Somesvara III (the Chalukya king who reigned between AD 1126–1138). Written for royal households, the *Mānasollāsa* contains "268 verses" on food preparations.

8. The cookbook-to-practice interaction that is also part of the modern culinary experience is a distinctive interaction (see Appadurai, "National Cuisine") bearing the mixed imprint of a European cookbook tradition, print literacies, and regional consciousness in the context of the modern nation-state. Most cookbooks, however, do not attempt to frame their information in "shastric" discourse.

9. Ramanujan, "Is There an Indian Way of Thinking?" p. 53.

10. A related term is *parampara*, "succession; lineage," which refers to a specific preceptorial line in a particular school of thought. The Sringeri guru parampara is the succession of gurus of the Sringeri matha beginning with Shankara. These gurus belong to the monastic order known as dashanami sampradaya, an order in which the names of ascetics bear one of ten suffixes (*dashanami* = with ten names). It is important to note that parampara (preceptorial line) and sampradaya (tradition) are used interchangeably. See Cenkner, *A Tradition of Teachers*.

11. Giridhara Shastry, e-mail communication to me, October 5, 2005.

12. Ramachandra Rao, *Consciousness in Advaita*, pp. 2–3.

13. Eliot, "Tradition and the Individual Talent," p. 38.

14. Janaki, "The Hand Gesture Patāka in Nāṭya," p. 206.

15. Quoted in Vatsyayan, *Bharata*, p. 38.

16. Janaki, "The Hand Gesture Patāka in Nāṭya,"p. 207. See also Cenkner, *A Tradition of Teachers*.

17. Zarrilli, "Between Text and Embodied Practice."

18. See Raheja and Gold, *Listen to the Heron's Words*; see also Prasad, "Anklets on the Pyal."

19. An adequate English equivalent of the concept of madi is in fact not possible, but generally, to be in madi is to maintain a physically sanctified state of the human body for ritual purposes.

20. Narayan, "Honor Is Honor."

21. Ibid. For contexts in which women's experiences are an exclusive focus of study, Narayan suggests that the continuum between silence and speech can be addressed in three ways: one, examining life stories narrated by various connected persons (as in a family); two, acknowledging how lifestory narrations are part of interpersonal processes between narrators and audiences; three, studying other folkloric forms of self-representation like songs and folktales.

22. Ramanujan, "Three Hundred Ramayanas," p. 46.

23. For Dharmashastric prescriptions on this subject, see Kane, *History of Dharmaśāstra*, vol. 2, part 2, pp. 803–805. In accordance with the belief that a sacred space must not be made impure by bodily wastes or by impure intentions, a menstruating woman keeps away for a few days from temple premises or worship spaces and does not attend ceremonial events. The practice is known by so much variation that it is impossible to document the full range of its observance, but it has also been rejected by many Hindu families, while many others are simply indifferent to its observance.

24. The kitchen is where the daily naivedya for the puja is made and, hence, like the puja room, is kept constantly clean and sanctified.

25. A sari worn in a special style.

26. Vinayaka Udupa of Sringeri emphasized the Vedic basis of shastra; for example, he said "Do the *sañdhyavañdane* everyday" is a broad vidhi (injunction) that comes from the Vedas.

27. Panduranga, May 2004.

28. Wittgenstein, *Philosophical Investigations* and *On Certainty*.

29. Wittgenstein, *Philosophical Investigations,* no. 19.

30. Ibid., no. 23.

31. Ibid., no. 219, 241.

32. Ibid., nos. 82–85.

33. Different from the tadige Gouri puja performed during the Gouri-Ganapati festival in August through September. The mangala Gouri vrata is performed by newly married women for five consecutive years for auspiciousness, a long married life, and the well-being of the family. The vrata is organized around the number sixteen (sixteen types of flowers, fruits, etc.). See McGee, "In Quest," for this vrata among Marathi women.

34. Noted by Kane, *History of Dharmaśāstra*, vol. 5, part 1, p. 367.

35. See Chakrabarti, *Religious Processes.*

36. Although the vrata is necessarily performed by married couples, only men performed the puja on this occasion. When I enquired about the absence of women, Putta Murthy said that the seating arrangement made many women feel awkward about sitting between their husbands and other men. While I have not inquired if this has changed since 1995, Putta Murthy had said that there was no rule whatsoever about women not attending. His dream, he had added, was to see women participate just as enthusiastically as in the mixed group bhajane (devotional singing) that took place in the evenings of the ten-day Ramanavami celebrations.

37. Wittgenstein, *Philosophical Investigations,* no. 217.

38. Ibid., no. 85.

39. *Kaṇe* could be used between women who are peers, irrespective of age, or by a woman addressing a younger woman. When a man says *kaṇe*, he is most probably talking to a sister. The masculine equivalent is *kaṇo.*

40. See Kanchipuram Shankaracharya's assessment of changes taking place in modern Indian society in *Hindu Dharma*, especially, "The Śāstras and Modern Life," pp.

113–120. See Fuller, *Renewal of the Priesthood*, for how professional priests in Madurai construct a complex, reflexive dialectic between "traditionalism" and "modernity."

41. Parry, *Death in Banaras*, pp. 193–194.

42. Ibid., pp. 193, 227.

43. Natarajan, *Jagadguru*, p. 93.

44. Vatsyayan, in *Bharata*, explores these questions with regard to the *Natyaśāstra*. See also the introduction by Blackburn and Ramanujan, in *Another Harmony*, for cycles of transmission and dissemination that transform the character of "texts" as they circulate through oral, written, and performed channels.

45. Studies of epic traditions and the folklore of India brilliantly capture these processes. See, for example, Wadley, *Raja Nal;* Flueckiger, *Gender and Genre;* Gold, *Carnival;* and Blackburn, *Singing of Birth and Death.* For how Tulsidas's Ramcharitmanas lends itself to the creation of many texts when contexts of its "use" change, see Lutgendorf, *Life of a Text.*

46. For an analysis of the varied ways in which "scripture" is conceptualized in Hindu life, see Coburn, "Scripture"; see also Gold, "Experiencing Scriptural Diversity," for how followers of *nirguṇa* (the formless divine) and *saguṇa* (divinity with specific form) traditions experientially construct their worlds of authoritative scriptures.

47. Sullivan, "Religious Authority of the Mahabharata," p. 384.

48. Hawley, "Author and Authority," pp. 287–288.

49. Carpenter, "Mastery of Speech," p. 31.

50. Kanchipuram Shankaracharya, *Hindu Dharma*, chapter 7.

51. See Wadley, "Vrats." For brahman women's motives and aspirations for undertaking vratas in Tamil Nadu, see McGee, "Desired Fruits."

52. Narayana Rao, "Purāṇa," p. 114.

53. Pollock, "'Tradition' as 'Revelation,'" pp. 395–417.

54. Kanchipuram Shankaracharya, *Hindu Dharma*, p. 114.

55. Said, *The World, the Text, and the Critic*, p. 39.

56. One needs to recall that, in the Hindu context, the invocation of a textual body in order to create new textual spaces is a not an unusual phenomenon. Anderson's notion of *imagined community* is helpful for understanding the imagination of a social collectivity around a political goal, but I hesitate to draw strong parallels because the textual space I refer to is primarily moral and aesthetic and not a national configuration.

57. Said, *The World, the Text, and the Critic*, p. 35.

58. Parker, "Text and Practice in South Asian Art," p. 10.

59. Reck, "The Invisible *Sāstra*, p. 410.

60. Ibid., p. 411.

61. Pollock, "The Idea of Śāstra," p. 19.

62. Ramanujan, "Three Hundred Rāmāyaṇas," p. 46.

63. Lakoff and Johnson, *Metaphors We Live By.*

64. Jonathan Parry reports a variant of this story in Varanasi; see *Death in Banaras*, p. 193.

5. *In the Courtyard of Dharma, Not at the Village Square: Delivering Ashirvada in Sringeri*

1. The Sanskrit etymology, shared in Kannada, is āśir= benediction and *vāda* = speech. The concept of ashirvada as blessing, outside its specific performance context in Sringeri, is, of course, pan-Indian. Ashirvada is sought from gurus, priests, or elders in a variety of festive and everyday contexts.

2. The performance of ashirvada at the conclusion of a ritual event is in fact not entirely unique to Sringeri, although the presence of the matha undoubtedly must have contributed to its unique character and the expertise that is brought to its performance. In some areas in the broader Malnad region the explanation is entirely in Kannada with no Sanskrit verses. Giridhara Shastry pointed out that among the Havyak brahmans of Dakshin Kannada, where ashirvada goes by the name of *āśirvacana,* the performance is highly attentive to the audience (sabhe), which is invoked formally with praise statements and mantras, and shlokas ("You are all great people"), and given honors (*sabha-tāmbūla*). The *āśirvacana* is a way of making formal the recognition that "society is supreme," a point that is especially appreciated given the geographical and demographic character of the place where one family (or a small group of families) makes a village. Interestingly, even the Vedic ashis saw so much variation that Jan Gonda writes, "there are no entirely identical accounts of the procedure, a fact that attests to the undeniable divergence of opinions and practices on the one hand and to the relative liberty of the authorities and the communities whose traditions they codified as well as to their inventiveness and ingenuity in coping with ritual difficulties"; *Prayer and Blessing,* p. 38.

3. See note 48 in chapter 1 for Hindu models of hospitality.

4. Kittel, *Kannada-English Dictionary,* p. 232.

5. For example, see Mills, *Rhetorics and Politics.*

6. Unlike, for example, with the North Indian *Dhola* tradition, which narrates religious themes but is not tied to ritual. See Wadley, *Raja Nal.*

7. Flueckiger, *Gender and Genre.*

8. Lit. "wheel of the goddess." A geometric Tantric diagram with a rich symbolism that is associated with shakti, divine feminine power.

9. "Water pot; pitcher; jar." In temple rites a pot of water, kalasha, topped with mango leaves and a husked coconut represents the deity during special pujas.

10. I am guided in part by the ethnopoetic terms spelled out by Tedlock, *Spoken Word*; and also Fine, *Folklore Text*: a speaker's emphases, pauses, ellipses, repetitions of phrases (entire stories in other instances), for example, could reflect the interpretive agency of a narrator, and I therefore present these to the extent I registered them. While the insights of ethnopoetics have helped sharpen my attentiveness to spoken language, I do not follow ethnopoetic conventions in transcription as fully as Tedlock does, as I find that a heavily marked-up text interrupts the "natural" fluency of the oral experience of it.

11. The text that follows was transcribed by S. R. Nagaraja mentioned in the vignette about Ramachandra Bhattru and Amrutamba, his parents. I gave Nagaraja a copy of my audio recordings of ashirvada, and he made extremely careful transliterations of the

oral texts. Using this for a basis and my own recordings and notes, I notated them in terms of performative aspects and also translated them. When possible, I cross-checked the transliterated text and my translation with performers. Since Nagaraja was the officiating priest at the Durga puja ashirvada, I worked closely with him and Prabhakara Bhattru to interpret this ashirvada. The text presented in this chapter is an instance of such collaborative synthesis.

12. *Devī Māhātmya* (DM), chapter 4, line 34. *See* Shastri, *Mārkaṇḍeya-Purāṇam* for translation.

13. DM, chapter 4, verses 35–37, ibid.

14. DM, chapter 11, from verses 52–53, ibid.

15. *Durgā Sūktam*, verse 1 (Part of the Rig Veda) Sanskrit text accessed at http://sanskrit.gde.to/all_pdf/durga-suuktam.pdf.

16. Special type of reciter of the Vedas.

17. For how the *Devī Māhātmya* functions a powerful liturgical text, see Erndl, *Victory to the Mother*; for textual studies, see Coburn, *Devī Māhātmya*; Lalye, *Studies in Devī Bhāgavatha*; Pintchman, in *Rise of the Goddess*, considers the wider historical context for the rise of goddess-centered theology.

18. The story of Aruna is mentioned in the eleventh chapter of the *Mārkaṇḍeya Purāṇa* in which Durga prophesies her return to destroy Aruna. It is mentioned in more detail in the tenth chapter of the *Devi Bhāgavata Purāṇa*. See Shastri, *Markandeya-Puranam.*

19. The repetition of a sacred mantra enjoined of initiated brahman males.

20. Dundes, "Metafolklore"; also Narayan, "Practice of Oral Literary Criticism."

21. Gonda, *Prayer and Blessing*, p. 145.

22. Ibid. for various statements of ashis from the *Maitrāyaṇi Samhita* and other Vedic texts. Also, see Heesterman, *Broken World of Sacrifice.*

23. In the sixteen acts known as upachara that constitute puja, ahvana, or "act of inviting," is the first act. However, Giridhara Shastry suggests that here the term simply means "invitation." "The tradition of inviting the guru to participate in the car festivals by the mahajana is reminiscent of the old days when the mahajana were in power"; e-mail communication to me, October 5, 2005.

24. Singer used this term to refer to the concerts, temple festivals, weddings, and so on that people identified as examples of their "culture" and, from the anthropologist's view, constituted recognizable and discrete units that could be studied; see Singer, *When a Great Tradition Modernizes.*

25. The fact that I was encouraged to acquaint myself with other formal genres of speaking also reminds me of a crucial argument that Ben-Amos made in 1976 that to understand a single genre it is necessary to locate it in the *system* of genres identified by the community or practicing group. For in-depth treatments that include such wide-angle views, see Gossen, *Chamulas in the World of the Sun;* Abrahams, *Man-of-Words;* Sherzer, *Kuna Ways of Speaking;* Briggs, *Competence in Performance;* and Flueckiger, *Gender and Genre.*

26. Putta Murthy, oral communication, 1995.

27. A pioneer in the call for documenting indigenous discourse about indigenous genres was Bronislaw Malinowski (see *Magic, Science, and Religion*), who asked

myth-collecting anthropologists to *ask* "natives" for explanations of their myths in order to understand emic typologies. Without reviewing the career of this call here, I draw on performance-centered folklore theory, which, beginning in the 1970s, greatly enabled and fine-tuned methodologies in order to attend to indigenous interpretation. See Seitel, *See So That We May See;* and Zenani, *World and the Word.* For challenges encountered during this process, see Taggart, *Enchanted Maidens*; Abu-Lughod, *Veiled Sentiments.*

28. Although both men and women give ashirvada as blessing in everyday life, ashirvada performances are always delivered by male brahmans. Ashirvada performances require traditional study in the Vedas and other shastras, which, even today, is largely restricted to men.

29. Understood from the perspective of modern performance-centered folklore theory in which competence is a pivotal concept, competence presupposes a sense of the appropriate that "has to do with the distinguishing of what persons will do in particular contexts from what they can do in principle . . . the relation between the possible and contextually doable is itself specific to a community"; Hymes, *In Vain*, p. 83. See Briggs, *Competence in Performance,* for a full-length study that explores the concept of competence as indigenously understood by a northern New Mexican community.

30. For example, in an upanayana, it is the father who must initiate his son into the recitation of the Gayatri mantra. Sesha Bhattru's reference was to situations in which the practice is not observed by the father, who is then unable to himself initiate his son.

31. For example, the avatara stories in the *Viṣṇu Purāṇa* (especially Narasimha and Vamana avatara).

32. BJP candidates have been winning elections to the state and central assemblies in the recent political history of Sringeri. I tried to follow up on the priest's remark but was told pointedly by participants and performers to not attribute political agendas to the ashirvada tradition. The ashirvada tradition is seen as being located in the practice and ethos of Malnad upachara and not in right-wing inventions of traditions. Whether the ashirvada, being a popular and rich medium of transmission, will be hijacked by right-wing agencies remains to be seen.

33. The festival that celebrates Rama's birth and coronation after his epic fourteen-year exile.

34. Ingalls, Masson, and Patwardhan, *Dhvanyāloka*, p. 16.

35. Ramanujan and Gerow, "Indian Poetics," p. 128. The section on "Dramatic Criticism" is written by Ramanujan.

36. Ibid.

37. Ramanujan and Gerow, "Indian Poetics," pp. 128–129 (in "Dramatic Criticism").

38. See Chari, *Sanskrit Criticism*; Kane, *History of Sanskrit Poetics*; De, *History of Sanskrit Poetics.*

39. For this section I draw on the extensive accounts of the history of auchitya in Suryakanta, *Kśemendra Studies;* and Raghavan, *Some Concepts of the Alaṃkāra Śāstra.* For Anandavardhana's treatment of auchitya, I also draw on the translation by Ingalls, Masson, and Patwardhan, *Dhvanyāloka.*

40. Ghosh, *Nāṭyaśāstra*, chapter 19.

41. Raghavan, *Some Concepts of the Alaṃkāra Śāstra.*

42. Ibid, p. 226.

43. Dated by Kane, *History of Sanskrit Poetics.*

44. Warder, *Indian Kāvya Literature*, 1:100–101.

45. Translation in Ingalls, Masson, and Patwardhan, *Dhvanyāloka*, p. 428.

46. Ibid, p. 429–430.

47. Kshemendra, *Aucityavicāracarca.*

48. Translation in Raghavan, *Some Concepts of the Alaṃkāra Śāstra*, p. 251.

49. Kshemendra, *Aucityavicāracarca*, p. 70.

50. Ramanujan, "Relevance of South Asian Folklore," p. 109.

51. Chari, "Decorum as a Critical Concept."

52. See Aristotle, *On Rhetoric*, 3, ed. George A. Kennedy (New York: Oxford University Press, 1991); and Cicero, *De Oratore* 3, esp. 208–227; see Cicero, *On the Ideal Orator*, trans. James M. May and Jakob Wisse (New York: Oxford University Press, 2001).

53. See O. B. Hardison Jr., ed., *Horace for Students of Literature: The "Ars Poetica" and Its Tradition*, trans. Leon Golden (Gainesville: University Press of Florida, 1995).

54. John Milton, *Of Education, to Master Samuel Hartlib* (1644), in *Complete Prose Works*, ed. Don M. Wolfe, vol. 2 (New Haven: Yale University Press, 1953–1982).

55. Trimpi, "Decorum," p. 283.

56. In fact, A. K. Ramanujan's proposition that the akam/puram classification of Tamil "classical" aesthetics could be potentially applied to oral narrative as well is a wonderful example of the correspondences possible between literary and social aesthetics. See "Relevance of South Asian Folklore". Although such correspondences need to be contextualized in their indigenous environments, so that "external" interpretations are not imposed on practice, the process of establishing correspondences generates questions that could reveal surprising dialogues and help distinguish worldviews.

57. Quoted in Gerow, *Indian Poetics*, p. 221.

58. De, *History of Sanskrit Poetics*, p. 267.

6. Edifying Lives, Discerning Properties: Conversational Stories and Moral Being

1. The Indian way of referring to a person who has participated in India's struggle for independence from the British.

2. For a fictional account of the struggle in a Kannada-speaking town, see Rao, *Kanthapura.*

3. Some scholars have distinguished between "narrative" and "story," arguing that narratives are open-ended, whereas stories typically identify a beginning, a middle, and an end. Stories admit closure; see White, "Value of Narrativity"; Leitch, *What Stories Are*; and O'Neill, *Fictions of Discourse.* On the other hand, Ricoeur refers

to *narrative* and *story* synonymously (see especially *From Text to Action*). While I too use the terms interchangeably, it is possible to note, in the "narratives" I present, particular points at which a "story" commences and ends. At the same time, I maintain that, while stories perhaps structurally end, they linger beyond the narrative context and may not necessarily see closure in an individual's life.

4. Ricoeur, "Life in Quest of Narrative," p. 29.

5. Ricoeur, "Narrated Time," p. 338.

6. My emphasis to underscore that, unlike Plato, Aristotle does not consider mimesis as producing weak copies of original forms but as enhancing "meaning in the field of [human] action"; Ricoeur, "Mimesis and Representation," p. 138.

7. Ibid., p. 142.

8. Temporality, Genette says, is enacted in narrative through order (sequencing of events), through duration (tempo that mimes time span of real life), and frequency (relationship between happening and the number of times it is narrated). See Genette, *Narrative Discourse.*

9. Ricoeur, "Life: A Story in Search of a Narrator," p. 430.

10. Bharata, *Nāṭyaśāstra*, 1.112, translated in Chari, *Sanskrit Criticism*, p. 207. See Chari for more on this debate.

11. Chari, *Sanskrit Criticism*, especially chapter 9. See also Hiriyanna, *Art Experience.*

12. See Chari, *Sanskrit Criticism*, for an elaboration of Abhinavagupta's rejection of imitation.

13. Ingalls, Masson, and Patwardhan, *Dhvanyāloka,* Abhinavagupta, *Locana* 1.18, p. 191.

14. Gerow, *Indian Poetics*, p. 267.

15. *Instress* is Gerard Manley Hopkins's term to describe the apprehended "force" or "energy" that sustains the essence of a thing, event, or phenomenon. Hopkins called the distinctive essence itself *inscape*. In Hopkins, *Note-books and Papers*, p. 119. For Hopkins "the all-powerfulness of instress in its mode and the immediateness of its effect are very remarkable." Ibid., p. 226.

16. Bakhtin, *Dialogic Imagination*, p. 293.

17. Ibid., pp. 341–342.

18. MacIntyre, *After Virtue.*

19. See Hauerwas, *Community of Character*, for example.

20. Nussbaum, *Love's Knowledge.*

21. Ibid., p. 183.

22. Newton, *Narrative Ethics*, p. 11.

23. Ricoeur, "Life: A Story in Search of a Narrator," p. 430.

24. Newton, *Narrative Ethics*, p. 26.

25. Ricoeur, "What Is a Text?" p. 46.

26. Day and Tappan, "The Narrative Approach," p. 75.

27. See, for example, the excellent work on the dialogic and dramatic aspects of storytelling in everyday conversations: Ochs and Capps, *Living Narrative*; also Norrick, *Conversational Narrative*. See also Ben-Amos, "'Context'"; Bauman, *Story, Performance, Event.*

28. Ochs and Capps, *Living Narrative,* pp. 1–58.

29. Hymes, *In Vain.*

30. The coconstruction of narrative is especially emphasized in life-story literature. See, for example, Crapanzano, *Tuhami.*

31. Tirrell, "Storytelling," p. 118.

32. Rommetveit, *On Message Structure,* p. 29.

33. Rommetveit, "On the Dawning."

34. Mills, *Rhetorics and Politics,* p. 20

35. Ingarden, *Literary Work of Art,* p. 205.

36. Ibid., p. 89, also pp. 84–91.

37. Ingarden, *Cognition.*

38. Hanks, *Language,* p. 148.

39. Ricoeur, "Life in Quest of Narrative," p. 30. See also Luigi Pirandello's "Six Characters in Search of an Author," in *Six Characters in Search of an Author and Other Plays,* trans. Mark Musa (London: Penguin, 1995).

40. Ramanujan, *Folktales from India,* pp. 26–29.

41. In the sprawling precincts of the monastery, through which runs the river Tunga, are many shrines (samadhis) of previous gurus of the monastery who have passed on. Departing from the customary Hindu rite of cremation, renouncers are interred in a sitting position over which often a shrine is built (see Olivelle, *Saṃnyāsa Upaniṣads,* and *Rules and Regulations,* chapter 11). This site is known as a *samadhi,* a yogic term that also indicates the attainment of spiritual union of the individual self with a universal self.

42. Worship of Rudra (the fiery aspect of Shiva) that includes ritual bathing of the image with soothing and cooling substances like milk, honey, yogurt, and ghee.

43. Sharma, *Pilgrimage to Sringeri,* p. 21.

44. The spirit of a brahman who had indulged in evil practices in his lifetime.

45. Dodda Murthy, December 2001.

46. See chapter 4 for more on Chandrashekara Bharati.

47. See Aiyar, *Call of the Jagadguru*; also Sharma, *Pilgrimage to Sringeri.*

48. Sharma, *Pilgrimage to Sringeri,* p. 55.

49. These states of consciousness are described and discussed in the *Māṇḍūkya Upaniṣad* and the *Kārika* by Gaudapada; See Swami Nikhilananda, *Upanishads.* For a close parallel in Romantic literature on the subject of knowledge gained through "dreaming," see the poem "Expostulation and Reply" (1798) by William Wordsworth, in Harold Bloom and Lionel Trilling, eds., *Romantic Poetry and Prose,* pp. 127-128 (New York: Oxford University Press, 1973).

50. Shastric literature on the subject of worship attends to all aspects of the ritual, ranging from "substances from which images are made, the principal deities of which images were or are worshipped, the proportions of various limbs in manufacturing images, the consecration of images in temples, the ritual of image worship"; Kane, *History of Dharmaśāstra,* part 2, 2:712.

51. Ibid, p. 731.

52. See O'Flaherty, *Asceticism and Eroticism*; Nagar, *Siva in Art.*

53. Das, "Wittgenstein and Anthropology," p. 179.

54. See Eck, *Darśan*, for a brief but excellent review of some of the historical debates on Hindu "idol worship." See Eck also for more on the terms *murti* and *vigraha* used to refer to the sacred image ("embodiment" or "that which allows you to grasp the form of God"). See Waghorne and Cutler, *Gods of Flesh*, for culturally specific conceptualizations of sacred embodiment. Interesting in this context is S. T. Coleridge's definition of symbol: "characterized by a translucence of the special in the individual, of the general in the special, or of the universal in the general; above all by the translucence of the eternal through and in the temporal. It always partakes of the reality which it renders intelligible; and while it enunciates the whole, abides itself as a living part in that unity of which it is the representative"; From "Symbol and Allegory," in Coleridge, *The Statesman's Manual.*

55. Sharma, *Pilgrimage to Sringeri*; p. 47.

56. In Kannada *sukshma* is both a noun and an adjective and thus also means "subtlety."

57. The story of Trishanku is told in the first section (*Bālakāṇḍa*) of Valmiki's *Rāmāyaṇa*, sarga 56–59. See Goldman, *The Rāmāyaṇa.*

58. The practice of storing in a small sealed brass or copper container some water from the Ganga or from any *tīrtha* (place of pilgrimage) is common to many Hindus.

59. RB = Ramachandra Bhattru; L = myself; P = Prasad.

60. Narayan, *Storytellers, Saints, and Scoundrels.*

61. See Olivelle, *Saṃnāyasa Upāniṣads*; also his *Rules and Regulations.* Elucidations of sanyasa dharma include details such as how many houses a sanyasi should visit, how many handfuls to accept as alms, and so on.

222. Bauman and Briggs, "Poetics and Performance"; p. 69

63. It is important to note that narratives about "caste" identity are only one type among many others that treat subjects individuals consider important to their day-to-day lives.

64. There is no single theory of karma. For different philosophical approaches to the concept, see Hiriyanna, *Indian Conception of Values*, chapter 6; O'Flaherty, *Karma and Rebirth*; for ethnographic literature that explores how this concept (and related terminology) plays out in various Hindu communities or in the lives of individuals, see Daniel and Keyes, *Karma*; Narayan, *Storytellers*, and *Mondays*; Wadley, *Struggling with Destiny*; Feldhaus, *Water and Womanhood.*

65. The fourth age, current, in the recurrent cosmic cycle of time. The Puranas recognize four eras, each marked by successive moral decline, in which dharma becomes increasingly unsteady: The longest is krita yuga, or the "perfect" age, which lasts 1,728,000 human years, the treta yuga (the yuga in which Rama is believed to have lived) for 1, 296,000 years; the dvāpara yuga (depicted in the Mahabharata) for 864,000 years, and *kali yuga* for 432,000 years.

66. Also known as *darbha, durva.*

67. Shri Ramanujacharya, former principal, Sanskrit College, Hyderabad; oral communication, June 2005.

68. Kanchipuram Shankaracharya, "Signs and Omens," in *Hindu Dharma.*

69. H. C. Dasappa of Mysore; renowned Gandhian, freedom fighter, member of Parliament, and union railway minister.

70. Also renowned freedom fighter and minister in the first Mysore state government.

71. One of Dodda Murthy's favorite phrases. Dodda Murthy's travel stories are especially full of thick descriptions of food. Good food or food arrangements at places he visited were summed by the one phrase "*sogasāda aḍige* (delectable cooking)"!

72. Literally, "motherland." A prominent Kannada newspaper with nationalistic leanings. N. S. Lakshminarasimha Murthy, "Sevāgrāmadalli Nanna Anubhavagaḷu" (My experiences at Sevagram), parts 1 and 2, *Tāyināḍu*, June 30, 1952.

73. See Weber, *Gandhi as Disciple and Mentor*, chapter 6, for a discussion of the reasons for Gandhiji's move to Sevagram Ashram.

74. See Gandhi, *An Autobiography*, chapter 87 ("A Sacred Recollection and Penance"), in which he recounts how he regretted rebuking his wife Kasturba over her reluctance to clean pots and pans.

Ethics, an Imagined Life

1. See, for example, McKenzie, *Hindu Ethics*; Sharma, *Ethical Philosophies;* Hindery, "Hindu Ethics in the Rāmāyaṇa"; Creel, *Dharma in Hindu Ethics*; Jhingran, *Aspects of Hindu Morality;* and Tiwari, *Classical Indian Ethical Thought*. Examples of works that discuss topical issues in ethics include Coward, Lipner, and Young, *Hindu Ethics*; Crawford, *Dilemmas of Life and Death*; and Chapple and Tucker, *Hinduism and Ecology*.

2. The essays in the fall 2002 issue of the *Journal of Religious Ethics* illustrate this diversity in "prescriptive" discourse. See Clooney, "Fierce Words"; Dhand, "Dharma of Ethics"; Schweig, "Humility and Passion"; Vail "Unlike a Fool."

3. Richman, *Questioning Rāmāyaṇas*.

4. Blackburn and Ramanujan, *Another Harmony*.

5. Gold, *Fruitful Journeys*; Raheja, *Poison in the Gift*; Narayan *Storytellers, Saints, and Scoundrels*; Khandelwal, *Women in Ochre Robes*; Nabokov, *Religion Against the Self*; Fuller, *Renewal of Priesthood*.

6. See especially Waghorne, *Diaspora of the Gods*.

7. For example, in his *Riches and Renunciation*, Laidlaw shows that various practices such as dietary regulation and introspective penance along with sacred iconography and worship express how ascetic ideals are incorporated into lay Jain practice—defeating an assumption, long held in Western scholarship on Jainism, that there is a fundamental opposition between the Jain ideal of renunciation and this-worldly living.

Bibliography

Abbott, Justin E. *Bahina Bai: A Translation of Her Autobiography and Verses.* Foreword by Anne Feldhaus. Delhi: Motilal Banarsidass, 1985 [1929].

Abrahams, Roger D. *Everyday Life: A Poetics of Vernacular Practices.* Philadelphia: University of Pennsylvania Press, 2005.

——— "After New Perspectives: Folklore Study in the Late Twentieth Century." *Western Folklore* 52 (1993): 379–400.

——— "Phantoms of Romantic Nationalism" *Journal of American Folklore* 106 (1993): 3–37.

——— *The Man-of-Words in the West Indies: Performance and the Emergence of Creole Culture.* Baltimore: Johns Hopkins University Press, 1983.

——— "A Rhetoric of Everyday Life: Traditional Conversational Genres." *Southern Folklore Quarterly* 32 (1968): 44–59.

Abu-Lughod, Lila. "Fieldwork of a Dutiful Daughter." In S. Altorky and C. Fawzi El-Solh, eds., *Arab Women in the Field,* pp. 139–161. Syracuse: Syracuse University Press, 1988.

——— *Veiled Sentiments: Honor and Poetry in a Bedouin Society.* Berkeley: University of California Press, 1986.

Achaya, K. T. *Indian Food: A Historical Companion.* Delhi and New York: Oxford University Press, 1994.

Agarwal, Madan M. *Six Systems of Indian Philosophy*. New Delhi: Chaukambha Sanskrit Pratisthan, 2001.

Aguilar, John. "Insider Research: An Ethnography of a Debate." In Donald Messerschmidt, ed., *Anthropologists at Home in North America*, pp. 15–26. Cambridge: Cambridge University Press, 1981.

Aiyar Balasubrahmanya, T. K. *The Greatness of Sringeri*. Srirangam: Sri Vani Vilas, 1951.

Aiyar, R. Krishnaswami. *The Call of the Jagadguru: Teachings of His Holiness Sri Jagadguru Sri Chandrashekara Bharati Swamigal of Sringeri*. Madras: Ganesh, 1957.

——— *Dialogues with the Guru: Talks with His Holiness Sri Chandrashekara Bharati Swamina, Late Shankaracharya of Sringeri Mutt*. Bombay: Chetana, 1957.

Aklujkar, Vidyut. "Sharing the Divine Feast: Evolution of Food Metaphor in Marathi Sant Poetry." In Ravindra S. Khare, ed., *The Eternal Food: Gastronomic Ideas and Experiences of Hindus and Buddhists*, pp. 95–115. Albany: SUNY Press, 1992.

Anderson, Benedict R. *Imagined Communities: Reflections on the Origin and Spread of Nationalism*. London: Verso, 1991 [1983].

Appadurai, Arjun. "How to Make a National Cuisine: Cookbooks in Contemporary India." *Society for Comparative Study of Society and History* 30.1 (1988): 3–24.

——— "Putting Hierarchy in Its Place." *Cultural Anthropology* 3 (1988): 36–49.

——— *Worship and Conflict Under Colonial Rule: A South Indian Case*. Hyderabad: Orient Longman, 1983.

——— "Gastro-Politics in Hindu South Asia." *American Ethnologist* 8 (1981): 494–511.

Appadurai, Arjun, and Carol Breckenridge. "The South Indian Temple: Authority, Honor, and Redistribution." *Contributions of Indian Sociology* n.s. 10 (1976): 187–211.

Apte, Vaman S. *Student's Sanskrit-English Dictionary*. Delhi: Motilal Banarsidass, 1993 [1890].

Ayyangar, Ramaswami M. S. *Studies in South Indian Jainism*. Delhi: Sri Satguru, 1982.

Bahadur, Krishna, trans. *Bahinabai and Her Abhangas*. New Delhi: Munshiram Manoharlal, 1998.

Bakhtin, Mikhail. *The Dialogic Imagination*. Ed. Michael Holquist. Trans. C. Emerson and M. Holquist. Austin: University of Texas Press, 1991.

——— *Rabelais and His World*. Trans. Hélène Iswolsky. Cambridge: MIT Press, 1968.

Bauman, Richard. *Story, Performance, Event: Contextual Studies of Oral Narrative*. Cambridge: Cambridge University Press, 1986.

——— *Verbal Art as Performance*. Rowley, MA: Newbury House, 1977.

——— "Differential Identity and Social Base of Folklore." In Americo Paredes and Richard Bauman, eds., *Toward New Perspectives in Folklore*, pp. 31–41. Austin: University of Texas Press, 1972.

Bauman, Richard, and Charles L. Briggs. "Poetics and Performance as Critical Perspectives on Language and Social Life." *Annual Review of Anthropology* (1990): 59–88.

Bauman, Richard, and Joel Sherzer, eds. *Explorations in the Ethnography of Speaking*. Cambridge: Cambridge University Press, 1974.

Belasco, Warren J. *Appetite for Change: How the Counter Culture Took on the Food Industry, 1966–1988*. New York: Pantheon, 1989.

Ben-Amos, Dan. "'Context' in Context." *Western Folklore* 52 (1993): 209–226.

Bhattacharya, Abheda Nanda. *Dharma-Adharma and Morality in Mahabharata*. Delhi: S.S., 1992.

Bhattacharya, V., trans., and I. Tripathi, ed. *Maharaja Nala's Pākadarpaṇam*. Banaras: Chowkhamba Sanskrit Series, 1983 [1915].

Blackburn, Stuart. *Moral Fictions: Tamil Folktales in Oral Tradition*. FF Communications 278. Helsinki: Academia Scientiarum Fennica, 2001.

——— *Singing of Birth and Death: Texts in Performance*. Philadelphia: University of Pennsylvania Press, 1988.

Blackburn, Stuart, and A. K. Ramanujan, eds. *Another Harmony: New Essays on the Folklore of India*. Berkeley: University of California Press, 1986.

Bose, Mandrakanta, ed. *The Rāmāyaṇa Revisited*. New York: Oxford University Press, 2004.

Bowring, Lewis B. *Eastern Experiences*. London: King, 1871.

Brettel, Caroline B., ed. *When They Read What We Write: The Politics of Ethnography*. Westport, CT: Bergin and Garvey, 1993.

Briggs, Charles L. *Competence in Performance: The Creativity of Tradition in Mexican Verbal Art*. Philadelphia: University of Pennsylvania Press, 1988.

Brown, Linda K., and Kay Mussell. *Ethnic and Regional Foodways in the United States: The Performance of Group Identity*. Knoxville: University of Tennessee Press, 1984.

Buhler, George, trans. *The Laws of Manu*. New York: Dover, 1969 [1886].

——— *Sacred Laws of the Aryas*. 2 Vols. Oxford: Oxford University Press, 1879–1882.

Bynum, Catherine. *Holy Feast and Holy Fast: The Religious Significance of Food to Medieval Women*. Berkeley: University of California Press, 1987.

Carpenter, David. "The Mastery of Speech: Canonicity and Control in the Vedas." In Laurie L. Patton, ed., *Authority, Anxiety, and Canon: Essays in Vedic Interpretation*, pp. 19–34. Albany: SUNY Press, 1994.

Carr, David. *Time, Narrative, and History*. Indianapolis: Indiana University Press, 1991.

Cenkner, William. *A Tradition of Teachers: Śaṅkara and the Jagadgurus Today*. Delhi: Motilal Banarsidass, 1983.

Census of India. Accessed at http://www.censusindia.net.

Chakrabarti, Kunal. *Religious Processes: The Puranas and the Making of a Regional Tradition*. New Delhi: Oxford University Press, 2001.

Chapple, Christopher, and Mary E. Tucker, eds. *Hinduism and Ecology: The Intersection of Earth, Sky, and Water*. Cambridge: Harvard University Press, 2000.

Chari, V. K. *Sanskrit Criticism*. Honolulu: University of Hawaii Press, 1990.

——— "Decorum as a Critical Concept in Indian and Western Poetics." *Journal of Aesthetics and Art Criticism* 26.1 (1967): 53–63.

Clifford, James. *Writing Culture*. Berkeley: University of California Press, 1986.

Clooney, Francis X. "Fierce Words: Repositionings of Caste and Devotion in Traditional Śrīvaiṣṇava Hindu Ethics." *Journal of Religious Ethics* 30 (2002): 399–419.

Coburn, Thomas. *Devī Māhātmya: The Crystallization of the Goddess Tradition.* New Delhi: Motilal Banarsidass, 1984.

——— "'Scripture' in India: Toward a Typology of the Word in Hindu Life." In Miriam Levering, ed., *Rethinking Scripture: Essays from a Comparative Perspective,* pp. 102–128. Albany: SUNY Press, 1984.

Coleridge, Samuel. T. *The Statesman's Manual.* In W. G. T. Shedd, ed., *The Complete Works of Samuel Taylor Coleridge.* New York: Harper, 1868.

Coomaraswamy, Ananda K. "The Nature of 'Folklore' and 'Popular Art.'" *Indian Art and Letters* 11 (1937): 136–177.

Coward, Harold, G., Julius Lipner, and Katherine Young, eds. *Hindu Ethics: Purity, Abortion, and Euthanasia.* Albany: SUNY Press, 1989.

Crapanzano, Vincent. *Tuhami: Portrait of a Moroccan.* Chicago: University of Chicago Press, 1980.

Crawford, Cromwell. *Dilemmas of Life and Death: Hindu Ethics in a North American Context.* Albany: SUNY Press, 1995.

Creel, Austin B. *Dharma in Hindu Ethics.* Calcutta: Firma KLM, 1977.

Cruikshank, Julie. *The Social Life of Stories: Narrative and Knowledge in the Yukon Territory.* Lincoln: University of Nebraska Press, 1998.

Cruikshank, Julie, with Angela Sidney, Kitty Smith, and Annie Ned. *Life Lived Like a Story: Life Stories of Three Yukon Native Elders.* Lincoln: University of Nebraska Press, 1990.

Cutler, Norman. *Songs of Experience: The Poetics of Tamil Devotion.* Bloomington: Indiana University Press, 1987.

Daniel, Valentine, and Charles Keyes, eds. *Karma: An Anthropological Inquiry.* Berkeley: University of California Press, 1981.

Das, B. K., ed. *Census of India, 1981: District Census Handbook, Chikmagalur District, Karnataka.* Bangalore: Government Central Press, 1984.

Das, Veena. "Wittgenstein and Anthropology." *Annual Review of Anthropology.* 27 (1998): 171–195.

Davis, Donald, Jr. *The Boundaries of Hindu Law: Tradition, Custom, and Politics in Medieval Kerala.* Turin: CESMEO, 2004.

——— "Dharma in Practice: Ācāra and Authority in Medieval Dharmaśāstra." *Journal of Indian Philosophy* 32 (2004): 813–830.

——— "Recovering the Indigenous Legal Traditions of India: Classical Hindu Law in Practice in Late Medieval Kerala." *Journal of Indian Philosophy* 27 (1999): 159–213.

Day, James M., and Mark V. Tappan, "The Narrative Approach to Moral Development: From the Epistemic Subject to Dialogical Selves." *Human Development* 39 (1996): 67–82.

De, S. K. *History of Sanskrit Poetics.* Calcutta: Firma KLM, 1976.

——— "Mahabharata as Mokṣa-śāstra." In S. Radhakrishnan, ed., *History of Philosophy Eastern and Western,* pp. 85–106. Vol. 1. London: Allen and Unwin, 1952.

De Nobili, Roberto. *Preaching Wisdom to the Wise: Three Treatises.* Trans., with introduction, Anand Amaldass and Francis X. Clooney. St. Louis: Institute of Jesuit Sources, 2000.

Derrett, J. Duncan M. *Religion, Law, and the State in India.* Delhi: Oxford University Press, 1999 [1968].

Devi, Konduri S. *Religion in Vijayanagara Empire.* New Delhi: Sterling, 1990.

Dhand, Arti. "The Dharma of Ethics, the Ethics of Dharma: Quizzing the Ideals of Hinduism." *Journal of Religious Ethics* 30 (2002): 347–372.

Dhavan, Rajeev. "Dharmaśāstra and Modern Indian Society: A Preliminary Exploration." *Journal of the Indian Law Institute* 34:3 (1992): 515–540.

Dirks, Nicholas B. *Castes of Mind: Colonialism and the Making of Modern India.* Princeton: Princeton University Press, 2001.

——— *The Hollow Crown: Ethnohistory of an Indian Kingdom.* Cambridge: Cambridge University Press, 1987.

Divine Discourses of His Holiness Jagadguru Sri Abhinava Vidyateertha Mahaswamigal. Madras: Vidyatirtha Foundation, 1994.

Doniger, Wendy. *Purāṇa Perennis: Reciprocity and Transformation in Hindu and Jaina Texts.* Albany: SUNY Press, 1993.

Douglas, Mary. *Implicit Meanings: Essays in Anthropology.* London: Routledge and Kegan Paul, 1975.

Dundes, Alan. "Metafolklore and Oral Literary Criticism." *Monist* 60 (1966): 505–516.

Durkheim, Emile. *The Elementary Forms of the Religious Life.* Trans. Joseph Ward Swain. New York: Macmillan, 1915.

Dwivedi, R. C. "Concept of the Śāstra." *Indologica Taurinensia* 13 (1985–1986): 43–60.

Eaton, Richard. *Essays on Islam and Indian History.* Delhi : Oxford University Press, 2000.

Eck, Diana, L. *Darśan: Seeing the Divine Image in India.* 3d ed. New York: Columbia University Press, 1998.

Eliot, T. S. "Tradition and the Individual Talent." *The Sacred Wood: Essays on Poetry and Criticism,* pp. 37–44. London: Faber and Faber, 1975 [1919].

Erndl, Kathleen. *Victory to the Mother: The Hindu Goddess of Northwest India in Myth, Ritual, and Symbol.* New York: Oxford University Press, 1993.

Falassi, Alessandro, ed. *Time Out of Time: Essays on the Festival.* Albuquerque: University of New Mexico Press, 1987.

Feldhaus, Anne. *Connected Places: Region, Pilgrimage, and Geographical Imagination in India.* New York: Palgrave, 2003.

——— *Water and Womanhood: Religious Meaning of Rivers in Maharashtra.* New York: Oxford University Press, 1995.

——— "Bahiṇā Bāī: Wife and Saint." *Journal of the American Academy of Religion* 50 (1982): 591–604.

Fine, Elizabeth C. *The Folklore Text from Performance to Print.* Bloomington: Indiana University Press, 1984.

Flueckiger, Joyce B. *Gender and Genre in the Folklore of Middle India.* Ithaca: Cornell University Press, 1996.

Forrest, G. W., ed. *Selections from the State Papers of the Governors-General of India.* Vol. 2: *Warren Hastings Documents.* Oxford: Blackwell, 1910.

Frazer, James. *The Golden Bough.* 3d. ed. London: Macmillan, 1907.

Fuller, Chistopher J. *The Camphor Flame: Popular Hinduism and Society in India.* Princeton: Princeton University Press, 1992.

——— *The Renewal of the Priesthood: Modernity and Traditionalism in a South Indian Temple.* Princeton: Princeton University Press, 2003.

Galanter, Marc. *Law and Society in Modern India.* Delhi: Oxford University Press, 1989.

Gandhi, M. K. *An Autobiography or the Story of My Experiments with Truth.* Trans. M. Desai. Ahmedabad: Gandhi Book Centre, Navjivan, 1940.

Genette, Gérard. *Narrative Discourse: An Essay in Method.* Trans. Jane Lewin. Ithaca: Cornell University Press, 1980.

Georges, Robert. "Timeliness and Appropriateness in Personal Experience Narrating." *Western Folklore* 46 (1987): 115–120.

Gerow, Edwin. "The Persistence of Classical Esthetic Categories in Contemporary Indian Literature: Three Bengali Novels." In Edward C. Dimock, Edwin Gerow, C. M. Naim, A. K. Ramanujan, Godern Roadarmel, and J. A. B. van Buitenen, eds., *The Literatures of India: An Introduction,* pp. 212–238. Chicago: University of Chicago Press, 1978.

——— *Indian Poetics.* Weisbaden: Harrassowitz, 1977.

Ghosh, Manmohan, trans. *The Nāṭyaśāstra: A Treatise on Ancient Indian Dramaturgy and Histrionics Ascribed to Bharata-Muni.* Calcutta: Manisha Granthalaya, 1967.

Gnanambal, K. *Religious Institutions and Caste Panchayats in South India.* Calcutta: Anthropological Survey of India, Government of India, 1973.

Goffman, Erving. *The Presentation of Self in Everyday Life.* Garden City, NY: Doubleday, 1959.

——— *Frame Analysis An Essay on the Organization of Experience.* Cambridge: Harvard University Press, 1974.

Gold, Ann Grodzins. *A Carnival of Parting: The Tales of King Bharthari and King Gopi Chand as Sung and Told by Madhu Natisar Nath of Ghatiyali, Rajasthan.* Berkeley: University of California Press, 1992.

——— *Fruitful Journeys: The Ways of Rajasthani Pilgrims.* New York: Oxford University Press, 1988.

Gold, Daniel. "Experiencing Scriptural Diversity: Words and Stories in Hindu Traditions." In Steven T. Katz, ed., *Mysticism and Sacred Scripture,* pp. 210–231. Oxford: Oxford University Press, 2000.

Goldman, Robert P., trans., and introduction. *The Rāmāyaṇa of Vālmīki,* vol. 1: *Bālakāṇḍa.* Princeton: Princeton University Press, 1984.

Gonda, Jan J. *Prayer and Blessing: Ancient Indian Ritual Terminology.* Leiden: Brill, 1989.

——— *The Ritual Sūtras*. Weisbaden: Harrassowitz, 1977.

Gossen, Gary. *Chamulas in the World of the Sun*. Cambridge: Harvard University Press, 1974.

Gottschalk, Peter S. *Beyond Hindu and Muslim: Multiple Identity in Narratives from Village India*. New York: Oxford University Press, 2000–2001.

Greatness of Sringeri. (author unknown) Mumbai: Tattvaloka, 1993.

Griffith, Ralph T. H., trans. *The Hymns of the Ṛgveda*. Ed. J. L. Shastri. New Delhi: Motilal Banarsidass, 1973 [1896].

Grimes, John, ed. and trans. *The Vivekacūdāmani of Śankarācārya Bhagavatpāda: An Introduction and Translation*. Burlington, VT: Ashgate, 2004.

Gumperz, John J., and Dell Hymes, eds. *The Ethnography of Communication*. Washington, DC: American Anthropological Association, 1964.

Gupta, Akhil, and James Ferguson. *Anthropological Locations: Boundaries and Grounds of Field Science*. Berkeley: University of California Press, 1997.

Halbfass, Wilhelm. *Tradition and Reflection: Explorations in Indian Thought*. Albany: SUNY Press, 1991.

Halloran, Michael S. "Aristotle's Concept of *Ethos*; or, If Not His, Somebody Else's." *Rhetoric Review* 1 (1982): 58–63.

Hanks, William. *Language and Communicative Practices*. Boulder: Westview, 1996.

Hansen, Kathryn. *Grounds for Play: The Nauṭankī Theatre of North India*. Berkeley: University of California Press, 1991.

Hauerwas, Stanley. *A Community of Character: Toward a Constructive Christian Social Ethic*. Notre Dame: University of Notre Dame Press, 1981.

——— "The Self as Story: Religion and Morality from the Agent's Perspective." *Journal of Religious Ethics* 1.1 (1973): 73–85.

Hawley, John Stratton. *Three Bhakti Voices: Mirabai, Surdas, and Kabir in Their Times and Ours*. Oxford: Oxford University Press, 2005.

——— "Author and Authority in the *Bhakti* Poetry of North India" *Journal of Asian Studies* 47.2 (1988): 269–290.

Heesterman, J. C. *The Broken World of Sacrifice: An Essay in Ancient Indian Ritual*. Chicago: University of Chicago Press, 1984.

——— "Householder and Wanderer." In T. N. Madan, ed., *Way of Life: King, Householder, Renouncer*, pp. 251–271. New Delhi: Vikas, 1982.

Herndon, Marcia. "Insiders, Outsiders: Knowing Our Limits, Limiting Our Knowing." *World of Music* 35 (1993): 63–80.

Herzfeld, Michael. *Poetics of Manhood: Contest and Identity in a Cretan Mountain Village*. Princeton: Princeton University Press, 1985.

Hindery, Roderick. "Hindu Ethics in the Rāmāyaṇa." *Journal of Religious Ethics* 4 (1976): 287–322.

Hiriyanna, A. *Art Experience*. New Delhi: Manohar, 1997 [1954].

——— *Outlines of Indian Philosophy*. Delhi: Motilal Banarsidass, 1993 [1932].

——— *Indian Conception of Values*. Mysore: Kavyalaya, 1975.

Hopkins, Gerard Manley. *The Note-books and Papers of Gerard Manley Hopkins*. Ed. Humphry House. London: Oxford University Press, 1937.

Hymes, Dell. *"In Vain I Tried To Tell You": Essays in Native American Ethno-poetics.* Philadelphia: University of Pennsylvania Press, 1981.

——— "The Ethnography of Speaking." In T. Gladwin, ed., *Anthropology and Human Behavior.* Washington, DC: Sturtevan, 1962.

Ingalls, Daniel. H. H., Jeffrey. M. Masson, and M. V. Patwardhan. *The Dhvanyāloka of Anandavardhana with the Locana of Abhinavagupta.* Cambridge: Harvard University Press, 1990.

Ingarden, Roman. *The Literary Work of Art: An Investigation on the Borderlines of Ontology, Logic, and Theory of Literature.* Trans. George G. Grabowicz. Evanston: Northwestern University Press, 1973 [1931].

——— *The Cognition of the Literary Work of Art.* Trans. Ruth Ann Crowley and Kenneth R. Olson. Evanston: Northwestern University Press, 1973 [1937].

Janaki, S. S. "The Hand Gesture Patāka in Nāṭya." In Jonathan Katz, ed., *The Traditional Indian Theory and Practice of Music and Dance,* pp. 187–209. Brill: Leiden, 1992.

Jhingran, Saral. *Aspects of Hindu Morality.* Delhi: Motilal Banarsidass, 1989.

Kamat, Jyotsna. *Social Life in Medieval Karnataka.* Bangalore: Abhinav, 1981.

Kamath, Suryanath. *Historiography of Karnataka: Seminar Papers.* Bangalore: Mythic Society, 1991.

Kambar, Chandrasekhara. *Singarevva and the Palace.* Trans. Laxmi Chandrasekhar. New Delhi: Katha, 2002

Kanchipuram Shankaracharya Pujyasri Chandrashekararendra Saraswati Swami. *Hindu Dharma: The Universal Way of Life.* Trans. Sri R.G. K. Mumbai: Bharatiya Vidya Bhavan, 1995.

Kane, P. V. *History of Dharmaśāstra.* 5 vols. Poona: Bhandarkar Oriental Research Institute, 1962–1975.

——— *History of Sanskrit Poetics.* Delhi: Motilal Banarasidass, 1971.

Kapchan, Deborah. *Gender on the Market: Moroccan Women and the Revoicing of Tradition.* Philadelphia: University of Pennsylvania Press, 1996.

——— "Performance." *Journal of American Folklore* 108 (1995): 479–508.

Katz, Jonathan. *The Traditional Indian Theory and Practice of Music and Dance.* Leiden: Brill, 1992.

Keane, Webb. *Signs of Recognition: Powers and Hazards of Representation in an Indonesian Society.* Berkeley: University of California Press, 1997.

Keith, Arthur. B. "The Science of Love." In A. B. Keith, *A History of Sanskrit Literature,* New Delhi: Motilal Banarsidass, 1993 [1920], pp. 467–470.

Khandelwal, Meena. *Women in Ochre Robes: Gendering Hindu Renunciation.* Albany: SUNY Press, 2004.

Khare, Ravindra S. "Anna." In Sushil Mittal and Gene Thursby, eds., *The Hindu World,* pp. 407–428. New York: Routledge, 2004.

——— "The Seen and the Unseen: Hindu Distinctions, Experiences, and Cultural Reasoning." *Contributions to Indian Sociology* 27.2 (1993): 191–212.

——— "Indian Hospitality: Some Cultural Values and Social Dynamics." *Cultural Heritage of the Indian Village.* British Museum Occasional Paper no. 47 (1991): 45–61.

——— *Normative Culture and Kinship: Essays on Hindu Categories, Processes, and Perspectives*. New Delhi: Vikas, 1983.

——— *Culture and Reality: Essays in the Hindu System of Managing Foods*. Simla: Indian Institute of Advanced Study, 1976.

——— *The Hindu Hearth and Home*. New Delhi: Vikas, 1976.

Khare, Ravindra S., ed. *The Eternal Food: Gastronomic Ideas and Experiences of Hindus and Buddhists*. Albany: SUNY Press, 1992.

Khare, Ravindra S., and M. S. A. Rao, eds. *Food, Society, and Culture: Aspects in South Asian Food Systems*. Durham: Carolina Academic, 1986.

Kittell, F. *A Kannada-English Dictionary*. Mangalore: Basel Mission Book and Tract Depository, 1894.

Klokke, Marijke J, ed. *Narrative Sculpture and Literary Traditions in South and Southeast Asia*. Leiden: Brill, 2000.

Krishna, Daya. *Indian Philosophy: A New Approach*. Delhi: Sri Satguru, 1997.

Krsnadasa Kaviraja Gosvami. [*Śriśricaitanyacaritāmṛta*] *Caitanya Caritāmṛta of Kṛṣṇadāsa Kavirāja: A Translation and Commentary*. Ed. Tony Stewart. Trans. Edward C. Dimock. Oriental Series 56. Cambridge: Department of Sanskrit and Indian Studies, Harvard University, 1999.

Kṣemēndra. *Aucityavicāracarcā*. In Suryakanta, *Kshemendra Studies*. Poona: Oriental Book Agency, 1954.

Kulke, Hermann, "Mahajanas, Mahants, and Historians: Reflections on the Early History of Vijayanagara and Sringeri." In Anna Dallapiccola and S. Zingel-Ave Lallemant, eds., *Vijayanagara: City and Empire*, pp.120–143. Stuttgart: Steiner Verlag Wiesbaden, 1985.

Kuvempu (K. V. Puttappa). *Malenāḍina Citragaḷu*. Mysore: Udayaravi Prakāśana, 1933.

Laidlaw, James. *Riches and Renunciation: Religion, Economy, and Society Among the Jains*. New York: Oxford University Press, 1995.

Lakoff, George and Mark Johnson *Metaphors We Live By*. Chicago: University of Chicago Press, 2003 [1980].

Lakshminarasimha Murthy, N. S. "Sevāgrāmadalli Nanna Anubhavagaḷu" [My Experiences at Sevagram]. Parts 1 and 2. *Tayināḍu*, June 30, 1952.

Lalye, P. G. *Studies in Devī Bhāgavata*. Bombay: Popular Prakashan, 1973.

Lariviere, Richard W. "Dharmaśāstra, Custom, 'Real Law' and 'Apocryphal' Smṛtis." *Journal of Indian Philosophy* 32 (2004 [1997]): 611–627.

——— "Justices and Panditas: Some Ironies in Contemporary Readings of the Hindu Legal Past." *Journal of Asian Studies* 48.4 (1989): 757–769.

Lath, Mukund. "Ancient Dance: Towards Reviewing the History of Art in India." *Jan Samachar*, January 25, 2003. Accessed at http://www.jansamachar.net/display.php3?id=#=606

——— "Tandu: The First Theoretician of Dance." In Jonathan Katz, ed., *The Traditional Indian Theory and Practice of Music and Dance*, pp. 173–186. Leiden: Brill, 1992.

Leitch, T. *What Stories Are: Narrative Theory and Interpretation*. State College: Pennsylvania State University Press, 1986.

Lévi-Strauss, Claude. *The Raw and the Cooked.* New York : Harper and Row, 1969.

Liddell, Henry George, and Robert Scott, eds. *A Greek-English Lexicon.* Revised Henry Stuart Jones. Oxford: Clarendon Press, 1996.

Lingat, Robert. *The Classical Law of India.* Trans. J. Duncan M. Derrett. New Delhi: Oxford University Press, 1998.

Ludden, David. *An Agrarian History of South Asia.* Cambridge University Press, 1999.

Lutgendorf. Philip. *The Life of a Text: Performing the Ramcaritmanas of Tulsidas.* Berkeley: University of California Press, 1991.

McGee, Mary. "Bahiṇābāī: The Ordinary Life of an Exceptional Woman, or, the Exceptional Life of an Ordinary Woman." In Steven J. Rosen, ed., *Vaiṣṇavī: Women and the Worship of Krishna,* pp. 133–169. New Delhi: Motilal Banarsidass, 1996.

——— "In Quest of Saubhāgya: The Roles and Goals of Women as Women as Depicted in Marathi Stories of Votive Devotions." In Anne Feldhaus, ed., *Images of Women in Maharashtrian Literature and Religion,* pp. 146–170. Albany: SUNY, 1996.

——— "Desired Fruits: Motive and Intention in the Votive Rites of Hindu Women." In Julia Leslie, ed., *Roles and Rituals for Hindu Women,* pp. 71–88. Rutherford: Fairleigh Dickinson University Press, 1991.

MacIntyre, Alasdair. *After Virtue.* Notre Dame: University of Notre Dame Press, 1984.

McKenzie, John. *Hindu Ethics: A Historical and Critical Essay.* Oxford: Oxford University Press, 1922.

Macnaghten, F. W. *Considerations on the Hindoo Law, as It Is Current in Bengal.* Serampore: Mission, 1824.

Madan, T. N. "The Ideology of the Householder." In T. N. Madan, ed., *Way of Life: King, Householder, Renouncer,* pp. 223–250. New Delhi: Vikas, 1982.

Maine, Henry. *Village Communities in the East and West.* London: John Murray, 1871.

Majumdar, J. K. *Raja Rammohun Roy and Progressive Movements in India.* Calcutta: Art, 1941.

Malamoud, Charles. *Cooking the World: Ritual and Thought in Ancient India.* Trans. David White. Delhi: Oxford University Press, 1996.

Malinowski, Bronislaw. *Magic, Science, and Religion, and Other Essays.* Garden City, NY: Doubleday, 1954.

Mani, Lata. *Contentious Traditions: The Debate on Sati in Colonial India.* Berkeley: University of California Press, 1998.

Marriott, McKim. "Caste Ranking and Food Transactions: A Matrix Analysis," In Milton Singer and Bernard. S. Cohn, eds., *Structure and Change in Indian Society,* pp. 133–172. Chicago: Aldine, 1968.

Marriott, McKim, ed. *Village India: Studies in a Little Community.* Chicago: University of Chicago Press, 1955.

Martin, Nancy M. "Mirabai: Inscribed in Text, Embodied in Life." In Steven J. Rosen, ed., *Vaiṣṇavī: Women and the Worship of Krishna,* pp. 7–46. New Delhi: Motilal Banarsidass, 1996.

Matilal, Bimal K. *Mind, Language, and World: The Collected Essays of Bimal Krishna Matilal.* Ed. Jonardon Ganeri. New Delhi: Oxford University Press, 2002.

Mayne, John. D. *A Treatise on Hindu Law and Usage.* Ed. V. M. Coutts-Trotter. 9th rev. ed. Madras: Higginbotham, 1922 [1878].

Merleau-Ponty, M. *Phenomenology of Perception.* Trans. Colin Smith. London: Routledge, 1962.

Mesquita, Roque. *Madhva's Unknown Literary Sources: Some Observations.* New Delhi: Aditya Prakashan, 2000.

Mills, Margaret A. "Feminist Theory and the Study of Folklore: A Twenty-Year Trajectory Toward Theory." *Western Folklore* 52 (April 1993): 173–192.

——— *Rhetorics and Politics in Afghan Traditional Storytelling.* Philadelphia: University of Pennsylvania Press, 1991.

Mohanty, J. N. *Classical Indian Philosophy.* New Delhi: Oxford University Press, 2002.

Monier-Williams, Monier. *A Sanskrit-English Dictionary.* New Delhi: Motilal Banarsidass, 1986 [1899].

Moon, Penderel. *Strangers in India.* London: Faber and Faber, 1944.

Mulla, Dinshah F. *Principles of Hindu Law.* Bombay: Tripathi, 1974 [1912].

Nabokov, Isabelle. *Religion Against the Self: An Ethnography of Tamil Rituals.* New York: Oxford University Press, 2000.

Nagar, Shantilal. *Siva in Art, Literature, and Thought.* New Delhi: Indus, 1994.

Nagaraj, D. R. "Tensions in Kannada Literary Culture." In Sheldon Pollock, ed., *Literary Cultures in History: Reconstructions from South Asia,* pp.323–382. Berkeley: University of California Press, 2003.

Nakhleh, Khalil. "On Being a Native Anthropologist." In G. Huizer and B. Mannheim, eds., *The Politics of Anthropology: From Colonialism and Sexism to the View from Below,* pp. 343–352. The Hague: Mouton, 1979.

Narayan, Kirin. "'Honor Is Honor, After All': Silence and Speech in the Life Stories of Women in Kangra, Northwest India." In David Arnold and S. Blackburn, eds., *Telling Lives in India: Biography, Autobiography, and Life History,* pp. 227–251. Bloomington: Indiana University Press, 2004.

———. In collaboration with Urmila Devi Sood. *Mondays on the Dark Night of the Moon: Himalayan Foothill Folktales.* New York: Oxford: Oxford University Press, 1997.

——— "The Practice of Oral Literary Criticism: Women's Songs in Kangra, India." *Journal of American Folklore* 108 (1995): 243–264.

——— "How Native Is a 'Native' Anthropologist?" *American Anthropologist* 95 (1993): 671–686.

——— *Storytellers, Saints, and Scoundrels: Folk Narrative as Hindu Religious Teaching.* Berkeley: University of California Press, 1989.

Narayanan, Vasudha. *The Vernacular Veda: Recitation, Recitation, and Ritual.* Columbia, SC: University of South Carolina Press, 1994.

——— *The Way and the Goal: Expressions of Devotion in the Early Śrī Vaiṣṇava Tradition.* Institute for Vaishnava Studies (American University), Washington, DC and Cambridge, MA: Center for the Study of World Religions (Harvard University), 1987.

Narayana Rao, Velcheru, trans. *Śiva's Warriors: The Basava Purāṇa of Pālkuriki Somanātha*. Princeton: Princeton University Press, 1990.

——— "Purāṇa." In Sushil Mittal and Gene Thursby, eds., *The Hindu World*, pp. 97–115. New York: Routledge, 2004.

______ "A Rāmāyaṇa of Their Own: Women's Oral Tradition in Telugu." In Paula Richman, ed., *Many Rāmāyaṇas: The Diversity of a Narrative Tradition in South Asia*, pp. 114–136. Berkeley: University of California Press, 1991.

Natarajan, A. R. *Jagadguru Sri Chandrashekara Bharati Mahaswami: Mystic and Seer*. Bangalore: Ramana Maharshi Centre for Learning, 1994.

Nath, Vijay. *Dana: Gift System in Ancient India (600 BC–AD 300)*. New Delhi: Munshiram Manoharlal, 1987.

Nelson, Hilde L. *Stories and Their Limits: Narrative Approaches to Bioethics*. New York: Routledge, 1997.

Nelson, John H. *Indian Usage and Judge-Made Law in Madras*. Kegan Paul: London, 1887.

——— "Hindu Law at Madras." *Journal of the Royal Asiatic Society of Great Britain and Ireland* n.s. 13 (1881): 208–236.

Newton, Adam Z. *Narrative Ethics*. Cambridge: Harvard University Press, 1995.

Nilakanta Sastri, K. A. *The Culture and History of the Tamils*. Calcutta: Mukhopadhyay, 1964.

——— *A History of South India from Prehistoric Times to the Fall of Vijayanagar*. Madras: Oxford University Press, 1958.

Norrick, Neal R. *Conversational Narrative*. Amsterdam: Benjamins, 2000

Nussbaum, Martha C. *Love's Knowledge: Essays on Philosophy and Literature*. New York: Oxford University Press, 1990.

Ochs, Elinor, and Lisa Capps. *Living Narrative: Creating Lives in Everyday Storytelling*. Cambridge: Harvard University Press, 2001.

O'Flaherty, Wendy. *The Rig Veda: An Anthology*. New York: Penguin, 1981.

——— *Asceticism and Eroticism in the Mythology of Śiva*. New York: Oxford University Press, 1973.

O'Flaherty, Wendy, ed. *Karma and Rebirth in Classical Indian Traditions*. Berkeley: University of California Press, 1980.

Olivelle, Patrick. *Manu's Code of Law: A Critical Edition and Translation of the Mānava-Dharmaśāstra*. With the editorial assistance of Suman Olivelle. New York: Oxford University Press, 2005.

——— "Manu and the Arthaśāstra: A Study in Śāstric Intertextuality." *Journal of Indian Philosophy* 32 (2004): 281–291.

——— *Dharmasūtras: The Law Codes of Āpastamba, Gautama, Baudhāyana, and Vasiṣṭha*. Oxford: Oxford University Press, 1999.

——— *Rules and Regulations of Brahmanical Asceticism*. Albany: SUNY Press, 1995.

——— *Saṃnāyasa Upāniṣads*. New York: Oxford University Press, 1992.

——— "From Feast to Fast: Food and the Indian Ascetic." In Julia Leslie, ed., *Rules and Remedies in Classical Indian Law*, pp. 17–36. Panels of the Seventh World Sanskrit Conference, vol. 9. Leiden: Brill, 1991.

O'Malley, Padraig. *The Irish Hunger Strikes and the Politics of Despair*. Boston: Beacon, 1990.

O'Neill, P. *Fictions of Discourse: Reading Narrative Theory*. Toronto: University of Toronto Press, 1996.

Padmanaban, K. *Srimad Sankara Digvijayam by Vidyaranya*. Madras: Padmanaban, 1985.

Pandurangi, K. T., ed and trans. *Madhvacārya Mahabhāratatātparyanirṇaya*. Vol. 1. Chirtanur: Sriman Madhva Sidhantonnahini Sabha, 1993.

Paniker, K. A. *Indian Narratology*. New Delhi: Indira Gandhi National Centre for the Arts, 2003.

Pannikkar, Raimundo. *The Vedic Experience: Mantramañjarī (An Anthology of the Vedas for Modern Man and Contemporary Celebration)*. New Delhi: Motilal Banarsidass, 1994.

Parker, Samuel. "Text and Practice in South Asian Art: An Ethnographic Perspective." *Artibus Asiae* 63.1 (2003): 5–34.

Parry, Jonathan P. *Death in Banaras*. Cambridge: Cambridge University Press, 1994.

Patil, Channabasappa. *Panchatantra in Karnataka Sculptures*. Mysore: Directorate of Archaeology and Museums, 1995.

Patton, Laurie L., ed. *Authority, Anxiety, and Canon: Essays in Vedic Interpretation*. Albany: SUNY Press, 1994.

Pearson, Anne Mackenzie. *Because It Gives Me Peace of Mind: Ritual Fasts in the Religious Lives of Hindu Women*. Albany: SUNY Press, 1996.

Perrett, Roy W. *Hindu Ethics: A Philosophical Study*. Honolulu: University of Hawaii Press, 1998.

Petheram, W. C. "English Judges and Hindu Law." *Law Quarterly Review* 56 (1898): 392–404.

Pintchman, Tracy. *The Rise of the Goddess in Hindu Tradition*. Albany: SUNY Press, 1994.

Pollock, Sheldon. "Sanskrit Literary Culture from the Inside Out." In Sheldon Pollock, ed., *Literary Cultures in History: Reconstructions from South Asia*, pp. 39–130. Berkeley: University of California Press, 2003.

——— "'Tradition' as 'Revelation': Sruti, Smrti, and the Sanskrit Discourse of Power." In S. Lienhard and I. Piovano, eds., *Lex et Litterae: Essays on Ancient Indian Law and Literature in Honour of Oscar Botto*, pp. 395–417. Turin: Edizioni dell 'Orso, 1997.

——— "The Idea of Śāstra in Traditional India." In Anna L. Dallapiccola, ed., *Shastric Traditions in Indian Arts*, pp.17–26. Stuttgart: Steiner, 1989.

——— "Playing by the Rules: Śāstra and Sanskrit Literature." In Anna L. Dallapiccola, ed., *Shastric Traditions in Indian Arts*, pp. 301–312. Stuttgart: Steiner, 1989.

——— "The Theory of Practice and the Practice of Theory in Intellectual History." *Journal of the American Oriental Society* 105.3 (1985): 499–519.

Potter, Karl. *Encyclopedia of Indian Philosophies.* New Delhi: Motilal Banarsidass, 1995.

——— *Bibliography of Indian Philosophies.* Delhi: Motilal Banarsidass for the American Institute of Indian Studies, 1970.

Prakash, Om. *Food and Drinks in Ancient India.* Delhi: Munshiram Manoharlal, 1961.

Prasad, Leela. "Celebrating Allegiances, Ambiguated Belonging: Regionality in Festival and Performance in Śringēri, South India." In Rajendra Vora and Anne Feldhaus, eds., *Region, Culture, and Politics in India,* pp. 211–238. New Delhi: Manohar, 2005.

——— "Anklets on the *Pyal*: Women Present Women's Stories From South India." In Leela Prasad, Ruth B. Bottigheimer, and Lalitha Handoo, eds., *Gender and Story in South India,* pp. 1–33. Albany: SUNY Press, 2006.

——— "Conversational Narrative and the Moral Self: Stories of Negotiated Proprieties from South India." *Journal of Religious Ethics* 32.1 (2004): 153–174. Also see publishers' errata in 32.3 (2004).

——— *Scripture and Strategy: Narrative and the Poetics of Appropriate Conduct in Sringeri, South India.* Ph.D. diss., University of Pennsylvania, 1998.

——— ed. *"Live Like the Banyan Tree": Images of the Indian American Experience.* Philadelphia: Balch Institute for Ethnic Studies, 1999.

Radcliffe-Brown, A. R. *The Andaman Islanders.* Cambridge: Cambridge University Press, 1922.

Raghavan, V. ed. *Studies on Some Concepts of the Alaṃkāra Śāstra.* Madras: The Adyar Library and Research Centre, 1973.

Raheja, Gloria G. *The Poison in the Gift: Ritual, Prestation, and the Dominant Caste in a North Indian Village.* Chicago: University of Chicago Press, 1988.

Raheja, Gloria G., and Ann G. Gold. *Listen to the Heron's Words: Reimagining Gender and Kinship in North India.* Berkeley: University of California Press, 1994.

Rajan, M. A. S. *Land Reforms in Karnataka: An Account by a Participant Observer.* Delhi: Hindustan, 1986.

Ramachandra Rao, S. K. *Consciousness in Advaita: Source Material and Methodological Considerations.* Bangalore: SAVSSRA, 1979.

Ramanujan, A. K. *Folktales from India: A Selection of Oral Tales from Twenty-Two Languages.* New Delhi: Penguin India, 1993.

——— "Three Hundred Rāmāyaṇas, Five Examples, and Three Thoughts on Translation." In Paula Richman, ed., *Many Rāmāyaṇas: The Diversity of a Narrative Tradition in South Asia,* pp. 22–49. Berkeley: University of California Press, 1991.

——— "Is There an Indian Way of Thinking? An Informal Essay." In McKim Marriott, ed., *India Through Hindu Categories.* New Delhi: Sage, 1989.

——— "Where Mirrors Are Windows: Toward an Anthology of Reflections." *History of Religions* 28 (1989): 187–216.

——— "The Relevance of South Asian Folklore." In Peter Claus, J. Handoo, and D. P. Pattanayak, eds., *Indian Folklore II,* pp. 79–156. Mysore: CIIL, 1987.

Ramanujan, A. K., trans. *Speaking of Siva.* Harmondsworth: Penguin, 1973.

Ramanujan, A. K., and Edwin Gerow. "Indian Poetics." In Edward C. Dimock, Edwin Gerow, C. M. Naim, A. K. Ramanujan, Godern Roadarmel, and J. A. B. van

Buitenen, eds., *The Literatures of India: An Introduction,* pp. 128–143. Chicago: University of Chicago Press, 1978.

Ramasvamy Iyengar, Gorur. *Haḷḷiya Bāḷu.* Maisuru: Kāvyālaya, 1948.

Ramaswamy, Sumathi. *Passions of the Tongue: Language Devotion in Tamil India, 1891–1970.* Berkeley: University of California Press, 1997.

Ramesam, N. *Sri Śankarācārya.* Ponnur, Andhra Pradesh: Sri Bhavanarayanaswami Temple, 1971.

Rangarajan, L. N. "Introduction." In L. N. Rangarajan., trans. *Kautilya's Arthaśāstra,* pp. 13–41.. New Delhi: Penguin, 1992.

Rao, Raja. *Kanthapura.* New Delhi: Oxford University Press, 1993 [1938].

Rao, T. Ramalingeswara (Swami Advayananda Bharati). *Sringeri Revisited.* Vijayawada, India: N.p., 1968.

Reck, David. "The Invisible *Sāstra*: A Personal Memoir of Musical Study in India." In Anna L. Dallapiccola, ed., *Shastric Traditions in Indian Arts,* pp. 407–414. Stuttgart: Steiner, 1989.

Redfield, Robert. *The Little Community and Peasant Society and Culture.* Chicago: University of Chicago Press, 1960.

Redfield, Robert, and Milton Singer. "The Cultural Role of Cities." *Economic Development and Cultural Change* 3.1 (1954): 53–73.

Reynolds, Nedra. "*Ethos* as Location: New Sites for Understanding Discursive Authority." *Rhetoric Review* 11.2 (1993): 325–338.

Rice, Lewis. *Mysore Inscriptions.* New Delhi: Navrang, 1983 [1879].

Richards, Audrey. *Land, Labour, and Diet in Northern Rhodesia: An Economic Study of the Bemba Tribe.* Muenster: LIT with the IAI, c. 1995 [1939].

Richman, Paula, ed. *Questioning Rāmāyaṇas: A South Asian Tradition.* Berkeley: University of California Press, 2001.

——— *Many Rāmāyaṇas: The Diversity of a Narrative Tradition in South Asia.* Berkeley: University of California Press, 1991.

Ricoeur, Paul. *Time and Narrative.* Trans. K. McLaughlin and D. Pellauer. 3 vols. Chicago: University of Chicago Press, 1984–1988.

——— *From Text to Action: Essays in Hermeneutics.* Trans. Kathleen Blamey and John B. Thompson. Evanston, IL: Northwestern University Press, 1991.

——— "Life in Quest of Narrative." In David Wood, ed., *On Paul Ricoeur: Narrative and Interpretation,* pp. 20–33. London: Routledge, 1991.

——— "Life: A Story in Search of a Narrator." In Mario J. Valdes, ed., *A Ricoeur Reader: Reflection and Imagination,* pp. 425–437. Toronto: University of Toronto Press, 1991.

——— "What Is a Text?" In Mario J. Valdes, ed., *A Ricoeur Reader: Reflection and Imagination,* pp. 43–64. Toronto: University of Toronto Press, 1991.

——— "Narrated Time." In Mario J. Valdes, ed., *A Ricoeur Reader: Reflection and Imagination,* pp. 338–354. Toronto: University of Toronto Press, 1991.

——— "Mimesis and Representation." In Mario J. Valdes, ed., *A Ricoeur Reader: Reflection and Imagination,* pp.137–155. Toronto: University of Toronto Press, 1991.

Rocher, Ludo. "The Dharmaśāstras." In Gavin D. Flood, ed., *The Blackwell Companion to Hinduism*, pp. 102–115. Oxford: Blackwell, 2003.

——— "Orality and Textuality in the Indian Context." *Sino-Platonic Papers* 49 (1994): 1–28.

——— "Law Books in an Oral Culture: The Indian *Dharmaśāstras*." *Proceedings of the American Philosophical Society* 137.2 (1993): 254–267.

——— *The Purāṇas: History of Indian Literature: Vol. 2*. Ed. Jan Gonda. Weisbaden: Harrassowitz, 1986.

———. "The Kāmasūtra: Vātsyāyana's Attitude Toward Dharma and Dharmaśāstra." *Journal of the American Oriental Society* 105.3 (1985): 521–529.

——— "Father Bouchet's Letter on the Administration of Hindu Law." In Richard W. Lariviere, ed., *Studies in Dharmaśāstra*, pp. 15–48. Calcutta: Mukhopadhyay, 1984.

Rocher, Rosane. *Orientalism, Poetry, and the Millennium: The Checkered Life of Nathanial Brassey Halhed, 1751–1830*. Delhi: Motilal Banarsidass, 1983.

Rommetveit, Ragnar. "On the Dawning of Different Aspects of Life in a Pluralistic Social World." *Poetics Today* 4.3 (1983): 595–609.

——— *On Message Structure: A Framework for the Study of Language and Communication*. New York: Wiley, 1974.

Rosenwald, George. C., and Richard. L. Ochberg, eds. *Storied Lives: The Cultural Politics of Self-Understanding*. New Haven: Yale University Press, 1992.

Row, B. R., ed. *Selections from the Records of the Sringeri Mutt*. Mysore: Government Branch Press, 1927.

Rudolph, Lloyd, and Susanne H. Rudolph. *The Modernity of Tradition: Political Development in India*. Chicago: University of Chicago Press, 1967.

Said, Edward. *The World, the Text, and the Critic*. Cambridge: Harvard University Press, 1983.

Sanday, Peggy-Reeves. *Women at the Center: Life in a Modern Matriarchy*. Ithaca: Cornell University Press, 2002.

Sarma, Deepak. *An Introduction to Madhva Vedānta*. Burlington, VT: Ashgate, 2003.

Sarma, D. S. *Hinduism Through the Ages*. Bombay: Bharatiya Vidya Bhavan, 1973.

Sastry, K. R. R. *Śrī Śringēri Jagadguru and the Karnataka Samsthanam*. Madras: Śringēri Jagadguru Sanatana Dharma Vidya Samithi, 1966.

Sawai, Yoshitsugu. *The Faith of Ascetics and Lay Smārtas: A Study of the Śankaran Tradition of Śringēri*. Vienna: Institute for Indology, University of Vienna, 1992.

Schomer, Karen, and W. H. McLeod, eds. *The Sants: Studies in a Devotional Tradition of India*. Berkeley: University of California Press, 1987.

Schweig, Graham M. "Humility and Passion: A Caitanyite Vaishnava Ethics of Devotion." *Journal of Religious Ethics* 30 (2002): 421–444.

Seitel, Peter. *See So That We May See: Performances and Interpretations of Traditional Tales from Tanzania*. Bloomington: Indiana University Press, 1980.

Sen, Surendranath. "The Shringeri Letters of Tipu Sultan." In Surendranath Sen, *Studies in Indian History*, pp. 155–169. Calcutta: University of Calcutta Press, 1930.

Sharma, B. N. K. *The Brahmasūtras and Their Principal Commentaries: A Critical Exposition*. Vols. 1, 2. Bombay: Bharatiya Vidya Bhavan, 1971.

Sharma, I. C. *Ethical Philosophies of India*. New York: Harper and Row, 1965.

Sharma, M. S. M. *Pilgrimage to Sringeri*. Published by author. 1954.

Sharma, R. "Sri Śankaracharya Dakshinamnaya Sringagiri Śāradā Peetham 'Vyakhyana-cum-Dharma Simhasanam.'" N.p. 1972.

Shastri, Joshi K. L., ed. *The Mārkaṇḍeya-Purāṇam: Sanskrit Text, English Translation with Notes and Index of Verses*. Delhi: Parimal, 2004.

Shastry, A. K. "Śṛingēri Kaḍitas as Sources of Vijayanagara History." In G.S. Dikshit, *Early Vijayanagara: Studies in Its History and Culture*, pp. 153–161. Bangalore: BMS Smaraka Pratishthana, 1988.

——— *A History of Śṛingēri*. Dharwad: Karnatak University Press, 1982.

Sherzer, Joel. *Kuna Ways of Speaking: An Ethnographic Perspective*. Austin: University of Texas Press, 1983.

Shuman, Amy. "Dismantling Local Culture." *Western Folklore* 52 (1993): 344–364.

Singer, Milton. *When a Great Tradition Modernizes: An Anthropological Approach to Indian Civilization*. New York: Praeger, 1972.

——— "The Great Tradition in a Metropolitan Center: Madras." In Milton Singer, ed., *Traditional India: Structure and Change*. Philadelphia: American Folklore Society, 1959.

Skuy, David. "Macaulay and the Indian Penal Code of 1862: The Myth of the Inherent Superiority and Modernity of the English Legal System in the Nineteenth Century." *Modern Asian Studies* 32 (1998): 513–557.

Smith, Brian K. *Reflections on Resemblance, Ritual, and Religion*. New York: Oxford University Press, 1989.

Sontheimer, Gunter-Dietz. "Religious Endowments in India: The Juristic Personality of Hindu Deities." *Zeitschrift fur Vergleichende Rechtswissenschaft* 67 (1964): 45–100.

Srinivas, M. N. "Some Thoughts on the Study of One's Own Society." In M. N. Srinivas, ed., *Social Change in Modern India*, pp. 147–163. Berkeley: University of California Press, 1966.

——— *Religion and Society Among the Coorgs of India*. Oxford: Oxford University Press, 1952.

Stahl, Sandra D. *Literary Folkloristics and the Personal Narrative*. Bloomington: Indiana University Press, 1989.

Steele, Arthur. *Summary of the Law and Custom of Hindoo Castes Within the Dekhun Provinces*. Bombay: Courier, 1827.

Stein, Burton. *Peasant State and Society in Medieval South India*. Delhi: Oxford University Press, 1994.

Sternbach, Ludwig. *Maha-Subhashita-Sangraha*. Vol. 4. Hoshiarpur: Vishveshvaran Vedic Research Institute, 1980.

Stoker, Valerie. "Conceiving the Canon in Dvaita Vedānta: Madhva's Doctrine of 'All Sacred Lore.'" *Numen* 51.1 (2004): 47–77.

Stokes, Eric. *The English Utilitarians and India*. Oxford: Clarendon Press, 1959.

Sullivan, Bruce. "The Religious Authority of the Mahābhārata: Vyāsa and Brahmā in the Hindu Scriptural Tradition." *Journal of the American Academy of Religion* 62.2 (1994): 377–401.

Suryakanta. *Kshemendra Studies: Together with an English Translation of his Kavikānthabharaṇa, Aucityavicāracarca and Suvṛttatilaka.* Poona: Oriental, 1954.

Swami Nikhilananda. *The Upanishads: A Second Selection.* London: Phoenix House, 1954.

Swami Tapasyananda, trans. *Sankara Digvijaya: The Traditional Life of Sri Sankaracharya.* 2d ed. Madras: Ramakrishna Mission, 1983.

Taggart, James. *Enchanted Maidens: Spanish Folktales of Courtship and Marriage.* Princeton: Princeton University Press, 1990.

Talbot, Cynthia. *Precolonial India in Practice: Society, Region, and Identity in Medieval Andhra*, Oxford: Oxford University Press, 2001.

Tedlock, Dennis. *The Spoken Word and the Work of Interpretation.* Philadelphia: University of Pennsylvania Press, 1983.

Thapar, Romila. *Interpreting Early India.* Delhi: Oxford University Press, 1992.

——— *A History of India.* Vol 1. New York: Penguin, 1990.

——— *From Lineage to State: Social Formations in the Mid-first Millennium B.C. in the Ganga Valley.* Delhi: Oxford University Press, 1984.

——— *Ancient Indian Social History: Some Interpretations.* Hyderabad: Orient Longman, 1978.

Tirrell, Lynne. "Storytelling and Moral Agency." *Journal of Aesthetics and Art Criticism* 48:2 (Spring 1990): 115–126.

Tiwari, K. N. *Classical Indian Ethical Thought: A Philosophical Study of Hindu, Jaina, and Bauddha Morals.* Delhi: Motilal Banarsidass, 1998.

Toomey, Paul M. *Food from the Mouth of Krishna: Feast and Festivities in a North Indian Pilgrimage Center.* Hindustan, 1994.

Trimpi, Wesley. "Decorum." In Alex Preminger and T. V. F. Brogan, eds., *Princeton Encyclopedia of Poetry and Poetics*, pp. 282–283. Princeton: Princeton University Press, 1993.

Turner, V. *The Ritual Process: Structure and Anti-Structure.* Ithaca: Cornell University Press, 1969.

Vail, Lise F. "'Unlike a Fool, He Is Not Defiled': Ascetic Purity and Ethics in the *Saṃnyāsa Upaniṣads*." *Journal of Religious Ethics* 30 (2002): 373–397.

Valdes, Mario J., ed., *A Ricoeur Reader: Reflection and Imagination.* Toronto: University of Toronto Press, 1991.

Van der Veer, Peter. *Religious Nationalism: Hindus and Muslims in India.* Berkeley: University of California Press, 1994.

Vatsyayan, Kapila. *Bharata: The Natyasastra.* New Delhi: Sahitya Academi, 1996.

——— "Inaugural Address." In Anna L. Dallapiccola, ed., *Shastric Traditions in Indian Arts*, pp. 1–4. Stuttgart: Steiner, 1989.

——— "Cultural Patterns of India and the Performing Arts." In K. Vatsyayan, ed., *A Study of Some Traditions of Performing Arts in Eastern India: Mārga and Deśi Polarities*, pp. 4–33. Gauhati: University of Gauhati Press, 1981.

——— *Classical Indian Dance in Literature and the Arts.* New Delhi: Sangeet Natak Akademi, 1968.

Vaudeville, Charlotte, and Vasudha Dalmia. *Myths, Saints, and Legends in Medieval India.* New York: Oxford University Press, 1996.

Venkataraman, K. R. *The Throne of Transcendental Wisdom: Śrī Śamkarācārya's Śāradā pīṭha in Śringeri.* Sringeri: Sri Sharada Trust, 1990.

Venkataramanayya, N. *Studies in the Third Dynasty of Vijayanagara.* Madras: University of Madras, 1935.

Wadley, Susan. *Raja Nal and the Goddess: The North Indian Epic Dhola in Performance.* Bloomington: Indiana University Press, 2004.

——— *Struggling with Destiny in Karimpur, 1925–1984.* Berkeley: University of California Press, 1994.

——— "Vrats: Transformers of Destiny." In Valentine Daniels and Charles Keyes, eds., *Karma: An Anthropological Inquiry,* pp. 146–162. Berkeley: University of California Press, 1981.

Waghorne, Joanne P. *Diaspora of the Gods: Modern Hindu Temples in an Urban Middle-Class World.* New York: Oxford University Press, 2004.

Waghorne, Joanne P., and Norman Cutler, with Vasudha Narayanan. *Gods of Flesh, Gods of Stone: The Embodiment of Divinity in India.* Chambersburg: Anima, 1984.

Wagoner, Phillip. "Sultan Among Hindu Kings": Dress, Titles, and the Islamicization of Hindu Culture at Vijayanagara. *Journal of Asian Studies* 55.4 (1996): 851–880.

Weber, Thomas. *Gandhi as Disciple and Mentor.* Cambridge: Cambridge University Press, 2004.

White, Hayden. *The Content of the Form: Narrative Discourse and Historical Representation,* Baltimore: Johns Hopkins University Press, 1990.

——— "The Value of Narrativity in the Representation of Reality." *Critical Inquiry* 7 (1981): 5–27.

Wittgenstein, Ludwig. *Philosophical Investigations.* Trans. G. E. M. Anscombe. 3d ed. Oxford: Blackwell, 2001.

——— *On Certainty.* Ed. G. E. M. Anscombe and G. H. von Wright. Trans. Denis Paul and G. E. M. Anscombe. Oxford: Blackwell, 1969.

Zarrilli, Phillip. "Between Text and Embodied Practice: Writing and Reading in a South Asian Martial Tradition." In Anna L. Dallapiccola, ed., *Shastric Traditions in Indian Arts,* pp. 415–424. Stuttgart: Steiner, 1989.

Zenani, N. M. *The World and the Word: Tales and Observations from the Xhosa Oral Tradition.* Ed. Harold Scheub. Madison: University of Wisconsin Press, 1992.

Zimmermann, Francis. *The Jungle and the Aroma of Meats: An Ecological Theme in Hindu Medicine.* Berkeley: University of California Press, 1987.

Index

252*n*32; conduct and, 20, 21, 110; Malnad, 11, 25, 52, 236*n*47; normative model of, 185, 227, 243; in puja, 237*n*53, 251*n*23; Sringeri, 11, 12, 20, 21, 54–57, 58; translation of term, 11, 57; *see also* Hospitality; Normative concept(s); Shastra
Upakarma (sacred thread ritual), 115–17
Upanishads, 103, 149, 171, 226
Urvashi (celestial dancer), 27

Vaidyanatha, 114
Vaishnava, 74
Valmiki, 129
Varalakshmi puja, 128
Vedas: aural textuality of, 142; blessings and, 150, 151, 163, 167; classification of shastras and, 242–43*n5*, 242*n3*, 245*n*81; as divine, 103, 106, 137, 142, 143; on food, 122; intertextuality of, 102; as liberation, 101, 102; morality/shastra and, 135, 137, 160; as origin of theory, 100; rejection of, 104; sacrifice in, 163; shastras and, 106, 143; sound and, 142; tradition/guru and, 65, 104, 125
Verbal art, *see* Recitation
Vibhandaka, 27
Vidyaranya (12th guru), 67, 70; kings' indebtedness to, 70
Vidyāraṇya Vrittānta, 67
Vidyaranyapura, celebrations of, 51
Vidyatirtha, Abhinava; *see* Gurus of the matha
Vijayanagara, city of, 67
Vijayanagara empire, 67, 68, 74, 75, 238*n*9; *see also* Kings; Kingship
Virashaiva, 74; devotion/shastra and, 103–4
Vishishthadvaita (qualified nondualism), 102–3
Vishnu, 154, 158–59
Viveka, 22, 197, 229; *see also* Aviveka; Sukshma
Vrata, 136, 142, 248*n*33
Vyasa, 141

War, Mysore, 75
Weddings, 167–68
Wittgenstein, Ludwig, 118, 134, 135, 137, 196
Women: addressing, 248*n*39; authority of, 127, 138; customs/traditions and, 127, 128, 129–30, 136, 142, 144; documentation of personal experiences by, 127–28; dress code for, 207; in municipal council, 62; newly married, vratas for, 132–33, 136, 248*n*33; professions of, 48; vratas/worship by, 142
Worship: arati/oil lamp ceremony in, 71, 72, 239*n*27; daily, 136–37; goddess, 31, 50, 128, 150–60, 164–65, 231*n*2; in matha, 82, 83, 193; reparatory, 196, 210–11; shastras on, 195; of shivalinga, 196; of Tulsi, 129; women's vratas as, 142, 248*n*33
Writing/arts, history and, 126

Yajurveda, 167
Yuga, 101, 211, 256*n*65; *see also* Kaliyuga